Public Health for the 21st Century
The Prepared Leader

Louis Rowitz, PhD
School of Public Health
University of Illinois at Chicago
Chicago, IL

JONES AND BARTLETT PUBLISHERS
Sudbury, Massachusetts
BOSTON   TORONTO   LONDON   SINGAPORE

World Headquarters

Jones and Bartlett Publishers	Jones and Bartlett Publishers	Jones and Bartlett Publishers
40 Tall Pine Drive	Canada	International
Sudbury, MA 01776	6339 Ormindale Way	Barb House, Barb Mews
978-443-5000	Mississauga, Ontario L5V 1J2	London W6 7PA
info@jbpub.com	CANADA	UK
www.jbpub.com		

Jones and Bartlett's books and products are available through most bookstores and online booksellers. To contact Jones and Bartlett Publishers directly, call 800-832-0034, fax 978-443-8000, or visit our website www.jbpub.com.

Substantial discounts on bulk quantities of Jones and Bartlett's publications are available to corporations, professional associations, and other qualified organizations. For details and specific discount information, contact the special sales department at Jones and Bartlett via the above contact information or send an email to specialsales@jbpub.com.

ISBN-13: 978-0-7637-4778-7
ISBN-10: 0-7637-4778-5

Production Credits

Publisher: Michael Brown
Production Director: Amy Rose
Associate Production Editor: Tracey Chapman
Editorial Assistant: Kylah Goodfellow McNeill
Marketing Manager: Sophie Fleck
Manufacturing and Inventory Coordinator:
  Amy Bacus

Composition: Auburn Associates, Inc.
Cover Design: Kristin E. Ohlin
Cover Image: Courtesy of Photographer's Mate
  1st Class Jon Gesch/U.S. Navy
Printing and Binding: Malloy, Inc.
Cover Printing: Malloy, Inc.

Library of Congress Cataloging-in-Publication Data
Rowitz, Louis.
  Public health for the 21st century : the prepared leader / Louis
Rowitz.
    p. ; cm.
  Includes bibliographical references and index.
  ISBN 0-7637-4778-5 (pbk.)
  1. Public health administration—United States. 2. Public health
—United States—Forecasting. 3. Terrorism—United States—Preven-
tion. 4. Emergency management—United States. 5. Leadership
—United States.   I. Title. II. Title: Public health for the twenty-first
century.
  [DNLM: 1. Public Health Administration—trends—United States.
2. Disaster Planning—methods—United States. 3. Leadership
—United States.   WA 540 AA1 R882p 2006]
  RA445.R78 2006
  362.1'068—dc22
                                                                    2005008298

6048
Printed in the United States of America
10 09 08 07 06   10 9 8 7 6 5 4 3 2

Dedication

To the three women in my life—my wife Toni who has always encouraged my heart, and to our two daughters, Julie Rubey and Ruth Urban, and their families who help define the wonderful world of family and generational connection for me. They are the core of my strength.

Table of Contents

Preface

ONE AUTHOR'S REFLECTIONS

Writing a book is a learning experience for an author as, one hopes, it is for the readers of the book. This book addresses the important issue of health preparedness. As I began to write this book, I sometimes thought that I was peeling an onion. As each layer was removed, a new layer was revealed with all sorts of new questions and new events to guide my thinking. Many public health leaders have learned the basics of leadership and developed some of the basic leadership competencies. However, we have now realized that leaders need to learn the skills of public health preparedness and use new tools to bring a new public health approach into being. As we develop this new public health orientation, it is important to build upon the foundation of core functions and essential public health services as well as utilize our basic leadership tools. It is critical that we do not reinvent the wheel.

This book views preparedness in the wide, rather than the narrow, view of emergency preparedness and response. The key issue relates to the public health community being prepared for whatever public health challenges need to be faced. Our work is no longer primarily about what our local health department will do, but rather about what our community will do. Now, our perspective must be shared leadership—and also shared responsibility. Public health preparedness is all about the community; it is also about our quality of life. Public health preparedness is about new partnerships and relationships. It is about building social capital and thus the capacity of our communities to carry out programs and initiatives that promote health, prevent diseases, and protect our residents from harm.

This book is also about hope and strong beliefs that this country can survive any challenges or onslaughts that may occur. This is a country of strong beliefs and values related to freedom, support for all individuals, and the right of each resident to live in a safe and secure environment. As a country, we have many social and health concerns to address. Yet, our world seems to be shrinking. The catastrophe of the tsunami in the Indian Ocean at the end of 2004 demonstrated the vulnerabilities of our world and our inabilities to control natural disasters. Hundreds of thousands were killed, and we saw a demonstration of the importance of preparing for events that we cannot predict. On our own shores, we have experienced the impact of several strong hurricanes in the Southeast in the summer and early fall of 2004. It is clear that we are not really prepared for such catastrophic events, whether they are natural or are man-made such as the events of September 11, 2001. The challenges are great, and the need for leadership today is more critical than in the past. Our public health leaders must help us to address these concerns with knowledge, skills, collaboration, and humanity.

This book is divided into four sections. In Part I, we will look closely at the changing face of public health as a result of the events of September 11, 2001, examine the need to reenergize our communities to build on our strong ties to each other, and look at the emerging new directions for public health in the future. In Part II, we will look at the critical avenues public health must take to achieve emergency preparedness and develop response strategies. Part III addresses some of the new skills that this new public health leadership must require. Finally, in Part IV, the book will address the future and the need to create a vision to guide our work. In addition, this book will present the readers with case studies that include real stories (with changed names) and interviews with public health leaders utilizing a public health quiz format in which these leaders are asked to answer five questions related to the content of selected chapters in the book.

PART I

Overview to the Changing Field of Public Health

CHAPTER 1

The New Public Health: A Preparedness Approach

We cannot live in a post-September 11, 2001 world with a pre-September 11, 2001 mind.

—*Adapted from Angela Thirkell, 1933*

Not only has the world of the present radically changed since the horrific terrorist acts in the United States on September 11, 2001, but public health and its programmatic priorities have also radically changed since those events. Many traditional public health programs and priorities have become secondary, on a policy and funding level, to our expanding role in emergency preparedness and response activities. As a profession we now speak of public health preparedness, emergency response, surge capacity, and consequence management; tabletop exercises and drills; bioterrorism; new and reemerging diseases such as SARS, monkeypox, and West Nile virus; and growing federal deficits due to increasing military expenditures related to the war on terror, along with major state deficits as well. Despite these new considerations, prepared public health leaders struggle to protect the many other priorities of public health. It is still necessary to have restaurant inspections, immunization programs, environmental health protections, maternal and child health initiatives, adolescent pregnancy prevention programs, and all the other health requirements necessary to protect the quality of life of the citizens of our communities.

Public health leaders must fight on a daily basis to show that public health is more than bioterrorism and emergency preparedness. Reality needs to guide action. It is important to ask our policy makers and funders to not underestimate the need for emergency preparedness activities, but also to remember the other activities that guide public health on a day-to-day basis. To keep a perspective, it is important to ask the following questions:

- How many terrorist acts have occurred in our communities in the past year?
- How many cases of SARS, monkeypox, West Nile fever, pertussis, or other new diseases have we seen in the past year?
- How many people have died of influenza complications in our community in the past year (perhaps due to the shortage of flu vaccines)?
- How many teenage girls have become pregnant in the past year?

Public health is about many things. Perspective is important. Perspective helps the public health leader determine the priority of health issues to be addressed. However, the determination of priorities is affected by factors other than the needs of the local community. Priorities are also affected by funding streams, policy priorities, and community concerns. Preparedness and response have become a major priority in recent years, and major funding is associated with it. Of course, all funding considerations need to build public health infrastructure. Unless the system is maintained and strengthened, the public health enterprise cannot move forward, regardless of program priorities. Leaders must be the architects and the navigators of the system. The prepared public health leader must deal with crisis in both normal and not so normal times. The leader must utilize whatever knowledge, attitudes, and skills are necessary and appropriate to a given set of circumstances.

Today, almost all public health agencies and communities are concerned with preparedness. It is important to be ready to address any crisis or challenge that our communities might face. To be prepared is to be ready for action. To do this requires a professional public health workforce that is trained not only in traditional public health knowledge, practices, and skills, but that also understands crisis and its implications. These latter topics are not things that many of us learned in our professional and graduate training. Even our leadership development programs have not completely prepared us for the impact of crises and other emergencies on the functioning of our organizations and communities. The recent tsunami catastrophe of Christmas week 2004 in the Indian Ocean showed how the infrastructure of several countries can be affected by earthquakes and the tsunamis that can follow. The international public health system was not well prepared. That event has led to worldwide reaction and support for the affected countries. The public health implications of the disaster were extreme. However, the world reaction in early 2005 showed an international humanitarian response that was spectacular. The peoples of the world can come together in ways that are nothing short of amazing.

Public health leaders know that the efficacy of their work is dependent on the organization of the public health system as well as a strong foundation in the principles that guide public health practice. These foundation guidelines are critical for addressing all types of public health issues. It is not that the core leadership skills that were learned are not useful for crisis situations; they still continue to be critical and become enhanced in our need to build teams and coalitions, prepare mission and vision statements, prepare and carry out action plans, implement our public health programs and evaluate them, carry out the core functions and essential services of public health, work with our county and other health officials, and learn to communicate efficiently and effectively (Rowitz, 2001).

It will be necessary to add new skills to our leadership toolbox if public health is to strengthen its infrastructure and its readiness and preparedness capacity to address all the new concerns that our society needs to address. This book will explore many of these new issues and the skills necessary to be an effective leader in a preparedness environment. If we can borrow the motto from the Boy Scouts, the new marching song for public health is "Be Prepared." Exercise 1–1, "Social Forces of Change," will put some of these issues in perspective by helping readers examine public health before September 11, 2001, and today.

THE LEADERSHIP PYRAMID

Effective leaders are lifelong learners. To put this lifelong learning approach into perspective, it is useful to look at education and learning in a sequential manner. The following discussion is based on a new approach to leadership development conceptualized by Lichtveld, Rowitz, and Cioffi (2004).

Over the past 15 years, there has been increasing interest in developing a framework for training public health professionals in management and

---

EXERCISE 1–1 Social Forces of Change

Purpose: To explore changes in public health since September 11, 2001.

Key Concepts: Social forces, public health infrastructure, crisis, shifting
priorities

Procedures: Divide the class or training group into smaller groups of about
10 people. Provide a flip chart for the groups.

1. Each individual fills out the worksheet below.
2. The small group discusses the lists of forces of its members and lists the
   different forces at work on the flip chart.
3. The small group discusses the forces and the reasons for them.
4. The small group summarizes the discussion and comes up with the five
   forces before and after September 11, 2001, that influenced public
   health priorities.
5. Small groups discuss the forces they found with the group as a whole.
6. The large group then summarizes the small group priorities and comes
   up with their own social forces for change in the two time periods and
   how these changes will affect public health in the future.

Prior to 2001	Since 9/11/2001
1._____	1._____
2._____	2._____
3._____	3._____
4._____	4._____
5._____	5._____

---

leadership under the assumption that leaders help build a stronger public
health system. Yet there is controversy about whether leaders differ in the
realms of business and the governmental human services fields. It is clear
that as soon as there are two people in a room, one of the two will try to
take a lead role in determining the relationship between the two individuals. Although it is true that leadership is a universal phenomenon, it
takes different forms depending on the cultural and ecological context in
which it takes place. There is clearly a difference between the profit
motive in business and the social justice motive which drives much of the
public health enterprise. As we view the public health system in the middle of the first decade of the new century with all the new challenges that

public health now faces, it is necessary that the issue of leaders in public health be looked at from a new perspective. This model presents a perspective for a better understanding of leadership from the vantage points of leadership competencies, performance, capacity building, and best practices.

Public health leadership can be defined as "creativity in action" (Rowitz, 2001). It is the ability to see the present in terms of the future, while maintaining and learning from the past. Leadership is in part a visionary endeavor, but it requires fortitude and flexibility necessary to put the vision into practice through sharing the vision with others. Public health leadership includes a strong commitment to community with an awareness that public health must be a shared responsibility with community partners. The leader must respect the values of the community and always set high ethical standards for community-based practices. The public health leader respects and supports social justice concerns, but uses acceptable planning and organizational practices to design an effective and comprehensive public health agency. Public health leaders act within the core functions of public health and the essential services that drive the public health enterprise. In addition, the public health leader is prepared for any natural or abnormal crisis that might occur in the community. The leader is committed to lifelong learning and the need to develop competencies required to protect the health of the public.

Figure 1–1 presents the leadership pyramid as an inverted triangle. Each level of the pyramid requires a determination of the specific competencies necessary to master that level of the pyramid. The triangle is inverted to show that the breadth of the set of core public health skills that public health professionals need to have act as the foundation for all that follows. There are numerous approaches these days to the learning competencies needed to practice certain professional and administrative skills. The pyramid requires that we reorganize these competencies to fit each level of the leadership pyramid. As a public health workforce masters each level of the pyramid, performance should improve and the infrastructure of public health should strengthen. Performance management systems and performance standards guided by a set of principles (e.g., essential public health services) would monitor this process.

Training is the key to mastering these skills, which are necessary to build infrastructure. If public health professionals improve their skills and become more effective as a result, they have increased their personal skills,

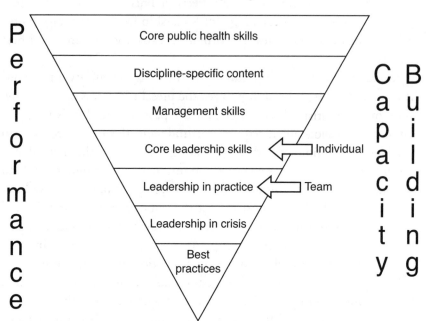

FIGURE 1–1 New Leadership Pyramid

which can then be translated into team-based and other collaborative processes. All of this would eventually improve the capacity of the total public health system. The bottom of the pyramid emphasizes the importance of best practices. The business community is not shy about discussing its best. Public health must begin to do the same. Quality assurance can then be newly defined by the following formula:

> Quality improvement = leadership competency as evidenced by best practices + high performance expectations + strategic capacity building

We can look for clues to the understanding of this quality improvement approach within the body of the pyramid. The first layer emphasizes the importance of an understanding and mastery of a set of core public health skills. Public health must have a public health workforce that is trained in public health principles and practice. Too many of our existing governmental public health workforce have no formal public health training. Recent discussions on credentialing have raised some of these issues, and proponents have argued that the public health system cannot be strengthened without this training. The set of competencies required for this level of the pyramid have been developed by a number of different organizations. All of this means that these skills will be required of all public health workers in the governmental public health sector.

Public health is a profession with a workforce from many different disciplines. Doctors, nurses, dentists, lawyers, business administrators, behavioral scientists, epidemiologists, biostatisticians, and many other discipline-specific experts are required if public health is to carry out its major responsibilities. The major message in level two of the pyramid is that the successful public health practitioner must blend the competencies of public health with discipline-specific competencies if public health is to function in an effective manner. Business learned these lessons long ago and has been able to build profit enterprises through the combination of sound business practices with discipline-specific expertise in many different areas.

The skills necessary to achieve competence at the first two levels of the pyramid are somewhat technical in nature. When the public health professional moves to level three of the pyramid, the tasks to be performed relate to making an agency run effectively and efficiently. Thus, a shift occurs when an individual decides to move into a management role. New sets of skills are needed. In addition, many public health professionals find that during their professional education they were not trained to be managers. Although business schools have been involved in the development of competencies for work in commerce, adaptation of these skills to the public sector needs to become more formalized. Management competencies are quite complex and require training in such diverse topics as time management, performance appraisal, strategic planning, office management, budgeting, and so on. A few certification programs now exist for public health management that do begin to build a public health competency-based management model. Illinois, Missouri, and Iowa have such systems in place.

The move from management to leadership is not as easy as it first appears. First, there is a shift from an agency focus to a systems focus. The manager looks inside the organization to make sure it is functioning efficiently and effectively. The leader looks outward and is concerned with how public health functions at a community and a national level. In addition, the technical skills required at levels one and two and the administrative task-oriented skills of level three become secondary to people and relational skill competencies. The core skills required to be an effective leader are also not taught in most traditional health science curricula. The national, regional, and state-based public health leadership institutes have been trying to fill this gap since the early 1990s. The National Public Health Leadership Network in collaboration with the Centers for Disease Control and Prevention have developed a framework of core public health leadership competencies which have been integral to the training of public health leaders. Public health leaders throughout the country have gone through these training programs. The philosophy of these training programs has been that leaders exist throughout the public health system, and that leadership can be taught.

Training without implementing the content of the training is nothing more than an academic exercise. Leadership development needs to be available for the practicing public health professional who can use these new leadership skills in the work and community context of their professional work. Leadership needs to be implemented to be effective. This may not be an easy task in environments that are resistant to change. Leaders needs to be students of the cultural setting in which they work. Each new skill will undergo some transformation as it is applied in the work and community setting. These new challenges may require skills beyond those that occur in most leadership development programs. It is at this level that such skills as collaboration, team building, community building, assets planning and mapping, emotional intelligence skills, and others come to play a key role in effective leadership.

The events of September 11, 2001, changed public health. Program priorities have changed. Bioterrorism specialists have become a critical component of the public health professional workforce. With these shifting priorities, it is clear that new leadership skills are needed to guide health departments. Public health preparedness and response have become the new priority for public health. Public health leaders have discovered that new skills are needed for the types of collaboration required to deal with crisis events in communities. Public health leaders need skills in not only risk management but also in health crisis communications. Forensic epidemiology has become a new specialty. Public health informatics is a new approach to the creation and use of data. Strategies are needed for working with families of the victims of a crisis event. New partnerships are required with the FBI, police departments, fire departments, hospitals and other health facilities, crisis agencies, community partners, and elected officials. Communicating with people who use different jargon has also become a major leadership challenge. Higher levels of emotional intelligence skills have become more critical. Bioterrorism leadership competencies are different than traditional leadership skills. It is a new type of leadership with more complex skills needed for working in environments of constant change.

The leadership pyramid presents a start on the development of a complex, new approach to the training of public health leaders. Leaders themselves will need to move from level to level in the development of their personal, team, agency, community, and professional skills. Whereas technical skills are usually required to get a person a job in an agency, people skills become more critical to job performance over the long run. Leadership development becomes a lifelong learning activity that leaders must commit to if best practices are to occur and if the infrastructure of public health is to be strengthened.

PUBLIC HEALTH INFRASTRUCTURE

Underlying all discussions of public health training and education programs (much of this section of the chapter is based on the 2002 CDC report *Public Health's Infrastructure: A Status Report*) is the rationale for why these programs are important. Public health professionals perform better when they not only have the skills and competencies necessary to make an agency run effectively, but also the vision and understanding of techniques to improve the health of people who live in their jurisdiction. Public health leaders provide the vision and direction for making these things happen. On one hand, we have the people who power the public health system. On the other hand, we have the structural components that make the system run. Public health infrastructure is embedded in the community and its organizational systems, the competencies for successful performance, and the relationships that are needed to carry out the mission of public health to improve the health of the public. Finally, public health is affected by the resources that aid public health professionals to perform well in their communities.

Public health infrastructure is part of a larger public health system. The Centers for Disease Control and Prevention (2002) have defined three major components of public health infrastructure that form the foundation of what has been called the Pyramid of Preparedness. The three elements that compose the pyramid are basic infrastructure, essential capabilities, and public health response. The pyramid is displayed in Figure 1–2. The bottom layer of the pyramid is composed of three components. Workforce capacity and competency refer to the knowledge and expertise of the public health workforce that comprise the federal, state, and local public health agencies that have been created—and continue to be created—to protect the public's health. To best serve the citizens of our country, the goal must be to have complete coverage of programs and services in every jurisdiction in the United States. Saying this, it is clear that the 500,000 professionals who work in public health are not sufficient in numbers to carry out this task. In addition, the public health workforce is aging; there is a clear possibility that many will retire in the next decade. In addition, many of these workers have learned public health on the job. Training is a necessity if public health is to do its job. Leadership at all levels of the public health system is critical if public health is to reach a level of preparedness required to address the challenges facing America today.

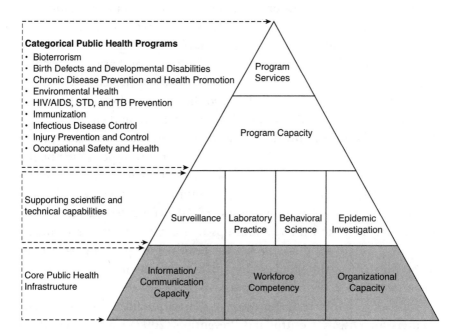

FIGURE 1–2 Pyramid of Preparedness

The second component of basic infrastructure relates to information and data systems. This component addresses the key issue of the need for information to guide the public health enterprise. Uniformity in the way data are collected as well as agreed-upon definitions for data elements are required. Training the public health workforce in data collection techniques is necessary as are the important skills related to the use of information. Up-to-date data guidelines are needed. These guidelines include recommendations, health alerts, and standards-based information and communications systems to monitor disease and enable efficient and effective communication among public and private health organizations, the media, and the public. It is clear that the more traditional approaches to data provided by epidemiological methods is no longer sufficient. It is for this reason that the new science of public health informatics is making such advances. For the public health leader, the skills of how to use information as well as the ability to judge the quality of the data to be used are more important than the data collection procedures. However, the prepared public health leader needs to know how to ask the appropriate questions about data. A basic background in epidemiology is thus required.

The third component of basic infrastructure relates to organizational capacity. Organizational capacity relates to the ability of public health to collaborate with others in coalitions, alliances, and partnerships to guarantee that the three core functions of assessment, policy development, and assurance, as well as all 10 essential services, are being met in every jurisdiction (Table 1–1). This means that public health leaders need to work with other professionals in public as well as private health care organizations to accomplish this. Organizational capability is enhanced by these relationships. Public health is a community issue, not just an agency-based one. As was pointed out above in the discussion of the leadership pyramid, public health leaders need many types of leadership skills if they are to be effective and prepared to address any health challenges in their communities.

The three components of basic infrastructure are clearly interrelated. A deficiency in one impacts the other two. CDC has argued that the goal of strengthening the basic public health infrastructure means the achievement of improvements in all three. In addition, leadership is required to bring about these improvements. The prepared public health leader is one who will see the systemic relationship between the three

---

Table 1–1 The 10 Essential Public Health Services

Assessment
  1. Monitor health status to identify community health problems.
  2. Diagnose and investigate health problems and health hazards in the community.

Policy Development
  3. Inform, educate, and empower people about health issues.
  4. Mobilize community partnerships to identify and solve health problems.
  5. Develop policies and plans that support individual and community health efforts.

Assurance
  6. Enforce laws and regulations that protect health and ensure safety.
  7. Link people to needed personal health services, and assure the provision of health care when otherwise unavailable.
  8. Assure a competent public health and personal health care workforce.
  9. Evaluate effectiveness, accessibility, and quality of personal and population-based health services.

Serving All Functions
  10. Research new insights and innovative solutions to health problems.

---

components of basic infrastructure and their relationship to the other two levels of the pyramid. The second level of the pyramid relates to the ability of the public health system to provide essential capabilities to respond more effectively to public health crises. These essential capabilities involve the knowledge, skills, and abilities related to surveillance. Public health needs 360° vision so that its leadership can be on the watch for all potential threats to the health status of people in its jurisdictions. An occurrence of a new threat in another part of the world can impact the local community in the future. These techniques of surveillance involve quantitative as well as qualitative factors. It means listening to the stories of our colleagues at a national or local meeting. It involves an awareness of the fears and concerns of people who live in our neighborhoods. It involves news reports from other parts of the world about an outbreak of SARS, a major earthquake and tsunami that kills hundreds of thousands of people in Southeast Asia, or some other emerging infectious agent.

The importance of our public health laboratories and the work they do to discover threats and potential threats is an essential public health capability. In recent years, there has been a need for public health laboratories to work with crime laboratories on potential bioterrorism activities. Communication as well as an understanding of chain-of-evidence techniques become critical. In fact, the whole new field of forensic epidemiology has developed to address these new concerns. The third essential capability involves the important role of epidemiology in public health's day-to-day activities. It is not that we don't know the importance of epidemiology in our work, it is the limited number of epidemiologists to do the necessary work. Small health departments cannot afford their own epidemiologist. Models for sharing this expertise are becoming important in our environment of preparedness. Part of our workforce development strategy should be to train the public health workforce in basic epidemiologic skills.

The tip of the pyramid involves the new vision of public health. Today, all of public health's work relates to responding to bioterrorism, emerging infections, and other health threats. This preparedness model needs to be expanded to include all those other concerns that public health has been addressing over the past decades. Water and air quality are still important. Restaurant inspections are still important. Teenage pregnancy is still an issue. Many other local issues continue to need to be addressed.

There are many issues that drive our agenda relative to strengthening public health infrastructure. There never seems to be enough money to do our jobs well. Public health still seems to lack importance among the public and the policy makers. Accountability for spending the taxpayers money is always an issue. When financial deficits occur at the federal, state, and local levels, public programs are often the first things to be cut. Although public health has made many advances in the past, it is almost impossible to predict when another public health breakthrough will occur. Policy makers are often complacent about funding public health programs unless a crisis or threat appears imminent. The fear of potential terrorist acts on American soil has led to the influx of money into the public health sector. More traditional public health programs continue to be underfunded. Public health professionals need to learn the valuable lesson that our business leaders learned long ago—all money builds infrastructure regardless of source. Whining does not serve us well. There will never be enough money. It is important to do the best we can with the resources that we have.

Public health is becoming an increasingly complex field. The scope and variability of the skills required to keep the public health system functional are quite extensive. These skills run the gamut from competencies and skills tied to the investigation of outbreaks to questionnaire design, interviewing techniques, population-based program development, lab specimen collection techniques, standards for effective community prevention services, and many other emerging techniques. When you add on all the skills necessary to be a successful manager and leader, the public health toolbox gets full. Despite these specialized competencies that are needed, many elected officials continue to believe that training programs are a frivolous expense.

There are also many global factors that affect infrastructure, including such things as the global movement of goods and people, antimicrobial resistance, global infrastructure gaps that prevent the containment of potentially lethal diseases, environmental and ecological changes such as deforestation and pesticide use, and the potential for bioterrorism. Public health leaders need to think globally even though they act within a local jurisdiction (Rowitz, 2001). The prepared public health leader is one who monitors the health issues of the world and is able to see the impact of these worldwide trends on local health conditions. Prepared leaders are visionary and always think of the future in developing local public health priorities.

Other issues of concern to public health leaders relative to building infrastructure include the necessity of building public health and emergency preparedness capacity at both the local and state level. It is critical that any enmity between state and local public health professionals be removed. Collaboration is necessary. In addition, a strong relationship between a local or state health administrator and their board of health (if one exists) and elected officials is also a critical partnership if communities are to become prepared for all potential health threats. Another important infrastructure issue is the defining role of the public health agency in the community setting. Public health agencies need to be seen as agencies that are responsive to the health needs of the entire population. If these agencies are to serve as coordinating centers for all public health concerns, then these agencies must develop collaborations with all other health providers in the community. Although it is often a social justice philosophy that drives many public health professionals into the field, it is sound management and leadership competencies that will strengthen the public health system.

Many infrastructure discussions involve the issue of service access and the elimination of health disparities. It is important to move beyond access issues to strategies to change the existing situation. The prepared public health leader knows that solutions need to be found in places other than the financial area. Arguments have accumulated that universal health coverage is the answer. It may be, but leaders know that universal health coverage is a long way off. So, the strategies that must be developed will require innovative approaches to health promotion and disease prevention as well as new collaborations to increase the health service coverage for the people in our communities.

New types of information are needed. Better data on the public health workforce are needed ranging from the composition of the workforce to the movement of public health professionals through the system. Performance appraisals based on individual assessment need to be changed to team performance appraisals, as so much of public health's work occurs in the community with our community partners. The views of expenditures with the concern of methods of determining costs for community-based activities also needs to be part of the public health infrastructure discussion. Public health leaders need to work with their business partners to develop new measures for this nontraditional form of activity.

A final issue of importance is tied to the program mismatch between mandated public health services and the 10 essential public health services previously shown in Table 1–1. First, the public and the policy makers often do not understand the essential services mode. It is clearly an approach that makes sense to the public health leader within the context of the public health system. The essential services are the driving force behind much of what is done in the public health system at a community level. The local public health agency may not carry out all 10 essential services, but all the community agencies involved in public health should carry them out collaboratively. Second, public health leaders know that it is specific mandated programs that are understandable to the public. The public understands the need for clean water and inspected restaurants. The essential services provide a framework for action for public health infrastructure. The prepared public health leader knows that he or she must communicate the results of these actions in a understandable way. The leader must stop being shy about marketing public health's good deeds and best practices. In Case Study 1–1, Dr. Bernard Turnock, director of the Illinois Department of Public Health in the 1980s and now professor of community health sciences at the University of Illinois at Chicago School of Public

CASE STUDY 1   A Public Health Practice Quiz for Bernard Turnock

1. How has public health practice changed since 2000?

   Public health practice has always been about identifying and addressing threats to health. Since 2000, there has been much more attention focused on health threats attributed to terrorism, but preparing for and responding to emergencies have long been major roles for public health practitioners. Public health practice has not really changed; however, there have been significant changes in the environment in which public health practice takes place, in terms of greater public visibility, expectations, and accountability.

2. Does the essential public health service paradigm make a difference in the way public health professionals practice public health?

   The essential public health services provide a framework for public health practice allowing standards to be established for individual and collective practice. Having a more formalized set of practice standards does indeed change what individuals and organizations do. After all, what gets measured gets done.

3. Why does the discussion of public health infrastructure development dominate the emergency preparedness and response dialogues?

   Preparedness and response are attributes of public health systems. Improving public health systems involves making positive changes in the structures and processes (i.e., the infrastructure) of those systems. You can't improve preparedness and response without focusing on public health infrastructure.

4. Do leadership development programs make a difference in the practice of public health?

   Leadership is essential to configure and guide the resources and relationships available for public health ends. Leadership development programs bring enhanced skills and attitudes to public health professionals even before they assume leadership positions. The net result is an ever-expanding corps of current and future leaders sharing common values and skills and greater consistency in and better results from modern public health practice.

5. Are leadership skills different in emergency preparedness and response than in traditional public health practice activities?

   Not really. Emergency preparedness and response are, and always have been, traditional public health practice activities. This role may not have been widely understood or appreciated prior to the events of 2001, but it is one that public health agencies have carried out since their inception.

Health, answers a public health practice quiz related to the issues raised in this chapter regarding the changes in the public health system in the last several years.

SUMMARY

It is important to tie concerns of lifelong learning for public health leaders with a continuing need to strengthen the infrastructure of public health in order to improve the health status of all citizens in our communities. The mission of this book is to develop leaders who will be prepared to address whatever situations affect the health of their constituents. It is imperative that the prepared public health leader recognize that there is more to being prepared than creating another bookshelf plan or conducting another tabletop exercise or drill. Prepared leaders need to consider the contextual issues that affect the public health system as well as specific competencies and skill sets that are needed for effective public health leaders now and into the future. The skills needed for public health in an emergency preparedness and response environment mean that prepared public health leaders need to develop not only the core public health leadership skills discussed earlier in this chapter, but also new skills that work in new program environments.

Figure 1–3 presents a graphic view of the skills this book presents as necessary to prepare our public health leaders for their new tasks. First, there are three critical dimensions to the public health infrastructure that require our attention. From a conceptual basis, strengthening the public health system is tied to our ability to build strong community relationships. Social capital concepts will be used to demonstrate this. Second, the recommendations of the latest Institute of Medicine Report on Public Health (2003) gives a series of recommendations to guide public health infrastructure development over the next decade. As strategies are developed to implement the recommendations of this report, the public health system as a whole will undergo change. In addition, crisis management techniques become imperative to address emergency preparedness and response, as well as utilizing the principles of social capital development and the Institute of Medicine's recommendations. These issues will be addressed in the remaining chapters of Part I and in Part 2. Part 2 will also explore new partnerships, new forms of collaboration, and issues related to public safety.

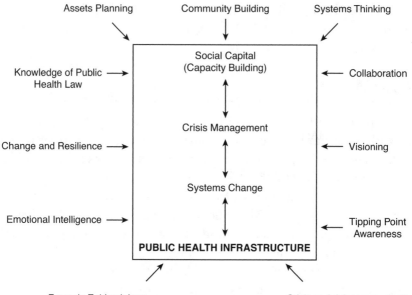

FIGURE 1–3 The Skills of the Prepared Public Health Leader in Crisis

Part 3 of this book will look in detail at the skill sets needed by the prepared public health leader. The specific skill sets involve the following:

- A better understanding of systems thinking and complexity
- People-smart strategies tied to the development of emotional intelligence skills
- Better understanding of public health law
- Health communication strategies
- Tipping point awareness
- Forensic epidemiology
- Prepared leaders
- Techniques for building communities
- Change strategies

The final section of the book will discuss some emerging concerns for the prepared public health leader and the importance of visioning.

REFERENCES

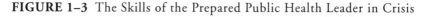

Centers for Disease Control and Prevention. (2002). *Public health's infrastructure: A status report for the Appropriations Committee of the United States Senate by the Department of Health and Human Services*. Atlanta, GA: Author.

Essential Public Health Services Working Group of the Core Functions Steering Committee. (1994). *Core functions and essential public health services.* Washington, DC: U.S. Public Health Services.

Institute of Medicine. (2003). *The future of the public's health in the 21st century.* Washington, DC: The National Academies Press.

Lichtveld, M., Rowitz, L., and Cioffi, J. (2004). The leadership pyramid. *Leadership in Public Health, 6,* (4), 3–8.

Rowitz, L. (2001). *Public health leadership: Putting principles into practice.* Sudbury, MA: Jones and Bartlett.

CHAPTER 2

The Social Capital Perspective

I have erected a monument more lasting than bronze.

—Edna Miller, A Chicago high school Latin teacher, 1955

In the years since the 1970s, Putnam (2000) has reported extensively that social ties and strong community identifications have declined. The reasons for the decline have been due to changes in social, economic, and technological factors. The American people just seem to be less involved with each other than they were in the past. Some of us live in suburban bedroom communities far from our places of work or our daily activities. Our social life also seems to take place out of our residential communities. We often do not know our neighbors even though we may have lived in our homes and apartments for several years. We do not get involved in many local activities unless our real estate taxes go up too high or our schools threaten to cut services and programs for our children. In fact, many of our citizens do not even vote. Our children spend much of their time before television sets or computer screens. It is for these reasons and many others that our level of community involvement has shown a measurable decline. Thus, Putnam and others who view the American landscape talk about this decline in our social capital. This chapter discusses social capital and the importance of it for a renewed American perspective. The prepared public health leader needs to understand the ramifications of building social capital in order to address critical issues in emergency preparedness and response as well as all other community-based concerns of the public health system.

Klann (2003) made distinctions between management and leadership in a crisis-prone environment. Crisis management relates mainly to operational issues. It involves the management of an organization during a crisis and the development and testing of crisis plans. Since September 11, 2001, public health agency administrators have become preoccupied with emergency preparedness and response activities. On the other hand, crisis leadership is a more expansive set of activities involving the human response to a crisis. Crisis leadership involves three major sets of activities. These three sets of activities include communication (see Chapter 11), clarity of vision and values (see Chapter 16), and caring relationships. Caring relationships involve the display of true sincerity and authenticity, development of strong and viable community relationships, strong relationships strengthened by sharing experiences with each other, and solving problems together. It is these latter activities that build social capital. Leaders need time to reflect on their actions and examine the emotional impacts of these activities and events on them personally.

DEFINITION OF SOCIAL CAPITAL

To successfully address the issues of bioterrorism and other threats as well as all public health concerns, it is clear that the secret to success lies in our collaborative efforts. None of the above challenges can be solved unless it is done with other partners. Collaboration is all about building social capital in our communities. Social capital refers to the synergistic effects of working together to strengthen communities and especially the public health system. Social capital refers to the value-added impact of working together to create positive change in our communities. Social capital comes into being through the combination of the following:

- The institutions, relationships, and cultural context in which such relationships are built
- The values and norms that impact these relationships
- The influence of our prepared leaders
- The social networks that evolve through teams, coalitions, alliances, and partnerships

Social capital comes into being through action. Social capital is the glue that strengthens our communities so that they can survive any crisis that may befall them.

Social capital can be distinguished from physical capital and human capital (Putnam, 2000). Physical capital simply refers to physical objects, and human capital refers to the properties of individuals. Physical and human capital involve the process of being trained to use tools and learning skills that enhance individual productivity. For example, a physical capital object might be a hammer which allows a carpenter to do his work. A college education or a bioterrorism preparedness workshop can increase individual productivity (human capital). If the individuals work collectively to improve the communities in which they work, we are beginning to build social capital. Thus:

Social capital = physical capital + human capital + collaboration

Exercise 2–1 will allow you to experiment with some of these principles by constructing a team flag.

Social capital involves both vertical as well as horizontal associations between organizations and people. At a horizontal level, people develop

---

EXERCISE 2–1 The Flag

Purpose: To understand how working in teams or other collaborative groups begins to build social capital

Key Concepts: Social capital, team-building, collaboration, and coalition

Procedures: Divide the class or training group into smaller groups of eight people. Give each group construction paper of one color (purple, orange, or green). Have each group (for 10 minutes) discuss how to build a flag with their one color. Discuss the difficulties of doing this with the group as a whole.

Put together three groups—a purple group, an orange group, and a green group. There may be several of these groups in the larger group.

1. Have each new combined team name their country or community.
2. Determine five major values that will serve as the foundation for your country or community.
3. Design and build your flag with construction paper and tape which includes your major color and two other colors from a package of different colors.
4. Discuss in your team how the new combined coalition built the flag and how it demonstrates social capital formation.
5. Discuss the process and social capital concepts in the group as a whole.

identification with others. At this level, personal ties are strong, and there is often both a common purpose to the interactions with relationships and roles that are clearly delineated. Vertical ties cross organizations and community diversity. These bridging relationships require extensive negotiation to learn how to work together when different roles and relationships define these different cultural groups and organizations (business as well as human service agencies). These vertical and horizontal associations must also be seen relative to the political environment of the local, state, national, and international levels. Actions at all levels of the political spectrum can affect local social capital formation and relationships. This latter issue is especially relevant in the arena of emergency preparedness and response.

Social capital is a productive resource that affects the productivity of all other resources within a community (Mattesich & Monsey, 1997). Social capital takes three forms. The first form involves information sharing which uses social relationships to gather information to address personal as well as organizational issues. The second form is built on the important consideration of trust. Trust gets built through positive social relations and may lead to reciprocal relationships as a positive norm within the community. If an individual is in crisis or fearful, he or she will get the help they need. The third form builds on the cultural norms and values of the community. Tradition plays a critical part in this form. The norms of cooperation and social expectation can be found in all the major institutions in the community, and the values and norms of cooperation are passed on in families, churches and faith-based agencies, schools, and other social entities of the community. All three forms of social capital are reinforced through social support, social networks, honors and awards, and community celebrations of various kinds. Those who do not go along with the accepted standards of behavior relative to collaboration are punished or ostracized.

There is much confusion over the definition of social capital (Kreuter & Lezin, 2002). There are five major themes in the definitions. First, social capital is most usually defined by its function. Second, the term is sometimes seen as relationship based. It is not a property of individuals, but rather is a property of the way the individual relates to others. The third theme involve actions to pursue shared objectives within the structure of the relationship that is created through collaboration. The fourth theme involves the creation of networks with norms and rules and regulations that allow the participants to work together in an effective manner. Trust building and reciprocity are critical components in this theme. The fifth theme involves the ability of the network to garner and command scarce resources.

Ultimately, the critical decision in the use of such a concept as social capital relates to the issue of why it seems to work. There are at least four reasons for this (Lin, 2001). First, the flow of information seems smoother in organizations and communities with high levels of social capital. It is through communication and interaction that social relationships develop and grow. First responders during a crisis must know how and to whom to communicate what they see. Second, these social ties seem to influence the individuals who make decisions about everything from hiring a particular person to passing a critical piece of legislation. Developing social ties between the prepared public health leader and his and her partners opens the channel of communication during a crisis. Working together is easier with people with whom you have developed social ties than with people with whom you have little connection. Third, these social ties are seen by organizations and their representatives as evidence of the social credentials of the individual which in turn tie that individual to other community organizations and networks.

In other words, the prepared public health leader needs to develop relationships with other community leaders and organizations in order to gain trust and credibility. The role of public health during a crisis needs to be negotiated with these partners. If these things are done early, then social capital is built and emergency response activities run more smoothly with an awareness of the critical role of public health during a crisis. Lin's fourth reason for why social capital works is that it reinforces the roles of each participant and organization in normal and not so normal community events. Not only are these relationships reinforced, they also gain recognition.

BUILDING SOCIAL CAPITAL

Although it is imperative that the prepared public health leader builds social capital with other leaders in the community, if biological or other threats are to be addressed in an efficient manner, it is not so simple a matter to do. There are conflicting agendas at play between people, organizations, political entities, communities, states, and so on. These conflicts and tensions often work against collaboration and infrastructure development. Building social capital can be a very difficult process in which many interconnecting relationships significantly affect the outcome of normal and not so normal events. The prepared public health leader needs to understand how his or her community functions. Most communities are diverse. Diversity here has a very wide meaning. It refers not only to its traditional meanings related to age, racial–ethnic groupings, gender differences, and educational differences; it now also refers to nontraditional family relationships, transorganizational relationships, and relationships with new partners such as the police, FBI, and fire department. The differences are demonstrated in many ways such as language, cultural differences, values, norms, and relationships during crisis.

Social capital can be seen as working at the two levels of sociocultural context (the ecological level and the institutional infrastructure level). At the sociocultural level, bonding social capital relates to those factors which affect group, neighborhood, or community solidarity. People who are similar in values and other demographic characteristics such as race and ethnicity seem to bond together more readily than those who differ in these demographic characteristics (Kreuter & Lezin, 2002). Bridging social capital refers to creating social capital among those individuals or organizations that differ in their values and characteristics. The social distance between people with different values and goals makes bridging social capital a more complex endeavor (Putnam & Feldstein, 2003). Social capital in the bridging situation does not occur automatically. The prepared public health leader needs to know how to collaborate, be resilient in adapting to change, have strong people skills, have strong public health credentials, and be knowledgeable about critical elements of bioterrrorism preparedness and response. Bridging social capital is a critical activity for the prepared public health leader.

Hofstede (1997) presented a model which should help the prepared public health leader better understand how these various relationships become defined. There are four dimensions that demonstrate the reasons for cultural variability. The first dimension is power–distance relationships. Power–distance refers to whether individuals or organizations see power as distributed unequally or not. This dimension also relates to how individuals think about their ability to influence decision-making activities. If certain groups for organizations feel distant from the power structure of the community, they may disengage from the process and become reactive to the decisions made. In fact, it appears that the level of inequality in a society may be unconsciously endorsed by the followers as well as the leaders. If individuals act as different and as unequal to other individuals or groups, this inequality gets reinforced in the fabric of the community and sometimes the society as a whole. Arguments abound that in a democratic society, all individuals can become involved in decision making regardless of the diversity of their group or organization. The prepared public health leader will probably see both of the above reactions to the use of power and authority in the communities they serve. The prepared public health leader must practice the skills of cultural competence if he or she is to address the diverse parts of the community.

The second dimension in the model relates to masculinity-femininity. Every society and every community acts in terms of expected gender roles. Masculine societies have very strong concepts of the male and the female role. Males tend to be assertive and dominant in these cultures and women more submissive. To be successful in these societies, women have become more assertive and dominant as well. Societies which are defined by feminine concepts tend to be more nurturing and more relationship oriented. These societies often blur gender roles. With the diversity in culture, we often find major differences in the gender role orientation of different groups that the public health leader serves. Some occupations have a strong masculine orientation, such as the military, the police, and fire professionals. Public health professionals and many social agency professionals take a more cooperative and nurturing approach that fits more under the concept of femininity. The prepared public health leader must relate to many individuals and groups with different orientations. An important issue for the prepared leader is how to push a caregiving agenda in a community that is more masculine in orientation.

Individualism–collectivism is the third dimension. This is a critical dimension in public health. Public health has argued strongly for the importance of working with others to accomplish tasks. Teams, coalitions, alliances, and partnership structures are utilized. The level of commitment of the group members is stressed. Leadership development programs teach collaborative skills and argue for the importance of shared leadership to accomplish our mission (Rowitz, 2001). Concerns about bioterrorism preparedness and response emphasize the importance of collaboration if our communities are to remain safe. On the other hand, we live in a society in which the ties between individuals are loose. We stress individualism and competition. Trust is a trait that is hard to maintain. Social capital declines in this environment. Thus, there is an inherent tug-of-war in American society between our strong individualistic heritage and the critical need to emphasize collectivism and cooperation to address the problems of today and the terrorist threats that seem to dominate our political agendas.

The fourth dimension involves what Hofstede calls uncertainty avoidance. Societies and communities differ in their tolerance for ambiguity and uncertainty. Cultures which rank low on this dimension are cultures in which people feel comfortable with the unknown. High uncertainty cultures are those in which formal rules guide action and in which uncertainty expresses itself in high anxiety and often fear. Americans today seem to be more anxious and fearful than before September 11, 2001. Our tolerance for uncertainty is clearly in decline. The high fear factor in many of our communities affects the ability of the prepared public health leader to address concerns of the people in his community. Mental health concerns as well as bioterrorism preparedness and response issues are now predominant in our public health planning activities. A key issue for many of our community residents is how to keep their families safe in this uncertain environment.

Building social capital as a means to address our present concern with terrorism threats means that it is necessary to address methods for working together to solve our community's concerns. With the Hofstede model in mind and Putnam's arguments about the critical nature of social capital building, review the Hickernoodle City case study and see the issues that arise when a terrorist act occurs and how one community might handle it (Case Study 2). Determine the role of a prepared public health leader in the scenario. What might have been done differently?

PATTERNS OF SOCIAL CAPITAL

The prepared public health leader is one who is able to integrate conceptual as well as research findings into a practical application. Some of the lessons that we can learn from the social capital thinkers include the following:

1. Social capital involves the development of social networks, reciprocities that grow out of these networks, and the values that accrue from the achievement of mutual goals (Schuller, Baron, & Field, 2000).
2. Communities work more effectively when residents trust their neighbors and their leaders, when residents become involved in community work and strive for common community goals, and

CASE STUDY 2   A Haze over Hickernoodle City: Biodefense Readiness in a Community

Margaret Beaman, RN, PhD
Peg Dublin, RN, BSN
Amy Lay, MPH
Jack Morgan, PhD
Gage Rosti, BS
Ellen Vonderheide, MBA

Chemical terrorism has recently surfaced as a major threat as terrorist groups have become more sophisticated in their methods. An attack of this nature can result in many casualties and severely strain the emergency response and health care system, as well as disrupt the normal operations of a city. Public health departments and their communities must be prepared for such disasters. One of the three core functions of public health is the assurance of the public's health and safety (Institute of Medicine, 1988). Disaster preparation also addresses the Healthy People 2010 Goal 23 to ensure that federal, tribal, state, and local health agencies have the infrastructure to provide essential public health services effectively.

This case study is a fictional account of the November 16, 2001, release of poisonous gas in the subways of Hickernoodle City, with a population of 1.4 million. The case is based on the facts of the sarin poisoning on the Tokyo subway (Ohbu et al., 1997). Hickernoodle City, like many communities, has collaborated with its state agency to develop a biodefense plan for combating terrorist acts of biological, chemical, and irradiation destruction. A release of sarin gas in the Hickernoodle subway system in November 2001 tested the functionality of the city's disaster plan. As a result of two simultaneous releases of the poisonous gas within two trains during rush hour, over 5000 persons were exposed and became symptomatic. Because of the magnitude of the problem, the state Emergency Management Agency became involved to assist the Hickernoodle City emergency respondents to activate the Emergency Operations Center (EOC). The effectiveness of this community's response to disaster unfolds through analysis of this fictitious, yet conceivable, scenario. This case study reflects the diagnosis and investigation of health hazards in the community, one of 10 essential public health services. The assessment focuses on identifying health, fiscal, administrative, legal, social, and political barriers that impede the community's ability to successfully handle mass disasters. The critical analysis of the health delivery system includes an evaluation of system capacity; public health leadership; and collaborations, strategic planning, and imperative local roles in disaster preparedness. This assurance exercise aims to achieve

continues

CASE STUDY 2   *continued*

the Healthy People 2010 Goal 23 of ensuring that federal, tribal, state, and local health agencies have the infrastructure to provide essential public health services effectively.

Hickernoodle City is a major metropolitan city in the Midwest. It has a mass transit system consisting of about 20 major passenger rail lines serving the distant city and suburbs which feed into five train stations near the downtown area. Over 100,000 passengers use this system daily. Each of these stations is connected to an extensive subway system serving the city. The rail stations are large, partially enclosed buildings that interconnect rail and subway lines.

The Facts

On Thursday, November 16, 2001, the Metro Commuter Southline train that served Hickernoodle City was unusually crowded due to the arrival of the Dalai Lama, who was scheduled to appear at a 10 a.m. rally in the city center. The train was filled with families and college students anxious to be in the presence of such a revered spiritual leader. At approximately 7:35 a.m., people on the third car noticed a paper bag had been left behind by an exiting passenger. Several people were later able to recall seeing an oily substance seeping from the bag. Within seconds, all of the 65 or 70 people on that car began coughing, eyes were tearing, and many were gasping for air. When the train stopped at the Southside Rail Station eight minutes later, two dozen people had lost consciousness and were lying on the floor of the car; others piled out onto the platform and collapsed. Most of the victims were vomiting and in a daze. Over the next minutes, fumes from the third railcar seeped into adjacent train cars and soon several hundred people were coughing, their eyes were watering, and they were complaining of pain in their eyes.

As people streamed out of the cars at the station, panic began to set in among the crowd of 3000 passengers in the rail station; many people were screaming. The stationmaster ordered the entire train evacuated and called for emergency personnel to arrive on the scene. Before emergency personnel could arrive, security guards at the station pulled 45 people out of the cars and placed the victims on the train platform. Those who could walk found their way outside and many collapsed on the sidewalk. Those who could speak described feeling intense pain in their eyes and everything looking dark, as if they were wearing sunglasses. Some described a sudden pain when taking a breath, as if they had been shot. Because of the large numbers of children on the train, there were a disproportionate number of children among those who had lost consciousness. Parents were frantically trying to find help for their children while they experienced breathing difficulty themselves.

continues

CASE STUDY 2   *continued*

By the time the paramedics and firefighters arrived at 7:55 a.m., there had been four fatalities, three of whom were children under the age of five. Emergency personnel found persons losing consciousness, foaming at the mouth, convulsing, stumbling, and exhibiting respiratory problems. They quickly determined that some form of chemical emission had occurred on the train. To reduce continued exposure, emergency workers put on protective masks as they removed persons from the train. The immediate area was ordered evacuated and a hazardous material (HazMat) team assembled to enter the site.

Meanwhile, first respondents began treating others who were unable to evacuate the area by applying mask-valve-ventilator devices and providing oxygen. Atropine injections were prepared for those convulsing and nearing unconsciousness. However, many of the respondents were not certified paramedics, and under law, were not allowed to administer the prophylaxes; they were only able to provide protective masks and oxygen, until those supplies began to dwindle. Some personnel, without knowing the exact cause and venue of contamination, were afraid to provide mouth-to-mouth resuscitation for fear of receiving secondhand exposure. A number of the victims had to remain struggling for air.

Emergency Operations Center

Thirty minutes after the incident began at the Southside Station, a similar incident involving a chemical emission began to unfold on the Northwest line at the Westside Station about five miles away. When that train arrived at the Westside Station dozens of dazed passengers stumbled from the train coughing and gasping for air. At least 10 people had lost consciousness in the railcar.

This time the Emergency Medical System (EMS) director was notified and he quickly called the Hickernoodle Emergency Operations Center (HEOC) into action. The HEOC, upon realization that a terrorist-related incident may have occurred, notified the State Department of Health emergency officer who arranged for the EMS chief to come to duty. The chief of EMS and Highway Services began notifying the point of departure (POD) designated disaster hospitals. Because the incident occurred in two EMS regions of Hickernoodle City, two POD disaster hospitals (I and II) were notified and warned of a possible influx of patients. As required by protocol, POD Hospital I, which had already begun receiving patients, contacted all participating and resource hospitals to assess emergency department (ED) availability, number of beds, units of blood, and inventory of ventilators and other supplies.

The area hospitals took inventory and began faxing in the required forms to the POD hospitals, which would forward the information on to

continues

CASE STUDY 2   *continued*

the state department who would coordinate resources for the remaining disaster time. The POD hospitals fax lines could not handle the influx of reports. Emergency personnel at POD Hospital II, confused about which health department was to receive their inventory and resource information, began faxing their information to the local health department. The EMS chief, upon receiving some faxes from POD Hospital I, started rerouting ambulances according to the hospital information faxes. Many hospitals had recorded limited supplies and shortages of staff, yet the ambulances kept coming since the EMS chief had not yet received their list of inventory. Before long, emergency rooms began running out of ventilators, oxygen, antidotes, and beds. One by one they started going on bypass, refusing to take any patients that arrived via ambulance.

Meanwhile back at the scene, Hickernoodle City Mayor Edgar M. Weekly ordered all rail and subway trains to stop at the next station until further notice and for trains and stations to be evacuated. The media arrived and began interrogating anyone willing to report on the situation. The state health department director notified the state and federal bureaus of investigation of the event. The mayor contacted his director of communications to coordinate communication responses that could calm the public. Fact sheets were obtained from the local health department on the likely agent of distress, and messages on avoiding secondary contamination were prepared. Hospitals were ordered to redirect the media to the state health department emergency director who would provide updated reports on casualties, patient conditions, and so forth.

The local health commissioner was disgruntled as she heard from an inside source that hospitals were simultaneously going on bypass and sending ambulances way out of their transport area. The city was running out of participating ambulances. The EMS director asked the fire chief to locate private ambulances in the area. However, the private ambulances refused service since a contract or payment couldn't be provided up front. As hundreds of patients arrived at emergency departments, hospitals continued to go on bypass. The local commissioner called the POD hospitals to order that no hospitals remain on or resort to bypass status. As emergency rooms became saddled with patients for whom no supplies, beds, or nurses to perform triage were available, the chief of EMS was notified. Appalled and angered by the commissioner's order, she contacted the emergency services medical director and they began calling hospitals to assess their conditions. Those lacking supplies and manpower were allowed to redirect ambulances. Some hospitals called other hospitals in their region and asked to borrow supplies in order to treat current ED patients. However, because no regulations mandate the sharing of sup-

continues

CASE STUDY 2   *continued*

plies, even in a time of crisis, hospitals were hesitant to loan away equipment they might need themselves.

About five hours after the initial incident was reported, specially trained FBI agents in chemical and biological terrorism began investigating the scenes at the train stations. Air and fabric samples from the rail cars were collected as well as remaining passenger items. Of particular interest was a backpack from the Southside Station and an open package from the Westside Station; both contained canisters capable of delivering gases. Neither the city nor state laboratories were capable of analyzing chemical warfare agents. Therefore, military planes out of O'Ryan International Airport were used to transport the samples to the FBI crime lab in Maryland for analysis. A medical alert was sent out to regional health care agencies and local health departments to report any cases showing symptoms of nerve agents. As media began reporting the incident to the public, hospitals also began receiving the "worried well." In addition, persons at the stations or on trains where the crisis had occurred began paying attention to their breathing difficulties, tightness of chest, or other mild symptoms that had previously been attributed to being in an excited or panicked state. They began worrying about the extent of their exposure.

The following day, the FBI lab reported that traces of sarin gas had been found in the rail cars and in the blood of victims. The canisters in the backpack and package were believed to be the means of dispersal. All rail and subway lines remained closed for three and one half days. Sample collection at the attacked stations and adjoining tunnels and stations began on Friday, November 17, for clearance testing of the affected structures. On Saturday, November 18, Mayor Weekly announced that limited rail service would be available on Monday, November 20. Those stations and lines directly affected by the attack would remain closed until they were determined to be safe for use. Increased security would be implemented by all public transportation agencies and a long-range security plan would be developed.

As questions about inappropriate ambulance transport times, numbers of hospitals on bypass, inadequate supply of ambulances, and other issues arose, the commissioner, anxious to pinpoint blame for the crisis, announced that a senate hearing would take place to investigate the disaster response.

Human Toll

A total of 750 people from both trains were taken to area hospitals the day of the attack. Symptoms of the victims included complaints of headache, shortness of breath, severe pain when breathing, uncontrollable shaking, watery eyes, and foaming at the mouth. Many of the victims who had lost

continues

CASE STUDY 2   *continued*

consciousness remained unconscious for 24–48 hours. A second wave of 250 people were seen in area emergency departments (EDs) over the next three days with similar symptoms as well as severe anxiety. Complaints of panic attacks, insomnia, and intense nervousness were reported. In all, there were seven fatalities, three of whom were young children. While most of those seen at area hospitals were released, 46 people remained hospitalized for up to 10 days.

In the days, weeks, and months following the incident, many persons present or near the incident complained of nervousness, jitters, excessive dreaming, insomnia, increased tension, restlessness, some gastrointestinal effects, and trouble concentrating.

Over the next six months, many of the victims took advantage of mental health services offered in the community. Mental health workers reported that many of the victims had persistent sleeping problems including waking after only 2–3 hours and nightmares. Other symptoms included difficulty concentrating, hyperexcitability, and fear of being in confined spaces. Area mental health professionals reported symptoms of post-traumatic stress among a significant number of people seeking services, including panic attacks, recurring flashbacks (of the incident), inability to enter the subway, obsessive thoughts about the possibility of another terrorist attack, and inability to experience pleasure. In addition to victims experiencing psychological effects of the attack, many of the emergency personnel and hospital staff who had attended the victims were experiencing anxiety symptoms. The demand for mental health services exceeded the availability of services, and officials needed to request assistance from other cities. Area businesses experienced unusually high rates of absenteeism and loss of productivity among employees impacted by the attack.

Public Relations

On Friday, November 17, articles appeared in three of Hickernoodle's major papers. The *Hickernoodle Sun Times'* headline read "Chemical War Zone at Southside Station." The *Sun Times* had a reporter at the Southside Rail Station who wrote a very descriptive account of the victims and the scene inside the Southside Station. The reporter described the scene as a "chemical war zone," with rescue workers appearing in moon suits to treat victims. He also mentioned that some of the rescue personnel were refusing to provide mouth-to-mouth resuscitation to some of the victims for fear of exposure.

The *Hickernoodle Tribune*'s headline read "Passengers Attacked with Nerve Gas." The reporter for the *Tribune* managed to interview victims at one of the hospitals, along with the hospital personnel. The personnel at the hospital mentioned the victims had been attacked with nerve gas. However, at

continues

CASE STUDY 2   *continued*

the time, they could not determine exactly which kind. The *Tribune*'s article also mentioned the confusion between the hospitals and the state and local health departments as to who was to receive inventory and resource lists. With this confusion many victims were being rerouted to different hospitals or to hospitals that were already at capacity. "These victims were spending far more time riding around in an ambulance than they should have."

The headline for the *Hickernoodle Daily* read "City Transportation Paralyzed by Terrorist Attacks." The *Daily* not only gave detailed descriptions of the victims and overcrowding of the hospitals, but also took the angle of the major public transportation system being shut down. The *Daily*'s reporter spoke with passengers stranded at both the Southside and Westside stations. The state of panic led to bigger traffic problems, with taxis, press, and emergency vehicles all trying to get to the stations.

Three local news networks were broadcasting live from the scene of the attacks. The reporters were talking to anyone they could—both victims and witnesses. Each of the networks also interviewed patients and emergency room personnel. One station had spoken with an ambulance driver who had been rerouted to three different hospitals. One of the other networks picked up on the packages and blood being flown out of state to be tested.

Each of the newspapers and the TV stations reported that a nerve gas or agent had been released in the two stations. Fact sheets were obtained from the local health department on the signs and symptoms to watch for and how to avoid secondary contamination. The biggest communication problem was incomplete information being publicized. The FBI, the city of Hickernoodle, and the local and state health departments simply did not have enough information to share with the public.

Hickernoodle City, the local and state health departments, and the FBI called a joint press conference on the afternoon of the 16th. The press conference was the first to confirm there was some form of terrorist attack on two morning trains. It was not yet known if the attack was of domestic or international origin. The chemical agents used in the attacks had not yet been identified. The second issue emphasized during the press conference was the frozen train service for the Southside and Westside stations for at least 24 hours.

Effect on Structural Systems

The attack caused great strain on the medical providers, both public and private, as well as taxing the transportation system, police, fire, and communications personnel. Although Hickernoodle City had practiced disaster preparedness, they had never dealt with a disaster of this magnitude.

continues

CASE STUDY 2   *continued*

The timing of the disaster, at the height of rush hour, tended to compound problems related in getting to the attack sight, as did the lack of knowledge as to the agent used in the attack. Other confounding problems became apparent as the amount of devastation and the human toll mounted. A lack of trained medical professionals, both in the public health sector and the private sector, to effectively handle the volume of injured and dying soon became apparent. A lack of available hospital beds for use in overnight observation and intensive care and the lack of a plan to evacuate the city in an orderly fashion all contributed to the confusion and hysteria.

With the shutdown of the rail system, transportation into and out of the city on surface streets soon became grid locked. As the news of the attack spread throughout the city, people poured out of their offices into the streets in an attempt to leave. This increased the difficulties in moving the victims from the triage site to the hospitals and transporting replacement medical personal into the triage areas. The Office of Emergency Management was activated to deal with some of the transportation issues. They were able to secure air transportation for the serious victims and bus transportation for the less serious victims and medical staff. The police were assigned the task of crowd control. They were also empowered to clear the roads to and from area health facilities.

Communication among the emergency personnel, government officials, and the public was the greatest problem. The government officials, not wanting to cause mass hysteria, withheld vital information in the treatment of the victims. By doing this they not only delayed the administration of the proper reagent, but also caused secondary exposure to some of the first responders. Transportation agencies, not wanting to be closed for an extended period of time, were slow in divulging the extent of the damage caused by the attack. Lastly, the sheer volume of the disaster pressed the communications system to its limits.

The number of people affected in the attack exceeded the bed capacity for the city's hospitals requiring transportation to outlying facilities. Budgetary constraints imposed by the elected officials earlier in the quarter caused a reduction in the medical staff used to tend to the needy. The staff reductions, in turn, increased the time it took for the victims to be seen. This in turn caused the milder cases to progress into more severe cases, which in turn increased the price of treatment.

The lack of knowledge as to the causative agent used in the attack increased the number of secondary exposure illnesses. A failure to communicate to the first responders the nature of the substance that they were encountering at the attack site caused them to be ill prepared. Of the

continues

CASE STUDY 2   *continued*

emergency personnel who responded in the first wave, 50% became ill with sarin poisoning symptoms. The lack of decontamination facilities caused the spread of sarin poison from the attack site to the medical facilities. Members of the medical team that had had no contact with the attack site, other than treating the victims, were reporting mild symptoms.

To stem the cost of providing services, the mayor of the city requested the governor to declare a state of disaster. Once this was done, the Federal Emergency Management Agencies became involved. This allowed the city to receive funding to pay for medical services, transportation services, improve communications, and cleanup activities. It also expanded the range of professionals available to provide assistance in dealing with the problems associated with the attack.

Because this was an act of terrorism, the FBI became involved. Their investigation slowed the return to normal by keeping the subway system closed. Their actions caused increased congestion and gridlock conditions as people looked for other means of transportation.

Post-traumatic stress symptoms were evident in many of the victims in the weeks following the attack. Cases that were followed cited a fear of the underground transit system. In addition to the nightmares, they reported fears of being trapped underground. Revenues from the subway operations fell off dramatically since the attack also.

Closing

Although this is a fictional account, the majority of the facts could be realized in an actual community. The community had a disaster plan, but it was not detailed enough to account for a disaster of this magnitude, a bioterrorist attack with chemicals, or potential problems at any point in the sequence of events. This disaster demonstrated the need for increased training at the worst-case scenario. level. Any disaster planning must include all potential agencies involved, including the media. A strong communication system is vital to keep everyone informed at the appropriate level, to prevent panic, and to increase cooperation. Strong disaster plans are a vital component of a sound public health infrastructure.

Case Study 2 References

Institute of Medicine, Committee on the Future of Public Health. (1988). *The future of public health*. Washington, DC: National Academy Press.

Novick, L. F., & Marr, J. S., (Eds.) (2001). *Public health issues in disaster preparedness: Focus on bioterrorism*. Gaithersburg, MD: Aspen.

continues

CASE STUDY 2   *continued*

Ohbu, I., Yamashine, A., Takasu, N., Yamaguchi, T., Nakano, K., Matsui, Y., et al. (1997). *Sarin poisoning on Tokyo subway* [electronic version]. In *Southern Medical Journal*. Retrieved from http:www.sma.org/smj/97june3.htm

Tucker, J. (1997). National health and medical services responses to incidents of chemical and biological terrorism. *Journal of the American Medical Association, 278,* 362–368.

US Department of Defense. (1997). *Fact sheet on exposure limits of sarin (GB).*

Web Sites

Agency for Toxic Substances and Disease Registry 2002. *Managing Hazardous Material Incidents.* http://www.atsdr.cdc.gov/2p-emergencyresponse.htm. Accessed April 4, 2002.
   Center for Disease Control. (2002). *Public health preparedness and response.* Retrieved April 4, 2002, from http://www.bt.cdc.gov/
   Includes information on many biological and chemical agents.

Centers for Disease Control. (2002). *The public health response to biological and chemical terrorism: Interim planning guidance for state public health officials.* Atlanta: CDC.

US Department of Health and Human Services. Retrieved April 4, 2002, from http://www/bt.cdc.gov/documents/planning/planningGuidance.pdf

Environmental Protection Agency. (2002). Retrieved April 4, 2002, from http://www.epa.gov/ebtpages/emergencies.html
   Lists the chemical emergency preparedness sites.

Federal Emergency Management Agency. (2002). *Preparedness.* Retrieved April 4, 2002, from http://www.fema.gov/pte/gaheop.htm
   Information for planning a response.

when people share a civic culture oriented toward cooperation and service (Rotberg, 2001).

3. Societies and communities that have a high level of social involvement that translates into social capital can function at higher levels than societies and communities where residents are not socially involved (Rotberg, 2001).

4. To build social capital, it is necessary to see and meet the individuals with whom you will work in many different settings and groups. Trust builds up from this "redundancy of contact" (Putnam & Feldstein, 2003).

5. People who live in communities with high social capital tend to be healthier than people who live in communities with less social capital (Putnam, 2000).
6. Social capital increases when it is used. The more social capital is used, the more it gets produced (Cox, 1995).
7. After September 11, 2001, people showed an increasing interest in public affairs. Trust in the government grew. Television viewing also increased. Still, evidence is more involvement in organizations did not significantly increase (Putnam, 2002).

It should be clear that communities work best when they use their resources effectively and efficiently and when social capital gets built. When one individual does work or engages in any solo activity, the primary beneficiary is that individual. There may be indirect effects on the physical and human capital of the community. If we want to see an effect on social capital, then two or more people have to be involved. When a young man and a young woman meet, they test each other and try to discover each other's traits. This dating process may or may not lead to a more permanent relationship. If it does, it may lead to marriage, which is a form of social capital building in which the two people decide to create a mutual household where resources will be shared. A marriage creates synergy in which the relationship generally becomes enriched and enhanced as the social ties increase. Social capital increases and will continue to do so if the couple have children. As this family unit reaches out to other family members, friends, and neighbors, social capital begins to expand and increase. As paths cross and interconnect with other neighborhood and community groups, more social capital is generated. Thus, social capital can be an ongoing process although it may not always be a smooth one.

Similar to the above example, the prepared public health leader needs to develop social ties throughout the community. These ties and relationships will be with individuals and organizations. The new public health environment requires that relationships develop with not only traditional health professionals and health organizations, but also with nontraditional partners such as businesses and the chamber of commerce, local FBI agents, police and fire department professionals, local emergency preparedness officials and agencies, elected officials, the media, and grassroots organizations. The more partners that we have, the more complex the relationships and the greater the potential for building social capital. The prepared public health leader should be spending much of his or her time in community-based activities and should delegate more managerial responsibility in the local public health agency to others. The leadership skills necessary for the new work of public health will be discussed in later chapters.

This book takes an expanded view of social capital. Building social capital can occur at all levels of the community:

- The personal level, such as families
- Grassroots organizations promoting community interests and values
- Transorganizational networks made up of public health as well as other health and social service agencies
- Emergency preparedness and response collaborations
- Community-wide networks

It is through social capital that we build the infrastructure of our communities generally and the public health infrastructure specifically.

An interesting variation on this was discussed by Marcus (unpublished paper). He pointed out that the challenge for public health leaders in this new age of preparedness is as much about developing relationships prior to a terrorist event as it is working with new organizational partners after a terrorist event. He has called these new working relationships "connectivity." Connectivity involves interdependent agencies and organizations and their leaders working to explicitly map out and coordinate linkages during the preparedness phase of planning to ensure they can work together during and after a crisis. This connectivity model is a practice approach to building social capital that builds on the need to develop relationships that will work during a terrorist event. It is necessary to break down silos if collaboration is to work. To train leaders to better connect, Marcus developed a program called Walk in the Woods that uses negotiation strategies to resolve conflict, shape solutions, and build constructive relationships.

SOCIAL CAPITAL AND HEALTH PROJECTS

Four interesting projects were funded through the Special Interest Projects of the Prevention Research Centers funded by the Centers for Disease Control and Prevention. The four projects were undertaken in

2001 and 2002 to determine the indicators of social capital for different racial and ethnic communities. Researchers from the Prevention Research Center at Tulane University took the lead in coordinating a multisite project to identify these indicators of social capital and capacity-building processes. The investigators at each of the four sites tested the indicators with different population groups. The four teams have developed a large-scale survey that community agencies and state health departments can use to measure community capacity and social capital that will help in health promotion and health improvement programs for community residents. The analysis of these projects are still underway but should give public health professionals some information they can use to understand how social capital affects health status.

Illinois researchers are studying urban ethnic groups. They are specifically trying to identify the characteristics of community-based health promotion campaigns that define the processes among community residents and organizations in four Chicago neighborhoods that may enhance the ability of the community to reach its health goals. The assessment of social capital in this study is limited to community grassroots organizations in these four neighborhoods. One interesting neighborhood project involved the development of community trust and social participation in community programs in Puerto Rican communities affected by HIV/AIDS (Kelley, Molina, & Concha, 2003). A collaboration developed between the University of Illinois at Chicago Prevention Research Center, the Puerto Rican Cultural Center, and its Vida/SIDA (AIDS and Life Program). The mission of the Vida/SIDA program is to decrease the incidence of HIV infection in the Puerto Rican community and also to enhance the quality of life of those who are already diagnosed with the disease. Community programs of all kinds work to bring the community together. Another goal of the program is to promote the arts, history, and culture of the Puerto Rican community. The researchers have tested whether an understanding of local social capital concepts of trust, social ties and connections, and the role of community-based organizations can impact the health status of community residents.

Tulane University, in partnership with Xavier University, studied inner-city African-American communities. St. Louis University researchers are working with rural African-American communities. The final project involves the study of social capital in Native American tribal communities in the southwest United States. Communities that promote strong involvement of their members *as* a community help to build the social capital of that community.

SUMMARY

It has been the purpose of this chapter to present a perspective that can be used in emergency preparedness and response initiatives. To understand the context in which first responders will act, it is necessary to know the human, physical, and social capital resources of the community. To successfully respond to a crisis of whatever type, the prepared public health leader must know how his or her community functions. The leader must know how to work in an ecological context because different communities respond differently to crisis. The social capital model is a useful one for this exercise.

REFERENCES

Cox, E. (1995). *A truly civil society*. Sydney, Australia: Australian Broadcasting.

Hofstede, G. (1997). *Cultures and organizations*. New York: McGraw-Hill.

Kelley, M., Molina, A., & Concha, J. (2003). The Chicago Puerto Rican community responds to the HIV/AIDS crisis, *The Acosa Update, 17* (4), 13–14.

Klann, G. (2003). *Crisis leadership*. Greensboro, NC: Center for Creative Leadership.

Kreuter, M., & Lezin, N. (2002). Social capital theory. In R. J. DiClemente, R. A. Crosby, and M. C. Kepler (Eds.), *Emerging theories in health promotion practice and research*. San Francisco: Jossey-Bass.

Lin, N. (2001). *Social capital: A theory of social structure and action*. New York: Cambridge University Press.

Marcus, L. J. (Unpublished). Connectivity and national preparedness. Resolving conflicts and building collaboration to enhance system readiness.

Mattesich, P., & Monsey, B. (1997). *Community-building: What makes it work*. Saint Paul, MN: Amherst H. Wilder Foundation.

Putnam, R. D. (2000). *Bowling alone*. New York: Simon and Schuster Touchstone Books.

Putnam, R. D. (2002). *Bowling together: The American Prospect*. 13, 3. Retrieved from www.prospect.org/print/V13/3/putnam_r html

Putnam, R. D., & Feldstein, L. M. (2003). *Being together*. New York: Simon and Schuster.

Rotberg, R. I. (2001). *Patterns of social capital*. New York: Cambridge University Press.

Rowitz, L. (2001). *Public health leadership: Putting principles into practice*. Sudbury, MA: Jones & Bartlett.

Schuller, T., Baron, S., & Field, J. (2000). Social capital: A review and critique. In S. Baron, J. Field, & T. Schuller (Eds.), *Social capital: Critical perspectives*. New York: Oxford University Press.

CHAPTER 3

The Changing Public Health System

We must sustain our commitment to a healthier nation through education, investment, and political will.

Jo Ivey Boufford and Christine K. Cassell, Co-Chairs
Committee on Assuring the Health of the Public in the 21st Century
Institute of Medicine, 2003

The events of September 11, 2001, changed public health forever. Today, everyone talks about preparedness—but the talk is primarily about preparedness related to preventing and responding to bioterrorism events. This book takes a wider view of preparedness in that public health agencies need to be able to address any type of crisis that may impact their communities. Preparedness also requires that the public health leader take a community-oriented approach to the challenges facing public health rather than the more traditional agency focus. If preparedness is about the entire structure of public health, then the prepared public health leader needs to be concerned about all of public health and not just bioterrorism preparedness and response. To take this wider view, public health needs an agenda. This chapter will look at public health's agenda. The quote that started this chapter states public health's critical mission in a succinct manner.

DILEMMAS OF THE PUBLIC HEALTH WORKFORCE

As pointed out in the last chapter, building social capital is about strengthening the social relationships between people. Strengthening the public health infrastructure that forms the foundation of the public health system is also about people. The public health workforce is both aging and also lacking in the skills necessary to build public health in the 21st century. Not enough young people are entering the field. An investment in people is critical. We need to train the present workforce and try to get them to delay retirement until we can get more people to choose public health careers. The development of lifelong learning opportunities oriented to the new skills needed to address a constantly changing public health landscape needs to occur. The present trend toward investment in learning management systems is a step in the right direction. These systems can create online registration processes for both online and face-to-face courses. All such courses need to be competency based. These systems also allow for the creation of a continuous learning record for all individuals who register for any course. In addition, these systems allow for ongoing needs assessments of future course needs, as well as gaps in an individual's learning requirements.

Politicians must stop passing early retirement buyouts for the public health workforce if public health is to continue to do its work. Deficits in state and local budgets have led to this phenomenon. The governmental workforce in many places is shrinking. Early retirement programs leads to the abolition of positions. A shrinking workforce is not conducive to building public health infrastructure or the public health system. Late in 2003, the Association of State and Territorial Health Officials surveyed the senior health officials of the 57 states and territories as well as the District of Columbia about public health workforce trends (ASTHO, 2004). ASTHO reported a significantly growing shortage of public health employees in a majority of the states. State budget deficits in this first decade of the 21st century have exacerbated the problem. A shrinking workforce complicates the work of public health leaders who are trying to strengthen the infrastructure of public health in their communities.

Some specific findings from the ASTHO survey included information on the aging public health workforce whose average age is 46.6 years. It was projected that the rate of retirements will be as high as 45% before the end of the first decade of the new century. In some parts of the country, the public health employee turnover rate is as high as 14%. In addition, the current vacancy rates are almost 20% in some of the states. In fact, the governmental public health workforce is older than the workforce in other parts of the governmental sector. The governmental public health agencies reported the most significant shortages in the areas of nursing, environmental health, epidemiology, and laboratory science. Low salaries complicate the process of filling the personnel shortage areas. The private health and health care sector pays significantly better than the public sector. These shortages also affect leadership capacity. Most states are now affiliated with a state and regional public health leadership institute in order to fill this gap. If we do not expand the public health workforce and provide training to increase the competencies of the workforce to address potential natural and man-made events, it will not be possible to be prepared for coping with these crisis events. The prepared public health leader needs a competent, well-trained workforce if public health preparedness is to become a reality.

Reports on the workforce status of local public health agencies show that there are often more public health professionals in actual numbers working in metropolitan health departments than the number of public health professionals working in state health departments (Fraser, 2003). The average number of full-time equivalent employees in local public health agencies is about 13. Specifically, this translates into about 31 staff in metropolitan area local public health agencies, 18 in suburban departments, and 12 in rural health agencies (Hajat, Stewart, & Hayes, 2003). Fraser (2003) recognized the realities of present-day economics but saw it as an opportunity to determine the type and number of public health professionals who will be needed in the future to effectively carry our public health preparedness activities. It is a time to review the structure of our public health system, and leadership will be needed to explore issues related to how the public health system can be structured in the future.

Public health preparedness is defined by both the governmental public health workforce and public health's community partners (Lichtveld & Cioffi, 2003). Table 3–1 summarizes and reviews some of the major competencies needed by a prepared public health workforce as gleaned from a number of key public health documents released from 1988 to 2002. Fifteen competency areas are defined, ranging from managerial and lead-

Table 3–1 Identified Needs for Public Health Workforce

Competency/Content	IOM 1988[a]	Healthy Communities 1996[b]	Faculty Agency Forum[c]	Competencies Developed 2001–2002, Council on Linkages[d]	Performance Standards; Core Functions; Essential Services[e,f]	The Future of the Public Health in the 21st Century (2002)[g]	Who Will Keep the Public Healthy? (2002)[h]
Managerial skills	✓		✓		All of the above	✓	✓
Leadership skills	✓	✓			All of the above	✓	✓
Technical professional skills	✓			✓			
Citizen participation	✓	✓				Community-based participatory research	Community-based participatory research
Minority health	✓					Health disparities	Health disparities
International health	✓					Global health	Global health
Modern disease (e.g., AIDS)	✓						
Assessment skills	✓	✓	✓	✓	All of the above	✓	MPH
Policy skills	✓	✓	✓	✓	All of the above	✓	MPH
Assurance skills	✓	✓	✓	✓	All of the above	✓	MPH

Competency/Content	IOM 1988[a]	Healthy Communities 1996[b]	Faculty Agency Forum[c]	Competencies Developed 2001–2002, Council on Linkages[d]	Performance Standards; Core Functions; Essential Services[e,f]	The Future of the Public Health in the 21st Century (2002)[g]	Who Will Keep the Public Healthy? (2002)[h]
Law	✓	✓	✓	✓	Performance standards	✓	✓
Managed care		✓			Private sector	Private sector	Private sector
Partnerships and interactions		✓				✓	
The ten essential services		✓		✓		✓	
Communication skills			✓				✓
Cultural skills			✓				✓

[a]Institute of Medicine. (1988). Retrieved from www.nap.edu/books/0309038308.html
[b]Healthy Communities. Retrieved from www.hospitalconnect.com/communityhlth/resources/hlthycommunities.html#GuidesTools
[c]Faculty Agency Forum. Retrieved from http://bookstore.phf.org/prod119.htm
[d]Council on Linkages Core Competencies. Retrieved from www.trainingfinder.org/competencies/list.htm
[e]*Performance standards.* Retrieved from www.phppo.cdc.gov/nphpsp/index.asp
[f]Core functions–Essential services. Retrieved from www.phppo.cdc.gov/nphpsp/10EssentialPHServices.asp
[g]The future of the public's health in the 21st century. Retrieved from www.nap.edu/books/030908704X/html
[h]Who will keep the public healthy? Retrieved from www.nap.edu/books/030908542X/html/R1.html
Source: Lichtveld and Cioffi (2003).

ership skills to skills related to cultural competency. There are six strategic elements related to the development of the public health workforce:

- Collect more detailed information about the composition of the public health workforce.
- Clearly define the competencies necessary for public health practice today. Then the competencies need to be tied to specific educational and training materials to ensure that the competencies will be attainable.
- Develop integrated learning management systems to better document the learning experiences of the public health professional workforce.
- Incentives for learning must be integrated into the lifelong learning models that are critical for public health preparedness.
- Programs must be evaluated.
- The necessary financial support must be provided.

Lichtveld and Cioffi (2003) looked at these six challenges from the perspective of building a science base, of the implications to policy, and the critical need to tie training to practice. The summary of this analysis can be found in Table 3–2.

1988 INSTITUTE OF MEDICINE REPORT

There are many health professionals who believe that most technical reports make little difference. When the report is released, there is a flurry of press coverage and sessions at annual professional meetings about the report and its recommendations. Much criticism often occurs. Is the public health system really in disarray? Some critics may argue that the recommendations are unrealistic. Then, with time, the pretty salmon-colored report goes on the shelf and is lost among the flurry of new reports that get released. The IOM's 1988 report on *The Future of Public Health* did make a difference and affected the direction of public health throughout the 1990s and still is affecting public health in the 21st century as the follow-up report is being discussed. Most if not all prepared public health leaders have a copy of this report and use it frequently as a guide to public health practice. Every page of the report has had an impact on public health. To put the report in perspective, Table 3–3 lists 10 infrastructure impacts of the report. Other writers may select other issues, but the following list does point to some of the report's significant impacts.

Table 3-2 Challenges and Implications for Public Health Workforce Development

Strategic Element	Science	Policy	Implications for Practice
Monitor workforce composition and project needs	Without a scientific base upon which to develop a standard ratio of workers to area, the use of workforce target numbers is arbitrary.	New policy is needed that defines a standard ratio of workers needed per unit area.	Currently, only estimates of the number and composition of the workforce have been generated, which creates difficulty in projecting resource needs for program implementation.
Identify competencies/ Develop curriculum	Key scientific gaps still exist in many disciplines, hampering development of discipline-specific competencies.	Policy leading to national acceptance of standardized, competency-based training with built-in incentive structures (certification/credentialing) is needed.	Competencies must be translated into integrated training to ensure that public health professionals understand each other's skills, thereby improving coordination of multidisciplinary efforts.
Integrate learning system	Only limited data exist regarding distributed learning delivery systems and adult learning performance.	Strategies should be developed to integrate the several existing federal, state, and local academic learning systems.	The infrastructure, networks, and awareness of learning systems varies significantly among agencies.
Provide incentives to ensure competency	No national system of incentives (including certification and credentialing) exists to ensure competency. Any such system should include strategies to promote lifelong learning.	Policy is needed to encourage recognition of specialized training and to allow portability of that recognition across state lines in emergency situations.	Development of models for career ladders and other incentives for staff (recognition, pay increase, promotion potential) needs to parallel implementation of new learning requirements.

continues

Table 3–2 *continued*

Strategic Element	Science	Policy	Implications for Practice
Conduct evaluation and research	A knowledge base linking individual competence to organizational performance and health outcomes is not well developed.	Evaluation strategies should be based on relationships among individual competence, organizational performance, and health outcomes.	Lack of feedback from evaluation makes it difficult to determine capacity and preparedness of the workforce.
Ensure financial support	Evaluation and accountability efforts are critical to public health's demonstration of its essential worth to the nation and to achieve recognition of the cost–benefit in expenditure of resources on public health programs.	To foster dual use of the nation's public health network, DHHS must ensure that various federal programs working to enhance the nation's public health preparedness work in collaboration.	Sustainability of core funding continues to be a prime concern for the public health infrastructure. While the influx of bioterrorism funds can further the development of public health workforce capacity, it could result in a resource drain on nonbioterrorism public health programs.

Table 3-3 1988 Institute of Medicine Top 10 Infrastructure Impacts

1. Clearer mission for public health
2. Promotion of the public health core functions model
3. Why every state should have a health department
4. Creation of public health leadership institutes
5. Support for nationwide health objectives
6. Importance of public health law
7. Emphasis on improving access to care
8. Increasing importance of collaborative relationships
9. Importance of training programs for the public health workforce
10. Promotion of a systems perspective for public health—community responsibility versus agency responsibility

---

Clearer Mission for Public Health

The report reviewed the history of public health in the United States in order to put into perspective the definition and contemporary mission of public health, which was to fulfill society's interests in assuring conditions in which the American people can be healthy. It is clear from the way the mission was stated and from the report as a whole that the mission related to the community as a whole. The health of the public needed to be seen as a shared responsibility. The word *public* itself implied a community perspective. Assuring conditions for health would also seem to have implied that public health is affected by personal health behaviors; environmental health concerns such as air quality, water quality, and potential toxic agents; economic downturns; behavioral health concerns; natural and not so natural crisis events; and programs and services consistent with the values that guide community life.

Promotion of the Public Health Core Functions Model

When public health professionals think of the 1988 report, the major idea that is most often mentioned relates to the delineation of the three public health core functions of assessment, policy development, and assurance. These three functions have become the foundation for a governing paradigm of public health (see Table 1–1). The assessment function relates to the need for information to guide the public health enterprise. This is the function that relates to data collection and analysis, issues related to how data are used, epidemiology, biostatistics, health screening and status information, laboratory analysis, and the whole new field of public health informatics which has evolved since the 1988 report was published. The development of many new assessment tools have also occurred since 1988.

Why Every State Should Have a Health Department

An important policy was determined when the recommendation was made: every state and territory should have a health department with a director with cabinet level status. This is still a critical dimension of public health system development, in spite of the movement to state human service superagencies in the 1990s with public health being a component of these agencies. The superagency model has left the directors of public health without cabinet level status in many instances. The superagency decision has often been made for political reasons and an assumption that the model will save money. This has not often been the case. Public health leaders have struggled in these agencies to define the state public health mission and the state funding necessary to carry out the mission. Many American governors are resistant to raising the taxes necessary to support a strong public health system as well as a strong educational system.

Creation of Public Health Leadership Institutes

The report recognized the critical issues related to public health leadership as well as the rapid turnover in the leadership of the field. Public health leaders are the major spokespeople for communicating to the public the various health risks and problems. These leaders also must make strong arguments for the expenditure of funds to address these problems. They need to build constituencies to support their work (see Increasing Importance of Collaboration Relationships). They also need to support the continuing need for scientific research to find ways to either cure or ameliorate these public health problems and risks. The major dilemma here is that many of the individuals who are appointed to high level governmental positions have little or no specific public health training. A medical degree is not sufficient. Public health administrators need leadership development training that not only introduces them to public health but also the skills and tools necessary to be an effective public health leader (Rowitz, 2001). Since 1988, the Centers for Disease Control and Prevention in concert with Schools of Public Health have supported the development of a national public health leadership institute and a number of state and regional institutes as was pointed out in Chapter 1.

Support for Nationwide Health Objectives

Public health professionals have tended to support a national public health agenda with national objectives. A process was implemented to develop a national set of health objectives for the year 2000 and then again for the year 2010. Although public health has made strong arguments in support of these national agendas, they have been difficult to implement because of fiscal restraints. The 2000 report was discussed much during the 1990s, but there have been barriers and problems surrounding the implementation plans for the 2010 objectives. Without political and legislative support for the plans, implementation as well as follow-through are almost impossible to attain. Public health leaders have not always been successful in their advocacy for public health agendas. It is important that leaders do not give up on a national agenda. A national agenda is critical to the strengthening of the public health system and the implementation of a national public health practice agenda.

Importance of Public Health Law

The 1988 report made us aware of the importance of public health statutes and laws. The concern raised in 1988 was that the public health laws in the various states needed to be revised in terms of the clear delineation of the roles and responsibilities of health officers and state agencies related to public health activities. The report also noted the necessity of updating the disease control measures for contemporary health care problems. It has become increasingly apparent over the intervening years how important these laws and statutes are and how they affect the manner in which the public health system operates and determines its priorities. Much discussion has been occurring since the happenings of September 11, 2001, on the development of a model statute related to bioterrorism events as well as statutes to revise public health laws in the states. A prepared public health leader clearly has to understand how the legal code works and also understand the nuances of public health laws and statutes. These issues will be further discussed later in this book.

Emphasis on Improving Access to Care

There has been continuing concern in the United States about the inability of segments of the population to have access to health and public health services. Public health agencies at the local level are often providers of last resort. The 1988 report strongly argued for the assurance of high-quality services that included personal health services. These services were supposed to be available to all community residents. In the many years since the report was published, this access issue still is a challenge for the health and public health system. The failed attempt to gain support for universal health care by the Clinton administration during the 1990s has only exacerbated the problems. Millions of people lack health insurance—both employed and unemployed individuals. Another interesting twist in the access issue has been the recent movement towards eliminating health disparities. This new wrinkle adds the cultural dilemma of cultural diversity and the lack of cultural competency by many in the health professions in working with patients and clients with different racial and cultural characteristics. The prepared public health leader knows the importance of cultural awareness and works with others to improve these culturally diverse relationships. There is another important dimension to the access issue: the health of the public needs to be seen within the ecological context of the community because many solutions to the access problem need to be developed at the local level by the public health leader and his or her community partners.

Increasing Importance of Collaboration Relationships

The above discussion leads to the eighth infrastructure impact of the 1988 report. Collaboration is critical. Public health is a shared responsibility. The major work of public health occurs outside of the walls of the local or state health agency. The authors of the report stated that the goals and objectives of public health cannot be addressed by the health department alone, but needs to occur collaboratively with private health and social organizations, health practitioners from the community, other public agencies, and the community at large. The involvement of grassroots leaders is also important if the public health agenda is to be met. An important dimension tied to collaboration involves the critical need for the state health apparatus to work with local communities to support local service capacity especially when many of these local communities have difficulty in raising revenue to support local health initiatives. If public health is local in operation, then it is important that no resident of the community be unable to gain access to public health programs and services.

Importance of Training Programs for the Public Health Workforce

As pointed out several times in this book, the public health workforce needs training. The skills that we learned in school in the last century are or may no longer be sufficient to help us function efficiently and effectively in the new century. To increase the capacity of the public health system, it is clear that an investment in the public health workforce is important. The 1988 report pointed out that one important way to provide this training would be to involve the schools of public health at various universities in these training activities. This would significantly improve academic and practice linkages. The development of educational and training opportunities for the public health workforce has been growing in recent years partly because of the terrorist events of September 11, 2001 and because of the need to prepare the workforce for its critical public health roles in emergency preparedness and response. There are also ongoing discussions about the development of a certification process for public health workers.

Promotion of a Systems Perspective for Public Health

In many ways one of the more significant impacts is the gradual shift from an agency-based public health perspective in the 1980s to a community or systems-based approach today. The systems perspective points to a community focus for public health with responsibility shared by the public health agency, its community partners, and every resident of the community. It is a "big picture" approach. However, it was noted that many communities do not have a well- integrated public health system in operation. Many relationships between agencies is competitive. There is clearly duplication of services and programs. This continues to be a problem today, although shrinking budgets and deficits may require more consolidation and collaboration.

Clearly, the 1988 report significantly affected the modern view of public health. There was an awareness that strong public health leadership is needed if the public health system is to become stronger and more effective. It is also clear that the public health leader needs to spend more time out in the community working with other leaders to create and implement the changes necessary to strengthen public health infrastructure and to bring about a more effective public health system for every American community.

1996 HEALTHY COMMUNITIES REPORT

An interim report was released in 1996 to record the progress in implementing the recommendations of the 1988 report and to account for the health care concerns related to the growth of managed care in the 1990s (Institute of Medicine, 1996). Distinctions were made in the report about the differences between personal health services and community interventions. In many instances, local health departments found themselves delivering personal health services as well as community interventions when these personal health services were not available through other health care providers to segments of the community. In fact, at least one health department in Florida experimented with creating its own health maintenance organization to serve the poorer segments of its service area (Rowitz, 2001). Some local public health agencies have argued that the delivery of personal services has provided the local health agency with revenue to run its community programs. Revenue for these community programs is often hard to obtain. Public health leaders had to become quite entrepreneurial in the 1990s if their agencies were to continue functioning at a high level of efficiency. These leaders began to apply for various grants and contracts to supplement limited local revenue sources.

The relationship between managed care and public health became contentious during the 1990s. The 1996 report tried to clarify the role of public health agencies in the changing health care environment. First, public health agencies were and still are the primary source of information on the health status of the population, emerging disease risks, and determinants of health. Second, public health agencies can work with managed care entities in planning and policy development. Third, public health agencies can provide specialized services such as family case management and other enabling services to all residents of the service community regardless of where these residents receive their health care. Finally, managed care organizations can gain assurance and oversight assistance from local health departments. The report pointed out that the core functions perspective would strengthen the relationship between public health agencies and their local health care partners.

The report also clarified the increasing role of local public health agencies in community partnerships. A critical role for governmental public health agencies was seen to involve the identification and work with *all* organizations that might impact the health of the public. The rationale given was that the public health agency has the knowledge and skills within it to understand and communicate the comprehensive array of factors that affect the health of the community. Part of this knowledge relates to the governing paradigm of public health. The core functions of assessment, policy development, and assurance have been further clarified through the delineation of the 10 essential public health services. These core functions and essential services help to organize information and help public health leaders in their work with communities.

The 1996 report also recognized the importance of training public health professionals. It specifically noted the advances in training public health leaders through the Centers for Disease Control and Prevention initiatives related to public health leadership and the general training of public health workers through the Public Health Training Network. Public health leaders need to be equipped with skills necessary to carry out the core functions and essential services of public health. These skills range from knowledge about communication, strategic planning and continuous quality improvement, cultural competency skills, conflict resolution and negotiation skills, and mentoring techniques (Rowitz, 2001).

The report also pointed out that progress in reaching the objectives of the 1988 report was slow in occurring. However, the report also stated that the recommendations of the original report were still relevant and should still guide the development of future public health programs. There was also an awareness that the core functions model was not understandable to everyone and needed to be translated into language that other partners, and even elected officials, can understand. There clearly remained the issue of limited resources to carry out the public health agenda. Public health supporters then and now still struggle to gain acceptance and revenue for the public health agenda, even though bioterrorism and other terrorist threats have increased the visibility of public health's role in prevention of these crises. Funding has increased in recent years for these initiatives.

THE FUTURE OF THE PUBLIC'S HEALTH IN THE 21ST CENTURY

At the beginning of the new report (IOM, 2003), recognition was given to the effects of the events of September 11, 2001, on the public health system. It seemed clear that the governmental public health system was not prepared for dealing with terrorist or bioterrorism events. Years of political neglect, budget cuts, political agendas that were oriented towards the protection of the private sectors of the economy, the aging of the governmental public health workforce, and the lack of public health training of this workforce all added up to a lack of preparedness on the part of public health. Thus, the United States is vulnerable on many fronts: from emerging infectious disease and the lack of research to protect the public to the types of social and environmental conditions that undermine the health of the public. All these factors have drawn attention to the need for support and the strengthening of the public health system. This report addressed these priorities. Although it is true that there has been increasing support for public health in recent years related to emergency preparedness and response, many of the traditional public health programs and services still tend to be severely underfunded. It is critical to remember that there is more to public health than bioterrorism. Despite many criticisms of the recommendations of this report, the report goes a long way in addressing and creating an agenda for public health in the future. Some of these issues are discussed by Dr. Hugh Tilson, Senior Advisor to the Dean at the University of North Carolina School of Public Health at Chapel Hill, in Case Study 3. Tilson has taken a major leadership role in defining the agenda for public health in the future.

The report proposed six areas of action and change:

1. The adoption of a population health approach based on the multiple determinants of health
2. Building and strengthening public health infrastructure
3. Collaboration with all segments of the community
4. Accountability related to the assurance of high-quality public health programs and the availability of these programs for all who need them
5. Building an evidence-based public health system
6. Improvements and enhancement of communication within the public health system

The report presented 34 major recommendations. Table 3–4 presents 10 key recommendations from this report that have important implications for the prepared public health leader and for the future of public health more specifically. This report needs to be taken seriously. Although criticism and discussion are necessary, the next step in addressing the

CASE STUDY 3   A Public Health Practice Quiz for Hugh Tilson

1. To build the public health infrastructure in the future, what strategies can be employed to get young health professionals to choose a career in public health?

   We need a national public health service that permits a single civil service status for all public health employees—federal, state, and local— with transferability of benefits and suitable salaries.

2. You have served on both IOM committees for the *Future of Public Health* reports as well as the *Healthy Communities* interim reports. What do you think were the major impacts of the 1988 report?

   The 1996 IOM Commission and Public Health Roundtable (for which I was cochair) held hearings and learned of dozens of remarkable strides attributed by opinion leaders and implementers. Most impressive was the alignment of the field around the construct of "assure, assess, and develop policy" as the nondelegable core functions of public health.

3. How do we go about developing strategies to implement the recommendations of the 2003 report in light of the events of September 11, 2001?

   The implementation of the 2003 IOM report is already ongoing and of great importance to the future of public health. Among major steps already underway, perhaps none is more important than a strong, nationwide consensus that the "10 essential services," embodied in the public health system performance standards, and embodied in the recommendations for public health infrastructure in the IOM report, form the backbone of the health-prepared community, and that public money spent to improve preparedness should be directed to build the public health infrastructure.

4. What types of skills will the prepared public health leader need to be able to implement the recommendations of the 2003 report in light of the events of September 11, 2001?

   Another fundamental recommendation of the 2003 IOM report is that the public health workforce must not only *be* competent, but must organize to demonstrate and credential that competence, and then continuously train public health professionals to maintain and upgrade their competencies. While there are many "new" competencies urged in the IOM report on education of public health professionals and many more which could be specified, the core public health practice competencies already well negotiated and widely agreed upon by the Council on Linkages will remain the essentials for the next decades.

continues

CASE STUDY 3   *continued*

5. How can our national public health organizations help in pushing the public health agenda?

   Without concerted effort by the national associations responsible for one or more of the recommendations of the IOM reports and the public health system they reflect, we will fall short of our full potential. Whatever individual commitment each public health organization makes, it will be important for the American Public Health Association to revisit the medicine–public health link, for the Association of State and Territorial Health Organizations (ASTHO) to advocate for a National Public Health Services Corps, for the National Association for County and City Health Organizations (NACCHO) to build on the "operational definition" of a local agency, and for the Council on Linkages to advance the public health systems research agenda, just to name a few. The key will be for these organizations to all agree to meet regularly and help each other be accountable for follow-through.

recommendations of the report must involve the development of strategies to bring the vision of the report to fruition. Strong public health leadership is needed if this is to occur. The logic of the report can be seen in Figure 3–1. The major assumption that undergirds the report is the belief that the United States population is not as healthy as it could be. The explanations for this can be seen in both systems problems and in societal norms and influences. To address these concerns, governmental public health agencies must work with other community partners to create the changes necessary to create a healthier society. Strong public health and community leadership is needed to make this happen. Societal norms and influences need to change. The public health system also needs to change. This will partly occur through changes in public policy. To create an outcome that promotes health in all our communities, there clearly needs to be improvements in population health and the elimination of health disparities.

A key recommendation is the creation of a national commission to review all existing public health laws and proposals that are being developed related to model statutes for public health and for emergency health powers. There are many inconsistencies in our laws at the federal, state, and local level. A national commission could work to develop a framework for public health law in this country. However, it is important to listen to local public health providers and others about how law impacts the

Table 3-4 Ten Key Recommendations of the 2003 Institute of Medicine Report of Public Health

1. Create a national commission to review public health law.
2. Expand workforce development activities to increase competencies of public health workers to carry out the core functions and essential public health services—including a possible credentialing scenario.
3. Emphasize and continue to train public health leaders to function in an emergency preparedness environment.
4. Emphasize communication skills as a core public health set of competencies.
5. Build the public health information infrastructure.
6. Develop methods for the assessment of public health infrastructure and its ability to carry out essential public health services to every American community.
7. Develop a public health practice research agenda.
8. Build collaborative relationships within communities.
9. Improve media relationships.
10. Increase prevention activities.

day-to-day operations of public health programs and service. There is also a need to recognize that law reform is a complex process integrally tied to the total functioning of a democratic society. A major challenge involves the fact that bioterrorism acts often cross state boundaries. Differences in laws in different states need to be reconciled.

There has been much discussion over the aging of the public health workforce and the lack of training of the workforce. A major set of recommendations in the report involved this issue. Strong arguments were made for training that was competency based. In 2000, the Council on Linkages Between Academia and Public Health Practice came up with the following list of core public health competencies:

1. Analysis and assessment
2. Policy development and program planning
3. Communication
4. Cultural competency
5. Community dimensions of practice
6. Basic public health sciences
7. Financial planning and management
8. Leadership and systems thinking

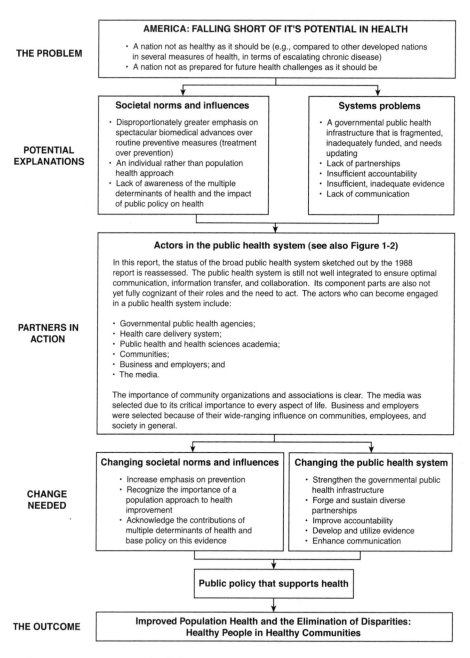

FIGURE 3–1 Framework of the 2003 IOM Report

The direction of training programs is toward linking these competencies to the core public health functions as well as to essential public health services. The goal of training is to have support persons in a public health agency who understand public health at the fundamental level and also public health leaders who are experts in their fields (Tilson & Gebbie, 2004).

The third recommendation relates to the need to train public health leaders. The report recognized the progress made in the training of public health leaders beginning in the early 1990s. The development of leadership competencies are critical for carrying out the work of public health. The National Public Health Leadership Network has developed a public health leadership competency framework that has served as a guide for the development of public health leadership training programs around the country. The model developed by the network was created in 1996 with an awareness that competency frameworks must not be etched in stone. They must be modified and updated as new realities enter into our public health agendas (Rowitz, 2001). The network continues to examine these competencies to make sure they represent the needs of public health practice today. Wright and her colleagues (2000) presented the following list of major competency areas for public health leaders:

1. Core transformational competencies
2. Political competencies
3. Transorganizational dynamics
4. Team-building competencies

This competency framework recognized early on the importance of collaboration in public health. Transformational competencies include skills related to visioning, creating a mission, development of change strategies and becoming a change agent. Political competencies involve skills in working within the political structure of the community, state, and federal systems. Political competencies also affect policy development, conflict resolution and negotiation skills, ethics and value-based strategies, along with marketing and education skills. Transorganizational competencies include the understanding of organizational dynamics, interorganization collaboration techniques, social forecasting methods, and scenario building. Team-building competencies include skills in the development of teams, coalitions, alliances and partnerships, group facilitation techniques, mediation roles, and ability to work with others. Subcompetencies are included under all of the four major competency categories.

The leadership framework also recognized the importance of communication in public health. Communication skills are a core public health set of competencies. The IOM report supported the need for strong communication skills both for internal functioning of governmental public health agencies and for external relationships with community partners and the public. One of the important activities for public health professionals is the transmission of information about health issues to outside sources, including the media. Communication skills include the use of all the new information technology sources that are at our disposal today. Messages given need to be culturally appropriate and suitable for the literacy levels of the audience for whom the message is being sent. Different language is needed for different audiences. Public health leaders need to become communication experts. Communication is a complex process with mastery needed in over 18 different communication skill areas (Rowitz, 2001). In general, the communication of public health information is important as a mechanism for getting information from the community about the health concerns that it has. It is also important as a mechanism for getting information to the public about health risks to the community from disease outbreaks and from disasters both natural and man-made.

Communication with the media is becoming more and more critical. The prepared public health leader needs to be able to communicate with the press as well as be able to be the voice of public health in television and radio interviews. Public health leaders can develop trusting relationships with journalists and other media people and provide accurate information on health risks to the community as well as interpret new research findings. Most television stations, for example, now have health reporters and editors. The goal of public health communication is to provide accurate and up-to-date information during a crisis. Communication improvement skills for the prepared public health leader are discussed more specifically in Part 3.

The fifth key recommendation involves the infrastructure of public health information. The report noted all the changes occurring in the information technology area over the last decade with the realization that public health information systems have lagged behind technology advances in other sectors. With proposed advances in technology, as well as bioterrorism grants to local health departments with the partial goal of improving information systems, it should be possible to build the information capabilities of the public health system over the next decade. These advances should also help build public health infrastructure by supporting and improving public health monitoring and disease surveillance activities. Prepared public health leaders need to learn how to use these new technologies as well as to develop competency in the use of data for program development and policy development. Specifically, the report recommended development and implementation of a national health information infrastructure. One cautionary note was discussed by the authors of the report. They warned that the public health information system needs to be as comprehensive as possible if it is to be the most useful. A silo-based bioterrorism information system would not be the most optimal information system for public health.

The next recommendation seems to be an extension of a recommendation from the 1988 IOM report, with the addition of the essential public health services component. This recommendation involved the importance of assessment as a public health function in the building of the infrastructure of public health. There is agreement that the core functions and essential public health services paradigm is an infrastructure building model. The paradigm defines the activities of public health. The model allows comparisons to be made across governmental public health agencies. It doesn't obliterate the fact that each community will carry out these activities in different ways, but it does say that these activities need to be carried out if public health is to be strengthened. The essential public health services model creates a structural system for public health and serves as a guide for the prepared public health leader in carrying out the public health agendas in his or her community. It is not meant to replace the need for governmental public health agencies to provide the many mandated services that they routinely provide, such as maternal and child health programs and restaurant inspections. The structural framework allows public health agencies to see the big picture in their work.

The report expands the assessment function to include the following:

1. Evaluation of federal, state, and local public health funding mechanisms
2. Study of the adequacy and capacity of the system to address the health needs of the public
3. Development of a funding and technical assistance plan to assure sustainability of public health programs and services

4. Continual evaluation at the state and local level of public health capacity through community-wide health assessments and implementation of a performance standards review of the state and local public health system

The seventh key recommendation involves the importance of developing a public health practice research agenda. Public health practice offers many opportunities for research related to the public health system as well as the factors which will guide policy decisions for public health practice. There are a number of groups that are looking at the issue of public health practice research, including the Centers for Disease Control and Prevention, the Council on Linkages Between Academia and Public Health Practice, the Association of Schools of Public Health and its Public Health Practice Council, the National Public Health Leadership Network, and other public health professional organizations. A coordinated plan needs to be developed to address the different perspectives of each of these organizations.

Some of the specific areas to be addressed in the development of a practice research agenda include monitoring the types and levels of the public health workforce and the effectiveness of various training initiatives; studies of how to develop and evaluate public health infrastructure; financial investments necessary to sustain a comprehensive public health system; performance of the essential public health services at the state and local levels; effectiveness of governance related to public health activities; participatory research related to improvements in health status of the public; and analysis of effectiveness of prevention programs.

Building on recommendations from previous IOM reports, the 2003 report emphasized the importance of seeing public health in a community context. The eighth recommendation emphasized the importance of collaboration. Because community-based organizations are so close to the people they serve, it is imperative that public health agencies work with these organizations and other grassroots community leaders. Without collaboration, the system will not work. These community-led efforts should include such activities as developing inventories of community resources, community assessment of needs, determination of gaps in service, formulation of collaborative response to these determinations of need, evaluation of outcomes related to community health improvement programs, and programs to increase service access for all segments of the population, and, of course, to eliminate any health disparities that may exist. Governmental public health agencies also need to provide technical assistance to community organizations and work collaboratively to obtain external funding to provide critical service and prevention programs for the community.

Recognizing the critical importance of leadership to collaboration, a collaborative leadership project was developed as part of the Robert Wood Johnson Turning Point Initiative. A training manual was prepared to train collaborative leaders (Turning Point, 2004). The training program involves the following six modules:

1. Assessing the environment
2. Creating clarity
3. Building trust
4. Sharing power
5. Developing people
6. Self-reflection

The prepared public health leader must become competent in these six areas if collaborative techniques are to be mastered. Exercise 3–1 will give you the chance to self-reflect on the issue of virtue. Virtue generally refers to the important concerns related to moral excellence and living the values by which a society defines itself.

An interesting collaborative effort involves the development of a Syndemics Prevention Network through the National Center for Chronic Disease Prevention and Health Promotion at the CDC (CDC, 2004). The Syndemics Prevention Network was developed to find ways to improve community health and to work towards health equity. Syndemics has been

---

EXERCISE 3–1   Self-Reflection

Purpose: To better understand on a personal level the virtues that make excellent leaders

Key Concepts: Self-reflection, virtues (moral excellence), ethics, values

Procedures: List 10 ideal virtues for people living in the United States today. Put a checkmark by the virtues which you believe refer to you. How can you improve your leadership behavior so that all 10 virtues become virtues by which you live your life?

defined as two or more afflictions which interact synergistically to contribute to an excess burden of disease in a population. A syndemic orientation would require the partners in the activity to inquire extensively into the various conditions that create and sustain health. The collaborative effort would also need to question and determine how these various health conditions might differ among various groups. The goal of these activities would be to find ways to remove those conditions that perpetuate health disparities. The network specifically involves the development of a national group of partner organization and community leaders, researchers, health officials, and others to work with CDC to find new prevention opportunities and strategies for energizing people throughout the public health workforce. The network wants to determine, using this collaborative approach, whether syndemics can alter public health science and action. The network is concerned with answering the following questions:

1. What is a syndemic?
2. What principles characterize a syndemic orientation?
3. Under what conditions is it appropriate to use this orientation?
4. What advantages and limitations are associated with this new orientation?
5. What procedures are available for planning and evaluating initiatives to prevent syndemics?
6. How can the public and the public health workforce be prepared to adopt the syndemics orientation?

Exercise 3–2 is an exercise related to the use of this model.

The ninth recommended priority of the IOM report involves the critical issue of improving media relationships. The skills associated with risk and crisis communication are discussed more fully in Chapter 11. The report recognized that public health leaders have often been ineffective in working with representatives from the mass media. In addition, many public health activities do not attract media attention. Most of us have heard that when public health is successful, nothing happens. Nothing tends to lack interest for the media. One of the more interesting recommendations in the report pointed to the value of developing an evidence base related to media influences on health knowledge and behavior in addition to the promotion of healthy public policy.

Finally, and probably the most important, set of recommendations related to the need to increase our public health prevention activities.

EXERCISE 3-2   A Problem in Syndemics

Purpose: To explore the relevance of syndemics for public health practice

Key Concepts: Syndemics, epidemic control, community health improvement

Procedures: A syndemic orientation implies that a key mission for public health is to move beyond epidemic control to incorporate community health improvement techniques in the process. There has been a significant increase in adolescent pregnancy in your community over the last decade. Explore some of the syndemic issues involved and also develop strategies for ways to reduce the rates. Using this new orientation might help your community coalition to better define the conditions under which categorically organized interventions can be effective, as well as the extent to which fragmented programs might themselves be a barrier to the goal of protecting the public's health.

1. Divide the class or training group into smaller groups of eight, each of which represents a community coalition
   A. Local health department administrator
   B. Director of family planning agency
   C. Principal of local family planning agency
   D. President of high school parents' organization
   E. Adolescent mother
   F. Member of county board of health
   G. Local business leader
   H. Minister, priest, rabbi, or other religious leader

2. Using a combination of procedures such as those listed below, address the problem, plan program strategies, and determine ways to document achievement:
   A. Determine differences in epidemic control (attribution) and systems change or community health improvement issues (contribution factors).
   B. Expand traditional outcome measures to include other community outcome issues based on culture and other factors.
   C. Define the conditions for a healthy community.
   D. Develop strategies for monitoring progress using a navigational model rather than a traditional steering model.
   E. Document changes in the community as a result of new strategies being implemented.

3. Develop a 2-page community syndemics plan for the problem and then present it to the group facilitator to present to the mayor of the community.

The committee behind the report felt that the majority of funded research through the various National Institutes of Health were for biomedically based research activities. There is clearly work that needs to occur on the prevention front. One specific recommendation related to an increase in funding levels for the CDC-funded Prevention Research Centers. Some of the most influential prevention research has been carried out by these centers over the last decade. The innovative Special Interest Projects (SIP) have also added to our knowledge base. Each of the prevention research centers focus on projects related to a public health theme. Yet, these programs and centers have been underfunded. Increased funding is necessary for these centers.

In addition, it was strongly argued that National Institutes of Health funding should be increased for population and community-based prevention research that addresses the following:

1. Identifies population-level health problems
2. Involves a definable population and also operates at the level of the whole person
3. Evaluates the application and effects of innovative programs and services as well as new discoveries on the actual health and health status of the population
4. Concentrates on the behavioral, psychological, and environmental factors associated with primary and secondary prevention of disease and disability in populations

To this latter point should be added the factors involved in tertiary prevention activities as well.

SUMMARY

This chapter has been all about leadership. Any success that the public health profession will have in accomplishing the recommendations of these various reports require not only prepared public health leaders but also a prepared public health workforce. A vision of the future of public health requires a template for guiding the agenda of public health. The various reports discussed in this chapter provide such a template. The additional requirements of emergency preparedness and response create an overlay to this agenda. This overlay will be discussed in detail in Part 2 of this book.

REFERENCES

Association of State and Territorial Health Officials. (2004). *State public health employee workers shortage report.* Washington, DC: ASTHO.

Centers for Disease Control and Prevention. (2004). *Syndemics overview.* Atlanta: CDC Syndemics Prevention Network.

Council on Linkages Between Academia and Public Health Practice. (2000). *Core public health competencies.* Washington, DC: Public Health Foundation.

Fraser, M. P. (2003). Commentary: The local public health agency workforce: Research needs and practice realities. *Journal of Public Health Management and Practice, 9*(6), 496–499.

Hajat, A., Stewart, K., & Hayes, K. L. (2003). The local public health workforce in rural communities. *Journal of Public Health and Practice Management, 9*(6), 481–488.

Institute of Medicine. (1988). *The future of public health.* Washington, DC: National Academy Press.

Institute of Medicine. (2003). *The future of the public's health in the 21st century.* Washington, DC: National Academy of Science.

Institute of Medicine. (1996). *Healthy communities.* Washington, DC: National Academy Press.

Lichtveld, M. Y., & Cioffi, J. P. (2003). Public health workforce development: Progress, challenges, and opportunities. *Journal of Public Health Management and Practice, 9*(6), 443–450.

Rowitz, L. (2001). *Public health leadership: Putting principles into practice.* Sudbury, MA: Jones and Bartlett.

Tilson, H., & Gebbie, K. (2004). The public health workforce. In J. E. Fielding, R. C. Brownson, & N. M. Clark (Eds.), *Annual review of public health* (Vol. 25, pp. 341–356). Palo Alto, CA: Annual Review, Inc.

Turning Point Leadership Collaborative. (2004). *Collaborative leadership learning modules.* Seattle: Turning Point National Program Office.

Wright, K., Rowitz, L., Merkle, A., Reid, W. M., Robinson, G., Herzog, B., et al. (2000). Competency development in public health leadership. *American Journal of Public Health, 90*(8), 1202–1207.

PART II

Emergency Preparedness and Response

CHAPTER 4

Overview to Bioterrorism Preparedness and Response

We are life's way of getting things done. There is always
something that needs doing right here and now. So do it.

—*Rabbi Rami Shapiro*
Congregation Beth Or, Miami, Florida

Since September 11, 2001, it seems like most of our conversation in public
health relates to bioterrorism, emergency preparedness, and our response to
it. There is also conversation about the critical role of public health during
any crisis. Public health preparedness is all about the need to be ready for
any health crisis that a community may face. The major responsibility of
public health in a crisis or other emergency that includes terrorism events
similar to those of September 11, 2001, or the anthrax letters bioterrorism
events in the months following, must be seen in the context of the overall
mission of public health to promote and protect the health of the public. If
this is the case, then emergency preparedness is to be seen as an extension
of the public health mission and integral to public health.

A crisis is a disruption in the normal activities that guide the daily work
of public health. Crisis is an abnormal event or series of disruptive events
that threaten the total operation of an organization or threaten the functioning of a community or country. Thus, crisis and its aftermath are examples of system failure. It is the crisis event that triggers community
emergency response activities. I will use the words crisis, disaster, emer-

gency, and hazard interchangeably in this book although the meanings of these terms do show subtle differences, as discussed below. An excellent example of the role of public health in a crisis can be seen in the train derailment case discussed in Case Study 4. The case study takes place in a small rural county in the Midwest. The case study also includes a number of supporting documents in a series of short appendices attached to the case.

In terms of other relevant definitions, the World Health Organization and Pan African Emergency Training Centre (2002) made a distinction between a disaster and an emergency. A disaster refers to the occurrence of an event that disrupts the normal conditions of existence and causes a level of suffering that exceeds the capacity of adjustment that is usual for a given community. It is important to remember that people are the most affected by a disaster although structural damage may also occur. WHO defined an emergency as a time in which normal procedures for dealing with events are suspended and extraordinary measures need to be taken to overt further disastrous events. WHO further distinguished between a hazard which is a natural or human event that threatens to adversely affect human life, property, or activities to such an extent that a disaster occurs, and vulnerabilities in a population or community that may make a crisis event more severe. Vulnerabilities then refer to predispositions to suffer damage in a population or community from external events. As Figure 4–1 demonstrates, a disaster occurs when hazards and vulnerabilities meet.

The United Nations has used the following definition to refer to disaster preparedness (Disaster Management Training Programme, 1994):

> Disaster preparedness minimizes the adverse effects of a hazard through effective precautionary actions, rehabilitation and recovery to ensure the timely, appropriate and effective organization and delivery of relief and assistance following a disaster.

TYPES OF CRISIS

In two excellent books on crisis and crisis management (Mitroff, 2001, 2004), the discussion of crisis and its aftermath is seen as related to the type of crisis that is involved. Bioterrorism events relates to only one type of crisis situation. Crisis falls into several different groups. Each major type of crisis requires different response patterns. Table 4–1 reviews a typology of crisis developed by Mitroff (2001). It was noted that there are at least seven different classes of crisis. The first group of crises are economic in nature

CASE STUDY 4

Emergency Response of Public Health to a Train Derailment and Evacuation

Authors:
Barbara Black, MSN
Herb Bostrom
Jean Durch, RN, MPH
Holly Matucheski, BSN
Jane Peterson, RN, MSN, MA, RS

Introduction

Government leaders at all levels are increasingly turning their attention towards emergency preparedness efforts. According to this state's public health statutes, health departments, as part of local government, are obligated to provide emergency management in the areas of mitigation, preparedness, response, and recovery. Communities have suffered devastating fires, floods, storms, hazardous spills, and terrorism. Because of health departments' direct experience responding to these disasters, they have had to translate concepts and plans into concrete practices. They have generally accomplished this while collaborating with other entities such as the Department of Natural Resources (DNR), the American Red Cross, hospitals, police and fire departments, National Guard units, and the US Department of Agriculture.

This case study looks at operationalizing the abstract function of assurance into the public health practices needed when confronted with a train derailment and evacuation of more than 1900 residents of a small community and the surrounding area. It studies the assurance role of a local health department in a complex emergency involving multiple agencies and levels of response.

For the purpose of this study, the assurance function is divided into four practices:

- Manage resources and develop organizational structure through the acquisition, allocation, and control of human, physical, and fiscal resources, and maximize the operational functions of the local public health system through coordination of community agencies' efforts and avoidance of duplication of services.
- Implement programs and other arrangements ensuring or providing direct services for priority health needs identified in the community by taking actions that translate plans and policies into services.
- Evaluate programs and provide quality assurance in accordance with applicable professional and regulatory standards to ensure that programs are consistent with plans and policies, and provide feed-

continues

CASE STUDY 4   *continued*

back on inadequacies and changes needed to redirect programs and resources.

- Inform and educate the public on health issues of concern in the community, promoting an awareness about public health services availability and promoting health education initiatives that contribute to individual and collective changes in health knowledge, attitudes, and practices towards a healthier community.

As you consider this case study, try to determine how successfully the local health department carried out these practices. What practices are illustrated? What practices are missing and what else could the department have done to assure a healthy community?

Community and Health Department Background

Moogaritaville is a small Midwestern village with a population of 1700. It is situated in the heart of rural Past-Your-Eyes County, which has a population of 48,000. Agriculture and related services are the major industries of Moogaritaville and the surrounding area. The Udder Express Train runs daily through the heart of the village and serves the industries. Located near the banks of the Meandering River, Moogaritaville prides itself in its strong economy and pristine environment.

The Past-Your-Eyes County Health and Human Services Department (PCHHSD) is located 10 miles away from Moogaritaville in the city of Silage, the county seat. The health officer, who also leads the Health Services Division (HSD) of the department, serves on many community committees, including the Local Emergency Planning Committee (LEPC). The conservative Past-Your-Eyes County Board of Supervisors has not been willing to approve a position of environmental sanitarian, even though the health officer has requested it annually since 1990. While they do not have a formal environmental health service, the HSD does work closely with the State Health Department on environmental health issues. The organizational chart for the PCHHSD and HSD is included in Appendix A.

The PCHHSD has adopted a community health plan which incorporates some of the principles of the *Healthy People* national health promotion and disease prevention objectives. Reducing human exposure to toxic agents is one of the objectives of the community plan. The plan does not include objectives for the emergency response system.

continues

CASE STUDY 4 *continued*

Derailment Events

Monday, March 4, 1996

5:55 a.m. The Udder Express Train derailed in the middle of the village of Moogaritaville (see map, Appendix B, for location). A total of 36 railroad cars were derailed, which included 14 tanker cars loaded with liquid propane and two tanker cars loaded with sodium hydroxide. Two of the propane tanks ruptured, exploded, and began burning as a result of the derailment. The fire quickly spread to a feed mill adjacent to the tracks. The tankers loaded with sodium peroxide also ruptured.

6:00 a.m. Residents' calls began flooding 911, and the local volunteer fire department responded and attempted to put out the fire. At the same time, the sheriff directed the dispatcher to notify the management of the Udder Express Train. Realizing the magnitude of the problem, the dispatcher was contacted by the fire captain who had set up an Incident Command (IC) and notified the key personnel listed in the LEPC's Emergency Response Plan.

7:00 a.m. Local Udder Express personnel arrived at the scene. The initial plan of the IC was to put out structural fires and let the two propane tankers burn out. After learning more about the contents of the cars and the nature of the fire, the fire department and Udder Express personnel were concerned that a catastrophic explosion known as a BLEVE (boiling liquid expanding vapor explosion) would occur. This would result in a massive explosion, hurling fire and debris over a large area. Therefore, the fire captain with the support of Udder Express, halted firefighting efforts and moved his crew and the IC to a safer distance at a business outside of Moogaritaville. Simultaneously, law enforcement at the scene began an evacuation of the public. The American Red Cross was contacted to set up a shelter.

8:00 a.m. Law enforcement officials completely evacuated residents who lived within a half-mile radius of the wreck, a total of 399 ambulatory individuals. The key personnel on the LEPC roster began to arrive at the IC site. The health officer also arrived after having heard the announcement on the local radio station while on her way to work. A decision was made to establish an Emergency Operations Center (EOC) at the same location as the IC.

continues

CASE STUDY 4   *continued*

10:00 a.m.   Since the threat of explosion continued with the ongoing burning of the ruptured cars, all residents within a 2-mile radius were completely evacuated. The 1900 residents evacuated included residents of one nursing home and three community-based residential facilities (CBRFs). Of the 85 total residents from these facilities, one third were chronically mentally ill, one third were developmentally delayed, and one third were elderly. The residents were taken to the Sheltered Workshop in Silage, which was county owned. Even though there were few beds, it was chosen because many of the residents knew the site, and administration believed the residents would be returning to their facility within hours. Ambulances from adjacent communities and buses from the Sheltered Workshop assisted in the evacuation. Nursing home and shelter staff accompanied the residents and remained with them.

Udder Express officials directed residents to find rooms at motels in surrounding towns, assuring them that their expenses would be covered. Only a few residents showed up at the Red Cross shelter, but those who did received assistance with food, shelter, and other needs. Since Udder Express officials appeared very knowledgeable about the burning contents and were offering financial resources and assistance, they assumed the command of the IC.

11:00 a.m.   Two additional tankers caught fire. Also, as the volume of propane decreased in each tanker, the risk of a BLEVE increased. Therefore, the decision was made to wait and let all tankers burn out.

12:00 Noon   A decision was made to move the EOC to the courthouse in Silage, primarily because of the cramped quarters at the combined site. A meeting of key personnel in the EOC was held to brief members on the events so far. The derailment had captured media attention and reporters began to show up at the IC and the EOC asking about events at Moogaritaville. A primary media contact was designated at the EOC by the Emergency Government Director. The fire captain talked to media at the IC. The health officer called the HSD staff to the EOC to assist in manning telephones and to locate residents who had been dispersed to motels in a 35-mile radius. Home care nurses contacted evacuated patients and made arrangements for visits, special equipment, or other medical needs. Other residents, who mar-

continues

CASE STUDY 4   *continued*

	ginally managed in their homes prior to the evacuation, now needed assistance. Home care nurses provided assessments and planned for care.
2:00 p.m.	Evacuees expected to return to their homes within hours and left without taking medications, pets, or changes of clothing. With the fire still burning, individuals began to report needing their medications. The primary physician for many of the Moogaritaville residents was the one physician in private practice in the village. In addition, the prescriptions had been filled in the one local pharmacy. Since all had been evacuated, no records were available. The HSD personnel tracked down the evacuated physician and the local pharmacist to assist in assuring that prescriptions were correctly refilled at Silage pharmacies.
5:00 p.m.	Another tanker caught on fire. It became evident that nursing home and CBRF residents would not be returning to their facilities. The HSD helped secure cots and other needed equipment and supplies for the night. Farmers who owned farms in the evacuation zone expressed concern to the fire captain and sheriff that their cows needed to be fed and milked. As long as they agreed to only do what had to be done and return immediately, the IC permitted the farmers to enter the evacuation zone and feed and milk the cows. This decision was neither communicated to the EOC nor the public, and the farmers continued to tend to cows twice a day throughout the event.

The IC at the scene of the derailment continued surveillance and kept out other evacuees throughout the night. The EOC stayed open throughout the night in the courthouse to handle arising issues, including media releases.

Tuesday, March 5, 1996

The IC established daily briefings for the evacuees by the railroad and cleanup personnel in one location. The HSD, with the assistance of the State Health Department, prepared a press release on the health effects of propane and sodium hydroxide to allay the fears of the residents about long-term effects (see Appendix C). The HSD also prepared a letter to health care providers in the area to inform them about substances involved in the incident (see Appendix D).

Since few residents were coming to the Red Cross shelter, HSD staff accompanied railroad personnel to the area motels to talk with evacuees

continues

CASE STUDY 4   *continued*

and determine unmet needs. Surveillance and response continued at the IC and EOC.

It became evident that nursing home and CBRF residents would not be returning home soon. Space was available to house residents in a state-owned veterans home. The HSD contacted the State Nursing Home Regulators to get permission and a waiver to transport and house the residents at the veterans home. Community volunteers solicited by the HSD first cleaned the rooms in the vacant wing prior to their occupancy.

The dietitian of the HSD's WIC program consulted the State Health Department and arranged to give out early WIC drafts to evacuees who had left all their possessions at home and were in need of food assistance.

Wednesday, March 6, 1996

Poor reception was frequently experienced with wireless communication systems. The EOC was moved to Moogaritaville to be colocated with the IC to improve communication and utilize personnel efficiently.

The EOC began to plan for reentry. Subzero temperatures were expected later in the week and electric and gas remained shut off to homes. Officials predicted that if the evacuation continued, with fluctuations in temperature, water damage would occur to houses, resulting from freezing and rupture of pipes and from accumulated pet waste. They planned accordingly. The HSD and State Health Department developed a section of the reentry packet to be distributed to all evacuees at the time of reentry. This included the Health and Safety Recommendations for Reoccupying Your Home as well as a Household Public Health Profile (see Appendices E and F).

The PCHHSD director convened a group of professionals, including the health officer and evacuees, who met to assess the needs and attempt to solve problems. Called the Disaster Committee, the group included representatives from the HSD, social services, mental health, Salvation Army, Red Cross, Moogaritaville and Past-Your-Eyes officials and evacuees. The goal was to respond to needs while preventing duplication of efforts. As a result of the first meeting, a one-stop information and service center was set up before the weekend.

The Red Cross established a hotline to take calls at its shelter, fielding incoming inquiries about residents and to take pressure off of the HSD at the EOC. Since the HSD had no environmental staff, the sanitarian from the State Health Department arrived at the shelter to ensure proper handling of food. The sanitarian observed that a lot of food had been donated, and since there was limited storage space, some of the food was being stored in boxes outdoors. This was discouraged by the sanitarian, but the shelter staff did not see the problem. The health officer intervened, and the food was eventually moved indoors under protest.

continues

CASE STUDY 4   *continued*

Thursday, March 7, 1996

A controlled pet rescue was done. Pet owners entered the area in armored personnel carriers, dressed in protective clothing. Many pets were rescued, and in other cases where pets did not recognize their owners in the protective clothing, food was left in the home. The rescue seemed to have a calming effect on the evacuees and helped them cope with other inconveniences.

The Disaster Committee learned that evacuees at outlying motels were requesting more detailed information about the progress of the derailment response. Minutes of the IC briefings, and later video tapes, were faxed or sent to outlying sites for evacuees to view.

The shelter became a community center for evacuees with meals served and briefings occurring at the site. Public health nurses came at key times to talk to residents to determine if their needs were being met. Twenty-four-hour coverage was provided via a home care on-call system. Surveillance and response continued at the IC and EOC.

Friday, March 8, 1996

The IC observed that more tanker cars ignited and continued to burn for several days.

Saturday, March 9, 1996

The State Department of Natural Resources (DNR) representatives were a part of the IC and EOC teams. They monitored the impact of the derailment on the environment. An estimated 9000 gallons of sodium hydroxide leaked from the derailed tankers, flowed into the drainage ditch, and entered the Meandering River. By the end of this day, HazMat teams applied 4.5 tons of citric acid to the spill and affected area. DNR staff monitored surface water conditions of the Meandering River one mile downstream. They were concerned about impact to the ecosystem, if pH exceeded 9.5. The pH never reached that level; most readings were well below 9.5.

Sunday, March 10, 1996

The HazMat team entered the site and tapped into three intact tankers to remove propane contents and begin controlled burning. The team purged the now empty tanker cars with nitrogen. Other tankers continued burning. Throughout the week, other controlled releases of propane occurred. The IC and EOC continued surveillance and response throughout the week.

continues

CASE STUDY 4   *continued*

Sunday, March 17, 1996

Only two tankers remained containing propane. They were in an unstable condition and technicians were uncertain of the amount of propane they contained. A demolition expert was hired to place two sets of explosives on each car. The detonation of the first set of charges released pressure in each tank; the second which was detonated 35 seconds later created an opening in the base of each which allowed the propane to flow into a ditch, ignite, and burn.

Monday, March 18, 1996

The area was declared safe and cleanup at the site began. Approximately 13% of the homes were badly damaged. Building experts from the County Housing Authority accompanied evacuees to assist in inspecting their homes.

The reentry packet was distributed to all evacuees. The completed Household Public Health Profile was returned to the HSD following the incident (see Appendix F). All who requested follow-up, a total of 30 households, received a contact from the HSD.

Tetanus immunizations were offered to workers and evacuees to protect them as they began cleanup following the incident. The HSD and Solid Waste Division assisted the community in disposal of solid waste including household, animal, and construction waste.

Tuesday, March 19, 1996

The State Health Department sanitarians inspected the restaurants, delis, grocery stores, cheese factory, bakeries, and other public establishments. The goal was to reopen these establishments as soon as possible without compromising the safety of the public.

The State Health Department personnel also conducted sampling of selected residential walls and surfaces to ensure that there was no air deposition of hazardous substances released by the fires. The wall and surface tests were negative for hazardous substances.

The State Agriculture Department ordered that cows that had been in the hot zone be destroyed.

The village water plant was brought online. Residents were notified through the local media to boil their water until further notice given the length of time the system was out of service.

The DNR performed residential soil sampling for inorganic metals and polyaromatic hydrocarbons. The soil test results were negative for these substances.

continues

CASE STUDY 4   *continued*

Following the Incident

Two months after the event, the LEPC convened a meeting of all the key participants in the derailment for the debriefing. Lessons learned were shared and documented. A report of the incident was developed and discussed at subsequent meetings in order to plan for the next community emergency.

Many months passed before recovery was complete. Frequent contacts were made to residents regarding home repairs, water quality, and health issues. Several homes had to be razed and rebuilt due to the degree of damage. No ill health was reportedly caused by the incident.

Conclusion

This case study illustrates how a local health department fulfilled the assurance function in a complex, long-term emergency involving many other agencies. The four assurance functions examined include resource management, program implementation, evaluation, and public education. Both strengths and weaknesses of the local response were revealed.

Although beyond the scope of this study, it should be noted that the ongoing recovery process is as important as the initial response. Recovery from a disaster such as the train derailment described above is a long-term process which involves not only the responding agencies but the entire community. Resumption of previous day-to-day activities, as well as coping with the aftermath of the disaster, presents an ongoing challenge to both agencies and citizens.

Source: Munson (2003)

CASE STUDY APPENDIX A

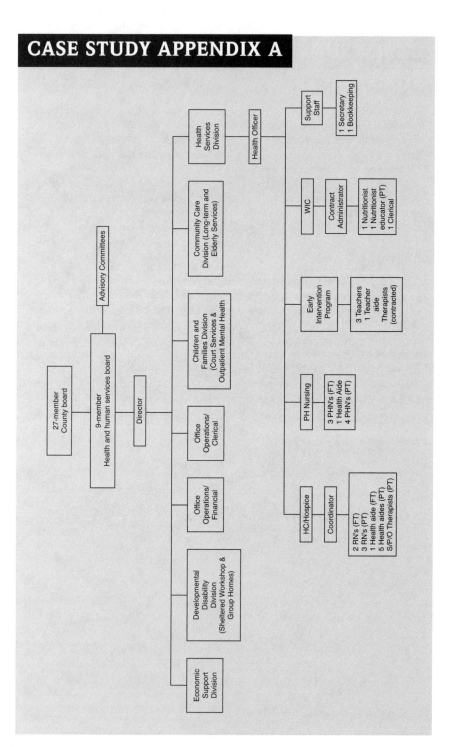

CASE STUDY APPENDIX B

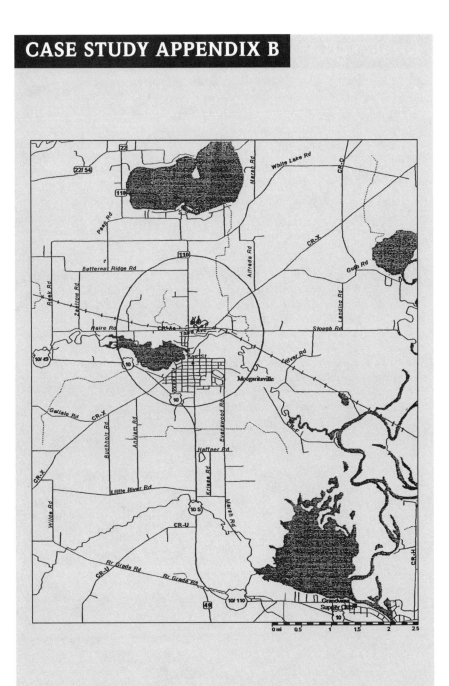

CASE STUDY APPENDIX C

Moogaritaville
Train Derailment

On March 4, 1996, a train derailed within the village of Moogaritaville. Because of the threat of explosion and the possibility that tank cars containing sodium hydroxide (lye) might be damaged by burning propane, people were evacuated from their homes. The fire at the derailment resulted from explosions of propane gas and the burning of wood.

As you return to your home, you may see ash and soot. These materials are not hazardous; however, they are messy and can be a nuisance cleaning up.

As you return you may smell smoke. As with any fire, people who are sensitive to smoke or people who have respiratory problems may experience some lung irritation. The smell of smoke will continue to be a nuisance, but we do not expect people to experience health effects from exposure to smoke.

If you do experience health effects that you believe are related to the fire, please contact your family physician. At your request, we will speak with your physician and provide information about the public health concerns associated with the emergency. Past-Your-Eyes County Health and Human Services is working closely with the State Bureau of Public Health to provide health information and assistance to concerned citizens.

Health Officer
Past-Your-Eyes County Health and
Human Services
811 Harding St.
Silage, IW 94981-2087
(715) 258-6385 (Moogaritaville Office)
(715) 258-4472 (Past-Your-Eyes Emergency Operations Center)

Emergency Coordinator
State Bureau of Public Health
4141 Lincoln Ave., Room 96
Jefferson, IW 35703-3044
(806) 662-7089

CASE STUDY APPENDIX D

Past-Your-Eyes County Department of
Health and Human Services
811 Harding Street
Silage, IW 94981-2087
(517) 258-6300
TDD (517) 258-6302
FAX (517) 258-6409

March 13, 1996
Dear Health Care Provider

As you are aware, an Udder Express train derailed in Moogaritaville at 6:00 a.m. on Monday, March 4, 1996. The derailment involved railroad cars of liquid propane (LP) and liquid sodium hydroxide (50%). Area citizens were evacuated for an extended period of time. There is no evidence that any toxic chemicals were involved in this incident.

Naturally, this situation has caused a great deal of anxiety among area residents. You may already be receiving questions about medical testing or examinations to evaluate health impacts. At this time we are not recommending any special testing. We are not aware that any unusual situations exist in any Moogaritaville area homes.

As these residents return to their homes they may encounter potential health hazards from food; drinking water; mold, mildew and spores caused by moisture; smoke particulate; lead-based paint; asbestos; household chemicals; electrical and physical hazards; and other public health concerns. Patients with asthma, allergies, or other respiratory disorders may manifest symptoms some time after initially returning to their residences.

The Past-Your-Eyes County Department of Health and Human Services and the State Department of Health and Social Services are committed to helping you help your patients. Andy Henderson, MD, the Chief Medical Officer of the State Bureau of Public Health, is available at (806) 662-1253 for direct consultation on any health effects or concerns that may come to your attention that may be related to this incident.

If you notice the onset of any unusual illnesses or infectious diseases that may be related to this incident, please call me directly.

I have enclosed for your information two public information notices that were given to area residents. Also enclosed are two reference sheets designed to help you quickly access the information you may need.

I hope this information is helpful. Please feel free to call me at (517) 258-6385 if you have any other questions or needs related to this incident.

Sincerely,

Health Officer
Past-Your-Eyes County Department of Health & Human Services

CASE STUDY APPENDIX E

Moogaritaville Train Derailment Evacuees
Residential and Commercial Reentry Plan
March 13, 1996

Objective: To conduct a door-to-door analysis of hazardous conditions and remedial measures needed to allow reentry of the general public. This process may take several days.

Before you return to your home, a team of experts, contracted by Land Construction Co., will inspect your house or business with you or your designated representative. This assessment will determine whether there are unsafe conditions to prevent you from returning to your home. If you are able to return to your home, it is because your home has been determined to be safe.

This assessment will be conducted by 20 individual teams that will be assigned sections. Each team will consist of:

1. Building owner or designee
2. Renter or lessee if a rental unit
3. Land Construction team leader
4. State gas representative
5. Plumbing subcontractor
6. Electrical subcontractor
7. HVAC subcontractor
8. Law enforcement

State Central Ltd. (WC) has retained Land Construction to act as the general contractor for repairs that may be required once the evacuated residents, merchants, and business owners of Moogaritaville return to their homes and businesses. Land has the size, experience, manpower, and equipment necessary to perform the job in the most timely and efficient manner, minimizing any further disruption to the residents and their families. Given the magnitude of the job, Land will engage all available qualified craftsmen in the area as subcontractors.

Hiring a single general contractor, which will bill WC directly for all repairs, to coordinate all the different craft work required will minimize the administrative and financial burden on the residents of Moogaritaville. *No money will be required of the residents*, as all financial arrangements will be addressed directly between Land and WC.

continues

CASE STUDY APPENDIX E *continued*

To enable all residents to return to their homes and businesses as soon as possible, Land plans to do the repairs in two stages. First, all residences and businesses will be repaired to the extent necessary to make them habitable and functional. In the case of residences, this will mean heat, water, and one working bathroom. After the initial repairs are completed on all structures, workers will return and entirely repair all affected homes and businesses.

WC anticipates that once the repairs are complete, residents of Moogaritaville will be satisfied with the quality and extent of the work done on their homes and businesses. All work performed by Land and its subcontractors are guaranteed by WC and Land. If you are unsatisfied with the quality or extent of the repairs performed, these disputes will be resolved by arbitration through the American Arbitration Association.

Since the extent of damage is unknown, WC and Land are unable at this time to give any estimate as to how long the first and second stages of repairs will take. As soon as the determinations are made, residents will be notified promptly. All repairs will be performed on the most expedited basis possible.

You may choose to retain a contractor of your own to perform any repairs necessitated by the derailment. Ultimately, you or your insurer will be reimbursed by WC for the reasonable and customary costs associated with necessary repairs performed by contractors other than Land. WC cannot, however, guarantee any work not performed by Land and its subcontractors. In the event you choose your own contractor, you should inform Land Construction of your decision and, furthermore, check with the appropriate consumer protection or licensing agency to ensure the contractor is reputable.

General Procedure

Assemble the evacuees at a designated location for a systematic reentry into town. Only one member or designated representative of each household or business will be allowed to join the inspection team. In the case of rental properties, the building owner and renter/lessee will be allowed to join the inspection. The elderly can be accompanied by a relative or friend. Transportation will be arranged for evacuees to their homes from the assembly area for the inspection process.

continues

CASE STUDY APPENDIX E   *continued*

Prior to team inspections, State Gas and State Electric have preparatory work that must be done. State Gas must first close all gas meters and purge the system. State Electric must restore power in the area of the train derailment. This preparatory work is estimated to take four to eight hours.

Once safe entry has been secured, the remaining team members will be prepared to enter the building and make assessments of damage repairs. Each structure will be categorized on the amount of work needed for occupancy to the following levels:

Level 1—No damage (green tag)
Level 2—Minimal damage, 4 hrs or less for repairs (blue tag)
Level 3—Intermediate damage, 16 hrs or less for repairs (orange tag)
Level 4—Major damage, 16 hrs plus for repairs (red tag)
Level 5—Uninhabitable (black tag)

Upon completion of the initial inspection, the home or business entrances will be tagged at one of the levels listed above. When the building is ready for occupancy, it will be tagged as such. This process will depend on an onsite agreement between owner, renter, and contractor as to the schedule of repairs.

Health and Safety Recommendations for Reoccupying Your Home

1. Moogaritaville's municipal water supply is under a boil water notice. Water should only be used for bathing and flushing toilets. To ensure your personal safety, you should take the following precautions:
   a. Boil all water used for drinking, cooking, or washing. Eating utensils should be boiled at a rolling boil for at least five minutes. Bottled water can also be used for drinking and food preparation purposes.
   b. Ice and beverages prepared with unboiled tap water should be discarded.
   c. You should follow these precautions until you receive notice that the water supply has returned to a safe condition.
2. Before you reenter your home, the pilot light of all gas appliances will be relit. Appliances not safe for relighting will be tagged as **DO NOT USE** and will be replaced at a later date. If the pilot has gone out for some reason, call the Land representative. Hotline: **411-644-2296**.
3. If you use your fireplace or wood burning unit for heating, be sure the flue is open and operating correctly. *Do not overload your fireplace. Do not burn fresh cut, treated, or painted wood.*

continues

CASE STUDY APPENDIX E   *continued*

4. If you decide to use electric heaters, be careful to place them away from items that can burn. Because of possible fire hazards, do not leave heaters unattended.

5. Food may have been damaged by extreme temperatures. Evaluate all food closely according to the following criteria. Remember that illness-causing bacteria may not be detectable by smell, taste, or appearance. *When in doubt, throw it out.*

   Frozen foods—Discard if not hard or solid. Check the food in the doors and upper levels of your freezer first. If these foods are leaky, food in lower levels may need to be discarded.

   Refrigerated foods—Discard outdated foods, foods that show decomposition or discoloration, and foods with a bad odor.

   Bottled or canned foods at room temperature—Discard if container is bulging, leaky, or rusted.

   Dry packaged foods—Discard if damaged by water or other liquids, or if color or texture has changed.

   Fruits and vegetables at room temperatures—Discard.

6. Because you may sustain a cut or puncture wound while cleaning your home, you should be protected against tetanus. Tetanus shots (Td) are recommended every 10 years and are available through the Past-Your-Eyes County Health and Human Services. The contacts for this service or any other health-related questions are:

   Health Officer, Past-Your-Eyes County Health and Human Services: (517) 258-6385

   Emergency Operations Center: (517) 258-4472

   Dentin Highbred of State Bureau of Public Health: (114) 448-5232

7. If there is a hazard or a situation that you are unsure of, or have any questions or problems concerning the above information, please contact Land Construction at (411) 644-2296.

Keep records of all items you discard so that you can be compensated for those items.

LAND RESIDENT HOTLINE
(411) 644-2296
(24 Hours)

CASE STUDY APPENDIX F

The Past-Your-Eyes County Health and Human Services Department wants to ensure that your health and safety concerns are addressed during and after your return home. To address those needs, we are asking that you take a couple of minutes to complete the attached Moogaritaville Household Public Health Profile. The information that you provide will assist our agency in focusing our resources to better meet your needs.

If you do experience health effects that you believe are environmentally related, please contact your physician. At your request, we will speak with your physician and provide any necessary information. Past-Your-Eyes County Health and Human Services is working closely with the State Bureau of Public Health to provide health information and assistance to the citizens of Moogaritaville. Should you have any questions, please feel free to contact the following individuals:

Health Officer
Past-Your-Eyes County Health and
Human Services
811 Harding St.
Past-Your-Eyes, IW 54981-2087
(517) 258-6385 (Past-Your-Eyes Office)
(517) 258-4472 (Past-Your-Eyes Emergency Operations Center)

T. A. Johnson
State Bureau of Public Health
4141 Lincoln Ave., Room 96
Jefferson, IW 35703-3044
(806) 662-7089

continues

CASE STUDY APPENDIX F   *continued*

Date _____/_____/_____

Moogaritaville Household Public Health Profile

Name _____
Head of Household

_____
PERSON COMPLETING THIS QUESTIONNAIRE (If other than head of household)

_____
ADDRESS
Moogaritaville HOME PHONE _____
Best time to contact? _____

1. How many individuals live at this address? _____

2. How many are children under the age of 7? _____

3. Does anyone in this household have;

    asthma?   Yes   No   allergies?   Yes   No

4. Does anyone in your household have a disability or other health conditions that requires special assistance?

    Yes   No

    If yes, please list the conditions:

    _____

5. Does anyone in your household have a disability which you feel may be aggravated by returning to your home?

    Yes   No

    If yes, please list type of disability:_____

6. Would you like someone from Past-Your-Eyes County Health to call you?

    Yes   No

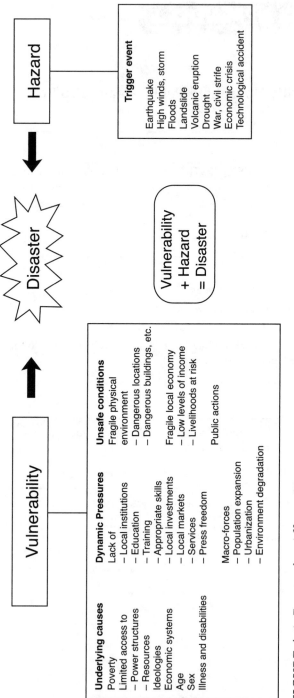

FIGURE 4–1 Factors that Affect a Disaster

Table 4–1 Major Crisis Types/Risks

Economic	Informational	Physical (loss of key plants and facilities)	Human Resource	Reputational	Psychopathic Acts	Natural Disasters
Labor strikes	Loss of proprietary and confidential information	Loss of key equipment, plants, and material supplies	Loss of key executives	Slander	Product tampering	Earthquake
Labor unrest	False information	Breakdowns of key equipment, plants, etc.	Loss of key personnel	Gossip	Kidnapping	Fire
Labor shortage	Tampering with computer records	Loss of key facilities	Rise in absenteeism	Sick jokes	Hostage taking	Floods
Major decline in stock price and fluctuations	Loss of key computer information with regard to customers, suppliers, etc. (Y2K)	Major plant disruptions	Rise in vandalism and accidents	Rumors	Terrorism	Explosions
Market crash			Workplace violence	Damage to corporate reputation	Workplace violence	Typhoons
Decline in major earnings				Tampering with corporate logos		Hurricanes

and include such things as labor strikes. In public health, an economic crisis relates to cutbacks in budget or loss of staff without an ability to rehire replacements. Although there have been increases in funding for emergency preparedness and response activities, other programs in public health have suffered from budget cuts and budget shortfalls.

The second group of crises are informational in nature. They deal with things such as tampering with public records, computer viruses that impact an entire agency's computer system, false information in files, privacy issues, and so forth. The potential for informational crises in public health are numerous and complex. Difficulties in sharing information across agencies is a problem. Different methods for collecting data as well as different data classification schemes all add to the potential for informational crises in the governmental public health sector. Federal and state guidelines related to the sharing or disclosure of health information to outside parties also create data problems. Misinterpretation of data is also important because it can create an inadvertent series of reactions to the report that can have crisis consequences.

Next, there are physical crises that involve the loss of property or key equipment through breakdowns or theft. This can lead to disruption in the normal flow of operations in an organization. Many universities report the loss of computers and computer laptops out of staff offices, for example. A power outage can affect activities. A lack of flu vaccine, as occurred in the fall of 2004, for people waiting for these immunizations during a potential influenza outbreak in a community is another crisis possibility. Public health agencies often struggle with a shortage of physical resources to carry out their work. The fourth group of crises relates to the human resources needs of organizations. These are the crises that occur when there is a sudden budget cut in programs, and programs and staff need to be eliminated or cut on short notice. These types of crises occur when a health administrator resigns or takes ill and the organization flounders because of a lack of competent leadership. A crisis occurs if there is a flu epidemic in the community and it leads to a rise in absenteeism in the agency because the primary program staff are out sick.

Many people ignore reputational crises, but they can severely cripple an organization or community. Here we are dealing with the effects of gossip, slander, misinformation during a crisis, rumors, and so forth. This is in many ways an extremely important group of potential crisis events. They cannot be ignored. For example, a rumor that a health administrator may be leaving when this is not true can create agency problems. There is one health department in the Midwest that had to deal with the impact of a staff member giving birth control devices to a teenage girl who it turned out was sent to the health department by her teacher–lover. Even though the staff member acted in the best interests of the girl, who was trying to avoid pregnancy, the image of the health department was eventually affected. The county board decided to not accept state family planning dollars for the agency as a result. Thus, it is possible that a reputational crisis can occur even when the public health agency is operating to protect the rights of the public. Crises and their occurrence are unexpected happenings.

Most of our discussions in public health in recent years are related to psychopathic crises, which include bioterrorism events, hostage taking in domestic and foreign places, workplace rage and violence, product tampering that affects the health of the public, foreign substances in the mail, and so-called weapons of mass destruction (biological warfare). The importance of the present typology is that psychopathic crises are only one group of crises, although much of the attention of public health is turned towards this class of abnormal events. The funding that public health agencies is receiving today is tied to this class. Public health preparedness models build on the military preparedness model related to these types of events. The argument that this book makes is that preparedness models do not need to be limited to psychopathic crises, but rather can be expanded and applied to all the crisis categories discussed in this section.

Public health has been most comfortable with the natural disaster form of crisis. We have dealt with these events on many occasions and have developed effective emergency preparedness and response plans for dealing with these natural disasters. For example, the Florida hurricanes of 2004 provide an excellent example of agencies working together to address the aftermath of one hurricane after another reaching landfall in Florida and other affected areas of the South. The earthquake and tsunami in southeast Asia during Christmas week of 2004 provide a second example where the emergency response was slow at first, but eventually involved worldwide response to the events.

Although public health agencies have worked well with fire departments and other emergency response groups during natural disasters, these relationships have tended to be jurisdictional in nature. Difficulties still exist when federal, state, and local entities need to work together. This becomes even more complex when the relationships cross state or national boundaries or have to involve federal agencies and international organizations, entities, and personnel as partners.

In the past, most disasters were caused by wars or natural events. Disasters in modern times have been natural as well as man-made. Mitroff (2004) reviewed many of these crises over time and noted that most of these modern-day crisis events occurred outside of the United States. Beginning with the Three Mile Island crisis in 1979 and the Tylenol poisonings in 1982, we have seen an increase in the number of crisis-related events in the United States as well as around the world. The events of September 11, 2001, changed the landscape of terrorism in that new forms of terrorism could now be waged against the United States by small terrorist groups. Table 4–2 shows some of these crises of modern times at a glance (Mitroff, in press). The table describes each of these major crises from the Three Mile Island nuclear plant disaster in 1979 to a number of other crises in 2003. The table also shows injuries, deaths, and damage from each of these events. All of these events had important public health implications for the population in the communities in which most of these crises happened.

It is unfortunate that the events of 2004 must now be added to the list, from the flu vaccine shortages in the fall of 2004, the Sudan holocaust-like crisis, the Florida hurricanes of the summer and fall of 2004, the Iraq terrorism activities of 2004 and 2005, and the southeast Asia natural disasters in late 2004. The prepared public health leader must be able to work with his or her community partners to address any future crises that may occur. It seems clear that these crises have been increasing and that they will continue to increase in the future. Organizations as well as communities need to be prepared. The additional issue of international terrorism adds new dimensions to the preparedness formula because not all countries of the world are equally prepared for crisis or emergency events.

LEVEL OF PUBLIC HEALTH PREPAREDNESS TODAY

There is growing evidence that the public health and its leadership are still not prepared to manage a large-scale emergency. In 2002, Congress enacted legislation as a response to the events of September 11, 2001, and the anthrax attacks that occurred later that year. The Public Health Security and Bioterrorism Response Act of 2002 was passed. This act was intended to provide guidance to public health officials at the federal,

Table 4-2 Major Crises at a Glance

Crisis	Date	Description	Injuries/Deaths/Damage
Three Mile Island	March 28, 1979	Malfunction at a nuclear power plant near Middletown, PA, caused the core of the reactor to overheat.	No injuries or deaths, but it was the most serious accident in U.S. commercial nuclear power plant operating history.
Tylenol poisonings	September 29 to October 1, 1982	Product tampering involving cyanide being inserted into Tylenol Extra Strength capsules.	Seven people in the Chicago area died. No one has ever been charged in this case.
Bhopal disaster	December 3, 1984	Industrial accident that killed thousands of people in the Indian city of Bhopal in Madhya Pradesh, following the accidental release of forty tons of methyl isocyanate (MIC) from a Union Carbide chemical plant located in the heart of the city.	The Bhopal accident killed more than 2000 people outright and injured anywhere from 150,000 to 600,000 others, some 6000 of whom later died from their injuries.
Space shuttle Challenger explosion	January 28, 1986	Space Shuttle Challenger explodes on take-off from the NASA Kennedy Space Center in Florida. The cause is later determined to be failure of an "O" ring due to extremely cold weather conditions.	All seven astronauts aboard the Challenger died.
Chernobyl disaster	April 25–26, 1986	One of the world's worst nuclear power accidents. The Chernobyl nuclear power plant, located 80 miles north of Kiev in the former Soviet Union (now Ukraine), went out of control resulting in explosions and a fireball which blew off the reactor's heavy steel and concrete lid.	The Chernobyl accident killed more than 30 people immediately, and as a result of the high radiation levels in the surrounding 20-mile radius, 135,000 people had to be evacuated.

continues

Table 4–2 *continued*

Crisis	Date	Description	Injuries/Deaths/Damage
Mad cow disease	1986 to present	Mad cow disease, or its scientific name bovine spongiform encephalopathy (BSE), is a fatal brain-wasting disease in cattle which was first identified in the United Kingdom (UK) in 1986. The disease can be passed from infected meat to humans, also causing brain damage and, eventually, death.	153 human cases reported worldwide; of these, approximately 100 people have died. Millions of cattle were slaughtered in an effort to eliminate the disease.
Pan Am flight 103	December 21, 1988	Pam Am flight 103 was blown out of the sky over Lockerbie, Scotland. Two Libyan citizens were later convicted of master-minding the bombing.	Deaths: 259 people on the plane and 11 on the ground
Exxon Valdez oil spill	March 24, 1989	The Exxon Valdez, an oil tanker, crashed into rocks in Prince William Sound, Alaska. Millions of gallons of oil contaminated the fragile ecosystem.	Animal deaths: 3000 sea otters, 250,000 sea birds, 300 harbor seals, 250 bald eagles, 22 orcas (killer whales), and billions of fish and small sea creatures. More than $2 billion was spent on the clean up, which was not completed until 1992.

continues

Chilean grape scare	April 1989	Chilean grapes were banned in the United States because of a terrorist threat and the finding of traces of a little cyanide on two grapes.	None.
LAPD– Rodney King beating	March 3, 1991	After a high-speed car chase in the San Fernando Valley, Rodney King, who is black, was beaten by white LAPD officers, as a sergeant directed from nearby. King sustained approximately 56 baton strokes, was kicked in the head and body, and stunned with a Taser stun gun. Some of the beating was captured on an amateur photographer's videotape, which was eventually viewed around the world.	None immediately (see the L.A. riots below).
L.A. riots	April 29 to May 4, 1992	The April 29, 1992, state court acquittal of the four officers involved in the Rodney King beating led to rioting that lasted six days. Thousands of people participated in the riots, and the violence and looting spread to other parts of Los Angeles County. Federal troops and the California National Guard were called in; the officers were subsequently tried on federal criminal civil rights charges. Sergeant Koon and Officer Powell were convicted of violating Rodney King's civil rights and sentenced to 30 months imprisonment.	54 people were killed, 2383 injured (221 critically), and 13,212 arrested. Property damage was estimated at more than $700 million for the county.

Table 4–2 *continued*

Crisis	Date	Description	Injuries/Deaths/Damage
World Trade Center bombing	February 26, 1993	A bomb exploded in a basement garage of the World Trade Center. In 1995, militant Islamist Sheik Omar Abdel Rahman and nine others were convicted of conspiracy charges, and in 1998, Ramzi Yousef, believed to have been the mastermind, was convicted of the bombing. Al-Qaeda involvement is suspected.	6 deaths and 1040 injuries.
Waco, Texas, standoff	February 28 to April 19, 1993	Agents of the Bureau of Alcohol, Tobacco and Firearms raided the Branch Davidian compound to serve arrest and search warrants as part of an investigation into illegal possession of firearms and explosives there. Gunfire erupted and a 51-day siege ensued which culminated on April 19, 1993.	Deaths of four ATF agents, and injuries to 16, on February 28th; the resulting fire in the compound at the end of the siege on April 19th killed 80 Branch Davidians, including 22 children.
Syringes in cans of Pepsi	June 10–17, 1993	Two reports in the Seattle–Tacoma area of Washington State that consumers found syringes in cans of Diet Pepsi led to a regional FDA warning; within 24 hours, reports of syringes in Diet Pepsi cans came in from disparate locations, resulting in widespread media coverage. With no reasonable explanation from a manufacturing standpoint, the FDA recommended a course of no recall.	No injuries were reported; Pepsi incurred $25 million in lost sales revenue.

Somalia	October 3–4, 1993	Battle of Mogadishu in Somalia: A deadly shootout developed into the largest firefight since the Vietnam War after two Black Hawk helicopters were shot down during a mission to capture two lieutenants of the Somalian warlord General Mohamed Farrah Aidid.	The battle ended with the eventual deaths of 18 of America's most elite soldiers, and the wounding of 75 others. Estimates of Somali deaths varied between 500 and 1500.
Texaco racism scandal	August 1994 to November 1996	A senior personnel manager in Texaco's finance department taped an August 1994 meeting at which he and three other executives disparaged black workers and discussed hiding and destroying documents that were vital to a pending discrimination case. This tape set off a racial scandal at Texaco.	Texaco settled the case for an estimated $176 million in cash and other considerations—the largest such settlement on record.
Orange County bankruptcy	December 6, 1994	Orange County, California, became the largest municipality in US history to declare bankruptcy after the county treasurer lost $1.7 billion of taxpayer money through investments in risky Wall Street securities.	No deaths or injuries
Kobe earthquake	January 17, 1995	Earthquake measuring 7.2 on the Richter scale struck Kobe, Japan.	5100 deaths; 300,000 people left homeless. The cost to restore the basic infrastructure of the city was about $150 billion dollars.

continues

Table 4-2 *continued*

Crisis	Date	Description	Injuries/Deaths/Damage
Barron's crisis	1995	Financial crisis at Barron's Bank brought about by risky Japanese investments which failed after the Kobe earthquake.	No deaths or injuries
Tokyo subway attacks	March 20, 1995	Act of domestic terrorism perpetrated by members of AUM Shinrikyo. In five coordinated attacks, AUM members released sarin gas on several lines of the Tokyo subway. This was the most serious terrorist attack in Japan's modern history.	12 deaths and 6000 injuries
Oklahoma City bombing	April 19, 1995	Domestic terrorist attack on the Alfred P. Murrah Federal Building in Oklahoma City, OK. The attack was in retaliation for the deaths in 1993 at the Branch Davidian compound in Waco, Texas.	168 people, including 19 children, died in the explosion. Timothy McVeigh was later convicted of the bombing and executed by the federal government.
Crash of ValuJet flight 592	May 11, 1996	Airplane disaster aboard a Miami-to-Atlanta flight. The plane crashed into the Florida Everglades shortly after takeoff; it was later determined that the crash was due to a cargo fire caused by oxygen canisters which were mistakenly labeled and improperly packed in the cargo hold.	All 110 people aboard the plane perished. As a result of the crisis, ValuJet was forced into bankruptcy. It was later reorganized as a new low-cost airline.
TWA flight 800	July 17, 1996	TWA Flight 800, a Boeing 747 bound for Paris, exploded shortly after takeoff from New York's Long Island. The FAA ruled that	All 230 people on board the plane perished.

Event	Date	Description	Outcome
		the explosion was caused by a spark of unknown origin in the fuel tank; there was much speculation that the plane was brought down by a shoulder-fired missile after 270 people provided the FBI with accounts of an unknown object which streaked up from the horizon and arced toward TWA flight 800 in the seconds before it exploded.	
US Army sexual harassment scandal	April to September 1996	Sexual harassment scandal involving 12 officers at the US Army's Aberdeen Proving Grounds near Baltimore, MD. The officers were accused of sexual abuses against females under their command, which included charges of rape, sodomy, and assault.	An Army hotline set up in November 1996 to field complaints of sexual harassment was flooded with about 5000 calls, resulting in 325 investigations of misconduct at army installations around the world.
Nazi gold	September 1996	Discovery of a paper trail linking gold in Switzerland to that which was looted by the Nazis between 1939 and 1945. The gold included bullion bars, trinkets from jeweler's shops, and gold from the teeth of those who died in the death camps. Calls issued to make restitution to the Holocaust survivors and/or their descendants.	The gold was worth around $400 million when it was looted ($3.9 billion in today's values). About three quarters of the money was kept in the Swiss National Bank and the remainder went to accounts in other countries.
LAPD Ramparts scandal	May 1998 to November 2000	A special task force was set up to investigate misconduct by more than 70 officers at LAPD's Rampart Station Antigang unit. The officers were investigated for either	L.A. City Attorney's office estimated that total Rampart-related settlement costs would total $125 million; the LAPD's elite

continues

Table 4-2 *continued*

Crisis	Date	Description	Injuries/Deaths/Damage
		committing crimes (routinely engaging in illegal shootings, beatings, perjury, false arrests, witness intimidation, and other misconduct) or knowing about them and helping to cover them up.	antigang unit CRASH was disbanded and court-ordered injunctions against gang members were suspended.
Attacks on US embassies	August 7, 1998	Near simultaneous terrorist attacks on the US Embassies in Nairobi, Kenya, and Dares Salaam, Tanzania. Seventeen individuals, including Osama Bin Laden, are charged with the crimes.	Kenya: 12 American diplomats, 34 Kenyan US embassy employees, and 167 citizens of Nairobi near the embassy at the time were killed, making a total of 213 dead Tanzania: 10 deaths and 70 injuries
Clinton-Lewinsky affair	August 1998	President Clinton, after nine months of near silence, admitted that he did have an affair with ex-White House intern Monica Lewinsky. The President was later impeached by the Senate, but was acquitted on the charges of perjury before the grand jury and obstruction of justice.	N/A
Turkey earthquake	August 17, 1999	An earthquake measuring between 7.4 and 7.9 on the Richter Scale occurs near Izmit, an industrial city about 55 miles east of Istanbul on the Sea of Marmara. At least 300 aftershocks followed in the first 48 hours.	More than 14,000 dead and 200,000 left homeless. Contractors were convicted of constructing shoddy buildings which were responsible for the deaths and injuries.

Ford-Firestone Tire Crisis	May to August 2000	Firestone tire recall is the most deadly auto safety crisis in American history. Most of the deaths occurred in accidents involving the Ford Explorer, which tends to rollover when one of the tires blows out and/or the tread separates.	More than 200 deaths and 800 injuries were linked to defective Firestone tires. The recall cost Ford $500 million in lost production. Both companies were the targets of a large number of lawsuits that likely will take years—and millions, if not billions—to settle.
California energy crisis	May 2000 to May 2001	By the early 1990s, electricity rates in California were on average 50% higher than the rest of the United States. The three major privately held utility companies (Southern California Edison, Pacific Gas & Electric, and San Diego Gas & Electric) spent $4.3 million on lobbyists and $1 million on political campaigns in their efforts to encourage deregulation. In 1995, the state legislature unanimously passed a bill to open the industry to competition, but consumers ended up paying almost twice the rate they did before deregulation, and suffering rolling blackouts.	Nearly 60 companies were allegedly involved in a price fixing scam that precipitated California's 2000–2001 energy crisis. A coalition including the CPUC and the state's attorney general demanded $7.5 billion in consumer refunds and almost $9 billion to cover the cost of emergency energy purchases.
Concorde crash	July 25, 2000	Concorde jet bound for New York crashed shortly after taking off from the Paris airport. It was eventually determined that the plane hit a metal strip on the runway, causing debris to burst underwing fuel tanks and start the fire that brought the plane down.	Deaths: 109 people on the plane, and 4 on the ground

continues

Table 4–2 *continued*

Crisis	Date	Description	Injuries/Deaths/Damage
USS Cole attack	October 12, 2000	Terrorist bomb attack against the USS Cole while it refueled in the Yemeni port of Aden.	17 sailors killed and 39 injured
9/11	September 11, 2001	Terrorist attacks carried out against the World Trade Center in New York and the Pentagon in Washington DC. Both buildings were struck by commercial airliners which had been highjacked by Al-Qaeda terrorists. A third airplane crashed into a field in Pennsylvania.	Death toll in the attacks: 2749 in the World Trade Center 189 in the Pentagon 44 in the plane crash near Shanksville, PA Total deaths: 2982
Anthrax attacks	September–October 2001	Bioterrorist attacks involving the mailing of anthrax spores through the US Post Office. Several attacks at various locations around the country resulted in numerous exposures, infections, and fatalities. Thousands were tested and 10,000 people in the United States took a 2-month course of antibiotics after possible exposure.	19 infections and 5 fatalities
Enron/Andersen	December 2001	Houston-based Enron went bankrupt in December 2001 amid revelations of hidden debt, inflated profits, and accounting tricks. Enron's auditor (Arthur Andersen)	The bankruptcy is one of the most expensive in history, generating more than $665 million in fees for lawyers, accountants, consultants, and examiners (according to

Martha Stewart insider trading scandal	December 27, 2001	was convicted of obstruction of justice, fined the maximum amount allowable by law ($500,000), and was given five years probation. Martha Stewart was found guilty of conspiracy, obstruction, and two counts of lying to investigators for covering up the circumstances surrounding her Dec. 27, 2001, stock trade of biotech company ImClone. Stewart is a good friend of ImClone's former CEO, and she sold $228,000 worth of ImClone stock the day before the Food and Drug Administration rejected the company's promising new cancer drug. the Texas Attorney General's Office). The bankruptcy plan proposes to pay most creditors about one fifth of the nearly $70 billion they are owed in cash and stock. Martha Stewart was sentenced to 5 months in prison, 5 months house arrest, and was fined $30,000 in July, 2004.
Pedophilia crisis in the Catholic church	2002	A national study of Catholic church records found that about 4% of US priests ministering from 1950 to 2002 were accused of sex abuse with a minor. The church hierarchy is also accused of systematically covering up the problem: roughly two thirds of top US Catholic leaders have allowed priests accused of sexual abuse to keep working. 4392 clergymen—almost all priests—were accused of abusing 10,667 people, with 75% of the incidents taking place between 1960 and 1984. Sex-abuse-related costs totaled $573 million as of 2002, but the overall dollar figure is much higher than reported because 14% of the dioceses and religious communities did not provide financial data, and the total did not include settlements made after 2002, such as the $85 million agreed to by the Boston Archdiocese.

continues

Table 4–2 *continued*

Crisis	Date	Description	Injuries/Deaths/Damage
WorldCom	June 25, 2002	WorldCom, the second largest long-distance provider in the United States, announced it filed bankruptcy. As a result of an internal audit, $4 billion in expenses had been improperly categorized as capital expenditures rather than as operating expenses. The effect was to overstate cash flow and profitability. Arthur Andersen was WorldCom's accounting firm.	17,000 WorldCom employees were laid off.
SARS	November 2002 to July 2003	Severe acute respiratory syndrome (SARS) is a viral respiratory illness caused by a coronavirus. SARS was first reported in Asia in February 2003. Over the next few months, the illness spread to more than two dozen countries in North America, South America, Europe, and Asia before the SARS global outbreak of 2003 was contained.	8098 people worldwide became sick with SARS during the 2003 outbreak. Of these, 774 died.
Columbia disaster	February 1, 2003	The space shuttle Columbia broke apart over western Texas on reentry to the earth's atmosphere. The accident was triggered by the incredible heat generated from atmospheric friction entering the interior of the left wing, causing it to melt from within	All seven astronauts aboard the shuttle died in the accident.

East Coast power outages	August 14–15, 2003	until it failed and broke free. When this occurred the shuttle spun out of control and disintegrated. A massive power blackout which spread through the northeastern United States and southern Canada. It was the biggest power outage in US history, and within three minutes, 21 power plants in the United States had shut down. At its peak, the outage reportedly affected more than 50 million people.	Three deaths were tied to the outage, and it cost New York City alone over a half billion dollars in lost revenue.
New York Stock Exchange crisis	August to September 2003	Problems with the corporate governance structure of the NYSE came to light when it was disclosed that Richard Grasso, NYSE president and chief operating officer, was going to receive a retirement package totaling $187.5 million. Many of the NYSE traders were angered that Grasso had extracted such a big pay package at the same time that their own paychecks were shrinking. The Securities and Exchange Commission began an inquiry and, after much pressure, Grasso resigned on September 17, 2003.	N/A
Mutual funds	October to November, 2003	Putnam, the fifth biggest mutual fund in the United States, was charged with improper trading by the Securities and Exchange Commission (SEC) and	N/A

continues

Table 4–2 *continued*

Crisis	Date	Description	Injuries/Deaths/Damage
		Massachusetts financial regulators. The SEC was criticized for slackness in overseeing the $7 trillion mutual funds industry, resulting in calls for a crackdown on some industry practices. Of specific concern are "market timing" practices which involve profiting from short-term trading in mutual fund shares, but can damage the value of the fund for long-term investors.	
US mad cow scare	December 2003	Mad cow disease was discovered in a cow in Washington state, prompting federal officials to recall more than 10,000 pounds of meat. The meat had been shipped to eight states and Guam. The diseased cow was determined to have originally come to the United States from Canada. A number of nations banned US beef imports once the case was announced.	N/A

state, and local level through cooperative agreement funding mechanisms to increase the ability of public health agencies to be prepared for potential bioterrorism activities through strengthening the public health system in the areas of emergency preparedness and response. State and local governments, including municipal health departments, were given funding to develop bioterrorism and other emergency response plans; purchase and upgrade equipment, supplies, and staff to manage national drug stockpiles necessary to enhance preparedness and response activities; conduct exercises and drills to test emergency response capabilities; improve surveillance methods; and train personnel in the use of early warning and surveillance networks to provide early detection.

Trust for America's Health reviewed our state of readiness at the end of fiscal year 2003 (2003) and for a second time in 2004 (2004). The trust noted progress in the area of completed bioterrorism planning documents, improvements in laboratory capabilities and upgrades, and improvements in communication systems. However, the trust felt that there were many concerns with our progress in improving our public health preparedness activities. Their concerns related to such factors as increasing state deficits and budget declines for public health, unspent federal aid, lack of preparation for pharmaceutical stockpiles, local health departments often left out of decision-making activities, and an increasing public health workforce crisis which has been noted earlier in this book. The trust presented a state preparedness evaluation process using the following 10 indicators (2004):

1. Spent or obligated at least 90% of fiscal year 2003 funds
2. State spending on public health increased or was maintained
3. Local concurrence with state's bioterrorism preparedness plan
4. Has less than 25% of the public health workforce eligible to retire within five years
5. Has sufficient BSL-3 Lab (Biosafety Level 3 Laboratory)
6. Has enough BT scientists to test for anthrax or plague
7. Has a disease tracking system in day-to-day use where information can be monitored via Internet
8. Has legal authority to quarantine
9. Increased the vaccination rates in older adults from FY 2002–2003
10. Has pandemic flu plan

Table 4–3 shows which states meet the indicator criteria in FY 2003. As can be seen, many states do not meet a number of the criteria. Most states met the criterion related to quarantine authority. A majority of states also met the criterion related to maintenance or increased spending for public health, the criterion on local concurrence with the state bioterrorism plan, and the criterion related to an increase in vaccination rates. What is disturbing about the second criterion listed is that a number of states decreased public health spending in FY 2003 when public health support was critical. Table 4–4 shows how many of the criteria are met by each state—from Alaska and Massachusetts, which met three criteria at the time of the trust survey, to Florida and North Carolina, which met nine of the criteria. This is clearly an improvement over the readiness of states as reported in the 2003 report. Despite some of these clear improvements, a number of states have argued that they are more prepared than the report states.

After reviewing progress towards readiness, Trust for America's Health (2004) made several recommendations for the future. These recommendations included the following from the 2003 report (numbers 1–3) and the 2004 report (numbers 4–7):

1. Public health agencies must be ready for all hazards, not just bioterrorism.
2. Establish health security requirements to ensure that all citizens are protected.
3. Convene a summit on the future of public health to develop a cohesive, national approach to public health protection.
4. Build a better bioterrorism preparedness game plan with an accountability standard for how money is spent.
5. Get back to basics; public health needs to address emergency preparedness and response issues as well as traditional public health concerns (expansion of 1 above).
6. Use practice drills to assess capabilities and vulnerabilities.
7. Limit liability to encourage vaccine development and protect health care workers.

Clearly, the trust report indicated the importance of strengthening the public health system in the United States. Strong public health leadership is required to make this happen. In Part 3 of this book, we will explore some of the skills needed by the prepared public health leader. Public

Table 4–3 State Preparedness Scores

States	1. Spent or obligated at least 90% of FY 2003 federal funds	2. State spending on public health increased or was maintained	3. Local concurrence with state's bioterror preparedness plan	4. Has less than 25% of public health workforce eligible to retire within 5 years	5. Has sufficient BSL-3 labs	6. Has enough lab scientists to test for anthrax or plague	7. Has a disease tracking system in day-to-day use where information can be monitored via Internet	8. Has legal authority to quarantine	9. Increased flu vaccination rates in adults 65 and older from 2002–2003	10. Has pandemic flu plan	11. 2003? Total Score
Alabama			✓	✓			✓	✓	✓		5
Alaska	✓		✓	✓		✓					3
Arizona		✓	✓	✓		✓	✓	✓		✓	5
Arkansas		✓	✓	✓			✓	✓			5
California	✓	✓		✓	✓		✓	✓	✓	✓	5
Colorado			✓		✓	✓	✓	✓	✓		6
Connecticut			✓	✓	✓		✓	✓	✓		6
Delaware		✓	✓					✓	✓		5
District of Columbia			✓	✓	✓			✓	✓		4
Florida	✓	✓	✓	✓	✓		✓	✓	✓		9
Georgia		✓	✓	✓			✓	✓	✓		6
Hawaii		✓		✓			✓	✓	✓		6
Idaho	✓	✓	✓	✓	✓			✓	✓		6

continues

Table 4–3 *continued*

States	1. Spent or obligated at least 90% of FY 2003 federal funds	2. State spending on public health increased or was maintained	3. Local concurrence with state's bioterror preparedness plan	4. Has less than 25% of public health workforce eligible to retire within 5 years	5. Has sufficient BSL-3 labs	6. Has enough lab scientists to test for anthrax or plague	7. Has a disease tracking system in day-to-day use where information can be monitored via Internet	8. Has legal authority to quarantine	9. Increased flu vaccination rates in adults 65 and older from 2002–2003	10. Has pandemic flu plan	11. 200? Total Score
Illinois	✓	✓					✓				5
Indiana	✓				✓			✓		✓	4
Iowa	✓	✓	✓	✓							6
Kansas	✓	✓	✓		✓		✓	✓	✓		7
Kentucky		✓	✓	✓		✓	✓	✓	✓		7
Louisiana		✓				✓		✓	✓		6
Maine	✓	✓	✓			✓	✓	✓			6
Maryland	✓		✓				✓	✓	✓		6
Massachusetts								✓		✓	3
Michigan	✓	✓	✓				✓	✓	✓	✓	6
Minnesota	✓	✓	✓			✓	✓	✓	✓		8
Mississippi		✓	✓	✓			✓	✓	✓		7
Missouri	✓	✓	✓		✓		✓	✓	✓		7
Montana		✓	✓			✓	✓	✓	✓		7

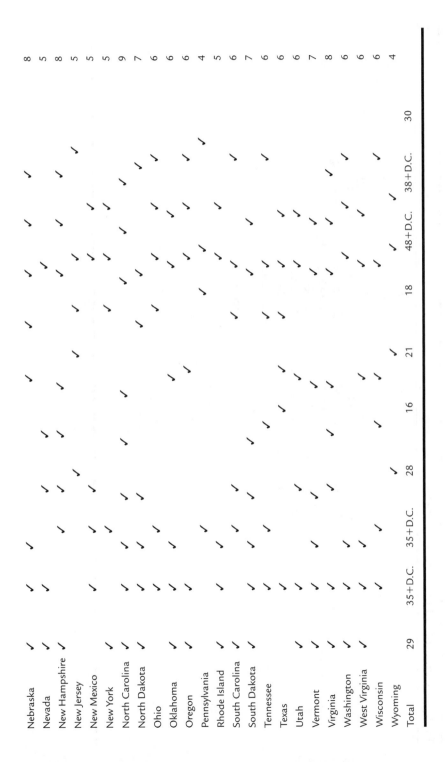

Table 4-4 Number of Indicators by State

9	8	7	6	5	4	3
Florida	Minnesota	Kansas	Colorado	Alabama	D.C.	Alaska
North Carolina	Nebraska	Kentucky	Connecticut	Arizona	Indiana	Massachusetts
	New Hampshire	Mississippi	Georgia	Arkansas	Pennsylvania	
	Virginia	Missouri	Hawaii	California	Wyoming	
		Montana	Idaho	Delaware		
		North Dakota	Iowa	Illinois		
		South Dakota	Louisiana	Nevada		
		Vermont	Maine	New Jersey		
			Maryland	New Mexico		
			Michigan	New York		
			Ohio	Rhode Island		
			Oklahoma			
			Oregon			
			South Carolina			
			Tennessee			
			Texas			
			Utah			
			Washington			
			West Virginia			
			Wisconsin			

health preparedness is also about crisis management. Some of these issues will be explored in the next section of this chapter.

MANAGING A CRISIS

As discussed earlier in this chapter, a crisis is an unstable time. Normal activities are disrupted. The outcomes are unpredictable. Usual agency or organizational processes are affected. Much of the writing about crisis and its effects relates to the impact of crisis on an organization and its levels of functioning. The rationale is somewhat easy to explain. Whether we are discussing the impact of a natural disaster such as a hurricane or a man-made terrorist event, it is the various governmental, nonprofit organizations, and other community organizations that are called upon to handle these events. Thus, the management of the crisis becomes critical to its amelioration or solution. Being a prepared public health leader may also mean being an effective manager as well.

Most discussions on management of a crisis see crisis management techniques as being different during each stage of a crisis. Crisis planning has a precrisis stage, a stage in which the crisis or disaster, either natural or man-made, occurs, a recovery phase, and some return to a new level of normality phase, which can start the entire planning and reaction cycle again. In discussing some of these issues, the time between crises seems to be shortening (Mitroff, 2004). There seem to be many more crises today than in former times. In addition, crises sometimes overlap or sometimes one crisis leads to another crisis. Thus multiple crises may be occurring simultaneously. Fink (2002) saw crisis management in the context of a 4-stage cyclical model. Stage 1 is the prodromal crisis phase which is basically a warning or precrisis phase. The important question to be answered is whether clues exist to a potential crisis. The events of September 11, 2001, have put Americans on constant alert for the possibility of an impending man-made disaster. The increases in crises since 1979 probably mean that we need to be constantly on the lookout for warnings signals (Mitroff, 2001). Signal detection may be one of the most important components in crisis management. If the prepared public health leader and his or her partners are vigilant in their signal detection efforts, many crises may be preventable.

The second stage is the acute crisis stage (Fink, 2002). At this stage, the crisis has occurred. The major concern at this stage is how to control the crisis. It is at this stage that fear levels increase. Deaths may occur.

Organizational structures collapse. It is here that the incident command system or its variations come into play to handle the crisis. This system is simply the model for the command, control, and coordination of a response to a community emergency which provides a well-defined structure for the coordination of the activities of community agencies and partners for dealing with the crisis (Turnock, 2004). These partners often include Federal Bureau of Investigation agents, local and state police, fire departments, local governmental agencies, public health leaders and their staffs, emergency medical system personnel, and many other community groups. The critical point here is that this system is basically a quasi-military model which is management based. Each participant knows his or her place in the system and his or her responsibilities in it.

The third phase in the model is the chronic crisis phase (Fink, 2002). Crises do not end abruptly. They have both short-term and long-term impacts. This is also the phase in which the crisis management team tries to lessen the long term impacts of the crisis. With September 11, 2001, and the anthrax letters in our background, this phase is also one in which major preparedness planning occurs to try to prevent future crises. In fact, it almost seems that there is a feedback loop at play here with the management strategies of the prodromal phase of activity. Fink talked about the importance of recovery and the need for people to get back to normal activities. An additional concern in this stage are all the possible legal actions that may occur as a result, which lengthen the time required for any final resolution of the crisis. An important example of the activities at this phase of a crisis included a law passed by the United States Congress in 2002 to establish the National Commission on Terrorist Attacks Upon the United States. President George W. Bush appointed the commission who held hearings in 2003–2004 and presented the final 9/11 Commission Report in 2004 with recommendations for changing the way the United States handles potential terrorist activities. The recommendations are controversial and will lead to a number of changes in the United States national security system and will do so as a result of the changes in the law early in 2005.

The fourth and final stage in the model is the crisis resolution phase. It is hoped the crisis is eventually resolved and life returns to some semblance of normality. However, the reality is that things are never quite the same. All crises leave some scars. New levels of adaptation must occur. Crisis resolution may actually trigger a new prodromal phases of awareness in which there is a need to prepare for other potential crisis or emergency events.

Fink (2002) also presented a model for crisis forecasting that is very useful for evaluating crisis events. The tool that he used is one called the crisis impact scale, which is a scale from 1–10. For any category of crisis, it should be possible to determine the potential for the crisis to escalate in intensity, the media or governmental scrutiny of the event, the impact of the event or potential event on the operation of agencies or organizations or the community, the impact of the crisis if it is an organizational one on the image of the organization, and the financial impact of the crisis. To develop a crisis impact scale, a score is determined for each of these variables or any others that are determined to be relevant from 0 (the lowest impact) to 10 (the highest). The scores are than added together and divided by the number of variables included in the index. The final score from 1–10 again gives a rough index of the impact of the crisis or the potential crisis on the agency or community.

Fink took this scale and tied it to a probability scale to create something which he called a crisis barometer. For each crisis or potential crisis, it should be possible to tie the crisis impact score with a probability of occurrence score. The Fink (2002) crisis barometer can be seen in Figure 4–2. The combination of these two scales can give an indication of the severity of the crisis or potential crisis. For example, a crisis such as a terrorist event would probably fall in the red zone which would be a high score on crisis impact and probability. It could also fall in the amber zone if the probability is lowered due to good preparedness activities. Although the barometer can be a useful tool, there are some cautions to keep in mind. It is important to plan for at least one potential crisis in each of the major crisis categories presented in Table 4–1, regardless of the low probability of that crisis category leading to a disaster within the near future (Mitroff, 2004). The prepared public health leader can learn much about disaster preparedness from simply being ready for any possible set of circumstances coming into being. Exercise 4–1 will give you a chance to work with the crisis barometer.

TWO MODELS OF DISASTER PREPAREDNESS

To understand the management concerns related to a crisis, an exploration of the preparedness or planning phase will be made followed by a discussion of some of the management activities related to recovery. There

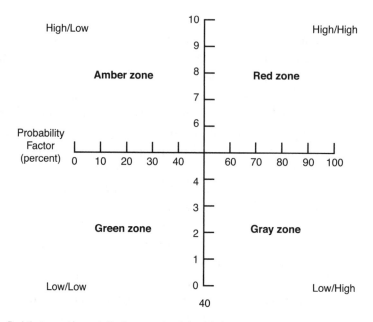

If you find that you have plotted your potential crisis into a danger zone, such as the Red Zone, with a high Crisis Impact Value and a high Probability Factor, your task as a crisis manager is to search vigilantly for alternative ways to plot yourself out of danger—and into opportunity—before the crisis strikes.

FIGURE 4-2 Crisis Barometer

are many different approaches to disaster preparedness. Many of these approaches take an organizational management perspective to demonstrate the factors and procedures that need to be taken into account in preparing an agency or company for a possible crisis of whatever type. Other approaches take a more systemic view of disaster. Whatever perspective is taken, there are clearly overlaps in the approaches. This section will view an approach taken by an organizational consultant and a second approach utilized by the Disaster Management Training Programme of the United Nations.

In preparing for a possible disaster, Blythe (2002) discussed how organizations plan for potential disruptive events in their organizations. One important distinction that was made involved the need to create two different crisis teams to address different aspects of a disaster. The first is a crisis management team for which seven steps were enumerated in putting this team together. The team needs to be multidisciplinary so that it

---

EXERCISE 4–1 Crisis Barometer

Purpose: To learn how to use the crisis barometer to make an initial evaluation of the probability and impact of a potential crisis

Key Concepts: Crisis, Crisis Barometer, crisis impact, flu pandemic, terrorism,
SARS

Procedures: With the copy of the Fink Crisis Barometer from Figure 4–2,
divide the class or training group into smaller groups of about 10
people. With your group, plot the following five crisis events, and
discuss your reasons for plotting them the way you did:

1. Thirty percent decrease in the budget of your agency
2. Flu pandemic this winter
3. Terrorist attack on a nuclear reactor plant
4. Appearance of a SARS case in New York City
5. Contamination of the water supply by a company in a small rural
community

---

represents all aspects of the organization. As a team, they need to develop
team decision-making strategies. As an organization sets up this special
team, it is important to first decide the parameters by which the team will
do its work. This becomes the scope of work. Second, the team needs two
types of leaders—a senior-level supporter of the team's work and also a
logistical person who can lead the team through the planning process in
an orderly manner. The selection of members is an important third step
because the team needs to represent all interests of the organization.
Fourth, a planning agenda needs to be created followed by a planning
budget for the team. An important limitation related to local planning
activities in health departments is that there often are no specific budgets
for the agency's planning activities. For example, some local health
departments have told me about the difficulty of getting local funding
bodies to financially support the critical activities related to carrying out
community health assessment activities. The sixth step in planning the
work of the crisis planning team is establishing a schedule of regular meetings and also a schedule of how these meetings are to be run.

The crisis planning team may need to be restructured when the crisis
management team has been designated. A crisis command center must be
set up. Procedures for handling the crisis are included in crisis plans and
crisis procedure manuals. If the crisis is primarily one which the organiza-

tion handles, procedures differ from a crisis that has strong community impacts. More will be said about these issues when we discuss crisis response. There is a critical need for an organization to consider the development of a humanitarian response team (Blythe, 2002). The crisis management team often does not have the time during a crisis to deal with all the issues related to working directly with the families of victims or injured people during a crisis. Thus, the creation of this humanitarian team is an important consideration in crisis planning and response activities.

Blythe (2002) presented a 6-step preparedness process that he named the "A,E,I,O,U, and Sometimes Y" approach. The A step involves the analysis of vulnerabilities. One of the tools for this activity could be the Fink Crisis Barometer discussed previously. This step is really concerned with the determination of foreseeable risks. If a crisis type has occurred previously, procedures and strategies may already be in place for dealing with them. Reality tells us that some crises or disasters are not predictable, and a process needs to be developed to address these events. There are ways to handle different crisis types (Mitroff, 2002, 2004, in press). Even though the crisis itself is unique, certain strategies can be developed to handle a new crisis event that has not happened before. In determining vulnerabilities, all crises involve people, finances, and reputation (Blythe, 2002). Reputation involves the issue of blame and how the organization will be viewed relative to the way it handles these unexpected happenings.

The E step involves the evaluation of existing procedures for crisis management. A 4-dimension evaluation strategy for a crisis was suggested (Blythe, 2002). First, there would be a determination of the foreseeable risks of a particular event. Second, a determination would be made of the types of controls that are already in place for handling this special type of risk. Third, it would then be necessary for the crisis planning team to determine if these controls could be enhanced in any way. Finally, a determination could be made of any new or additional types of controls that might be needed. Relative to the issue of controls and new methods that might be required, an organization needs to consider the issues of time needed to become prepared, money needed to implement the controls and other strategies, and the effort that these activities may require. One important strategy that is often used today to check these controls and strategies involves the use of exercises, drills, and other simulations.

The I step refers to the identification of new primary and secondary prevention preparedness procedures. This step involves a determination of types of possible incidents. For example, it is possible to use Table 4–1 as a guide. Next, ways and strategies to prevent these events are determined (primary prevention). A good example of this relates to airport security measures. If it is possible to screen all passengers for airlines prior to entering a plane, the chances of an explosion in the air due to a passenger carrying explosives on his or her person is greatly diminished. Secondary prevention activities involve the creation of strategies for what happens if a crisis occurs so that further damage is prevented. If we take the anthrax letter example, primary prevention activities would entail the screening of all mail in the mailroom before it is delivered to the staff of the organization. Secondary prevention techniques might be to give all staff biobags if a suspected letter is delivered to a staff member.

Next, it is important for the crisis planning committee to "organize" the plan (the O step). The issue of the relationship between the culture and values of an organization and the ways that the various controls fit that culture is an important consideration (Blythe, 2002). It is with this step that the issue of educating and training the staff of the agency becomes critical. The additional concern of the implementation of controls as well as the person who will be responsible for monitoring that implementation needs to be determined. The importance of values clarification in an organization is a necessary early step in the process (Rowitz, 2001). The values clarification activity can be used by organization leaders to work with staff to modify the organizational structure to accommodate these new crises protocols. It may well be necessary to modify the mission and vision of the organization to accommodate these changes. For example, a simple change in vision might be made. If the vision of the local health department is "Healthy people in healthy communities," it can be changed to "Healthy people in healthy and safe communities."

The U in the preparedness process refers to utilization of the plan. Utilization involves the creation or change of the crisis planning team into a crisis management team. It is here that the use of all those drills and tabletop exercises becomes important as a way to determine readiness. The debriefing and the lessons learned activities become important here. As it is not possible to determine when and if a disaster will occur, these drills and exercises need to become a routine part of the activities of the agency or organization. Crisis leaders may be different people from those who lead in normal times (Blythe, 2002). Some leaders handle stress better than other leaders. It is important to determine who the right leaders may be. Leadership is a complex phenomenon in that some leaders shine in crisis yet seem to be less effective in other times. An interesting example can be taken from the autobiography of Rudolph Giuliani (2002), who was mayor of New York City during the crisis of September 2001. Although there had been criticism of Giuliani as an effective mayor prior to September 11, 2001, most people agree with how effective he became as a crisis leader during and after terrorist events of September 2001.

The final planning step in the Blythe model referred to the need to scrutinize "yourselves," the Y step. This step involves the need to check at regular internals how well prepared the organization is for a potential crisis. It seems that the further away an organization is in time, the less the organization seems to be concerned about a potential crisis. What September 11, 2001, taught us is that a crisis can occur at any time. It is always necessary to monitor our organizations to determine preparedness and readiness. This approach needs to become a critical part of the culture of the organization. The top management of our organizations need to support these preparedness activities if they are to occur (Mitroff, 2002). Without this support, the plans will remain on the shelf, and preparedness will not become a reality.

A second disaster preparedness model that relates more to communities and countries was developed by the Disaster Management Training Programme in 1991 as a joint management effort of the United Nations Department of Humanitarian Affairs and the United Nations Development Programme with the aid of the Disaster Management Program of the University of Wisconsin. The purpose of the training module was to provide a framework for various countries and institutions to obtain the means to increase their capacity in emergency management in a development context. The model which was developed provides an excellent contrasting model to the Blythe model just presented. The framework on which the disaster preparedness approach is built contains nine components, as can be seen in Figure 4–3. Disaster preparedness was defined in the training program as a methodology to minimize the adverse effects of a hazard or crisis event through the utilization of effective precautionary actions, rehabilitation strategies, and recovery approaches that ensure a timely, appropriate, and effective organizational structure for the delivery of relief and assistance following a disaster.

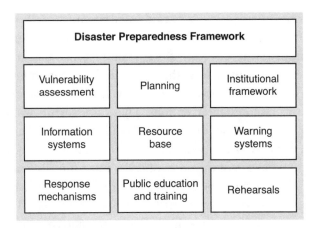

FIGURE 4–3 Vulnerability Assessment

Before exploring this model, it is useful to put it in a public health perspective. In 2001, CDC (Centers for Disease Control and Prevention) enumerated the key elements of a public health preparedness program. These elements included the following needs:

- An emergency preparedness plan to be in place prior to the emergency
- A hazards analysis of the types of events that might occur in a given community
- A plan of emergency activities in advance to ensure a coordinated response to the consequences of a potentially credible event
- A foundation and capability necessary for effective response to potentially credible emergencies
- The development of health surveillance, epidemiological investigation methods, laboratory capability, and diagnostic procedures to evaluate an emergency when it occurs
- The ability to implement the planned response quickly and effectively (consequence management)
- The stage of recovery from the emergency incident

Leadership is clearly required to develop this state of readiness.

The first of the nine components of the DMTP (1994) disaster preparedness framework involves the need for vulnerability assessment and analysis. Blythe (2002) also pointed out that this was an important preparedness component. Vulnerability is a determination of the probability of certain types of risks. It is a hazards analysis in the rubric of public health. It requires a continuous effort by public health professionals and other community leaders to assess the risks and hazards that a community faces in order to determine how these potential hazards and risks should be handled. Clearly, it is important to link vulnerability assessments with development or response interventions. These assessments will help community, state, and national leaders understand the utility of a national or local approach to given categories of emergency. Although local decision makers are pretty aware of the types of crises most probable in their local jurisdiction, they may not be aware of terrorist or biological threats that could impact their communities from an outside source. Bioterrorism and other unexpected events will often require state, national, or even international approaches to preparedness and response. At a local level, vulnerability assessments often provide clues to the types of disaster plans that need to be developed.

The planning component of the framework is also common to all disaster preparedness models. It should be clear that written plans are necessary to be successfully prepared. People need to not only know the rules, but also how to act during a potential emergency. Their roles and activities during an emergency need to be well defined. The written plan needs a set of clearly stated objectives; it should reflect the systematic sequence of activities that will occur during a response to a crisis, the assignment of specific tasks and responsibilities, and an implementation strategy to ensure that the objectives of the plan are met during an emergency. Table 4–5 shows the typical outline of a disaster plan. If the plan is to be a community-based one, then the planners need to include representatives from all the collaborating organizations that will be involved in the response phase of the emergency. If we follow Mitroff's advice earlier in this chapter, it is necessary to keep in mind that multiple plans may be needed for different types of crises and emergencies. Different collaborators may be involved in different types of disaster-planning activities. All plans need to be revisited after an emergency and recovery. In addition, the plans should be tested using exercises and drills that are based on the plan, and the plans should be revisited on a regular basis to determine if relevance still exists.

The third component of the model relates to the institutional framework that is put in place to respond to a crisis. A company or agency will probably develop a crisis management team model to respond to the emergency (Blythe, 2002). There is also a need for a humanitarian response team to work with the families of the injured or deceased. At a

Table 4–5 Typical Structure of a Disaster Plan

Introduction	Legislative authority
	Related documents
The Aim,	
definitions and abbreviations,	
The country (region, state)	Topography
	Climate
	Demography
	Industry
	Government organization
The threat	History
	Natural events (by type)
	Industrial accidents (by type)
Command and coordination	Powers and responsibilities at each level
	Command authorities and posts
	Description and role of emergency service
Planning groups	Arrangements for sectoral planning (such as medical, transport, and communications)
External assistance	Arrangements and authority for requesting assistance from outside the planning area
Emergency operations centers	
Activation of organizations	Warning systems
	Receipt and dissemination of warnings
Operational information	
Counterdisaster organizations	Government departments
	Defense ministry
	Local government
	Voluntary organizations
	Arrangements for liaison
Administration,	
financial procedures,	
supply	Emergency purchasing procedures
	Powers for requisitioning
Public information	Announcements (requiring action)
	Information releases
	Emergency broadcasting
	Multilanguage broadcasts
Subplans	Communications, police, fire services, medical, rescue, welfare, housing, public works, transport, power, registration, and tracing service

country level, there are, of course, different institutional arrangements that are created. In the United States, the general model that is used is one called the incident command system. This model will be discussed in the next section of this chapter. However, the model does vary from state to state, and different names may be used for the institutional arrangements that are created. Suffice it to say at this point, senior levels of government at the local, state, or national level need to sanction whatever responses model is selected. A focal point needs to be determined to ensure effective emergency preparedness and responses as well as to guarantee that a coordination of response activities is created. Whatever institutional arrangement is generated, roles and responsibilities need to reflect the expertise needed to address the emergency, the roles and responsibilities of all crisis management personnel must be clearly defined, and these roles and responsibilities have to be appropriate for the crisis being addressed. In order to create a more uniform system, the National Incident Management System (NIMS) was announced in 2004 to develop the nation's first standardized management approach to coordinate federal, state, and local lines of government for incident response.

The next component is an important one for public health and is always a part of any public health activity. It is information that drives the public health agenda. Information systems are based on community assessment methods, scientific research epidemiologic surveillance, laboratory diagnosis, demographics, and so on. The core function of assessment is clearly one function that public health must carry out on a day-to-day basis even during emergency situations. Assessment techniques related to hazards and risk analysis, crisis monitoring, and so on are all critical to public health preparedness. The development of early warning systems and leadership skills related to signal detection strategies are also important information mechanisms. Another important dimension of information is the need to share it in a disaster situation with other community partners (Landesman, 2005). Clearly, there are complexities related to this information sharing, and there is a need to work out methods and strategies to expedite the process.

The fifth dimension of the disaster preparedness framework relates to the resource base. It is always important to determine the resources necessary to handle terrorism whether it relates to the organizational capacity issues (Blythe, 2002) or by a community or country planning a disaster preparedness program. A number of factors need to be considered. First, what are the costs of a potential crisis for the organization, community, or country? At a community level, it is important to develop some type of crisis or disaster relief funding. The issue of how to access pharmaceutical stockpiles needs to be addressed. Costs of these drugs needs to be considered as well. The question of insurance coverage is another possible issue in disaster relief. In fact, the whole process of public health preparedness has both apparent and hidden costs. Relative to the issue of stockpiling is also the issue of stockpiling food reserves as well as drug reserves. You can undertake a very simple experiment with your community disaster partners if you are involved in such an effort presently by having your crisis team determine whether your community has a resource base strategy for a potential disaster.

The UN's Disaster Management Training Programme (1994) course next discussed the dimension of whether warning systems are in place. The critical issue here relates to whether a command center has been set up with telephones, cell phones, computers, fax machines, backup electrical generators, televisions, and battery operated radios. Is there a community-wide communications system developed? Are first responders trained? Are automobiles, trucks, ambulances, and other vehicles designated to work during the crisis immediately accessible? How will the public be warned? Has a surge capacity protocol been developed in case more hospital or medical services are needed for a given crisis? It is important to have alternate communications system available for the police, fire department, military, FBI, and any other critical governmental network support. There is also the need for redundancy in the provision of communication technologies in case of failures in a given system and the overall vulnerability of public communication networks (Landesman, 2005). There should always be a concern that a terrorist group might attack and immobilize the communication systems first.

The seventh dimension of the disaster preparedness framework relates to response mechanisms. Response is covered in more detail in the next section of this chapter. For now, it is enough to point out that response mechanisms need to be developed for a variety of hazards and need to include at a minimum the following mechanisms:

1. Evacuation procedures
2. Search and rescue procedures
3. Security procedures for affected geographic areas

4. Assessment and crisis management teams
5. Activation of public health and emergency medicine procedures
6. Activation of the various distribution systems (e.g., food and drugs)
7. Preparation of emergency reception centers and shelters
8. Activation of emergency programs for airports and other public transportation systems

The next dimension of the model relates to the importance of public education and training. It is not only the public health workforce that needs to be trained, it is the public that also needs to be prepared. There are many different approaches to the issue of education and training. For example, there are many computer-based training courses on emergency preparedness and response available for the public health workforce today. There are also face-to-face training and continuing education opportunities available for public health and other health professionals. For example, the state of Illinois Department of Public Health holds an annual bioterrorism summit each summer to present cutting-edge speakers discussing emergency preparedness and response. The summit also has break-out sessions to teach the participants about new program strategies as well as new preparedness tools and techniques. Public education of children in schools is one way to train the public. Extension programs from colleges and universities is another approach to distributing important information. Public service announcements can also be used to educate the public.

The final dimension of the framework relates to rehearsals, which are important to prepare the organization for potential disasters. Systemwide drills and exercises are also critical. An important national exercise was conducted in May of 2003. The exercise, called TOPOFF 2 (acronym for Top Officials), was a 5-day national exercise with Canadian partners to measure and analyze a response to a terrorist attack on Seattle and Chicago. Specifically, the exercise created a simulation based on a radiological device explosion in Seattle and a covert biological attack in Chicago. Twenty-five federal agencies in partnership with the American Red Cross were involved in the exercise. Some conclusions from the exercise were reported in a press release from the United States Department of Homeland Security in December 2003. One conclusion related to the necessity of improving communications, coordination, and connectivity during the response phase to a mass casualty incident. The need to collect information and the need to coordinate medical information placed a heavy burden on state and local authorities. A major positive finding was the ability of Chicago hospitals to carry out the requirements of the exercise on such a wide scale. Another finding of the exercise was the difficulty in disseminating a unified message during a crisis. Clearly, there is a need to improve communication systems. The exercise also helped agencies explore better ways to work together. Finally, the exercise did point to difficulties related to resource allocation among federal, state, and local entities.

These two disaster preparedness frameworks provide excellent approaches to dealing with emergency preparedness concerns at the organization or agency level as well as at the community, state, or national level.

PUBLIC HEALTH RESPONSE

When an emergency occurs, planning activities have hopefully been completed. Public health response is clearly about management strategies and addressing the emergency in a constructive way. Blythe (2002) discussed the immediate aftermath phase of a crisis. The impact has to be determined quickly. It is best to imagine that the worst has happened and then figure out what needs to be done. The crisis management team and the crisis structure has to be called into action. Plans have to be implemented to handle the events over the first 72 hours. This has to occur even prior to receiving the information on what happened specifically, how bad the event or events were, what has been done and what needs to be done, and the ultimate question of whether the crisis can escalate.

There are 10 immediate actions that need to be taken in any crisis (Blythe, 2002):

1. Evaluation of potential for continuing danger
2. Verification of the availability and quantity of emergency vehicles
3. Availability of information to determine the severity of the emergency
4. The cordoning off of the incident area and its perimeter, if appropriate
5. Implementing a notification process for the families of the wounded or deceased
6. Prevention strategies to prevent escalation of the crisis
7. Protocol for notification of individuals to assist in the emergency

8. Implementation of the communication procedures for the media
9. Determination of the legal and regulatory compliance process
10. Contact of any specialists that may be required

When a crisis occurs, it is important to contain the crisis as soon as possible. In an organization, this involves the activation of the crisis management team and a crisis command center. At a community level, the activation of the incident command system is a comparable activity to what occurs at the organization level. The community response activity will be discussed further later. What the crisis management group should do is determine and accurately document the emerging facts of the event. The development of a log of evolving facts itemizes what the emerging fact is, the time each fact was seen and verified, and the person who discovered it. The crisis team should also prioritize its activities with the determination of who takes the lead on addressing any priority. There should also be a determination of an end time for a priority to be carried out. The goal of all response activities is to restore order as soon as possible.

Whereas preparedness is a planning and proactive stance, response is about reaction. Public health's involvement in response has often been tied to the issues of emerging infections and bioterrorism. Landesman (2005) discussed nine specific roles for public health in responses situations:

1. Development and utilization of multidisciplinary protocols for collaborative activities between public health agencies and their community and health agency partners
2. Determination of the specific symptoms of various emerging infections and the activation of public health surveillance systems
3. Increase laboratory capacity, upgrade public health laboratories, and develop communication criteria for a laboratory response capability that distributes information on suspected bioterrorism agents to the appropriate sources.
4. Development of methods to deliver diagnostic and bioterrorism treatment protocols to the medical service community
5. Make sure response protocols are in place to reduce morbidity and mortality from a crisis event by stockpiling antibiotics and other drugs, using quarantine procedures if necessary, delivering medical services as necessary with surge capacity procedures available, using humanitarian notification procedures, and a well-considered crisis communication network.

6. Develop, test, expand, and implement the Health Alert Network (national network to link state and local public health agencies and community and governmental partners by Internet to get information on crisis events quickly).
7. Procedures for the handling of victims
8. Development of training programs for the public health workforce
9. Procedures for the resolution of public health legal issues relating to disasters

In the United States, the major process for response is tied to the activation of an incident command system or a number of variations of it. The models are built upon a military approach to the handling of a crisis. A number of online courses are available to managers and leaders on the incident command system from the Department of Homeland Security and the Federal Emergency Management Agency, or FEMA (2004). The following comments on the system come from the Basic ICS course offered online. The incident command system is an organizational structure utilizing command, control, and coordination approaches to response. The ICS model provides a means to coordinate the efforts of individual agencies (for our purpose, public health agencies as well) as the system works towards the primary goal of stabilizing the incident and protecting life, property, and the environment. The ICS has proved over time to be effective in the response to hazardous materials (HazMat) incidents, planned events, natural hazards response, law enforcement incidents such as potential riots outside a political convention facility, lack of a comprehensive resource management strategy, fires, multiple casualty incidents, multijurisdictional and multiagency incidents, air, water, and ground transportation incidents, search and rescue missions, pest eradication programs, and private sector emergency management programs.

As can be seen in Figure 4–4, the basic structure of the ICS system has five components. The command function is directed by the incident commander whose job it is to manage the response to the crisis event. For many incidents, the commander is the senior first responder to the event. Since ICS is a management system with the roles and responsibilities of all participants well determined, it is worthwhile to list 12 of the management process activities involved in the system:

1. Establishment of command structures and procedures
2. Assurance of responder safety

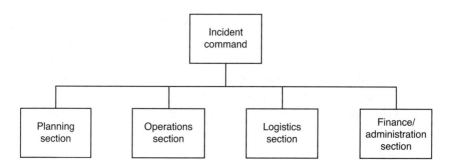

FIGURE 4–4 Incident Command System Organization

3. Assessment of incident priorities
4. Determination of operational objectives
5. Development and implementation of an incident action plan
6. Development of an organizational structure appropriate to the incident
7. Maintenance of a manageable span of control for all levels of the system
8. Management of incident resources
9. Coordination of overall emergency activities
10. Coordination of partnership activities
11. Authorization and management of the communication of information
12. Maintaining cost and financial records for the incident

The second component of the basic ICS system relates to the planning section, which collects, evaluates, disseminates, and utilizes the information about the development of the incident and the status of resources. This section may also develop the incident action plan that lays out the response activities and the utilization of resources for a specified time period. The third component relates to the operations section, which has the responsibility for carrying out the response activities described in the incident action plan. In addition, this section directs and coordinates all ICS operations, assists the incident commander in the development of response goals for the incident, requests needed resources from the commander, and keeps the commander informed about the state of the response operation and the use of resources.

The next component in the basic structure is the logistics section, which has the responsibility for providing facilities, services, personnel, and materials to operate the requested equipment for the incident. The logistics section often has a medical unit to provide care for any incident responder who is injured. The final component of the system is the financial/administration section, which is responsible for tracking incident costs and reimbursement accounting. Each of the five components of the ICS can and often are expanded with the appropriate delegation of authority.

There is much discussion these days about an expanded model of ICS called *unified command*. This system brings together the incident commanders from all major organizations in the community or the state for the purpose of coordinating the response to a crisis event. This coordination does not preclude separate ICS activities related to specific jurisdictions. The unified command links the various ICS activities and allows the various commanders to make consensual decisions. The unified command becomes responsible for the overall response and the overall management of the event.

SUMMARY

It has been a major purpose of this chapter to give an overview to the whole field of emergency preparedness and response. As a field of practice, public health has many new responsibilities. Although much discussion of emergency preparedness and response has been about terrorist acts, the issues in a crisis are more complex. Types of crises have been reviewed and commentary given about the need to plan for different classes of crises. The planning-and-response approaches differ depending on the type of crisis. The one sure fact is that crisis and disaster events seem to be increasing. Readiness is clearly an important area of concern for the prepared public health leader. Crises go through a series of stages in which different activities occur. Discussions of the preparedness phase were viewed from the vantage point of an organization as well as from the perspective of a community or country. The discussion of response was viewed from both an organizational perspective and a community one. The incident command system basic model and its extension into a unified command model was discussed as a model which is utilized in the United States. It does seem clear that many approaches to emergency preparedness and response fit into traditional management perspectives. The leadership issues are also clearly important, and the remainder of this book will be concerned with the development of skills necessary to be a prepared public health leader in an ever-changing public health environment.

REFERENCES

Blythe, B. T. (2002). *Blindsided*. New York: Portfolio (Penguin Putnam).

Centers for Disease Control and Prevention. (2001). The public health response to biological and chemical terrorism interim planning guidance for state public health officials. Atlanta, GA: CDC. Retrieved from http://www.bt.cdc.gov/documents/planning/planningguidance

Department of Homeland Security, FEMA. (2004). *Basic incident command system (IS 195)*. Emmitsburg, MD: Author.

United Nations Disaster Management Training Programme. (1994). *Disaster preparedness* (2nd Ed.). New York: Author.

Fink, S. (2002). *Crisis management: Planning for the inevitable*. Lincoln, NE: Authors Guild—Backinprint.com.

Giuliani, R. W. (2002). *Leadership*. New York: Hyperion Books.

Landesman, L. Y. (2005). *Public health management of disasters* (2nd Ed.). Washington, DC: American Public Health Association.

Mitroff, I. (2001). *Managing crises before they happen*. New York: Amacom.

Mitroff, I. (2004). *Crisis leadership: Planning for the inevitable*. New York: John Wiley and Sons.

Mitroff, I. (in press). *Why some companies emerge stronger and better from a crisis*. New York: Amacom.

Munson, J. (2003). Case study manual: Guidelines and protocol for case study development (2nd Ed.). (Monograph No. 1). *Leadership in Public Health*.

National Commission on Terrorist Attacks upon the United States. (2004). The *9/11 commission report*. New York: W. W. Norton and Co.

Rowitz, L. (2001). *Public health leadership: Putting principles into practice*. Sudbury, MA: Jones and Bartlett.

Turnock, B. (2004). *Public health: What it is and how it works*. Sudbury, MA: Jones and Bartlett.

Trust for America's Health. (2004). *Ready or not? Protecting the public's health in the age of terrorism*. Washington, DC: Author.

Trust for America's Health. (2003). *Ready or not? Protecting the public's health in the age of terrorism*. Washington, DC: Author.

World Health Organization and Pan African Emergency Training Centre, Addis Abada. (2002). *Disasters and emergencies: Definitions*. Geneva, Switzerland: World Health Organization.

Bioterrorism Competencies for Leaders

Knowing is not enough, we must apply.
Willing is not enough, we must do.

—Goethe

The Committee on Educating Public Health Professionals for the 21st Century, Board on Health Promotion and Disease Prevention (IOM, 2003), described a public health professional as an individual who was educated in public health or a related discipline and who is employed by governmental or nongovernmental agencies to improve health through a population-based focus. The committee also required the public health professional to have at least a baccalaureate degree. Among the specific tasks of the public health professional are designing and implementing programs to prevent the spread of infectious diseases, implementing research programs directed at the determination of effectiveness of health intervention programs, translating research into the solution of real-world health problems, collaborating with policy makers to translate science into practical policies and legislation, working in community settings to address community-identified public health problems, and ensuring and assuring that the public health system is prepared to respond to any crises that affect the health of the public, including terrorist and bioterrorist events. The public health professional must also learn management skills and become a prepared leader if public health is to be responsive to all the challenges that the above responsibilities entail.

Whatever suggestions or requirements that are designated for the education and training of public health professionals, it is important that schools of public health and other accredited public health and health professional schools include as part of their educational mission the preparation of individuals for senior-level positions in public health practice, research, and teaching (IOM, 2003). The education and training of public health leaders is critical for the future of the public health system. Leaders build, maintain, and nurture the system. Prepared public health leaders need the knowledge, skills, and attitudes to guide the public health system. It is an important expectation that our health professions schools take a lead in this effort. At the present time, only a few programs offer a course in public health leadership, although many states do offer these programs to working public health professionals. When these leadership courses are offered, they are usually only electives and not required learning experiences. This clearly needs to change. Leadership needs to be a set of learning experiences that leads to competencies that translate into more effective public health practice.

Some of the ways that this leadership development might occur were outlined in the IOM education report (IOM, 2003). One important way to train future leaders is to significantly expand the supervised practice and work–study opportunities for public health professional students. Different types of placement sites are state and local health departments, community-based public health programs, and various types of health agencies. Another possibility is to work for an elected official with a strong health agenda. Whatever the field experience, it is critical that faculty advisors play a key role in developing and supervising the experience. Underlying the above is a strong need for public health educational institutions to realize that public health practice is a key to understanding the workings of the public health system. Without an emphasis on education, research, and training in public health practice, educational programs will not reflect reality. Public health educational programs need to develop a flexibility and awareness of cutting-edge educational needs for working in the public health professions. It is important for these programs to also offer curriculum opportunities in emergency preparedness and response. It is amazing that many of these educational programs do not offer much on these critical emerging public health topics, although some of these programs do take these emerging issues as important in their curriculum-planning activities. When they are offered, they fall into the elective course category and not required course sequences. In fact, many schools have limited opportunity for public health professional and graduate students to take elective courses. Many educational programs need to expand their public health education and training opportunities to people who are already working in the community. Training through distance learning modalities as well as in more traditional continuing education and face-to-face approaches needs to be expanded.

THE ISSUE OF COMPETENCY

There has been increasing interest in recent years with the issue of competency in public health practice. Competency does not relate to just the content of academic or continuing education offerings. Competency is about how this new content gets used. The following formula for competency shows this relationship more clearly:

Competency = knowledge + practice + context − organizational constraints − political reality

A competency must demonstrate the use of new information and knowledge to create change. Despite this, organizations are resistant to change and the organization has to be pushed to allow the change to occur. Political issues can also impact the ability of the prepared public health leader to institute the changes necessary to make the organization adapt to new realities. Thus, competency is a complex demonstration of the use of new skills for effective change.

The Council on Linkages Between Academia and Public Health Practice (Public Health Foundation, 2001) defined core public health competencies as a set of skills, knowledge, and attitudes necessary for the broad practice of public health. From the council's Web site (www. TrainingFinder.org), core competency is tied to individuals who need to develop the skills necessary to carry out the 10 essential public health services. The levels of competency will differ for individuals at different levels of a public health organization. Thus, the level of mastery for the different competency domains vary for frontline staff in contrast to staff in supervisory or management positions. The three levels of skill were designated as *aware*, *knowledgeable*, and *proficient*. Table 5–1 shows the core

Table 5-1 Core Competencies for Public Health Professionals

Analytic/ Assessment Skills	• Defines a problem
	• Determines appropriate uses and limitations of both quantitative and qualitative data
	• Selects and defines variables relevant to defined public health problems
	• Identifies relevant and appropriate data and information sources
	• Evaluates the integrity and comparability of data and identifies gaps in data sources
	• Applies ethical principles to the collection, maintenance, use, and dissemination of data and information
	• Partners with communities to attach meaning to collected quantitative and qualitative data
	• Makes relevant inferences from quantitative and qualitative data
	• Obtains and interprets information regarding risks and benefits to the community
	• Applies data collection processes, information technology applications, and computer systems storage/retrieval strategies
	• Recognizes how the data illuminates ethical, political, scientific, economic, and overall public health issues
Policy Development/ Program Planning Skills	• Collects, summarizes, and interprets information relevant to an issue
	• States policy options and writes clear and concise policy statements
	• Identifies, interprets, and implements public health laws, regulations, and policies related to specific programs
	• Articulates the health, fiscal, administrative, legal, social, and political implications of each policy option
	• States the feasibility and expected outcomes of each policy option
	• Utilizes current techniques in decision analysis and health planning
	• Decides on the appropriate course of action
	• Develops a plan to implement policy, including goals, outcome and process objectives, and implementation steps

continues

Table 5-1 *continued*

	• Translates policy into organizational plans, structures, and programs
	• Prepares and implements emergency response plans
	• Develops mechanisms to monitor and evaluate programs for their effectiveness and quality
Community Dimensions of Practice Skills	• Establishes and maintains linkages with key stakeholders
	• Utilizes leadership, team building, negotiation, and conflict resolution skills to build community partnerships
	• Collaborates with community partners to promote the health of the population
	• Identifies how public and private organizations operate within a community
	• Accomplishes effective community engagements
	• Identifies community assets and available resources
	• Develops, implements, and evaluates a community public health assessment
	• Describes the role of government in the delivery of community health services
Basic Public Health Sciences Skills	• Identifies the individual's and organization's responsibilities within the context of the essential public health services and core functions
	• Defines, assesses, and understands the health status of populations, determinants of health and illness, factors contributing to health promotion and disease prevention, and factors influencing the use of health services
	• Understands the historical development, structure, and interaction of public health and health care systems
	• Identifies and applies basic research methods used in public health
	• Applies the basic public health sciences including behavioral and social sciences, biostatistics, epidemiology, environmental public health, and prevention of chronic and infectious diseases and injuries
	• Identifies and retrieves current relevant scientific evidence
	• Identifies the limitations of research and the importance of observations and interrelationships

Attitudes

• Develops a lifelong commitment to rigorous critical thinking

continues

Table 5–1 *continued*

Communica-tion Skills	• Communicates effectively both in writing and orally, or in other ways
	• Solicits input from individuals and organizations
	• Advocates for public health programs and resources
	• Leads and participates in groups to address specific issues
	• Uses the media, advanced technologies, and community networks to communicate information
	• Effectively presents accurate demographic, statistical, programmatic, and scientific information for professional and lay audiences
	Attitudes
	• Listens to others in an unbiased manner, respects points of view of others, and promotes the expression of diverse opinions and perspectives
Cultural Competency Skills	• Utilizes appropriate methods for interacting sensitively, effectively, and professionally with persons from diverse cultural, socioeconomic, educational, racial, ethnic, and professional backgrounds, and persons of all ages and lifestyle preferences
	• Identifies the role of cultural, social, and behavioral factors in determining the delivery of public health services
	• Develops and adapts approaches to problems that take into account cultural differences
	Attitudes
	• Understands the dynamic forces contributing to cultural diversity
	• Understands the importance of a diverse public health workforce
Financial Planning and Management Skills	• Develops and presents a budget
	• Manages programs within budget constraints
	• Applies budget processes
	• Develops strategies for determining budget priorities
	• Monitors program performance
	• Prepares proposals for funding from external sources
	• Applies basic human relations skills to the management of organizations, motivation of personnel, and resolution of conflicts
	• Manages information systems for collection, retrieval, and use of data for decision making

continues

Table 5-1 *continued*

	• Negotiates and develops contracts and other documents for the provision of population-based services
	• Conducts cost-effectiveness, cost-benefit, and cost-utility analyses
Leadership and Systems Thinking Skills	• Creates a culture of ethical standards within organizations and communities
	• Helps create key values and shared vision and uses these principles to guide action
	• Identifies internal and external issues that may impact delivery of essential public health services (i.e., strategic planning)
	• Facilitates collaboration with internal and external groups to ensure participation of key stakeholders
	• Promotes team and organizational learning
	• Contributes to development, implementation, and monitoring of organizational performance standards
	• Uses the legal and political system to effect change
	• Applies theory of organizational structures to professional practice

competency framework for public health professionals within the following skill categories:

- Analytic/Assessment Skills
- Policy Development/Program Planning Skills
- Communication Skills
- Cultural Competency Skills
- Community Dimension of Practice Skills
- Basic Public Health Sciences Skills
- Financial Planning and Management Skills
- Leadership and Systems Thinking Skills

A recent document pointed out that there are a number of key assumptions underlying the various discussions that deal with competency development in public health (Center for Health Policy at Columbia University School of Nursing and Association of Teachers of Preventive Medicine, 2004):

1. Competencies can be learned through formal training and education.

2. Public health workforce development will all be competency based.

3. Public health competency development will be tied to the essential public health services and the Council on Linkages core competency framework.

4. Competency-based public health workforce development programs will take different forms in different places.

5. Competency-based programs will integrate academic learning with practice learning.

6. Individual competencies will add value but not replace the need for organizational performance standards.

7. Competency sets should be relevant for the people trained and their positions in the organizations they serve.

8. The development of comprehensive public health workforce development programs will involve multiple and overlapping competency sets.

9. Competency statements describe acceptable levels of performance, skills needed to perform work tasks, and the actual conditions under which that work is carried out.

10. Individual performance needs to be measured over time because the impact of training will take time to be actualized.

11. Some measures of performance in the short run will need to be determined in educational institutions where students are evaluated at the end of courses.

12. Competencies are not etched in stone. They need to be updated and reviewed on a regular basis.

To see competency development more clearly as a process, Figure 5–1 presents a competency framework as a series of developmental phases. Each individual enters a learning situation with a cognitive map based on previous experiences. The individual then goes through a new learning experience in which he or she gains new information. This is the learner phase of the competency development process. The individual will then process that new information or new experience and classify it according to previous learning experiences that he or she has had. This second stage is a thus a processing phase. The new knowledge or experience then needs to be integrated with present skills, knowledge, and attitudes to create a revised cognitive map. This integration phase needs to be followed by an

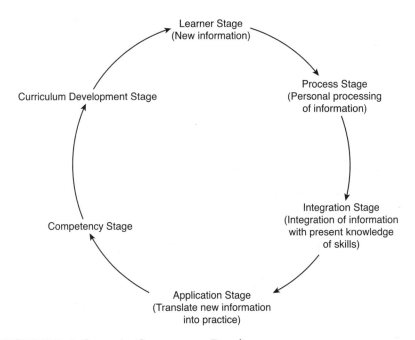

FIGURE 5–1 Stages in Competency Development

application phase in which the new information is utilized and tested within a real-world setting. If the new knowledge is successfully applied, tested, and evaluated, it is then seen as evidence of competency. As the need for further competency in public health is required, a curriculum development stage occurs in which present competencies are evaluated and the need for refinement or new levels of competency are determined in order to develop the needed new curriculum or education and training courses. As the curriculum gets developed and tested, the cycle begins again with individuals taking the new courses.

It should be evident by now that determining that a competency has been mastered and measuring whether the individual is using the new knowledge, skills, and attitudes is not a simple process. As noted above, the Council on Linkages designed their measure of competency on the three levels of awareness, knowledgeability, and proficiency. It is not really a simple task to quantify these three levels. It will be necessary to develop other measures of competency determination. Table 5–2 lists five possible ways to measure competency. In the leadership literature, there is much discussion of the 360° evaluation approach. This literature and the numerous instruments that have been developed involve a self-administered test

---

Table 5–2 Ways to Measure Competency

- 360° evaluation
- Performance standards tied to individual behavior and essential public health services
- Drills, exercises, and simulations
- Mentoring and coaching
- Self-reflection

---

where the individual evaluates personal leadership skills. Then other people who work with these leaders do the same evaluation. It is then possible to evaluate the relationship of self-evaluation to the evaluation of these same skills by others. It would seem that this 360° approach has the possibility of being applied in the public health competency arena where the individual can self-evaluate personal competencies in carrying out the 10 essential public health services and then can have others evaluate him or her on whether these competencies have been met.

A second example relates to public health's concern with performance measurement and standards. Performance measurement, management, and standards generally involve a system for determining whether an organization or community is meeting some set of standards for determining effectiveness of public health programs and practices. Performance standards in public health are often tied to whether public health at state, local, and governance levels is carrying out the 10 essential public health services at high levels of practice (CDC, 2003). If performance standards are our measures of public health practice, it should be possible to develop a modified version of these standards to determine the effectiveness of prepared public health leaders in carrying out these essential public health services utilizing the eight skill domains in the Council on Linkages framework, or in fact any other competency framework.

Another way to develop competency is through practice. Public health can expand its use of drills and exercises to test how public health workers are using their new knowledge, skills, and attitudes in simulated public health examples. Individuals will go through the exercises and drills and then evaluate the experience and how behavior can be changed in future simulations or real-life situations. Scenario-planning techniques can also be used to test new competencies. What occurs in scenario planning is to develop a series of exercises based on particular facts. Variations in the facts are made. These variations may involve how the workforce might behave in different types of crises hitting the same community with the same cast of characters. Testing the state of readiness in different crisis situations provides experiential learning for public health workers.

It might also be possible to measure competency through the development of mentoring or executive coaching programs. Benefiting from the experience of individuals who are expert in displaying and demonstrating competency in carrying out the essential public health services and managing and leading the community in a crisis situation, it should be possible to develop measures of effectiveness in carrying out public health practice activities. These mentors and executive coaches can then work with public health workers and leaders developing these new public health competencies.

Finally, self-reflection is an important indicator of success. Most of us can identify our deficiencies and our skills if we are honest enough. It is important for the future of public health for each public health professional to not only self-reflect, but also to develop a learning plan to address any deficiency or to engage in experiences necessary to effectively carry out the three core functions of assessment, policy development, and assurance and the 10 essential public health services.

COMPETENCY TO CURRICULUM

Dr. Kristine Gebbie of the Center for Health Policy at Columbia University has been a major proponent and supporter of a competency-based approach to education and training of the public health workforce. Case Study 5 presents a public health practice quiz with Gebbie about her perspective on competencies and the need to tie competencies to curriculum development. The new Competency to Curriculum Toolkit (Center for Health Policy, 2004) proposes nine steps that need to occur in the move from a determination of the competencies that may exist in the workforce or need to be developed to the determination of curriculum (see Figure 5–1):

1. Specify the audience for the training or education.
2. Develop learning objectives for the curriculum.
3. Determine the time that the learner has available for learning.

4. Determine the ways in which the learning will be measured and how this will occur.

5. Determine the expected outcomes and how the learner will translate the new information into a competency.

6. Determine the content of the learning and the resources needed for the learning experience.

7. Match the teaching methods and teaching modalities to the needs of the audience.

8. Develop the curriculum.

9. Evaluate the impact of the learning experience on the learner over time, if possible.

To develop a competency-based curriculum, it is first necessary to select the competency that the curriculum wishes to address. Table 5–3

CASE STUDY 5

A Public Health Practice Quiz for Kristine Gebbie

1. Why are competency frameworks useful?

   Competencies describe what we expect people to be able to do, either as a result of a learning/training experience, or as a part of job performance. Stated as such, with action verbs, competencies are much more measurable than some of the previous approaches (lists of content for training, or very general descriptions of work to be done in job descriptions) and therefore have become the expected norm in many educational and human resource circles.

2. There are now many different competency frameworks in public health. Should we try to consolidate them or should we encourage the development of many different competency frameworks?

   There are many frameworks for several reasons:
   a. We have just begun this work, and many enthusiasts have plunged in without waiting for anyone to set an overall standard or framework.
   b. Some sets are being developed at a very generalized level, and are most useful in the work setting; some are much more detailed and are most useful in the educational setting; we need both, but in most areas we need both ends of the spectrum.

continues

CASE STUDY 5   *continued*

    c. There are also some sets that need to be differentiated by what gen-
eralists need to know and what specialists need to know, and we are
not yet very good at this.
At some time we need a more complete road map to the various sets,
but I'm not sure we are yet ready to take up this task.

3. How can we measure competencies in individuals?
They can be measured by watching the individual perform the competency, by asking supervisors about the ability to perform, or by asking
the individual for his or her self-assessment. The first two are considered more reliable and useful than the third, though the third is the easiest to obtain.

4. What is the relationship between individual competencies and effect on
performance of organizations?
Organizations have capacity to perform that requires not only competent individuals, but the other components of infrastructure: systems
and relationships; data and information; and resources to support all
of the above. The specific performance of competency expected of individuals within the mission and specific responsibilities of an organization will depend on all of the above.

5. Should public health professionals take the lead in the incident command system in their local area, and if so, what kind of competencies
would they need?
Public health officials are a part of the overall emergency response in
their jurisdictions, and may well be appropriate incident commanders
for some types of emergencies. In any type of emergency, the public
health agency should be available to, and consulted by, the incident
commander regarding the public health aspects (immediate or potential) of the event, and the public health agency itself should activate its
internal incident command system to facilitate rapid and appropriate
response. Doing any of the above requires at a minimum the core public health competencies in emergency response.

lists the eight steps in the development of a competency-based curriculum. After the competency is selected, it is important to define key and
related words that are specific to the competency selected. Step 3 involves
the determination of the audience for whom the curriculum is being
developed. Since most competencies have subsets of competencies tied to
it, the next step in the process involves sequentially separating out these
subcompetencies. Step 5 relates to the development of learning objectives
for the curriculum. Next, strategies for the evaluation of these learning

Table 5-3 Steps to a Competency-Based Curriculum

Step 1 Select a competency.

Step 2 Define key words or phrases within the competency statement.

Step 3 Describe the target audience for the education program.

Step 4 Sequentially separate all required subcompetencies.

Step 5 Develop objectives (the desired learner behavior or state) for each subcompetency.

Step 6 Relate an evaluation procedure to learning objectives.

Step 7 Provide an example of relevant literature (content) from theory and practice for each subcompetency.

Step 8 Plan specific classroom or other learning experiences that encompass all identified learning objectives.

objectives are determined. The evaluation may involve anything from a written test to observed performance in a work setting. Step 7 involves a determination of resources which will be used to teach the learner the knowledge necessary to develop the competency. The final step in the process is the planning of specific classroom or other learning experiences that encompass all the learning objectives of the curriculum.

An excellent example taken from the Competency to Curriculum Toolkit relates to leadership (Center for Health Policy, 2004). One important competency for leaders that is listed under the Council on Linkages core competencies for public health professionals in Table 5–1 above involves the skills related to the development, implementation, and monitoring of organizational performance standards. Table 5–4 from the Toolkit shows the relationship between competency, subcompetency, and learning objectives. Exercise 5–1 gives you a chance to experiment with the Competency to Curriculum Toolkit.

LEADERSHIP COMPETENCIES FOR BIOTERRORISM AND EMERGENCY PREPAREDNESS

In addition to basic types of public health competencies as previously presented in Table 5–1, the events of September 11, 2001, have led to discussions about additional competencies that public health workers need to address for emergency preparedness and response activities. These new

Table 5–4 Relationship Between Competency, Subcompetency, and Learning Objectives

Competency	Subcompetency	Learning Objective
Contributes to the. . . Development of organizational performance standards (OPS)	Determines assets available for developing an OPS program as well as identifies gaps and deficits	• Discusses implications of theories and models of assessment approaches • Utilizes both qualitative and quantitative data-gathering techniques in a systematized approach • Identifies externally imposed requirements or standards and writes an OPS program justification using needs assessment data
	Prioritizes areas of need for OPS development	• Articulates the benefits of the OPS program • Takes reasonable inferences from community data • Defines desired outcomes, given a set of community data • Recognizes relevancy of community data for a particular performance standard • Evaluates existing performance standards for local use • Recognizes whether there are or will be sufficient community data to monitor each performance standard • Gives novel examples of garnering needed information (e.g., linking existing data sets, developing new partnerships with other public and private agencies to share data of mutual interest or developing new primary data collection strategies) • Considers external decision makers and community expectations

continues

Table 5–4 *continued*

Competency	Subcompetency	Learning Objective
	Uses a collaborative and inclusive approach in the development of OPS	• Recognizes that the choice of performance indicators is a political process and requires the participation of a broad constituency base • Identifies potential partners for collaboration including criteria for selection • Describes processes by which multiple partners could be involved • Demonstrates networking and group process skills to facilitate collaboration .
Contributes to the . . . Implementation of OPS	Analyzes the organization's culture (the integrated pattern of human behavior within an organization that includes thoughts, communications, actions, customs, beliefs, and values) and readiness in relationship to the OPS program goals	• Infers a relationship between the knowledge, attitudes, and skills of individual public health workers and the extent to which an organization is delivering the public health services and achieving the OPS program goals • Determines staff knowledge regarding performance standards • Distinguishes formal and informal aspects of the organizational culture • Identifies factors that influence organizational culture • Determines how the OPS program will influence and will be influenced by organizational culture
Contributes to the . . . Implementation of OPS	Assesses the political climate of the organization, community, state, and nation regarding conditions that advance or inhibit the	• Describes political factors that influence the OPS program • Analyzes sources of political pressures supporting and opposing the OPS program

continues

Table 5–4 *continued*

Competency	Subcompetency	Learning Objective
	goals of the OPS program	• Creates ways of adapting the OPS program within the political climate and develops resources, as feasible, within the identified system
Contributes to the . . . Implementation of OPS	Develops strategies to achieve the OPS program goals within the organizational culture	• Debates actions that may be used within the organizational culture
		• Communicates need for OPS to those who will be involved in implementing and monitoring the OPS program
		• Seeks ideas and opinions of those who will affect or be affected by the OPS program
		• Incorporates feasible ideas and recommendations into the planning process
		• Obtains commitments from personnel and decision makers who will be involved in the OPS program
		• Integrates concepts of continuous quality improvement throughout the implementation process
		• Ensures an operational, competency-oriented training program for staff responsible for implementing and monitoring the OPS program
		• Documents OPS program goals and interventions
Contributes to the . . . Monitoring of OPS	Designs specific plans to monitor the agency's performance including the impact on subgroup population disparities in health status and risk exposure to	• Defines the community to be monitored
		• Employs or develops appropriate data-collecting methods

continues

Table 5–4 *continued*

Competency	Subcompetency	Learning Objective
	determine if particular needs of vulnerable populations are being adequately addressed	• Uses strategies that are exemplary of OPS program implementation and monitoring in given settings • Identifies ways in which the implementation and monitoring component of the OPS program may need to be adapted to different settings • Predicts consequences if errors or changes in implementing and/or monitoring the program occur and documents OPS program outcomes
	Uses OPS outcomes to influence or shape health policy development	• Describes how OPS outcomes influence or shape health policy development • Drafts OPS policy intended to encourage administrative, regulatory, or legislative changes • Advocates for health policy development
	Revises OPS as necessitated by changes in community, state, and national data	• Compares actual OPS outcomes with the stated standards and desired outcomes • Assesses relevance of existing OPS to current needs • Participates in professional groups developing ongoing OPS

competencies must build upon the competencies necessary to carry out public health programs and services in normal times. Bioterrorism and emergency readiness competencies have been determined for public health leaders, public health communicable disease staff, public health clinical staff, environmental health staff, public health laboratory staff, medical examiners and coroners, public health information staff, and

---

EXERCISE 5-1 Development of a Training Course with the Development of Learning Objectives

Purpose: To develop expertise in the development of training and educational programs

Key Concepts: Competency, learning objectives, leadership competencies, curriculum development

Procedures:
1. Divide the class or training group into teams of 8-10 people.
2. Using Table 5-3, develop a training program with learning objectives for the leadership competency below from the Council on Linkages competency framework:

     Promote team and organizational learning.

---

other public health professional staff (CDC and Center for Health Policy at Columbia University, 2002). Competencies have been developed related to preparedness and planning, response and mitigation, and recovery and evaluation. Table 5–5 lists the competencies for a prepared public health leader. The competencies are described quite specifically in the ways that a public health leader is supposed to perform during crisis situations. The prepared public health leader clearly has to utilize all the other skills required of leaders (Rowitz, 2001). This table outlines other skills and knowledge that are needed for effective leadership during crisis. The next part of this book discusses in depth the types of new skills that the prepared public health leader needs.

Table 5-5 Bioterrorism and Emergency Readiness Competencies for Public Health Leaders

Public Health Officials: Occupations in which employees set broad policies, exercise overall responsibility for execution of these policies, or direct individual departments or special phases of the agency's operations, or provide specialized consultation on a regional, district, or area basis. Includes department heads, bureau chiefs, division chiefs, directors, and deputy directors.

I. **Preparedness and Planning**

Core Competency 1. Describe the public health role in emergency response in a range of emergencies that might arise (e.g., "This depart-

continues

Table 5–5 *continued*

ment provides surveillance, investigation, and public information in disease outbreaks and collaborates with other agencies in biological, environmental, and weather emergencies.").

- **Communicate** public health information/roles/capacities/legal authority accurately to all emergency response partners (other public health agencies, other health agencies, and other government agencies) during planning, drills, and actual emergencies. (This includes contributing to effective community-wide response through leadership, team building, negotiation, and conflict resolution.)
- **Evaluate/Review** the public health laws of the jurisdiction on a regular schedule, to assess that they are current and up to date pertaining to bioterrorism (BT) events.

Core Competency 2. Describe the chain of command in emergency response.

- **Describe** the chain of command and management system (incident command system) for emergency response in the jurisdiction.
- **Maintain** regular communication with emergency response partners. (Includes maintaining a current directory of partners and identifying appropriate methods for contact in emergencies.)
- **Maintain** agreements with partners from within the jurisdiction and from other jurisdictions to allow the public health agency to secure assistance and other resources.

Core Competency 3. Identify and locate the agency emergency response plan (or the pertinent portion of the plan).

- **Ensure** that the agency (or agency unit) has a written, updated plan for major categories of emergencies that respects the culture of the community and provides for continuity of agency operations.
- **Identify** the needed components of a public health BT response plan that is integrated with the overall emergency response plan for the agency.
- **Ensure** that all BT plan components are developed by appropriate and knowledgeable staff *by applying the following competencies*:
  - **–Integrate** the agency's BT response plan into the incident command or unified command system used by other responders (such as fire, police and EMS) in the jurisdiction.
  - **–Define** modifications to the agency's internal command notification and coordination structure required for BT response.
  - **–Design** BT-specific protocols for enhanced surveillance, including activating additional personnel (e.g., infection control practitioners, public health nurses, epidemiologists, and data entry clerks from other institutions, jurisdictions and/or agencies).
  - **–Establish** emergency communications roles and responsibilities for BT response.

continues

Table 5–5 *continued*

--Establish protocols for handling and distribution of the National Pharmaceutical Stockpile.

--Establish protocols to address public health surge capacity, including use of volunteers.

--Identify pharmaceutical, veterinary, or other resources required for consultation by the agency or jurisdiction during BT response.

--Use risk assessment of potential biological, chemical, or radiological hazards in the community to determine the roles and responsibilities of those involved in public health BT response.

--Generate regulations that provide the authority to conduct risk assessments in BT events.

--Generate plans to conduct risk assessments in public health emergencies.

--Specify safety measures to be taken by public health responders in a BT event, including use of personal protective equipment.

--Disseminate notifiable disease information, reporting requirements, and procedures to health care providers on a periodic basis.

--Ensure that laboratories within the jurisdiction or agency have BT response plans:

   ○ Identify Level A laboratories serving the jurisdiction or agency.

   ○ Ensure Level A laboratories can conduct "rule-out" testing, specimen packaging and handling, and referral of suspected biological threat agents to a higher-level laboratory.

   ○ Maintain contact and location information for Level B/C laboratories in the BT lab response network serving the jurisdiction.

- Maintain written plans for 24/7 availability of specific staff and specialists required during a BT event.

- Identify specific resources needed for response to critical biologic agents (Category A, B, C).

Core Competency 4. Describe his/her functional role(s) in emergency response and demonstrate his/her role(s) in regular drills.

- Identify your functional role in the agency's BT response plan.

Core Competency 5. Demonstrate correct use of all communication equipment used for emergency communication (phone, fax, radio, etc.).

Core Competency 6. Describe communication role(s) in emergency response within the agency, using established communication systems:

- Establish a public health communication infrastructure that receives and transmits data and information for decision support during a BT event.

- Establish secure communication pathways for use in a BT event, including computer security policies and safeguards against data loss.

continues

Table 5–5 *continued*

- **Establish** redundant communication mechanisms for immediate and reliable voice and secure data communication during a public health emergency.
- **Test** protocols for BT-specific communication and agency interaction at regular intervals with BT response partner agencies.

Core Competency 6A. Describe communication role(s) in emergency response with the media and with the general public.

- **Ensure** development and delivery of accurate event-specific, science-based risk communication messages to the public, to health care providers, to the media, and to the response community during a BT event.

Core Competency 6B. Describe personal communication role(s) in emergency response with family or neighbors.

- **Ensure** that the agency (or agency unit) regularly practices all parts of emergency response.
- **Conduct** workforce BT preparedness programs.
- **Evaluate** every emergency response drill to identify needed internal/external improvements.
- **Ensure** that knowledge/skill gaps identified through emergency response planning, drills, and evaluation are filled.

Core Competency 7. Identify limits to own knowledge, skill, and authority, and identify key system resources for referring matters that exceed these limits.

Core Competency 8. Recognize unusual events that might indicate an emergency and describe appropriate action (e.g., communicate clearly within the chain of command).

II. **Response and Mitigation**

- **Implement** the public health emergency response plan.
- **Implement** your individual BT response functional role.

Core Competency 9. Apply creative problem solving and flexible thinking to unusual challenges within his/her functional responsibilities and **evaluate** effectiveness of all actions taken.

- **Use** the agency BT incident command management structure.
- **Activate** emergency public health and infection control measures specific to the BT event.
- **Activate** enhanced active surveillance protocols to track the scope of the exposure or outbreak.
- **Identify** persons potentially exposed to a specific BT agent in need of public health and/or medical intervention.
- **Activate** the laboratory BT response plan.
- **Ensure** functioning of a system for rapid rule-out testing, referral,

continues

identification, confirmation, and characterization of biological threat agents, including rapid reporting of results, during a BT event.

- **Provide** public health support as needed for victims and responders within the jurisdiction's response.
- **Activate** a call-down roster using 24-hour contact information to reach BT response staff and consultants.
- **Communicate** the need for assistance during a BT event to appropriate resources.
- **Use** the agency's BT-specific public information plans, protocols, and materials in a BT event.
- **Use** established communication systems for coordination among the response community during a BT event.
- **Activate** redundant communication mechanisms for immediate and reliable voice and secure data communication during a public health emergency including two-way emergency communications.
- **Use** event-specific information and scientific principles of risk communication to inform the public, the media, health care providers, and the response community during a BT event.
- **Designate** a media spokesperson during a BT event.
- **Perform** your individual communication responsibilities during a BT event.

III. Recovery and Evaluation

- **Apply** appropriate science-based public health measures to ensure continued population protection appropriate to the biological threat involved.
- **Evaluate** every emergency response to identify needed internal/external improvements.
- **Ensure** that knowledge/skill gaps identified through emergency response evaluation are filled.

SUMMARY

This chapter has struggled with the complex issue of competencies in public health and the new competencies related to emergency preparedness and response. Although this chapter has not been specifically concerned with the issue of credentialing of public health workers and the accreditation of health departments, these latter issues are closely tied to the issue of competency development. Much discussion is occurring at the policy level about the pros and cons of credentialing and accreditation. These issues have been under discussion for a number of years. The issue of crisis has moved these discussions to the table, and more discussion will occur in the next several years.

REFERENCES

Centers for Disease Control and Prevention and Center for Health Policy (Columbia University School of Nursing). (2002). *Bioterrorism and emergency readiness: Competencies for all public health workers.* New York: Columbia University School of Nursing.

Center for Health Policy (Columbia University School of Nursing). (2004). *Competency-to curriculum toolkit: Developing curricula for public health workers.* New York: Columbia University School of Nursing.

Centers for Disease Control and Prevention. (2003). *National Public Health Performance Standards.* Atlanta, GA: Author.

Committee on Educating Public Health Professionals for the 21st Century. (2003). *Who will keep the public healthy.* Washington, DC, Institute of Medicine.

Council on Linkages Between Academia and Public Health Practice. (2001). *Core competencies for public health professionals.* Washington, DC: Public Health Foundation.

Rowitz, L. (2001). *Public health leadership: Putting principles into practice.* Sudbury, MA: Jones and Bartlett.

CHAPTER 6

New Partnerships

Collaboration improves performance.

—Kouzes and Posner, 2002

The prepared public health leader knows the secret to effective public health is involving community partners in carrying out the mission of public health to promote health and prevent disease. No leader can perform public health activities alone. In reviewing the Institute of Medicine reports on the future of public health which were discussed in detail in Chapter 3, the new public health needs to be seen in a new context (Gostin, Boufford, & Martinez, 2004). Throughout the 20th century, public health was seen primarily as a responsibility of government. Over the past several years, there has been a shift that has been discussed several times in this book concerning a change from an organizational to a community focus for public health. There has been an increasing engagement of nongovernmental partners in the public health agenda for the 21st century. Utilizing the IOM reports, it seems evident that the protection of the public's health cannot be assured by one governmental agency, but rather needs to involve many important community entities such as health care institutions, community organizations and grassroots leaders, businesses, the media, and academic partners (Gostin, Boufford, & Martinez, 2004). To ensure these critical partnerships are developed, the federal government needs to take a leadership role and ensure that every resident of the United States receives the needed health care coverage that they require. Both the federal and state levels of government support community-led public health efforts which help strengthen the collaborations that have been mentioned. Finally, it is necessary to build incentives into the system for the various partners, such as changes in the tax code to encourage the private sector to stay involved in the community-wide health promotion efforts. It was also recommended that the time devoted to public service announcements be increased to better inform the public of good and healthy behaviors. Finally, academic institutions need to be involved in these activities by providing real-life experiences for students as well as public health practice research activities.

Sometimes it is money that triggers collaboration. It is clear that there needs to be some incentives for individuals or organizations to collaborate with other individuals or organizations. The concerns with bioterrorism and other terrorist activities were issues of concern to public health and governmental agencies prior to September 11, 2001. Public health leaders have known that preparedness is critical to carrying out the agenda of public health as well as the unintended health threats that occur and need to be addressed quickly by public health agencies and their various community partners. Public health leaders have known for many years that the level of preparedness in their communities was affected by many factors, including shrinking public budgets, health access issues, concerns about prescription drug costs for seniors, limited interest in public health issues by the public, and competition for resources by other community agencies. In 1999, the Local Public Health Centers for Public Health Preparedness Project was initiated to link state and local public health agencies, schools of public health, and other community health partners to improve public health preparedness through training the public health workforce to improve competence and increase collaborations with other community partners.

To initiate the project, the Centers for Disease Control and Prevention selected three public health agencies to serve as local Centers for Public Health Preparedness—DeKalb County (Georgia) Board of Health, Denver Health (Denver County, Colorado), and Monroe County (New York) Health Department. Between 1999 and 2001, the following lessons were learned by these projects (National Association of City and County Health Officials [NACCHO], 2001):

1. Improvements in the infrastructure for public health bioterrorism preparedness and response capacity of the Local Centers not only improved preparedness capacity, but also improved routine public health functions and services.

2. The critical determination related to the implementation of new technologies tended to be administrative concerns as well as cultural acceptance concerns with less emphasis on the availability of these new technologies.
3. When new communication and information systems are introduced, it is important to determine how these new systems will be sustained over time.
4. The key to success for these preparedness programs related to the development and maintenance of community partnerships.
5. Education of first responders and the medical community to the important role of public health is critical.
6. Money builds infrastructure, and these Local Centers found that their local agencies administratively improved as preparedness programs were implemented.
7. Drills and tabletop exercises significantly aid in the development of bioterrorism plans. These exercises and drills also help measure local preparedness capacity.

The partnership activities of these Local Centers have been critical to their success. They have expanded their relationships with agencies at the local, state, and federal levels. Specifically, the three model sites developed strong partnerships with the Federal Emergency Management Agency, Environmental Protection Agency, Federal Bureau of Investigation, and the Department of Justice. At the state level, they have developed partnerships with their state health departments and/or state offices of emergency management. At the local level, they developed partnerships with hospitals, neighboring local health departments, municipal and county emergency medical services, police and fire departments, and other county and local agencies. These Local Centers recognized the importance of having prepared public health leaders as well as the critical need for partnership in emergency preparedness and response.

In a recent NACCHO report (2002), a number of local resource tools were reviewed from the Local Centers projects that were believed to be of use to other local public health agencies and partners who also are involved in improving their local emergency preparedness and response capacity. These tools are listed in Table 6–1. For detailed information on these tools, referral to the NACCHO report or direct contact with the Local Centers would be useful. These projects clearly serve as best practice

Table 6-1 Tools of Use for Bioterrorism Planning and Response for Local Centers Project

DeKalb County	Denver County	Monroe County
1. Bioterrorism Response Plan Model	1. Syndromic Surveillance	1. National Pharmaceutical Tabletop Exercises
2. West Nile Virus Response Plan Model	2. Colorado Electronic Disease Reporting System	2. Computerized Electronic Ambulance Run Reporting System for Syndromic Surveillance
3. Bioterrorism Tabletop Educational Exercises	3. Wireless Disease Reporting	3. Emergency Department Color Codes Module
4. Emergency Department Information System Analysis	4. Health Alert Network (HAN) Application	4. Protocol Regarding Response to Suspicious Packages
5. Pharmacy Resource Assessment—GIS Map of Local Resources	5. Handheld Device Data Collection Applications and Accompanying Tabletop Exercise Protocol	5. Bioterrorism 101 Internet-Based Course
6. Suspicious Package Orientation Folder	6. Handheld Device HIV Outreach	6. Bioterrorism—What is Public Health?
7. Web-Based References and Educational Materials	7. Redundant Response System Tools	7. Bioterrorism Management of Public Emergencies
	8. Bidirectional Communication and Notification System	8. Agents, Treatments, and Protection for the Health Care Worker
	9. Linkage with Local Public Health System Partners	
	10. Hospital Capacity and Inventory	
	11. Emergency Event Tracking and Notification	
	12. Public Health Emergency Information Lines	
	13. Internet-Based Learning Materials and Courses	
	14. Consequences of Weapons of Mass Effect Video	

examples for public health preparedness. In December 2003, five sites were named by NACCHO and CDC to become Advanced Practice Centers. These sites, which include the original DeKalb, Georgia, site, were funded by CDC to serve as learning laboratories to design and test creative and innovative ways to improve the emergency preparedness and response capacity of the United States. These five sites will be given resources to develop their public health emergency preparedness infrastructure and to provide technical assistance to other local health departments to develop and test innovative resources and technologies. These five sites include Georgia East Central Health District, Santa Clara County (California) Public Health Department, Seattle and King County (Washington) Department of Public Health, Tarrant County (Texas) Public Health Department, and DeKalb County. They will serve as formal demonstration and training sites for other local health departments and the CDC. The specific areas of focus for these five programs will be:

1. Partnerships and collaboration with first responders
2. Preparedness planning and readiness assessment
3. Workforce development and training
4. Risk communication and public education
5. Integrated communications and information systems

Partnership will be a critical element in all these projects. Leaders will need to be better prepared in the future if all the new critical concerns of public health are to be addressed.

OVERVIEW OF COLLABORATION

Before starting a discussion of collaboration and its benefits, it is important to present a few cautionary comments. First, it is critical to decide whether collaboration is the best direction to follow or not. There are situations in which an individual or an organization can accomplish more by going it alone. Second, collaboration should only be used in those situations in which working together has a synergistic effect. The issues of power, power relationships, and shared leadership often complicate any collaborative endeavor. Third, collaboration is often about the relationships between organizations and the people relationships need to be kept in perspective. Fourth, collaboration may occur within organizations and not between organizations and vice versa. Fifth, collaboration is more about the commitment of the members of the collaboration and less about the structure of the collaboration.

With these cautions in mind, collaboration can be defined as a mutually beneficial set of relationships that are well defined and that are entered into by two or more organizations in order to achieve some common goals (Mattesich, Murray-Close, & Monsey, 2001). The individuals who represent these collaborating organizations tend to be called members or partners. An important reason to collaborate is to achieve results that are more likely to happen when people work together than in situations where people or a specific organization would work alone (Winer & Ray, 1997). Working together also creates further collaboration opportunities. In most circumstances, collaboration becomes a continuing set of circumstances that provides a wide range of outcomes that empower people, organizations, and systems to change. Keeping collaborations active is not an easy task. Many collaborations have to struggle with such issues as unproductive meetings, shifting members from organizations, making the same decisions over and over again, lack of accountability, difficulty of maintaining a collaboration when funding ends, and difficulty of getting agencies to implement best practices throughout the system (Ray, 2002).

Ray developed a model called the nimble collaboration to orient collaborative activity towards results by emphasizing the premise of the collaboration, its promise, mission, vision, outcomes, evaluation criteria, and work plan. Another interesting approach has been called *collaboration math* which creates a structure for the collaboration based on the participants in the collaboration (Cohen, Aboelata, Gantz, & VanWert, 2003). Collaboration math requires a common set of definitions and categories that each partner to the collaboration fills out. A matrix is created based on the definition of the problem, key issues, available or needed data, funding issues, training needs, outside partners, and results which are anticipated.

There are many reasons to collaborate (Turning Point, 2004). Some of these reasons include a shared concern for an issue or community challenge and a strong belief that working together can address the challenge most effectively. A second reason is to pool power so the combined impact of several groups or agencies working together can have a substantial impact on the outcome. Third, when gridlock exists, working together will help the community or a specific agency get unstuck. Fourth, bringing together several groups or agencies to work together increases the chances for diversity issues to be addressed. Several agencies working together can also increase the ability of the various members to handle complex community issues. Exercise 6–1, which was developed by the Turning Point Leadership Collaborative, is an excellent way to explore the issue of collaboration.

EXERCISE 6–1 Reasons for Collaboration

Purpose: To learn the benefits of collaborative leadership techniques

Key Concepts: Collaborative leadership, cultural diversity

Procedures:

Roseland: Reasons for Collaboration

Roseland had always been a tranquil, quiet town. To the outside observer Roseland might be described as quaint. Most people in town knew each other, it was safe for children to play outside all over town, and town leaders were well meaning and eager to work on behalf of the town. There were not many entertainment options in Roseland—the diner, riding the local strip on week- ends, "hanging out" at the new book/video and coffee store on Main Street, or riding 30 minutes to the next town for a movie. Oddly enough, sleepy, little Roseland sat in the shadow of an intersection for two major interstates. Town people often talked of their amazement, and gratefulness, that the town did not take off in a boom of growth when the new interstates were built.

Early in spring 2001, people in Roseland began to notice a change in their sleepy, little community. Several of the town teenagers were becoming involved in drugs. These were not new kids in town; they were children of families who had lived in Roseland for several generations. Teachers and school administra- tors were talking about the change in the students. The local high school in Roseland had five drug arrests in the previous year on campus, as well as a more than 50% increase in violence in the schools in the last two years. The police were hinting at the presence of gangs in the community, and community members were shocked to see graffiti that looked much like what they saw on television as gang tagging. Usually business owners did not mind teenagers "hanging out" on Main street around their businesses, but lately there had been an increase in fighting and disturbing the customers. Community mem- bers in Roseland knew that times were different now than they were 10 or 15 years ago, and that teenagers were exposed to more temptations. However, they suspected that the change in Roseland was due to something more than just "changing times." These changes became the topic of many conversations around town and dominated many community meetings.

continues

EXERCISE 6–1 *continued*

One day a group of high school teachers were talking in the teachers' lounge, discussing the changes. They decided two things: (1) their children needed help, and (2) it was going to take more than just the school to accomplish the needed changes. These teachers went to their principal and talked about their idea. With the principal's blessing (and involvement), they then solicited the health department, police department, parents, churches, business leaders, a social service agency representative, and several youths to participate in a Saturday morning meeting.

The first meeting went well. They came to a general consensus that there was an issue regarding the youth. They agreed to work on the problem collaboratively, and they appointed people to tasks such as getting others involved, doing an assessment to understand the underlying issues at hand and their effects, and a commitment to always actively include teenagers in their group. The group became known as the Saturday Morning Breakfast Club. Over the course of the next year the Saturday Morning Breakfast Club conducted an assessment that discovered drugs were making their way into Roseland through the interstates and several businesses located at the interstate exits. This assessment was also able to document the change in Roseland youth and the effects these changes were having on youth performance in school, health, and crime rates. The collaboration used this information to apply for funding to begin a program they called Roseland Cares (RC). This is a collaborative effort to provide fun, safe, and affirming activities for teenagers in Roseland. It is based on a service model in which the teenagers get involved in service projects around Roseland. The program has only been in operation for six months. However, to date, more than 150 students are participating in the service projects.

1. Why did the people of Roseland initially collaborate?
2. What are your impressions of how or if the people in Roseland pooled power?
3. Discuss the collaboration's diversity.
4. Rate the complexity of Roseland's problem on a scale of 1 (not complex) to 10 (most complex), and discuss why people and organizations collaborate when issues are more complex.

Collaboration needs to be seen in relationship to three other strategies for working together (Himmelman, 2002). These three other strategies are networking, coordination, and cooperation. Time and circumstances will affect which of these strategies will be used. Table 6–2 shows the Himmelman matrix of strategies. Collaboration was defined as the

Table 6-2 Matrix of Strategies for Working Together

Definition	Networking	Coordinating	Cooperating	Collaborating
	Exchanging information for mutual benefit	Exchanging information for mutual benefit, and altering activities to achieve a common purpose	Exchanging information for mutual benefit, and altering activities to achieve a common purpose	Exchanging information for mutual benefit, altering activities, and sharing resources to achieve a common purpose
Relationship	Informal	Formal	Formal	Formal
Characteristics	Minimal time commitments, limited levels of trust, and no necessity to share turf; information exchange is the primary focus	Moderate time commitments, moderate levels of trust, and no necessity to share turf; making access to services or resources more user-friendly is the primary focus	Substantial time commitments, high levels of trust, and significant access to each other's turf; sharing of resources to achieve a common purpose is the primary focus	Extensive time commitments, very high levels of trust and extensive areas of common turf; enhancing each other's capacity to achieve a common purpose is the primary focus
Resources	No mutual sharing of resources necessary	No or minimal mutual sharing of resources necessary	Moderate to extensive mutual sharing of resources and some sharing of risks, responsibilities, and rewards	Full sharing of resources, and full sharing of risks, responsibilities, and rewards

exchange of information, or altering the way activities get done, a possible sharing of resources, and enhancing the capacity of the various partners to achieve the goals defined by working together. This latter point of mutual benefit is critical to any collaboration. Networking is the most informal of the four strategies and relates primarily to the sharing of information.

Many coalitions have this networking strategy as a primary goal for getting together. The coordination strategy incorporates the major goal of networking with the additional goal of altering activities. It is hoped that this strategy will reduce barriers for those seeking to access specific services. The last strategy relates to cooperation that incorporates the strategies of networking and coordination and adds the sharing of resources for mutual benefit. The major difference in cooperation and collaboration is the willingness of organizations to enhance the capacity of the various partners for the mutual benefit of all partners and to increase the chances of meeting the goals and purposes of the relationship.

The Center for Civic Partnership has also looked at the issue of collaboration. A distinction was made between collaborative actions covering such dimensions as connectivity, continuous assessment and planning, communication, capacity building, coordination of services, and collaborative initiatives and collaborative attitudes encompassing the six Cs:

- Commitment
- Consensus building
- Community outreach and involvement
- Conflict resolution
- Cooperation
- Change

Table 6–3 presents the details of these 12 activities. They are especially interesting when compared to the four strategies of Himmelman that are incorporated into these 12 actions and attitudes.

It is important to evaluate whether a group of individuals or organizations in a community are ready to work together. To this community readiness issue must be added the concern or evaluation of the community's capacity to change. Thurman (2001) has utilized community readiness theory to explore how communities can implement successful prevention programs using a step-by-step process. Communities can be defined in terms of nine stages of readiness (see Table 6–4). Once a collaborative group can define the stage in which a community can be located in the model, they then can develop the strategies to address ways to move a community to a higher level of readiness. Community readiness is only part of the evaluation that is necessary. It is important to determine individual, team, and organizational readiness levels as well (Ayer, Clough, & Norris, 2002).

Table 6–3 Collaborative Functions: the 12 Cs of a Collaborative

Collaborative Actions:

- **Connection**—Serving as the convener of its members to promote information sharing and networking.

- **Continuous Assessment and Planning**—Coordinating needs and resource assessments to provide current information on service delivery gaps, existing needs, and available community resources. Another collaborative function may be to convene and facilitate ongoing strategic planning activities.

- **Communication**—Acting as a clearinghouse for information exchange and dissemination for its members and with the media.

- **Capacity Building**—Building the knowledge and skills of individuals and organizations through trainings, providing information, etc.

- **Coordination of Services**—Coordinating services in the community to improve service delivery and availability, reduce duplication, and address service gaps.

- **Collaboration**—Participating in joint grant proposals and collaborative projects, pooled funding, shared resources and staff, and colocated services. Organizations and community members share risks, responsibilities, and rewards by working as partners. This requires a high level of trust and commitment to the collaborative process by decision makers and collaborative members.

Important Collaborative Attitudes:

- **Commitment**—Collaboration requires an ongoing commitment from all members.

- **Consensus Building**—Members agree upon a shared vision and participate in the development, implementation, and achievement of the collaborative's goals.

- **Community Outreach and Involvement**—A successful collaborative stays in frequent contact with the community it serves and involves community members in planning, decision making, and other collaborative activities.

- **Conflict Resolution**—Conflict is a natural occurrence in the collaborative process. Issues should be resolved immediately through a conflict resolution process developed and approved by collaborative members.

- **Cooperation**—Collaborative activities promote a more cooperative approach in decision making and service delivery and enhance relationships between individual agencies and community. Information and expertise are shared, but agency resources and authority are usually separately maintained and risks are minimal.

- **Change**—Change is both a prerequisite and a result of successful collaboration! True collaboration requires organizations and the community to think differently about how they do business and usually requires change in their current systems to achieve collaborative goals.

Table 6–4 The Community Readiness Model Identifies Nine Stages of Readiness

---

- No knowledge (formerly community tolerance) stage suggests that the behavior is normative and accepted.
- Denial stage involves the belief that the problem does not exist or that change is impossible.
- Vague awareness stage involves recognition of the problem, but no motivation for action.
- Preplanning stage indicates recognition of a problem and agreement that something needs to be done.
- Preparation stage involves active planning.
- Initiation stage involves implementation of a program.
- Stabilization (formerly institutionalization) stage indicates that one or two programs are operating and are stable.
- Confirmation/expansion stage involves recognition of limitations and attempts to improve existing programs.
- Professionalization stage is marked by sophistication, training, and effective evaluation.

There is the additional issue of a collaborative or a community's capacity to work together to create change (Chrislip & Larsen, 1994). First, it is necessary to clearly define the issues or the problems to be addressed. Second, the issue of leadership and who will lead the change effort is critical. It is here that power sharing and turf issues become prominent. The identification of appropriate stakeholders and partners with whom to address the issues is very important. It is necessary to make sure that *all* key organizations and community leaders are represented in the collaborative activity. The assessment of agreement between the stakeholders must also be evaluated. All possible solutions also need to be explored. Both the issue of the community's readiness to change, as well as the capacity of the community to change, are important. In the arena of emergency preparedness and response, it is important to recognize that change will occur whether a community or collaborative feels it is ready for the change or not. If community readiness issues and community capacity for change can be addressed as part of the planning and preparedness activities of the community, some of the response events will be easier to predict.

MODELS OF COLLABORATION

To put the discussion on collaboration in a structural context, Figure 6–1 portrays collaboration as a continuum. There are several dimensions to the continuum. First, there is the internal organization type of working together that is represented by the team. This type of working together can be collaborative or it can be like a committee or task force in which the chair of the group guides the process. From a collaborative perspective, the second dimension shows the team model to be weak from a community collaboration approach. Teams are used in many ways and leaders argue that they can be extremely effective in sharing leadership and responsibility (Rowitz, 2001).

External to the single organization, collaboration takes three major forms. First, there is the coalition which is created for information sharing and to bring together different community leaders and organizations to map out strategies for community change. Alliances are groups of health, health care, and public health organizations that combine forces to address key community or public health issues. These alliances, which are quite common, often develop informal contractual agreements to provide more comprehensive types of programs and services to their communities. Alliances may also add or delete members as programmatic needs change. The most structured organizational model is one based on written contracts with all details of the collaboration worked out in minute detail with possible legal consequences. These collaborations are called partnerships. With a continuum perspective like the one presented in Figure 6–1, variations of the three major models are possible. For exam-

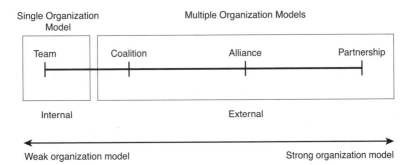

FIGURE 6–1 Models of Collaboration

ple, a coalition–alliance model may be created with elements of each structural type included in the collaboration

An interesting model that appears to have both the elements of a coalition and an alliance can be found in Case Study 6. In this case study, Willis, who was a faculty person in a Kellogg-funded health leadership fellowship program at the University of Illinois at Chicago called the International Center for Health Leadership Development (ICHLD), interviewed a graduate of the 2-year collaborative leadership fellowship, D. Tecumseh (Seh) Welch, about how training impacted her collaborative work with a Southern California coalition. One of the interesting issues to observe in the dialogue is the confusion over the use of the words *coalition* and *partnership*. The case study does demonstrate that leadership development can make a difference.

COLLABORATIVE LEADERSHIP

Not all leadership is collaborative. Although all leaders need followers, all leaders do not feel that they need to share power or their decision-making authority. Collaborative leadership involves a leader who believes in engaging other leaders in working together for the common good (Turning Point, 2002). Collaborative leaders work together, convene appropriate stakeholders in the cause for which the group is brought together, and they also facilitate and find methods for sustaining their activities and interactions. Collaborative leaders also facilitate mutual enhancement of each other activities (Himmelman, 2002). Collaborative leaders have strong values and they are clear in stating them. Collaborative leaders also see commonalities and try to find common interests that bind them to their partners (Turning Point, 2002). These leaders are also expert in creating and refining their visions and in mobilizing others to work with them. They are also excellent mentors who work towards the development of others.

Himmelman (2002) has summarized some of the major characteristics of collaborative leaders. These characteristics can be found in Table 6–5. These 10 characteristics can also be seen as a framework for a set of competencies for collaborative leaders. All sorts of skills are involved from the use of values to drive action, persuasion, mentoring and training, risk taking, information sharing through telling stories and other techniques, community-organizing skills, training other leaders, communication

CASE STUDY 6

Creating Win-Win: Leveraging and Strengthening Coalition Resources: An Interview with D. Tecumseh Welch

Marilyn A. Willis

D. Tecumseh (Seh) Welch received a Bachelor of Science degree in mechanical engineering from the University of Santa Barbara and a law degree from its College of Law in 1997. One year later, she was actively addressing the issues of inequity and lack of trust that have negatively impacted the health and quality of life of Native Americans and Alaska Natives. To achieve her personal and professional objective of making an effective, ongoing, positive contribution to the Native American community, she has assumed leadership roles in a wide range of projects at the national, state, and local levels.

Ms. Welch is the founder and executive director of American Indian Health & Services (AIH&S), in Santa Barbara, California. AIH&S has as its mission "to improve the health and general welfare status of urban American Indians within Santa Barbara County by providing quality comprehensive health care services that are culturally appropriate, accessible, and socially responsive, while preserving the American Indian culture and identity." From its small beginnings in 1996, Ms. Welch expanded the program and spearheaded the development of the organization to its current level of coordinated medical, dental, outreach, and referral services for Native American and Alaska Native residents, before leaving in 2003.

In this leadership story, Welch briefly reflects on her activities during the late 1990s, her decision to submit an application to a leadership fellowship, and the primary objective she achieved through her participation. She then goes on to discuss her role in initiating a successful oral health project—The Dental Access Response Team Proposition 10 (DART/P-10).

Marilyn Willis (MAW): Seh, obviously you were a leader prior to joining the Health Partners Leadership Fellowship. To what extent, though, were you involved in collaborative projects during that time?

Tecumseh Welch (SW): Actually very little. I had been part of the local HIV/AIDS coordinating council, but that was more so in name only, not a true partnership or coordination. That was really about politics around the table, and essentially I had very little experience with true partnership or true collaboration.

MAW: What specifically attracted you to a collaborative leadership program?

SW: I certainly felt that there had to be something more than getting together and just stroking each other's egos, there had to be more definitive ways of operating to address disease or other issues at hand, something more than just chasing funding. When the information for this

continues

CASE STUDY 6 *continued*

leadership program came across my desk, I was very excited to learn about an opportunity to foster what my gut had already been telling me, a chance to learn how to develop actual win-win situations so that we could move forward and pass the organizational ego, the collaborative ego, and make true progress towards the goal that we were all supposedly there to address—improved health status for our community.

MAW: What insights did you gain about yourself once you became involved?

SW: One of the things I definitely discovered was internal balance. I had been struggling so hard to try and make things work. Often I asked myself, "Well, isn't it really about health care—and not about how much money a certain organization receives over some other organization?" I was pretty naive. I really thought that we were all about providing health care, or we were all about providing car seats for infants, or all about whatever the topic was.

I learned to create win-win situations so that we could all be far more productive. Internally, my own personal growth resulted in more balance. I didn't feel like I was crawling uphill so much all by myself. I realized that there are tools—tools that I now have after the fellowship—tools that I can put into place to move in the direction where all parties feel so much better and are so much more positive about the outcome.

First Year of a New Partnership

MAW: I knew that when you returned to your health center, you became involved in several new health initiatives. Can you highlight a program of which you are particularly proud?

SW: Well, there are several. However, one that really sticks out in my mind is our dental program, DART/P-10. We had a huge need here in California, particularly Southern California, regarding cavities in little kids, particularly kids under six years old. And the reason for dental problems in children is really two fold. I mean, the parents think that, "Oh, we don't have to worry about these teeth; they're going to fall out anyway." And the child isn't educated enough or developed enough in his or her own character to be able to understand the necessity of brushing twice a day.

MAW: Who is involved in the DART/P-10 collaboration?

SW: One of the things we did was step back and say, "We can't do this as an American Indian organization—we can't do it by ourselves—and who else is interested in dental issues?" That's creating a partnership. Pick out the areas of common interest and the allies you have in your own community.

We had several interested parties: the Santa Barbara County Health Department, local parish nurses, the Santa Barbara County Dental Society, and a few private dentists. I asked everyone to come together so

continues

that we could talk a bit about common goals and see how we might be able to begin to educate the community, begin to educate possible funding sources regarding the problem, about the critical need for dental care for the under six-year-old population.

MAW: Were you able to successfully get this program funded?

SW: The program has been funded by a cigarette tax here in the state of California (Proposition 10). Proposition 10 is an additional tax per pack of cigarettes that has been levied and those additional dollars come to the different counties in the state. Our county in Santa Barbara receives a very large sum of money from Proposition 10 funds. This group that I put together was able to educate the county health department, and ultimately the Santa Barbara County Board of Supervisors was convinced to put money aside and focus on the dental needs of children under six years old.

The collaboration or coalition that I was able to put together was already poised and well situated and ready to receive the money so that we could very quickly begin implementing a program. That program has many different tiers, and there were a lot of issues around the table that we had to work out as a coalition if we wanted to be successful.

MAW: What do you think really helped you to get through this process? I know initially you assumed a leadership role, but how did it progress once you brought the people together?

SW: One of the things that tends to bring people together is funding, or available financial rewards for their agency or their own cause; so, that's definitely one motivating factor that kept people at the table. The second one was the skills and talents that I had developed through leadership training that allowed me to create win-win situations around the table so that we could all come together and apply for funds.

Now, it turns out that after about the first six to eight months, I had to step back as the person who had the initial vision. I had to step back as the leader or the facilitator because of politics that started happening and shifted things around the table. We turned to the local dental society so that they could be the lead agency, and they began running the meetings and the communication, making sure we had meetings every month and taking minutes. And those are things we had to flush out during the first year of our partnership. How do you communicate? Communication is absolutely one of the basic foundations in any collaboration, especially if you're going to share the responsibilities, the rewards, and the benefits of providing a service.

MAW: When you think of your key challenges, what issues would you place at the top of the list?

continues

SW: Certainly, I think the key challenges were to come to terms with the organizational egos gathered around the table, the individual egos around the table, and kind of figuring out the pecking order. There's always a natural kind of pecking order that's human to human. But then you bring in agency baggage and historical factors such as how many staff you have and how many this and how many that. A key factor was trying to sort out all of this. I'm not so sure that we have it all sorted out yet, but I do know that we are actually providing services.

Personally, I think one of the key factors that I needed to realize was that even though I have the vision and even though I know that I have the leadership skills, sometimes being a good leader is about letting go and fostering the other leaders around the table so that everyone has ownership of the program or the project.

MAW: Were there any areas or topics that were not acceptable in the partnership?

SW: Yes, absolutely. There are a number of topics that ended up being taboo. One of them, for example, was evaluation. How are we going to evaluate whether this program is a success? Some individuals really felt that I, in particular, was asking them to be accountable as individuals. And I was really asking for us as a partnership to be accountable so that we could actually attract additional dollars.

I was looking at evaluation as a positive thing. How do we collect our data? I know that we were serving almost 400–500 children, but if we don't keep data on those children—you know, ask questions like: What is their income? What dental problems are we treating? How many of them have baby bottle tooth decay? How many of them are actually showing up for their appointments?—If we don't collect data like this, we will never make progress toward the larger, more long-term goal. And that's really the difference and the true meaning of collaboration and coalition: to have a long-term effect on whatever the issue is. Otherwise, you're really much more of a task force.

MAW: That sounds like one opportunity for training. Did you train any of the partners or community persons regarding this particular project?

SW: I actually did share quite a bit of information that I learned, but I still don't think that they necessarily bought into the fact that we are there to deal with an issue—dental services for kids—versus getting from one funding cycle to another funding cycle. I can begin to see the shift in a few of the key players. Certainly the Santa Barbara County Health Department has a longer-term vision and so does the county dental society. I'm not so certain about some of the other community-based organizations, and that may be because of their internal organizational structure or the length of time that they have been involved in some of these issues.

continues

CASE STUDY 6   *continued*

I think many times, some community-based organizations end up strug-gling year by year, sometimes project by project, just to keep their doors open. And when you're in a financial situation where you're struggling to keep your doors open and your lights on, looking at a long-term effect five years down the road seems almost an impossible dream.

MAW: Well, that's one thing good about having a collaboration because certain partners have the talent to accomplish certain objectives, and if you put the two together, those who are involved in the service as well as those who can have the opportunity to achieve other goals, the end result is a much more effective and outcome-oriented program.

SW: Absolutely. And that is exactly the reason that we decided to bring the university into our coalition to do the evaluation. They weren't con-nected to any one of the organizations in the coalition directly. They were a neutral party. They also brought those initials behind their name, their expertise in developing an evaluation form with which we could collect particular data throughout the project, and each one of us could collect that data and pool it together. That really helped a lot of people get over the anxiety of evaluation, and we began looking at our partnership together versus its individual components.

Continued Growth and Development

Welch found the first year of the DART/P-10 coalition to be very inter-esting, with many lessons learned from the struggles the group faced. The coalition continued to grow and develop during the second year; at the time of this writing, the coalition was confident that funding would be received for a third year.

SW: Another lesson is that politics plays a huge role in determining who an organization chooses to send as a representative to the coalition. If the organization is not very invested in the topic, it sends employees who don't have authorization to commit the organization to anything that the coali-tion is doing. Once you start to move up the ladder, once the executive directors and the program directors are at the table, it become much more effective and much more rewarding for all the partners.

The other thing that I've learned about is organizational egos and indi-vidual egos. It's like having another extended family. You have to try to fig-ure it all out and realize and learn about new friendships. You can learn, "What's the button?" for a particular person or organization. For example, you may know that they lost funding from some grant, and they don't ever want to bring that up. There are taboos that we don't necessarily want to talk about.

MAW: It sounds like you've increased your sensitivity and are tuning in to other people's problems. I think sometimes we get involved with our

continues

CASE STUDY 6   *continued*

own projects and we want to see certain things accomplished, and we don't pay as much attention to each other from an organizational point of view—you know, not from a personal, friendship point of view. Could you add a little bit more about recognition from the community? Were you able to achieve recognition from certain community groups?

SW: We have been recognized by several different groups. The Latino community has recognized our work within their community. We've also been recognized by the California Dental Association. I think it most rewarding that we've been recognized by the community as one of the heroes in providing direct dental services. You know, some of the programs that we offer teach kids proper brushing techniques—don't saw your teeth in half, brush up and down and in circles. We also teach about flossing. Many people don't really know how to floss properly. It's very easy once you learn how to handle the darn floss. Even I have been retrained. And we teach parents about baby bottle tooth decay. There's no simple way to prevent cavities, not only in those teeth that are going to go away, but in the new permanent teeth as well.

We also offer a treatment. We provide fillings for cavities and fluoride treatments, regular cleaning, and some other basic services on a regular basis. One of the best things that we've implemented in the dental chair occurs when a child comes to the dentist for the very first time. Sometimes the dentist is perceived as a scary person. I don't know where they learn this, but every kid thinks the dentist is the bogeyman. So at the very first appointment in our dental program, we don't do anything. They come in and they just walk around the dental chair and they get to hold the drill and they get to do different things. They get to sit in the chair and that's it. And the other key thing is we don't give them suckers afterwards. So we really try to make their first visit a positive experience. Now, some of the kids won't even leave the waiting room—and that's okay. The dentist comes out to the waiting room and sits on the couch and we talk together. They talk together about brushing. We can teach them to brush their teeth when they're sitting on the couch just as well as when they're sitting in the dentist's chair. And just visually looking at their teeth, without any X-rays or anything can tell a dentist an awful lot.

The other key piece to this is we screen for diabetes in those under six-year-old kids. You can see signs of diabetes in a person's mouth way before you can see it in their eating or drinking preferences or other signs and symptoms of diabetes. We have had our dentists specially trained in diabetic dental care. At first people thought, "Oh you're crazy, that'll never work." Well, it turns out it works really well.

MAW: And you also go into the homes!

continues

CASE STUDY 6   *continued*

SW: Yes, we do home visits because many people work during the day; particularly if they're working a couple of part-time jobs, they can't afford to take the time off. If they do take the time off, they don't get paid and then their employers start the routine of saying, "If you want this job, you need to show up or I'll find somebody that does." The pressures go on and on. If people take time off of work to take their child to the dentist for preventive care, then they're actually losing money. Well, one of the things that we've found is that there's no better way to do dental education, particularly about proper brushing and flossing techniques, than to do it in the home.

We take new toothbrushes and we go to the home and we teach them how to brush their teeth right there in their environment, in front of their sink. And if they don't get it quite right, we'll review it with them. But it's in their environment and they're not scared. In addition, we're able to take a look around and make sure that their environment is safe. For example, we also use our access through our dental education program to check if the family has a smoke alarm. It's very simple. It doesn't always have to be just about dental care.

It doesn't have to be just about the obvious. Coalitions and collaborations allow you freedom. Once the trust is built, you're allowed the freedom to be creative and assist other organizations in reaching goals. Our goal as a health agency involved in this coalition is to prevent dental caries and other health-related issues that get started because of bad oral hygiene. Another one of the partners, the Santa Barbara County Health Department, brought their WIC program to the coalition to talk about good nutrition and how that has an effect on dental development. Now that helps the WIC program and it helps us.

Then, we had a third group come in and that's who brought the smoke detector idea to us. And we said, "Well, why not? If we're already in the home all we have to do is look up." How would the fire department or the injury prevention specialists get into a person's home? But we are there with our free toothbrush program going into the home, teaching the child—and oftentimes the parents—proper brushing and flossing techniques and talking to the family about baby bottle tooth decay. Literally, all we have to do is look up. Do you know how many children die each year, how many family homes burn down because they don't have a smoke alarm?

Quite frankly, we have been able to create this coalition and move it forward because I brought skills and talents back home that I learned during the ICHLD fellowship, and I had the will to implement them locally. Now all of us in this collaboration are moving forward and helping our own community.

continues

CASE STUDY 6   *continued*

MAW: Throughout this conversation it seems to me that you have created a high level of trust among the partners. I can hear it in the nature of how you describe your approach to communication. How do you think you went about creating that level of trust?

SW: That goes back to those creating win-win situations. If you and I were involved in a project and if it was all about me, you wouldn't trust me. But if every now and again I say, 'Now what about you?' it begins a trust relationship. It's very simple really. Once both partners realize that you're going to look out for yourself—and you have to be honest about that—but once the other partner realizes that you're going to look out for them too, it becomes so much easier.

MAW: Well, you know it also sounds like you created a level of respect too, respect for the talents and resources of your other collaborators.

SW: I certainly hope so. I don't know if I've always been able to project that. It's difficult work, it really is. You know, that first year I felt like I was running up against the wall, but all of a sudden, things started turning around and we started seeing changes. I think that there have been just a few really uncomfortable situations in the coalition, and not all of the original partners are still at the table, but we have to have faith in each other and move forward as we all have the same vision and goal.

MAW: Are there any other accomplishments or thoughts that you want to mention?

SW: Within any true partnership—and this is a true partnership—you really need to exchange information and be flexible concerning activities. You've also got to share all the common purpose stuff—share resources, share the capacity for mutual benefit, share the risks and the liabilities, as well as the benefits, the positive aspects, the successes. There has to be an atmosphere of respect for the talents and resources of the various folks around the table—they are the ones directly responsible for the services we provide to our clients.

You know, so far this year (2002), we've treated 410 children and educated 1100 about dental care. We've been recognized by the community and we've got mechanisms in place to support the communication necessary for success, and some problem-solving mechanisms are now routine. I think we can point towards other accomplishments as well. For instance, people are starting to look at our coalition and say, "Well, hey, if they can do it, we can do it." And that has got to be the biggest accomplishment ever. We've really built the bridges that are so important for long-term collaboration.

skills, and an ability to use humor in stressful situations. All of these competencies and characteristics are useful for all leaders. All collaboration is used for community betterment and also for the empowerment of others. Collaboration strategies are used to produce policy change and to make improvements in the local delivery of programs and services.

Table 6–5 Some Collaborative Leadership Characteristics

1. A commitment to improve common circumstances based on values, beliefs, and a vision for change that is communicated both by "talking it and walking it"

2. An ability to persuade people to conduct themselves within ground rules that provide the basis for mutual trust, respect, and accountability

3. An ability to respectfully educate others about the relationship of processes to products and outcomes about the relationship of organizational structure to effective action

4. An ability to draw out ideas and information in ways that contribute to effective problem solving rather than ineffective restatements of problems

5. A willingness to actively encourage partners to share risks, responsibilities, resources, and rewards and to offer acknowledgments of those making contributions

6. An ability to balance the need for discussion, information sharing, and storytelling with timely problem solving and keeping focused on responding to action-oriented expectations of those engaged in common efforts

7. An understanding of the role of community organizing as the basis for developing and expanding collaborative power

8. A commitment to and active engagement in leadership development activities, both informal and formal, that can take the collaborative process to higher levels of inclusiveness and effectiveness

9. An ability to communicate in ways that invite comments and suggestions that address problems without attacking people and, when appropriate, draws upon conflict resolution and win-win negotiating to resolve differences

10. A very good sense of humor, especially whenever collaborative processes get ugly or boring or both

Ayre and a panel of public health department leaders in 2002 as part of the Turning Point Leadership Development National Excellence Collaborative discussed the topic of building understanding and information sharing. The panel believed these skills would help address the challenges to building collaborative leadership in public health. Several key themes emerged (Turning Point, 2002):

1. Collaboration and its leadership aspects can best be seen at a local level where there seems to be greater accountability.

2. Collaboration is vital to the work of public health, which is a population-based activity.
3. Individuals define collaboration differently. Federal, state, and foundations funders also may define it differently from local leaders who practice collaboration on a daily basis.
4. Because different leadership styles are required for different situations, collaboration may not be the best approach in every circumstance.
5. If collaborations are beneficial, it becomes critical to nurture them over time by supporting the various members when they need it.
6. Collaboration can be unpredictable in that different members may have different agendas that take precedence to the collaborative activity, or unexpected happenings may occur.
7. It is important to deal with the collaboration skeptics.
8. Collaboration skill development needs to be included as a key competency for leadership development programs.

LEADERSHIP IN CRISIS

Most discussions of collaboration present their discussions of collaboration as a continuous process that begins small and expands over time. These discussions have not been oriented toward crisis events such as those that occurred in the United States on September 11, 2001. Collaborations in public health occurred between public health agencies and leaders and community partners who also had strong health and health care agendas. Terrorist and bioterrorist events occurred and public health leaders now find they have new partners in Federal Bureau of Investigation officials, federal and state emergency preparedness personnel, police, fire professionals, bomb experts, elected officials, and many others. It is almost like the biblical story of the Tower of Babel in which everyone speaks a different language and there is chaos. New types of collaboration are necessary for preparedness planning and for individuals to become prepared public health leaders. The purpose of collaboration in the emergency preparedness phase of activity often relates to presenting a rationale for why public health should be at the table if a crisis occurs. Whereas the personal relationships appear to be as important as the institutional ones when collaboration occurs in fairly normal times, the institutional relationships are a critical component of emergency preparedness.

When a crisis or other emergency occurs, collaboration ends. As Figure 6–2 shows, the issue during the crisis relates to who is in charge. In a bioterrorism or disaster event, the incident command system or the unified command system are management systems in which all roles and responsibilities have been defined prior to the event. The leadership style required is a command and control one. The crisis must be handled and contained. Relationships between individuals change, and it is critical that each individual in the chain of command follows orders and protocols. Once the response is made and the crisis is over, then the various partners to the original collaborative come back together, review the events, and refine the system for the next possible crisis. Thus, there has been a change in our views of collaboration in crisis from a continuous process of growth and decline in normal times to a form of collaboration which is broken during a crisis event and reestablishes itself after the event. Prepared public health leaders need to be flexible and adaptable to changes in circumstances. It is possible that leaders during a crisis will not be the same individuals who are leaders in normal times.

It is clear that the models of collaboration during crisis are changing (Drath, 2001). The issues are less about conflicting agendas than they are about sharing work to address a problem of concern to the whole community. Of course, we are well aware that there are many global connections, but the connections at the local level are also extensive. There should be respect for diverse views without letting these views prevent necessary action from taking place. Leadership may need to be shared for

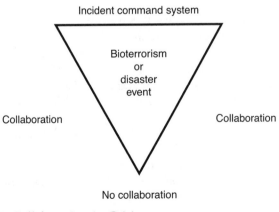

FIGURE 6–2 Collaboration in Crisis

success. Relationships are important, and relational dialogue skills will be required. The way that relational dialogue works is for those people who share the work to create new leadership approaches based on new methods for constructing the direction of the work, the commitments that are needed, and adaptive approaches to the challenges that the crisis or emergency presents (Drath, 2001).

SUMMARY

This chapter has discussed the important leadership issue of collaboration and how beneficial collaboration can be in many circumstances. The discussion also observed that collaboration may not always be the best leadership model to use. It was also pointed out that crisis situations change our views of how to work together. New partners are needed to address issues of emergency preparedness and response. Leadership relationships change during a crisis. Prepared public health leaders need many new skills to add to their repertoire. Many of these new skills will be discussed in Part 3 of this book.

REFERENCES

Ayre, D., Clough, G., & Norris, T. (2000). *Facilitating community change.* Boulder, CO: Community Initiatives.

Center for Civic Partnerships. (2002). *Collaborative functions: The 12 C's of a collaborative.* Sacramento, CA: Center for Civic Leadership.

Chrislip, D., & Larsen, C. (1994). *Collaborative leadership.* San Francisco: Jossey-Bass.

Cohen, L., Aboelata, M. J., Gantz, T., & VanWert, J. (2003). *Collaboration math.* Oakland: CA: Prevention Institute.

Drath, W. (2001). *The deep blue sea.* San Francisco: Jossey-Bass.

Gostin, L. O., Boufford, J. I., and Martinez, R. M. (2004). The future of the public's health: Vision, values, and strategies, *Health Affairs, 23* (4), 96–107.

Himmelman, A. (2002). *Collaboration for a change.* Minneapolis, MN: Himmelman Consulting.

Mattesich, P. W., Murray-Close, M., Monsey, B. R. (2001). *Collaboration: What makes it work* (2nd Ed.). St. Paul, MN: Amherst H. Wilder Foundation.

National Association of County and City Health Officials [NACCHO]. (2001). *Local centers for public health preparedness: Models for strengthening public health capacity (Year 2 report).* Washington, DC: Author.

National Association of County and City Health Officials [NACCHO]. (2002). *Local centers for public health preparedness: A resource catalog for bioterrorism and emergency preparedness*. Washington, DC: Author.

Ray, K. (2002). *The nimble collaboration*. St. Paul, MN: Amherst H. Wilder Foundation.

Rowitz, L. (2001). *Public health leadership: Putting principles into practice*. Sudbury, MA: Jones and Bartlett.

Thurman, P. (2001). *Community readiness: A promising model for community healing*. Oklahoma City, OK: University of Oklahoma Health Sciences Center (Center on Child Abuse and Neglect).

Turning Point. (2002). *Academics and practitioners on collaborative leadership*. Seattle, WA: Author.

Turning Point. (2004). *Collaborative leadership: Collaborative leadership learning modules*. Seattle, WA: Author.

Winer, M., & Ray, K. (1997). *Collaboration handbook*. St. Paul, MN: Amherst H. Wilder Foundation.

CHAPTER 7

Concern of the Community for Safety

A leader should be anticipating all the time.

—*Rudolph W. Giuliani*

Even though it often appears that the public has little respect for elected officials or the people who work for governmental agencies, during a crisis the public immediately turns to these people who serve the public. Crises of all types disrupt both family and community life activities. Especially since September 11, 2001, families keep asking public health and other officials about how to keep their families safe. Public health leaders now find themselves addressing not only health and safety issues but also issues related to mental health and distress. A critical second set of questions that the prepared public health leader has to address is the set of concerns related to community and family preparedness for emergencies. This chapter will address some of these issues as they are critical to promoting the health and welfare of all residents of our communities Case Study 7 presents the observations of Linda Landesman, a public health leader working in New York City who deals with these critical public health issues on a day-to-day basis.

In a recent press release from the Columbia University National Center for Disaster Preparedness at the Mailman School of Public Health (2004), the researchers reported a crisis of confidence in the federal government's ability to protect Americans. The study was commissioned in July 2004. Specifically, about three quarters of Americans are concerned that another terrorist attack is coming and think that the federal government will not

CASE STUDY 7 A Public Health Practice Quiz
for Linda Landesman

1. What is unique about the public health orientation to the psychological consequences of terrorism in contrast to the mental health orientation to these problems?

   Public health interventions are aimed at protecting or intervening with the community while mental health is interested in improving the community by focusing on the clinical picture that the individual, family, or group presents. Public health actions often follow a careful look at data or science to determine the best intervention. Only in the most recent years has the mental health profession moved towards a population-based approach. This has been driven, in part, by broadening their management practice because of the interface with managed care companies who examine mental health costs by monitoring data.

   With sophisticated data systems, it is possible to identify cohorts of patients and predict what their response to terrorism might be. With inherently elevated levels of depression in the U.S. population, we know those who were depressed before the event and who develop anxiety after a terrorism event. Clinicians have learned from the public health approach and can now plan better by looking at such data. The combined use of the World Trade Center Health Registry (Registry) is a good example. The Registry, organized by the New York City Department of Health and Mental Hygiene (NYCDOHMH), tracks 70,000 people: NYC residents near the trade center site, those present when the Twin Towers collapsed, and emergency responders to the disaster. With continued financial support, NYCDOHMH will monitor this group over the next two decades. When analyzing the data collected through the registry, NYCDOHMH found that these residents and emergency workers reported "symptoms of psychological distress" at a level 60% higher than the New York City average (Santora, 2004). This data will be used by both the public health and mental health communities to determine the type and number of interventions needed. Mental health practitioners will organize and deliver the identified clinical services.

2. How can mental health and public health leaders work together to provide a more unified approach to mental health issues in terrorism?

   As a practicing clinician, the gap between hospital and prehospital mental health services was what initially interested me in emergency preparedness. In the early 1980s, with the formation of ASTM Committee F-30, the first national EMS consensus standards development activity, Blanche Newhall and I fought to have a single paragraph requiring mental health services included in the EMS standard for disasters. We were part of a small voice that understood the need for public health and mental health professionals to be integrated within the

CASE STUDY 7 *continued*

team that prepared for and responded to emergencies. Since then, many U.S. disasters and considerable research have demonstrated that major emergencies have long-term mental health impacts. Yet, it wasn't until terrorism struck on American shores that there was a true societal interest in intervening in more than a cursory, time-limited way. Even so, mental health is often an afterthought.

In some states, mental health is organized as a human services agency, in other states it is part of the department of health, and in others public health is a stand-alone agency. As a result, mental health and public health are often not well integrated into emergency response until there is a disaster and the community understands the need to include these disciplines in the response and recovery. Dedicated effort is needed for a unified approach to mental health issues in terrorism. By partnering in their planning efforts, mental health and public health leaders can enhance their effectiveness. This might be accomplished by including each other in the organizational structure of response activities. As an example, mental health could be asked to provide behavioral services when a point of dispensing site is established for mass prophylaxis. Public health could be asked to participate in the organization of victim assistance centers established following a community emergency. By working together and building upon established relationships, the human service elements of a response can be strengthened.

3. How closely are public health agencies working with mental health agencies on emergency preparedness and response activities?

There are a variety of models that exist in practice. Some communities, such as New York City, have merged their public health and mental health departments. This organizational structure facilitates a close working relationship, including mental health as a component of the health department's incident command structure and as a full partner in the DOHMH-based emergency operations center. This integration and the community's ability to organize and provide services are enhanced by the wealth of mental health providers in the metropolitan New York City region. In contrast, many areas of the country have an insufficient number of mental health providers, even for commonly occuring problems. So these communities are dependent on outside resources following emergencies.

Despite the deluge of external resources that occurs to stricken communities, it is best if the planning process calls for the provision of emergency mental health services solely by local mental health providers. Following the events of 9-11-01, mental health and public health professionals in the metropolitan region of New York City saw

continues

CASE STUDY 7   *continued*

that many who sought service in the early days of that response were best served by providers who had an extensive understanding of local resources. Despite a plethora of providers who came to New York to help, providers and administrators didn't have the time to provide training or credentialing for those coming from outside the region. Many of the early needs following a disaster are for concrete services, so providers need to know which agencies provide which services and who to call to make nonfrustrating, helpful referrals. The first task of a social worker new to an agency is to organize a list of resources and contacts. Even if that list is prepared in advance, how does an outsider tell a victim how to get there if landmarks are destroyed?

However, many areas in the country do not have enough mental health providers. Without local capacity to provide even core mental health services, communities are dependent on outside personnel to meet postcrisis demand and need. In all states, the American Red Cross has mental health units trained to conduct assessments of the mental health needs of a community following a disaster. Plans in these regions should include coordination with these groups.

4. What are the political ramifications of family involvement in community emergency planning activities?

Family involvement can only improve a community's preparedness efforts. Recent surveys suggest that citizens do not believe that their government will take care of them following an emergency. If citizens are more knowledgeable about the efforts that are in place and understand what various responding agencies will do in an emergency and what, as individuals, they should do to protect themselves and their families, then citizens are likely to feel more confident and to be more cooperative with government officials. Further, community preparedness can be enhanced when responsive government adapts or expands plans so they map with community expectations and needs. None of this, however, is easy. It requires all to listen carefully and to be open to changing behavior and to taking on new tasks. Some communities will be more successful at cooperative planning than others.

The randomness of disasters makes any of us a potential victim. It is only human nature to want to protect one's family during these times, and families are a natural support system for each other following a disaster. Having a family disaster plan in place can provide peace of mind, enabling public health professionals to report to and remain at work for long shifts if necessary. At a minimum, family disaster plans should include all members knowing where to go, having an out-of-state contact to call, having adequate emergency supplies, and ensur-

continues

CASE STUDY 7   *continued*

ing that elderly or infirm relatives have redundant supports who will look after them in the event of an emergency. As a collaborative, public health and the emergency management community should encourage the development of a personal/family disaster plan.

5. Should we train community volunteers to work in community crisis response activities?

When a crisis happens, there is always a spontaneous arrival of volunteers who want to help. By definition, disasters are emergencies that can't be managed with routine resources, so planning for what is known as "surge capacity" will improve a community's response. it is beneficial to have an advance structure in place that organizes that effort to both maximize the volunteer resource and to provide the volunteers with meaningful and constructive opportunities to assist their communities.

Once a crisis has begun, no one has time to train volunteers on how to be helpful. Further, a procedure is needed to manage all who arrive on the scene. Without oversight, multiple problems can complicate a response, ranging from injured volunteers to looting, such as that which occurred in the shops under the World Trade Center and in the surrounding restaurants and stores that were abandoned during the collapse. It is often referred to as a "disaster within a disaster."

The Federal Emergency Management Agency (FEMA) and National Voluntary Organizations Active in Disaster (NVOAD), a membership group of national nonprofit organizations, have worked to formalize management training for disaster volunteers. Organizations such as the Volunteer Center National Network connect unaffiliated volunteers with the needs of a stricken community.

One of the initiatives through the US Department of Homeland Security has been the recruitment and training of volunteers at all levels. Through collaborative planning, the Citizens Corps mobilizes local citizens to help their communities respond and recover from disasters. The Medical Reserve Corps (MRC) was established to recruit local medical providers who can augment local public health capacity during large scale emergencies. The MRC has attracted practicing and retired physicians, nurses, and other health professionals as well as other citizens interested in health issues.

Local community leaders develop their own MRC units and identify the duties of the MRC volunteers according to specific community needs. For example, MRC volunteers may deliver necessary public health services during a crisis, assist emergency response teams with patients, and provide care directly to those with less serious injuries and

continues

CASE STUDY 7 *continued*

other health-related issues. MRC volunteers may also assist with ongoing public health needs (e.g., immunizations, screenings, health and nutrition education, and volunteering in community health centers and local hospitals).

The decision to strengthen the response system through volunteers is not without complications. If the expectation is that a community will always look to volunteers to meet its health and safety needs in emergencies, it is easier for governments to maintain a staffing level at or below that needed to provide daily services. The trend toward smaller government could translate into never providing sufficient personnel to meet a community's needs. *Without core capacity, organizations cannot provide surge capacity in times of emergency.* Further, citizen volunteer groups attract many of the same folks—the medical personnel in disaster medical assistance teams and emergency medicine or the staff of emergency medical services, the fire services, and the National Guard are often the same people. While redundancy is desired in disaster preparedness, this type of redundancy is a game of musical chairs. If a call-up is needed, someone will be shorthanded when the same volunteers are listed for more than one organization. While this is more likely to occur in smaller communities, an examination of the MRC volunteers in our biggest cities will also demonstrate this inherent risk.

Linda Young Landesman, DrPH, MSW
New York, New York

Case Study 7 References

Santora, M. (2004, November 23). Thousands near 9/11 attack reported ill effect, US says. *New York Times*, 9.

be able to protect local areas from these attacks (a drop to 53% confidence in 2004 from 62% confidence in 2003). Only 39% of Americans think that the health care system is ready to respond to a biological, chemical, or nuclear attack. In addition to this lower confidence, 63% of families in the United States do not have a basic emergency plan. An interesting finding in this study was related to the American transportation systems. There is more confidence in security at airports than there is at other types of transportation sites. It was also found that 59% of the population will not evacuate immediately during, or preparatory to, a crisis even if told to do so by officials. A large percentage of parents (48%) said that they were not aware of the emergency preparedness plans at the schools of their children. In fact, only 21% of residents of the United States seem to know about the emergency preparedness and response plans that exist in their communities.

REDEFINING READINESS

A very important study by the Center for the Advancement of Collaborative Strategies in Health at the New York Academy of Medicine explored the issue of terrorism planning from the viewpoint of the American public (Lasker, 2004). This study explored how the public would respond to official instructions related to terrorists releasing smallpox or detonating a dirty bomb. After preliminary work with focus groups and various officials, a large sample of over 2500 people were surveyed. The study used smallpox and dirty bomb scenarios to place respondents in situations in which they would be told what to do. The findings were quite profound in that the percentage of people who would follow the protective instructions were lower than would be needed for protective levels determined by the officials. Specifically, it was found that only about 40% of the sample would go to a vaccination site during the smallpox outbreak and only about 60% would go to a shelter during a dirty bomb explosion. Other factors probably came into play in the reactions of the public—fear of side effects of the vaccine in the smallpox example, and worry about other family members and where they might be in the dirty bomb example.

This study made some very important recommendations about future planning efforts related to the public. It is important to listen to the concerns of the public and not rely only on the experts' untested assumptions about how the public will react. The prepared public health leader needs to meet with all segments of the community during the planning phases of emergency readiness development. Using focus groups in communities may be a very good technique to use. It is also important to realize that communities differ, and different communities may react to crises in different ways. The issue of trust is very important in that community residents are less likely to listen to officials or follow instructions when there is little trust in these officials. It is interesting to note in both of the reports cited above that most community residents are unaware of community preparedness plans or activities. Despite this lack of awareness, it does appear that the public recognizes that sound planning can reduce the harmful effects of an emergency. The public also seems to be interested in community-level planning. They just want to be involved in those planning activities.

In New York City and Washington, DC, where communities experienced the effects of the terrorist events of September 2001, about two fifths of the population said that they were interested in helping governmental officials and agencies develop plans for the future. In places not directly affected by a terrorist event, about one third of the population shows this same strong interest in helping. If the public is to be involved in future planning activities, prepared public health leaders have to guarantee the public that their opinions matter. The public wants to influence the planning activities and be involved in activities that can or may directly affect its welfare in the future.

There are a number of issues that have been raised that affect community readiness. Some of these issues include the following:

- Families are confused by the varied emergency preparedness activities going on around them.
- Families and other community residents do not feel secure in their home environments.
- The public continues to get conflicting messages, and they lack trust in official governmental agencies and their leadership.
- The public does not think that their opinions matter, and they think they are being excluded from the emergency preparedness and responses planning activities.
- No one seems to want to handle the mental health issues that concern local residents.
- Residents aren't sure that there is anything they can do to feel safer.
- A growing lack of trust in law enforcement officials complicates the planning efforts.
- Some diverse population groups think that they are being unjustly persecuted.
- Public health agencies struggle to be recognized as part of the preparedness team.

The prepared public health leader should then involve the public in a number of ways:

- Organize focus groups composed of members from all segments of the community and community officials to work together to define key preparedness issues and concerns.

- Develop community-wide coalitions to address different preparedness concerns with community residents on each committee.
- Develop an ongoing community assessment process for public health including information related to community health education and preparedness activities.
- Develop community-wide drills and exercises to prepare the public for a potential emergency.
- Ensure that the public understands the emergency preparedness community plan and how the incident command system will work during an emergency.
- Train community residents as members of a humanitarian response team during a crisis.

Competency-based community education approaches are as critical for the public as they are for the various professional workforces. Knowledge alone is clearly not sufficient. Until knowledge is put into action within the context of the community, a competency cannot develop.

MENTAL HEALTH ISSUES

There is growing concern about the psychological impact of crises of all kinds. When lives are disrupted, stress of all kinds occur. Some people are more resilient and seem able to deal with unusual events better than others. Leaders clearly need to show this resilience (Conner, 1992). The role of public health in addressing these psychological issues is to help restore order so that people can function at a psychologically and socially acceptable level as quickly as possible (Landesman, 2005). Prepared public health leaders are also critical in the reduction of the occurrence and severity of adverse mental health outcomes caused by natural and manmade disasters. The methodology for doing this is complex because of the separation of mental and physical health domains in our society in the past. It has become increasingly clear that public health professionals and mental health professionals need to work together to address these critical concerns for community health. Another important public health role related to aiding the community towards speedy recovery and prevention of long-term problems is through health education about normal stress reactions to crisis and how to handle this stress (Landesman, 2005).

In late October 2001, a group of disaster mental health experts from six countries were brought together in Virginia to address the impact of early psychological interventions within four weeks of a disaster event in order to define best practices in understanding and working with the people affected by mass violence or disaster (NIMH, 2002). Early intervention strategies were defined as preparation, planning, education, training, and service provision evaluation. The conference participants agreed that the best efforts to carry out early mental health assessment and intervention should be conducted relative to the hierarchy of needs related to the issues of survival, safety, security, food, shelter, health concerns, mental health triage for emergencies, orientation to emergency services available in the local area, humanitarian communication concerns, and other psychological first aid methods. Psychological first aid includes such techniques as protecting survivors from further harm, reducing physiological arousal, mobilizing support for those most in need, keeping families together, providing information, and using risk communication techniques.

Some of the best practice concerns for mental health include the following:

- Early, brief, and focused psychotherapeutic intervention
- Cognitive behavioral approaches to reduce stress
- Early intervention in the form of one-on-one discussion of events that have occurred (may have limited effect over time)

It is clear that this whole area of psychological intervention needs to be further explored and developed. There are questions related to the effectiveness of many techniques that are presently used. This evolving area needs testing and further development. Table 7–1, from the report of the conference, is a good guide to timing of early interventions on the basis of our present state of knowledge. The table does look at interventions from the preincident phase to the return-to-life phase (two weeks to two years after the event).

PUBLIC HEALTH STRATEGY ON PSYCHOLOGICAL CONSEQUENCES OF TERRORISM

Whereas mental health professionals take a strong clinical perspective on the psychological impact of disasters, the public health strategy is often quite different. In a recent 2003 Institute of Medicine (IOM) report on these issues, it was strongly pointed out that the psychological impact of

Table 7–1 Guidance for Timing of Early Interventions

Phase	Preincident	Impact (0–48 hours)	Rescue (0–1 week)	Recovery (1–4 weeks)	Return to Life (2 weeks–2 years)
Goals	Preparation, improve coping	Survival communication	Adjustment	Appraisal and planning	Reintegration
Behavior	Preparation vs. denial	Fight/flight, freeze, surrender, etc.	Resilience vs. exhaustion	Grief, reappraisal, intrusive memories, narrative formation	Adjustment vs. phobias, PTSD, avoidance, depression, etc.
Role of All Helpers	Prepare, train, gain knowledge	Rescue, protect	Orient, provide for needs	Respond with sensitivity	Continue assistance
Role of Mental Health Professionals	**Prepare** Train Gain knowledge Collaborate Inform and influence policy Set structures for rapid assistance	**Basic Needs** Establish safety, security, survival Ensure food and shelter Provide orientation Facilitate communication with family, friends, and community Assess the environment for ongoing threat/toxin	**Needs Assessment** Assess current status, how well needs are being addressed Recovery environment What additional interventions are needed for: • Group • Population • Individual	**Monitor the Recovery Environment** Observe and listen to those most affected Monitor the environment for toxins Monitor past and ongoing threats Monitor services that are being provided	**Treatment** Reduce or ameliorate symptoms or improve functioning via • Individual, family, and group psychotherapy • Pharmacotherapy • Short-term or long-term hospitalization

continues

Table 7–1 *continued*

Role of Mental Health Professionals	Psychological First Aid	Triage
	Support and be a "presence" for those who are most distressed	Clinical assessment
	Keep families together, and facilitate reunion with loved ones	Refer when indicated
	Provide information and education (i.e., services), foster communication	Identify vulnerable, high-risk individuals and groups
	Protect survivors from further harm	Emergency hospitalization or outpatient treatment
	Reduce physiological arousal	**Outreach and Information Dissemination**
	Monitoring the Impact on Environment	Make contact with and identify people who have not requested services (i.e., "therapy by walking around")
	Observe and listen to those most affected	**Outreach and Information Dissemination**
	Monitor the environment for stressors	Inform people about different services, coping, recovery process, etc., (e.g., by using

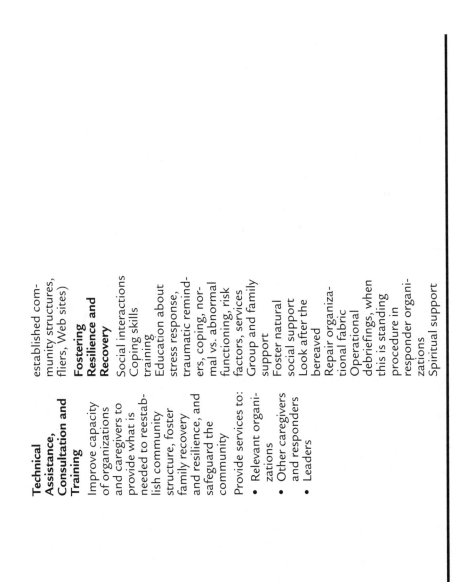

Technical Assistance, Consultation and Training

Improve capacity of organizations and caregivers to provide what is needed to reestablish community structure, foster family recovery and resilience, and safeguard the community

Provide services to:

- Relevant organizations
- Other caregivers and responders
- Leaders

established community structures, fliers, Web sites)

Fostering Resilience and Recovery

Social interactions

Coping skills training

Education about stress response, traumatic reminders, coping, normal vs. abnormal functioning, risk factors, services

Group and family support

Foster natural social support

Look after the bereaved

Repair organizational fabric

Operational debriefings, when this is standing procedure in responder organizations

Spiritual support

terrorism encompasses multiple levels of consideration from the emotional concerns discussed above to behavioral, cognitive, and eventually to community reactions. Every individual who observes or is impacted by a terrorist event will have some psychological reaction. The committee who prepared the report stated that prepared public health leaders as well as other community leaders will have to optimize the overall health and well-being of the population in the communities they serve by preventively addressing the potential impact of terrorist events and then addressing real impacts throughout the phases of a terrorist or other disaster event. It will be important for the United States Department of Health and Human Services (DHHS) and its various subdivisions such as the National Institutes of Health, the Substance Abuse and Mental Health Services Administration (SAMHSA), and the Centers for Disease Control and Prevention to work together to develop evidence-based techniques, training programs, and innovative psychological prevention and treatment programs for all sorts of crisis events, ranging through their pre-event to postevent phases. These activities may also be enhanced through the involvement of the Health Resources and Services Administration, Public Health Training Centers, Academic Health Centers, Centers for Public Health Preparedness, and the National Public Health Leadership Development Network, all of whom are involved in the training of public health workers and other health professionals. Exercise 7–1 brings the health and mental health leaders of a large city together to develop a coordinated plan for health and mental health reactions from a terrorist or bioterrorist event.

Utilizing the classic epidemiologic model of agent, host, vector, and environment, the IOM Committee (2003) looked at a framework for psychological impacts. In terrorism, then, the *agent* would be the violent act or threat, the *host* would be the affected people or populations, the *vector* is the terrorist or injurious agent, and the *environment* is the physical or social jurisdiction affected by the agent. Thus, a violent act in a community against a population would have psychological impacts. To make a coordinated response to these events, the infrastructure of the community needs to be strengthened relative to the coordination of agencies and services, preparedness training for staff and for management and leadership, more effective coordination of communication networks, adequate financing of the emergency preparedness and response system, and always supporting knowledge and evidence-based services. Without these

---

EXERCISE 7-1 Big Town Crisis Health Plan

Purpose: To explore the mental health concerns related to a terrorist or bioterrorist event in a large city

Key Concepts: Mental health, family preparedness, community preparedness, family security

Procedures: Human services organizations in Big Town have been asked by the mayor to develop a proposal for a coordinated plan for addressing the mental health and physical health needs of the residents of Big Town if there is a terrorist or bioterrorist event. The local public health administrator is asked to convene a meeting with representatives of the community's mental health agencies, social agencies, health agencies, and the emergency medical service network to develop a plan for addressing mental health issues during an emergency.

1. Divide the class or training group into teams of ten.
2. Each team of ten will be composed of five mental health and five public health representatives, and will address the issues posed by the case. Each individual in the exercise will choose one of the two agency perspectives.
3. Each team will develop a 2-page preliminary proposal related to the physical and psychological needs of the public during a crisis.
4. Each team will make a five minute presentation to the mayor on their proposal.

---

elements, the public health response will be weak, and psychological impact concerns will not be well addressed.

The committee adapted the Haddon injury prevention matrix (1972, 1980) to the issue of psychological consequences of a terrorist event. Table 7–2, from the 2003 IOM report, utilizes the epidemiological model previously discussed as related to a terrorist event (agent) on the affected individuals and population (host), the terrorist and injurious agent (vector), and the physical and social environment (environment) to the preevent, event, postevent, and desired end-result phases of the terrorist or other crisis event. This model can be used by federal, state, and local planners and leaders to address and evaluate the community's planning and preparedness activities in terrorist and other emergency events. This evaluation will be critical if leaders are to be prepared for the psychological impact of these crisis events.

Table 7-2 An Example Public Health Strategy: Preparing for the Psychological Consequences of Terrorism Example of a public health plan to assist in preparation for and response to the psychological consequences of a terrorism event utilizing phases and factors adapted from the Haddon Matrix.

Phases	Factors		
	Affected Individuals and Populations	Terrorist and Injurious Agent*	Physical and Social Environment
Preevent	**Biological–Physical** • Stockpile vaccinations, antibiotics, antidotes • Train emergency, medical, and public health professionals in spectrum of skills necessary to respond to incidents • Conduct baseline health surveillance **Psychological** • Integrate psychological and mental health into all public health and emergency preparedness plans • Design and implement psychological first aid training • Prepare materials for media and public education • Identify groups of special interest	**Biological–Physical** • Make chemical, biological, radiological, and nuclear weapons difficult to obtain • Decrease information and dissemination about how to produce weapons • Make buildings safer, and trains and planes less likely to be hijacked, and develop inherent detection systems in potential agents • Decrease available resources and disrupt terrorist groups **Psychological** • Describe prevention efforts in biological–physical areas and achieve positive publicity • Explain consequences for terrorists	**Biological–Physical** • Ensure that buildings, planes, water, food, etc., are tested and protected **Psychological** • Develop an effective risk communication strategy • Identify and train spokespersons • Inform the public about prevention and safety efforts • Provide information that educates populations about expectable responses and coping strategies that will increase community resilience **Sociocultural** • Develop terrorism response plans

Event

Biological–Physical
- Implement public health–mental health response
- Provide basic needs
- Provide appropriate interventions

Psychological and Sociocultural
- Implement psychological first aid
- Affected population responds appropriately and takes action to minimize exposure to agent, including implementing disaster behaviors

- Train all relevant health professionals in disaster mental health and psychological consequences of terrorism
- Train other relevant service providers

Sociocultural
- Identify population characteristics important to intervention
- Develop mapping of populations, potential targets, and community resources
- Identify and implement methods for educating the public
- Ensure adequate public health and mental health care systems

Biological–Physical
- Develop systems to interdict during an event
- Describe to the public the available organizational and communication systems

Psychological and Sociocultural
- Consider how to mobilize trauma workers and notify survivors of services in the absence of functioning communication systems

Sociocultural
- Study conditions that foster terrorism
- Make certain there are lawful ways for terrorists to communicate legitimate concerns

Biological–Physical
- Respond to alarms
- Respond to surveillance system
- Dispatch emergency personnel and involve public health and medical care systems
- Monitor immediate threats

Psychological and Sociocultural
- Communicate risk and proposed response effectively

- Ensure the community is appropriately represented in prevent planning
- Address and ensure equity in the allocation of resources

continues

Table 7-2 *continued*

Phases	Factors		
	Affected Individuals and Populations	Terrorist and Injurious Agent*	Physical and Social Environment
	• Distribute information appropriate to the event		
Postevent	**Biological–Physical**	**Biological–Physical**	**Biological–Physical**
	• Minimize secondary consequences	• Respond quickly to seek out and punish those responsible	• Evaluate effectiveness of emergency plan and disaster response
	• Triage and treat as necessary	• Decrease availability or toxicity of agents used in the attack so that the next attack will not be so deadly	• Mitigate ongoing health risk and secure physical infrastructure
	• Recover, identify, and bury dead		• Monitor ongoing threat
	Psychological	**Psychological**	**Psychological**
	• Continue psychological first aid	• Communicate deterrent information	• Limit secondary exposure
	• Conduct individual, group, and population assessments to identify specific needs in response to event including the assessment, triage, and treatment of psychological injury	**Sociocultural**	• Adjust risk communication, emphasizing the positive
	• Consider intervention needs of special populations	• Identify better ways to decrease activity of terrorists	• Devise a public mental health strategy to assist communities, groups (workplace and schools), families, and individuals to cope with trauma reminders
	Sociocultural		**Sociocultural**
	• Communicate that preparedness helped decrease impact of the attack		• Establish strategies for community healing

	• Publicize availability of targeted services to appropriate segments of the population • Produce public information and warnings • Promote family and community cohesion	• Minimize loss of life and impact of disease processes • Minimize spread of infectious agents • Minimize destruction of buildings and infrastructure • Provide an environment that allows for rapid recovery and rehabilitation	• Minimize disruption in daily routines of life • Enhance community cohesion	
Desired End Results	• Mitigate or prevent adverse consequences including: • Distress • Negative behavioral change • Psychiatric illness • Poor job performance or loss of job • Physical injury • Increase positive adaptive behaviors • Facilitate post-traumatic growth • Increase empowerment			

*Although factors related to the terrorist and injurious agent include elements that may have psychological consequences (for example, decreasing information and dissemination about how to produce weapons may make the public feel more safe and decrease anxiety), they are not addressed in this report. These are factors likely addressed by the infrastructure's law enforcement sector, rather than public health, emergency, or medical services. The intent of illustrating these items in this table is to present an example of the full array of factors that warrant the joint attention of all systems responsible for the health and safety of the public in preparation for and response to terrorism events.

STATE MENTAL HEALTH PLANNING TEAMS

It should already be clear that the prepared public health leader needs to be involved in the activities related to protecting the mental health of affected population in emergency preparedness and response. It should also be clear the public health leaders need to work with mental health experts on many of these concerns. The Disaster Technical Assistance Center of the Substance Abuse and Health Services Administration has been working with state mental health authorities to prepare for and design a methodology for the mental health response to any emergency or hazard event. A guidance document (SAMHSA, 2003) was prepared after a review of its content by more than 30 state mental health directors. Interviews were held with a number of key informants at the federal, state, and local levels. National focus groups were convened. In addition, documents from the Federal Emergency Management Agency (FEMA) were reviewed as well. The document was also developed using an all-hazards approach that was developed to serve as a method for effective response to any hazard that threatens a jurisdiction. Strategies have been developed for mitigation during response and recovery as well. The one thing that became clear as various states were examined was that there was much variation between states on compliance to this all-hazards approach.

To help the states, SAMHSA (2003) and its partners are developing a planning worksheet document to aid the states in their mental health planning efforts. Table 7–3 is a shortened version of this planning document and includes 16 action items and accompanying examples of planning strategies. As with public health leaders, it is clear that mental health leaders need to collaborate with many community partners to make sure they are part of the emergency preparedness and response team.

FAMILY SECURITY ISSUES

With fear levels about the possibility of terrorist events reccurring again in the United States in the near future, it becomes imperative that families receive information that can help relieve some of these fears. The American Academy of Pediatrics (2004) has developed a family readiness kit to help families prepare for potential crisis events. The kit lists four steps that a family can take to prepare for a disaster or terrorist event. The

Table 7–3 State Mental Health Authority All-Hazards Planning Worksheet

I. Planning

Action Item	Planning Strategies
1. Ensure the State Mental Health Authority (SMHA) is on the call-down list from: • Governor's office • Mayors' offices • State Emergency Management Agency (SEMA)	Have mental health interests and presence represented at State's Emergency Operations Center. Carefully select a credible and competent representative.
2. Develop supportive relationship with SMHA commissioner and senior management.	Educate about importance of dedicated staff to coordinate disaster mental health services, funding sources, etc.
3. Review and understand: • State Emergency Operations Plan • SMHA All-Hazards Plan	Be familiar with *Federal Response Plan*, which can be obtained from the Federal Emergency Management Agency's (FEMA) Web site, Review Emergency Support Function #8. Please note that the *Federal Response Plan* is currently under revision and will be known as the *National Response Plan*. The initial *National Response Plan* and its final version can be found on the Department of Homeland Security Web site.
4. Ensure these groups/issues are addressed in SMHA All-Hazards Plan: • Consumers • Children • Elderly persons • Hearing and/or vision impaired • Disabled and/or special medical needs populations • First responders • Ethnic minorities/refugees	Include procedures for continuing services to special, at-risk populations without interruption. Develop a comprehensive community profile to include demographic information on subgroups and special populations.

continues

Table 7–3 *continued*

I. Planning

Action Item	Planning Strategies
• Persons who are homeless • Substance abusers/persons who are chronically mentally ill • Domestic violence/trauma survivors • People with mental retardation/developmental disabilities • Others as demographics mandate	
5. Develop grant application/ disaster management team with the following expertise: • Fiscal/contracts • Public information office • Human resources • Behavioral health • Mental retardation/ developmental disabilities • Administrative support	Review content, eligibility requirements, and submission timelines for various funders such as FEMA, SAMHSA, the Health Resources and Services Administration (HRSA), the Centers for Disease Control and Prevention (CDC), etc. Determine data and narrative needs. Bookmark Web sites and identify other content resources (annual reports, block grant, etc.). Develop a library of resources to include standard language and/or templates for use in funding applications. After the disaster, begin gathering preliminary damage assessment information from FEMA, SEMA, and the American Red Cross (ARC); start needs assessment, survey community mental health centers, and keep commissioner and medical director informed of findings.
6. Send disaster coordinator or other key staff to FEMA's annual Crisis Counseling Program (CCP) training in Emmitsburg, Maryland.	Network with neighboring and experienced state disaster coordinators for tips and networks for state-to-state technical assistance (TA) and support. Get to know your SEMA and FEMA region representatives.

continues

Table 7-3 *continued*

I. Planning

Action Item	Planning Strategies
7. Develop and coordinate the following cadre lists and protocols: • List of state employees and specialized teams (rapid response team, crisis management team, etc.) with current contact information and special skills • List of prescreened volunteers who are trained and trusted to deliver crisis response services • Activation plan for notifying, mobilizing, transporting, and deploying preidentified staff/teams/volunteers to response site(s)	Maintain and exercise these lists, databases, and protocols on a regular basis. Work with various licensing boards to ensure rapid access to licensing information and to design a mechanism for a reliable database or procedure that permits only qualified disaster workers to participate in the response.
8. Contact the Emergency Mental Health and Traumatic Stress Services Branch (EMHTSSB) at the Center for Mental Health Services (CMHS) and/or the Substance Abuse and Mental Health Services Administration's Disaster Technical Assistance Center (SAMHSA DTAC) for TA and have your commissioner contact the National Association for State Mental Health Program Directors (NASMHPD) for support services that may be available postdisaster.	Enlist EMHTSSB and/or SAMHSA DTAC as needed to assist pre- and postdisaster by arranging state-to-state TA, providing program consultants, conducting trainings, and arranging meetings.
9. Plan for all hazards, but pay special attention to these aspects of terrorism response: • Be prepared for accelerated response pace and mental health workers to be first responders.	Keep in mind that there won't be time to wait in a terrorism response. Create informational messages in advance for use under various scenarios. Link first with primary care and first responders. Remember that terrorism impacts *everyone* in the affected area; impacts include

continues

Table 7–3 *continued*

I. Planning

Action Item	Planning Strategies
• Plan to spend more money for media outreach. • Hire or work with agency's public information staff from day 1 of the event. • Hire more mental health professionals vs. paraprofessionals (1:4 in terrorism vs. 1:6 in natural disaster). • Consider special circumstances in predominantly urban, diverse areas where terrorists may strike	economic, transportation, tourism, infrastructure, etc. Know that the different segments of the community will respond in unique ways at different times. Use the media as an effective vehicle for delivering information related to mental health and emotional issues; have talking points drafted and supply these to the governor, congressmen, or anyone who may conduct a press conference about the disaster.
10. Work with the SMHA public affairs staff on the public information and education messages you want to provide during critical times.	Prepare templates, public service announcements, messages, and distribution methods for critical information, i.e., consequences of specific bioterrorist agents, what to do for children, typical stress reactions, etc. Provide flyers and Web site links. Consider multicultural and multilingual needs of the community.
11. Develop or obtain public information and educational materials.	Promote resilience by reminding the community to go about their daily lives, keep their schedules, and participate in their regular activities. Educate the community about normal reactions to abnormal events. Take advantage of existing mental health materials developed by states for various disasters, in multiple languages, and targeting a wide range of special populations. Contact SAMHSA DTAC, which houses an extensive resource library of state-developed materials and SAMHSA publications.

continues

Table 7–3 *continued*

I. Planning

Action Item	Planning Strategies
12. Participate in disaster training exercises with SEMA and other partners as well as resource review.	Make sure commissioners, disaster coordinators, and medical directors are aware of and identify staff to participate in local/state exercises and training opportunities with SEMA, public health, education, ARC, and other groups as identified above. Link with SAMHSA DTAC for regular review of disaster literature, Web sites and information on grants and workshops that may be funded through SAMHSA, FEMA, CDC, the Department of Justice, etc.
13. Work with your SEMA and check the response priorities outlined in your agency's all-hazards plan.	Link with the Emergency Management Agency and provide staff as agreed to at the emergency operations center and other locations.
14. Anticipate the following: • Unrequested volunteers (in-state and out-of-state)	Assign someone to take names and contact information. Have a pre-screened, trained cadre of local volunteer professionals available.
• Donations	Devise a system to manage donations. The local community may want to donate money, food, clothing, or other supplies to victims, survivors, and their families. If the disaster receives national media coverage or is of a particularly large scale, donations may be made from across the country.
• People wanting something to do	Have a list of small but meaningful tasks for employees and volunteers.
• FEMA, CMHS, ARC, Salvation Army, and other "sanctioned" disaster organizations showing up	Know the leaders and understand their organizational culture and response roles in advance. Coordinate SMHA crisis response with ARC. Contact the local ARC,

continues

Table 7–3 *continued*

I. Planning

Action Item	Planning Strategies
	Salvation Army, and FEMA offices for complete information on the program; be familiar with anticipated mental health needs, shelter operations, and FEMA disaster recovery centers. Review fact sheets and program guidance documents on organization Web sites.
• Overdedication of management and staff	Devise shift limits and promote stress management and physical well-being. Provide regular stress management training and staff debriefing and help prevent diminished effectiveness and burnout by ensuring staff get adequate rest. For strategies, review chapters on stress management in the *Training Manual for Mental Health and Human Service Workers in Major Disasters*.
• Flexibility and creativity in response	Recruit indigenous workers knowledgeable about the affected community. Tailor services to needs and cultural traditions of community. Not everything will be a success—if a service does not work, try something else. For strategies, review sections on developing culturally sensitive services in *Developing Cultural Competence in Disaster Mental Health Programs* and *Training Manual for Mental Health and Human Service Workers in Major Disasters*.
15. Develop training plan on disaster response and recovery for your local providers.	Crisis counseling is a specialized service that requires distinct training. Conduct trainings regularly and update your training plan and curricula.

continues

Table 7–3 *continued*

I. Planning

Action Item	Planning Strategies
16. Obtain and organize funding, resources, and staff for the long term, and plan accordingly.	Consider that the psychological impact may continue for 3–5 years; one third of those directly impacted and 10% of those in the vicinity of the event will have ongoing post-traumatic stress disorder (PTSD) and/or depression. Think long term to ensure adequate services and staffing.

first step is to find out what could happen to your family during a disaster and what your community has done to prepare for a potential disaster. If an impending disaster is imminent, it is necessary that families know what do. It is critical, for example, that families follow evacuation warnings when they are given. The Florida hurricanes of 2004 provided an example of some residents of a community not following evacuation orders. A major challenge to emergency preparedness and response workers is community resistance to emergency warnings and recommendations.

The second step to family safety readiness is the development of a family readiness or disaster plan. All family members need to be involved in this activity. Couch (2003) recommended the development of a number of checklists for this plan including a family emergency evacuation and escape plan with steps, family home hazard checklist, a disaster supplies kit, automobile getaway kit, and a procedures checklist to follow when the family is away from home. It is important for families to have discussions on all these issues. With regard to the family disasters supplies kit, the kit needs to include such things as fresh water, enough prescription drugs if necessary, some packaged or canned food, fresh clothing, blankets, first aid kit, cellular phone, credit cards and/or cash, extra car keys, important family documents including photo albums, and so on.

The third part of family safety readiness involves another checklist that includes such things as the following:

- Make copies of important documents and put them in a bank safe deposit box.

- Take a home safety course.
- Check insurance coverage.
- Buy emergency supplies and put them in a readily accessible place.
- Designate safe places to go in the house for natural and not so natural disasters.
- Determine items that could fall or break during a disaster and move them to a safer place.
- Help children understand how and when to turn off utilities.
- Plan home escape routes.

The final part of the safety readiness plan is to practice and maintain your family plan. The American Academy of Pediatrics recommends this latter step involves testing the smoke and carbon dioxide detectors regularly, reviewing the family plan every six months, carrying out family disaster drills, making sure children remember procedures every month or so, and replacing any stored food on a regular basis. It is clear that families as well as communities need to be prepared. The family procedures listed in this section can easily be expanded into a neighborhood or block plan. People do better when they are prepared. This does not mean that there will not be a psychological impact of a disaster event. It only means that preparation may lessen some of the extreme effects of the event.

A MODEL FOR VOLUNTEERS

An interesting volunteer model is demonstrated by the Medical Reserve Corps which is a component of the Citizens Corps (DHHS, 2004). The Medical Reserve Corps (MRC) came into being in 2002 with the purpose of strengthening communities through the establishment of a system of medical and public health volunteers who would offer their expertise to the community throughout the year and during periods of crisis. The goal of the MRC is to supplement existing medical emergency and public health responses in the community. Table 7–4 gives a partial list of who can become a member of the volunteer corps (DHHS, 2003). The corps gives what has been termed surge capacity to the community in that extra personnel and resources are often needed by a community during a crisis. MRC volunteers do outreach and prevention, help in immunization programs, blood drives, case management, and care planning, and can also

Table 7–4 Who Can Volunteer?

Volunteers can be active, inactive and/or retired health professionals, students in the health professions, and others.

Volunteers can include (but are not limited to):

- Physicians (MD and osteopathic)
- Nurses (registered nurses, nurse practitioners)
- Dentists and dental assistants
- Mental health practitioners
- Veterinarians
- Epidemiologists
- Pharmacists
- Physician assistants
- Public health advisors/experts
- Health educators/communicators
- Public relations experts
- Health care administrators
- Technicians (including pharmacy, radiology, dental)
- Licensed practical nurses and nursing assistants
- Former military personnel who had medical/health training and experience while in the service
- Trained health interpreters
- Microbiologists
- Laboratory technicians
- Nutritionists
- Environmental engineers
- Environmental health specialists
- Industrial hygienists
- Psychologists
- Substance abuse counselors
- Health information/medical records specialists
- Medical equipment experts
- Toxicologists
- Social workers
- Medical supply experts
- Occupational and physical therapists
- Clergy

help in the coordination of activities with the local emergency response program structure.

A checklist to guide community action in working with the local MRC can be found in Table 7–5. This checklist shows that the MRC has a critical technical assistance function related to assessing community needs and

---

Table 7–5 Action Steps Checklist

Remember: these are only suggestions. We offer them as a quick reference guide and as something to stimulate your own thinking through some of the complexities you may face in your MRC unit. You may choose to follow a different approach.

Assessing Your Local Situation

☐ Find out how your MRC volunteers can supplement existing medical emergency and public health response efforts in your area.

Conducting a Risk and Needs Assessment

☐ Consider the specific medical and public health-related risks and needs that affect your community.

☐ Interview potential response partners and other community organizations to learn more about their work and where they see needs for volunteer support.

☐ Identify some possible approaches to those risks and needs that will involve your MRC volunteers.

☐ Start with what you know best about your community. You don't have to tackle everything at once. Your MRC's contribution can grow over time.

Considering All the Components

☐ Always keep the big picture in mind. Even if it's impossible to handle all at once, you'll still be better prepared to meet your next challenge.

☐ Explore ways to coordinate with local response partners.

☐ Consider what your volunteers will need to develop capabilities and commitment to your MRC.

☐ List the things you will need to establish and maintain a strong administrative organization. What resources will you require to sustain your MRC?

Developing a Rough Plan

☐ Sketch out a plan that touches on all the key points. You can always revise it.

☐ Include a mission statement, objectives, an action plan, an organizational chart, and a budget.

☐ Make a preliminary list of potential response partners and other organizations that might be willing to champion your MRC. Who can you count on?

Table 7–5 *continued*

☐ Note any ongoing issues that will require advocacy (e.g., liability protection for volunteers, integrating MRC volunteers into existing systems, credential verification procedures, etc.)

Securing Broad-Based Community Support

☐ Get others in your community to buy into your vision for the MRC. You cannot achieve it alone.

Negotiating with Response Partners

☐ Identify partners with a shared mission or who are engaged in work that complements what your MRC volunteers can provide.

☐ Make sure your MRC activities don't conflict with other organizations' domains. Negotiate workable compromises.

☐ Come to a solid agreement to work together, even if you still have to iron out the details.

☐ Get letters of intent. Use them to continue building your network.

☐ Stay in touch with the prospects that are more difficult to cultivate. It can take time to understand the MRC's role in any community.

☐ Keep the conversations moving forward.

Enlisting Champions for Your MRC

☐ Identify champions who will actively support your MRC effort.

⇒ *Approach local government officials, corporations, private sector businesses, prominent individuals or leaders in your community, and so on.*

☐ Get letters of support. Use them to continue building your network.

☐ Stay in touch with the prospects that are more difficult to cultivate. It can take time to understand the MRC's role in any community.

☐ Keep the conversations moving forward.

Matching Resources to Operational Needs

☐ Determine how to get the resources necessary to make your MRC a reality.

Developing Monetary Resources

☐ Apply to grant programs (national and local foundations, state and federal government programs, and corporate charitable offices).

☐ Appeal directly to donors through mail or by making personal contact.

☐ Plan special fundraising events.

☐ Ask a fundraising specialist for help with determining what activities will work best in your community.

☐ Ask your response partners if they have access to funds that might be applied to cover the contributions made by your MRC.

☐ Let your response partners and community champions know what you need financially so they can direct you to other sources.

continues

Table 7–5 *continued*

Soliciting In-Kind Donations

☐ Identify resources that might be attained through a direct gift rather than by paying for it with funds.

⇒ *Your list might include office space, office equipment, a computer, software, programming and other support services, media placement, communications materials, etc.*

☐ Let your response partners and community champions know what you need so they can direct you to possible donors.

Seeking Out Specialty Expertise

☐ Identify the time-limited expertise that would help move your MRC forward.

☐ Don't be afraid to ask for help if you don't know how to do something. Many people are willing to help a worthy cause.

☐ Let your response partners and community champions know what you need by way of expertise so they can direct you to their contacts.

Optimizing Strategic Partnerships

☐ Be clear about the benefit your MRC volunteers bring to others—especially to you response partners.

☐ Look to see what your partners have that they might be willing to share or give to you for free or at a low cost.

⇒ *Partners may be willing to share training, access to legal and other expertise, office space or other administrative resources, the ability to conduct verification of credentials or background checks for volunteers, etc.*

---

planning community activities, securing broad-based community support, and matching resources to operational needs. Table 7–6 gives a listing of the types of training an MRC unit would need to address the many crisis concerns that communities might have (DHHS, 2003). As can be seen from the table, these training activities include such thing as clinical training, disaster training, and cultural competency training programs. It is apparent that a community needs to build on existing resources in an emergency. To be able to build a medical reserve volunteer corps in a community is a great advantage. To be able to add a citizens volunteer corps to the mix would clearly build the surge capacity of the community.

SUMMARY

It has been the purpose of this chapter to look at the complex issues of community safety from the vantage points of psychological impact, fam-

---

Table 7-6 Types of Training for Medical Reserve Corps

- Disaster response planning
- Knowledge of local, regional, and statewide emergency response capabilities
- Knowledge of the mechanics of disaster medical assistance teams (DMAT) and epidemiological surveillance teams
- Knowledge of working relationships between medical emergency teams and law enforcement personnel
- Basic triage of emergency patients
- Advanced cardiac life support
- Pediatric advanced life support
- Advanced trauma life support
- Basic burn care
- Knowledge about mental health issues that are likely to arise
- Knowledge of decontamination
- Recognition of clinical manifestations of infectious diseases
- Knowledge of quarantine procedures and quarantine facilities
- Experience with routine emergency equipment
- Knowledge of hazardous materials
- Experience with communication systems and technology
- Basic confined space medicine
- Basic medical care in an austere environment
- Basic knowledge of the management of the consequences of biological and chemical weapons use
- Cultural competence

---

ily safety and concerns, community readiness, and the use of volunteers. Part 2 of this book has looked in detail at some of the realities of public health in the 21st century. Part 3 of the book will review some of the new skills which the prepared public health leader needs to develop to work in this new public health world.

REFERENCES

American Academy on Pediatrics. (2004). *4 steps to safety readiness: Family readiness kit.* (Updated). Chicago: Author.

Columbia University National Center for Disaster Preparedness. (2004). Crisis of confidence [Press release]. New York: Author.

Conner, D. P. (1992). *Managing at the speed of change.* New York: Villard.

Couch, D. (2003). *The U.S. armed forces nuclear, biological, and chemical survival manual.* New York: Basic Books.

Department of Health and Human Services. (2003). *Medical Reserve Corps: A guide for local leaders.* Washington, DC: Author.

Department of Health and Human Services. (2004). *Getting started: A guide for local leaders.* Washington, DC: Office of the Surgeon General, DHHS.

Haddon, W., Jr. (1972). A logical framework for categorizing highway safety. *The Journal of Trauma, 12*(3), 193–207.

Haddon, W., Jr. (1980). Advances in the epidemiology of injuries as a basis for social policy. *Public Health Reports, 95*(5), 411–21.

Institute of Medicine. (2003). *Preparing for the psychological consequences of terrorism: A public health strategy.* Washington, DC: National Academies Press.

Landesman, L. Y. (2005). *Public health management of disasters* (2nd ed.). Washington, DC: American Public Health Association.

Lasker, R. D. (2004). *Redefining readiness: Terrorism planning through the eyes of the public.* New York: The New York Academy of Medicine.

National Institute of Mental Health. (2002). *Mental health and mass violence* (NIH Publication No. 02-5138). Washington, DC: U.S. Government Printing Office.

Substance Abuse and Mental Health Administration. (2003). *Draft state mental health authority all-hazards planning worksheet.* Bethesda, MD: Author.

PART III

New Leadership Skills and Tools

Systems Thinking and Complexity

It's the system stupid.

—Adapted from Bill Clinton's 1992 campaign speeches

All types of crises have effects on the community whether the crisis impacts one organization in the community or many organizations or residents of the community. The prepared public health leader knows that a crisis is the community's business and that the crisis needs to be addressed from the vantage point of the community. It is for this reason that systems thinking skills are so critical for successful leadership. To be a systems thinker, a leader needs to see and talk about situations in a way that helps others to better understand and carry out activities within organizations and agencies that impact the lives of people who live within the community. A prepared public health leader must see the big picture. An interesting demonstration of the complexities involved in the issue of infectious disease outbreaks related to monkeypox can be seen in Case Study 8. It demonstrates the systemic aspects of disease and the importance of knowing global disease trends and their potential application at the local level. What happens in one part of the world can impact other parts of the world very quickly.

CASE STUDY 8

Monkey on Our Backs: Identifying and Containing an Outbreak of Monkeypox on a Regional Basis

Authors:
Douglas Beardsley, MPH
Christine Borys, BSN, MPH
Cheryl Lee, BA, MS
Jean McMahon, MS, BSN
Heather Miller, BS
Larry Swacina, MS

Abstract

In the spring of 2003, it was discovered that prairie dogs originating from a pet distributor became infected with monkeypox (MP). The infected prairie dogs had been sold directly to distributors who in turn sold them to consumers in several neighboring states. Communicable disease personnel at various local health departments and the state department of public health began contacting pet owners to investigate possible MP cases in humans. Personnel from the state's department of agriculture and investigators from the Centers for Disease Control and Prevention were also involved in the investigation. Because this was the first time that MP had been seen in the Western Hemisphere, staff at all levels had many questions and came to the situation with a great deal of zeal and energy. All persons involved made every effort to be thorough, but this had the unintended effect of creating redundancy, uncoordinated effort, and lack of information sharing. As investigators worked with family members of infected individuals, they found that one investigator was literally leaving through the side door as another was coming in the front door. Pieces of information known to one agency, which potentially could have been critically important to the human investigation, had to be accidentally discovered at a later time by personnel from another agency. Fortunately, all of the persons exposed to MP made a full recovery and the cases were not widespread.

This case study will examine the events leading up to the incidents of human cases of MP and the events surrounding the investigation, containment, and remediation of the cases. The case will present policy questions surrounding legal authority to act, when to seek legal counsel, coordinating the activities within and between agencies, and developing incident

continues

CASE STUDY 8   *continued*

command and unified command approaches as applied to public health investigations.

The focus of this case study is to address the core function of policy development. According to the three core functions, this case study will explore the need for developing policy to address the steps needed to take action when a public health emergency that needs immediate and effective response arises.

Introduction and Background

Even before the catastrophic events of September 11, 2001, public health began to recognize the need for emergency preparedness plans related to potential bioterrorism events. For many state and local health departments, emergency preparedness and planning were neglected. Post 9-11, emergency response plans and training were accelerated. While new funding was in the pipeline for many of these activities, policy makers tried to emphasize that preparedness for an emergency should be a process of strengthening the overall infrastructure and competency of the public health system and should not become an activity divorced from day-to-day public health functions.

The investigation of a new or unknown disease and that of a potential bioterrorism event have many parallels. Both share a number of the same assumptions, procedures, and resources. Much of the training made available to local health departments (LHDs) emphasized the need to communicate and cooperate across various agencies and jurisdictions through the use of incident command. The rationale behind this concept was that an investigation might have already been initiated before knowing if an event was related to terrorism. Consistent communication on a regular basis with other agencies will facilitate more efficient and effective action when a public health emergency occurs.

Monkeypox is a rare viral disease caused by the monkeypox virus which belongs to the orthopoxvirus group of viruses. (Other orthopoxviruses that cause infections in humans include variola [smallpox], vaccinia [used for smallpox vaccine], and cowpox viruses.) It occurs mainly in the rain forest areas of central and West Africa. The disease was first discovered in laboratory monkeys in 1958. Blood tests of animals in Africa later found evidence of monkeypox infection in a number of African rodents. The virus that causes monkeypox was recovered from an African squirrel. Laboratory studies showed that the virus also could infect mice, rats, and rabbits. In 1970, monkeypox was reported in humans for the first time. In June 2003, monkeypox was reported in prairie dogs and humans in the United States.

In humans, monkeypox is similar to smallpox, although it is often milder. Unlike smallpox, monkeypox causes lymph nodes to swell

continues

CASE STUDY 8   *continued*

(lymphadenopathy). The incubation period for monkeypox is about 12 days (range 7 to 17 days). The illness begins with fever, headache, muscle aches, backache, swollen lymph nodes, a general feeling of discomfort, and exhaustion. Within 1 to 3 days (sometimes longer) after the appearance of fever, the patient develops a papular rash (i.e., raised bumps), often first on the face but sometimes initially on other parts of the body. The lesions usually develop through several stages before crusting and falling off.

Brief description of scenario

On June 7, Midwest State Department of Public Health (MWSDPH) informed the Simian County Health Department (SCHD) that it was investigating a potential exposure of monkeypox (MP) to customers of a pet shop in Primate County (a county in the same state about 60 miles west of Simian County. SCHD was asked to follow up with customers in its jurisdiction. SCHD was provided with information specific to its jurisdiction and was not made aware that similar investigations would be taking place in other counties. The only information shared between all parties was that the suspected exposure was through Gambian rats and prairie dogs, which had been sold by Rod's Pox Pets in Primate County.

On June 8, Simian County Health Department (SCHD) personnel contacted the family in their jurisdiction, which had bought a prairie dog at a swap meet. The prairie dog had originated from Rod's Pox Pets. The 9-week-old prairie dog appeared healthy when bought on 5/18/03. Sonny, the 10-year-old boy in the family, was the primary caretaker of the prairie dog and regularly played with and cuddled the prairie dog, in addition to the 1-year-old prairie dog he had raised. Upon arrival at the family's house, SCHD Communicable Disease (CD) investigators learned that inspectors from the State Department of Agriculture (SDOA) had already been working with the family for more than a week. One week after purchase, the new prairie dog had become ill, showing aggressive behavior, loss of appetite, eye discharges, and lesions on its face. Three days later the new prairie dog died and the father disposed of it in the trash. SDOA personnel had instructed the family to isolate the surviving prairie dog from other animals but had not given any instructions about human contact.

CD personnel educated the family on MP and took health histories of all family members. The family was strongly advised not to travel and to limit contact with others as much as possible until the incubation period for MP had passed in two more weeks. The family was somewhat upset because of a planned vacation the following week. Investigators were unsure if they had authority to "officially quarantine" the family or otherwise restrict their movements. The SCHD contacted the State Attorney's office to get clarification on the health department's authority to quarantine.

continues

CASE STUDY 8   *continued*

The State Attorney's office said they would check into the matter. Ironically, this happened to be an election year. SCHD was told the State Attorney would not be taking a position on this matter.

SCHD personnel followed up with the family by phone on a daily basis to monitor the family's health. On June 11, the CDC issued its first case definition of human MP for this incident. None of the family members reported any illness.

On June 12, SCHD personnel were unable to contact the family by phone. Investigators were sent to the family's home but no one was present. Neighbors told the investigators the family, father, mother, and their three sons, had left that morning on vacation to Montana for two weeks. When asked about the remaining prairie dog, the neighbor said the family told her that "some government agency" had taken the prairie dog and put it to sleep. SCHD personnel were not able to confirm this with SDOA until three days later.

The investigators then called the MWSDPH for recommendations on the situation, with the family away on vacation. During the course of the conversation, the MWSDPH advisor informed SCHD personnel of several cases of MP in Primate County. SCHD personnel were somewhat disturbed that they had not been informed of these cases. SCHD wanted more details on the signs and symptoms experienced to better detect a case and to provide physicians with this information. The MWSDPH advisor indicated that he thought CDC had contacted SCHD with this information since they were running the investigation.

Later that day, SCHD learned that several dead mice had been discovered at the family's residence a week earlier and were taken by CDC for examination. SCHD Environmental personnel were concerned that the mice might have been infected. The disease could potentially spread throughout the community and become permanently established in the rodent population. Results ultimately showed that the mice had died of rat poisoning and were not diseased.

In the meantime, the MWSDPH issued a press release on the monkeypox situation, including the current number of cases and the precautions being implemented. One of the cases included a 17-year-old youth in Primate County. The family contacted the television media, who in turn made assumptions prior to confirming facts with the Primate County Health Department (PCHD). The PCHD responded with a press conference to clarify the situation and provide accurate information. Daily updates were then provided.

On June 18, the family who left the state against medical advice visited the Mountain County Health Department (MCHD) in Montana. Sonny had developed approximately 20 lesions on his trunk and complained of

continues

CASE STUDY 8 *continued*

tender cervical lymph nodes. Sonny had pharyngeal lesions, which increased the chance of spreading the virus by air transmission whenever Sonny coughed. The MCHD strongly advised the family not to travel back to Midwest State but rather to seek medical care in Montana. The family decided to return to Midwest State, ignoring health department advice for the second time. This meant the family would spend over 24 hours in a car together, with the potential of spreading the virus to other family members by air transmission from coughing. The family also stopped frequently at fast food establishments en route.

The MCHD contacted SCHD to inform them of the contact with the family and that the family was en route to Midwest State against MCHD recommendation. On June 19, the family called SCHD and informed them they should be arriving the next day. They mentioned Sonny had a fever and was quite uncomfortable with the lesions and would need to see a doctor right away. The family informed SCHD that their insurance would only allow them to go to Simian Community Hospital (the Hospital).

SCHD personnel immediately contacted the Hospital to prepare for an infectious patient. While the Hospital had an infectious disease plan and had been participating in the county's emergency preparedness activities, including smallpox exercises, no personnel at the hospital had received the smallpox vaccine prophylactically. The Hospital was reluctant to admit a patient with MP. Prior to this event, the hospital had withdrawn their phase one emergency response smallpox vaccination program. After much deliberation and negotiation, the Hospital allowed a nonaffiliated physician who had received the smallpox vaccine to have temporary treatment privileges at their hospital to administer health care services to Sonny.

The family arrived at the Hospital and after initial examination, the child was admitted. The mother, exhausted from the long trip, became upset when seeing her child in pain and connected to multiple tubes and monitors. The distraught mother removed the tubes from the child. She attempted to leave with the child against medical advice and without signing required release forms. Security was called and physicially blocked the exit, at which point the mother reluctantly complied with medical treatment. Four days later the child was discharged and eventually made a full recovery without any long-term effects.

Conclusion

Even though this was a fictional account with a factual basis, the local health departments responded well and effectively within their jurisdiction. Each responding agency had a protocol for responding to such an event; however, there was an initial lack of communication and coordination within and between the agencies involved and a lack of an incident com-

continues

CASE STUDY 8 *continued*

mand structure. The situation was further complicated by misinformation in the media, family noncompliance with medical advice, questions on legal authority in the investigation protocols, political consideration expressed by the State Attorney's Office during election year, the lack of regulation of exotic pets, the lack of a timely response to address the wild mice population as a potential reservoir for MP, and questionable hospital adherence to their own emergency response plan.

This case not only points out the issue of systems analysis, it also shows the importance of collaboration at a local level in addressing the threats associated with the outbreaks of infectious disease. This latter point is extremely important because the importance of collaboration to bring about change is not directly addressed by writers in the discussion of systems thinking approaches. The systems approach becomes problematic because the systems thinker is often at odds with others within the home organization or with partners who do not think in a systems way (Addelson, n.d.). In addition, the tools of systems do not take into account the collaborative nature of social relationships. It is the social relationships within an organization or community that are the most important. The structure of the system is less important. If it is people who create the system, then the system will be fluid and ever changing. In actuality, people do create social structures and do collaborate, but the social structure and cultural norms and rules that guide action also are affected. The leadership challenge relates to the necessity of the leader working with his collaborators to use a systems framework to better understand problems so that the solutions become more comprehensive and more likely to work to improve the functioning of the community. To paraphrase an old popular song, the system and partners need to go together "like a horse and carriage."

THE FIVE LEVELS OF LEARNING

To begin, it is important to see systems learning and thinking relative to four other categories of learning in which leaders become involved. The five levels are (Senge, 1990):

- Personal mastery
- Mental models

- Shared vision
- Team learning
- Systems thinking

Systems thinking is a critical set of skills for leaders (Rowitz, 2001). A leader is extensively involved in change-oriented activities; therefore, the leader must master the techniques of thinking systemically because leaders recognize the interconnectedness of all organizations and people in communities. Systems analysis gets at root causes and separates symptoms from these root causes. The traditional forms of linear thinking that follow a cause-to-effect perspective is often an oversimplification of reality. The interplay of organizations and people require a more complex analysis of the various interrelationships that occur. Leaders monitor not only the changes that these relationships generate, but also the transformational patterns of these interactions.

Most of the important discussions of systems thinking and its relationship to the other four thinking disciplines comes from the work of Senge (1990). Systems thinking is tied to organizations and community collaborations of all kinds. Organizations and collaborations also seem to learn from the interactions of those who are part of these structures. This does not mean that individual learning is unimportant, but rather that all levels of learning affect the groups and organizations with whom we work. This has been extended to the importance of all these groups and organizations becoming learning organizations. It is important to recognize that the way an organization or collaborative does its work is really the product of how the individuals who compose these groups interact (Senge, Roberts, Ross, Smith, & Kleiner, 1994). The critical activities of these learning organizations is the translation of tested and evaluated experience into knowledge and information that the whole organization, collaborative, and perhaps even community can use.

Any group can determine if it is a learning organization or not by deciding and evaluating its present level of functioning and what changes would have to occur if it were to become a learning organization. In the incident command system, for example, a learning organization model can and should be implemented. It is important to evaluate how emergency response activities are carried out during an emergency. The learning that occurs and which would be evaluated after an event can then lead to improvements in the response activities in a later emergency. Drills and exercise events can also follow the learning organization approach. Learn from experience to improve the process of response in later events. The learning organization development involves the creation of two groups. The first group is composed of the followers of the vision of the group or organization. The second group deals with the realities of the organization or group, the exploration of divergent approaches and perspectives, the clarification of differences, the determination of learning priorities and the barriers to carrying out these priorities, and the implementation of action steps that can bring the reality group and the vision group together (Senge et al., 1994).

The five learning disciplines that impact the learning organization are discussed in the following sections (Senge, 1990).

Personal Mastery

Many leadership development programs are oriented to the increase and enhancement of personal leadership skills. This learning discipline involves not only increasing the leader's personal capacity to improve his or her organization and community but also empowers the leader to work towards increasing the skills of those individuals the leader supervises. The leader who masters this learning level is often guided by a personal vision and an ability to understand the realities of the environment in which he or she works. To better understand the idea of a personal vision, Exercise 8–1 gives you a chance to experiment with personal visions.

Mental Models

Mental models involve our view of the world as defined by such things as the values and culture perspective that guide our personal development. These mental models sometimes put blinders on us in that we see the world through these personal and family cultural orientations. These mental models can have a direct impact on our actions and decisions. Mental models also have an important emotional component. Organizations and other groups also develop mental models that over time affect the way these groups make decisions and take actions. Since September 11, 2001, public health professionals have been hearing about something called public health preparedness. Even though public health agencies have addressed emergencies in the past and have strategies and techniques for doing this, the new culture of public health preparedness is pushing for a change in the mental models that public health has used in

---

EXERCISE 8–1   Personal Vision

Purpose: To relate a personal vision to an action plan

Key Concepts: Personal mastery, vision, action plan

Procedures: Develop a written personal vision for the next five years incorporating the following dimensions:

1. My vision for my personal life
2. My vision for my career
3. My vision for improving my leadership skills
4. My vision for the development of a personal recreational plan
5. My vision for my spiritual development

Develop specific action steps to bring each dimension to reality.

---

the past. Public health agencies struggle to incorporate the new emergency and response techniques into the way they do business. Community partnerships are changing. All of these innovations mean old mental models are disintegrating, and there is now a transition phase toward acceptance of these new preparedness approaches into the way public health agendas do their work. To begin to explore these issues of changing mental models, do Exercise 1–1 on social forces of change. Then, explore in Exercise 8–2 the structural organizational differences in your agency between 1999 and the post-September 11, 2001, period.

Shared Vision

Creating visions is so important that visioning will be discussed in more detail in Chapter 16. It is important that a group or organization develop a shared vision to guide their action. Shared visions are about shared images of the future the group or agency wants to create. It also involves the development of guiding principles to make the vision come to pass. Shared vision puts all the members or participants on the same page. Exercise 8–3 explores the development of a shared vision.

Teams

Much has been written about the importance of teams in public health. This discipline involves the requirements for team learning. Team leader-

---

EXERCISE 8–2 Structural Change

Purpose: To explore how agencies and organizations change as a result of changes in societal priorities

Key Concepts: Social forces of change, system, organizational change, mental models

Procedure: Utilizing the results of Exercise 1–1 on social forces of change, explore the ways a local health department may or has adopted to these changing priorities:

1. Divide the class or training group into groups of 8–10.
2. Review the results of Exercise 1–1.
3. Apply the results of Exercise 1–1 to organizational changes in a local health department and present your results in a chart similar to that shown below.

Organizational Structure in 1999	Organizational Structure in 2005

---

ship skills incorporate the skills that an individual has learned at the personal level with the new skills required for working with teams and with learning skills related to sharing leadership with others (Rowitz, 2001). There is an important synergistic element in this learning discipline. Working together, leaders utilize intelligence and actions that are greater than the sum total of the contributions of an individual member. Despite our awareness of the importance of teams, conflicts often occur over issues about who is in charge. Exercise 8–4 gives you a chance to discuss the issue of power. The questions in the exercise were developed as part of

---

EXERCISE 8-3   Steps in Developing a Shared Vision

Purpose: To examine the shared vision level of learning as defined by Senge (1990)

Key Concepts: Shared vision, team learning

Procedures: You have been asked to develop a vision for your local health department. The health administrator appoints you and several other program heads to carry out the task. How would you do this and how would you get the president of your board of health and the director of your health department involved in the process.

1. Divide the class or training group into teams of 8–10 who are department heads.
2. Determine who will head the group and why he or she was chosen.
3. Discuss how to involve the health administrator of the agency and the president of the board of health in the process.
4. Develop the vision statement.
5. Develop a strategy for getting others in your agency to share the vision.

---

a training module on sharing power and influence that was developed as part of the Turning Point Leadership Development National Excellence Collaborative (2004).

Systems Thinking

The remainder of this chapter will address the fifth discipline of systems and systems thinking. Systems thinking is a high level of thinking involving all those forces and interrelationships that shape the behavior of organizations and communities (Senge, 1990). Systems thinking is all about change and how to manage and lead it more effectively. It also recognizes that global trends often impact local events and actions. It is the ongoing interaction of the parts that push the system forward and sometimes backwards (Senge et al., 1999). The system is affected by its organizational makeup, biological niches, family residents, technology, socioeconomic factors, national and international events, and everything else. Senge and his colleagues (1999) talked about the dance of change that related to the constant interplay between growth processes and the processes that limit growth.

EXERCISE 8–4 Power and Influence

Purpose: To explore collaborative leadership techniques related to power and influence

Key Concepts: Collaborative leadership, power, influence

Procedures: Divide the class or training group into smaller groups of 8–10 and discuss the questions below.

1. What is power? What is influence?
2. Do you think your definition would change if your were:
   • The opposite gender?
   • A different race?
   • Wealthier? Poorer?
   • Older? Younger?
   • From a different country?
3. Where does power come from?
4. *"Empowerment is the basis for collaboration."* Do you agree or disagree with this statement? Why?
5. Can power be shared? Who decides?
6. What is a collaborative leader's role when power is shared?

DEFINITION OF A SYSTEM

A single human being is a biological system. A local health department is a system. The incident command organization is a system. A basketball team is a system. A family is a system. Despite the disagreements that occur, the United States Congress is a system with two interesting and contrasting subsystems. A community is a system. Kim (1999) provided a succinct definition of a system as any group or organization with interacting, interrelated, or interdependent parts. These various parts form a unified whole with specific purposes and tasks to perform. All the parts of the system are interrelated and interdependent in some way. The parts must work together to function as a whole (Kauffman, 1980). Systems are clearly everywhere. There are living systems such as each human being, and there are human-made systems such as automobiles and washing machines. A distinction can be made between a system and a collection, which is a series of people or things which do not interact (Kim, 1999). For example, a kitchen is a collection of gadgets until a person enters it and turns it into a system. Although a bus and a driver compose a system, the passengers may only be a collection of people who enter the bus but do not interact. A system has a number of characteristics. In the newsletter *The Systems Thinker* (2002), the authors list five major characteristics of a system:

1. Every system has a purpose (mission) and every system is tied or related to other systems.
2. All parts of a system must be present or the system will not work properly. However, parts can be replaced or adapted to a new level of functioning. For example, one health administrator leaves a local health department and is replaced by a new administrator.
3. The arrangement of the parts is critical if the system is to work. If you put the wheels of a car on the front seat of the car instead of where they usually would go, the car will not drive.
4. Systems change because they constantly receive information that guides the system's operation. This is called feedback.
5. Systems can remain stable only if they make adjustments based on feedback.

Although the concept of a system is understandable to most people, the process of using a systems framework to guide the thinking of a leader is much more complex.

SYSTEMS THINKING

Despite the fact that most people are aware that they live in a complex society, they still think and deal with reality in a more linear way. Linear thinking can be tied to what researchers call cause-and-effect relationships. If event A occurs, then the effect of that event is outcome B, which may lead to effect C, and so on. In other words, a cause leads to an effect that becomes the cause of the next effect. This is a rather simplistic approach to the addressing of complex problems in the real world. It is here that the feedback factor enters the picture. As soon as it is realized that events and outcomes are interrelated, then things can be arranged so that A causes B, which causes C, which then causes A again. When C occurs, it causes information to be sent back to a person or organization that requires a determination of the meaning of the feedback and how it triggers the happening of the A event again. This concept of feedback leads the prepared public health leader to see the limits of linear thinking and the need to see all the complexities and interrelations in given events. Feedback also allows leaders to see how the organization or community is functioning relative to some desired state.

Systems thinking concentrates on the recognition of the interconnections between the parts of the system and synthesizing them into a new unified whole (Kim, 1999). If you think of a system as a jigsaw puzzle, you may have 500 pieces which form a unified whole. If the pieces do not fit for whatever reason, the systems thinker will rearrange the pieces until the puzzle is whole again. Systems thinking provides a different conceptual framework than linear thinking approaches (Senge, 1990). A body of tools and knowledge about systems have been created to help the leader develop systems thinking skills. Sweeney and Meadows (1995) have gone beyond a simple definition of systems thinking to a profile of a systems thinker. With an awareness that prepared public health leaders all need to be systems thinkers, systems thinkers are people who do the following:

1. See the big picture.
2. Remain flexible to address the need for change and an understanding of changing leverage points in complex systems.
3. Look for interconnections and interdependencies between people and organizations.
4. Explore how different mental models create different views of the future.
5. Be oriented more to long-term solutions than short-term ones.
6. Step back from situations (objectivity) to better understand complex cause and effect relationships.
7. Be prepared for unanticipated consequences and have strategies for addressing them.
8. Understand the structural issues that cause change, and be careful not to pin the blame on a specific person.
9. Understand and explain to others that conflicts with the system may take a long time to correct.

There is another interesting way to look at the relationship between linear and systemic thinking. Figure 8–1 looks at levels of perspective in linear and systems thinking relative to action modes (Kim, 1999). Most linear thinkers react to an event. The leader tries to resolve the impact of the event and come to some satisfactory outcome. Kim uses an example of

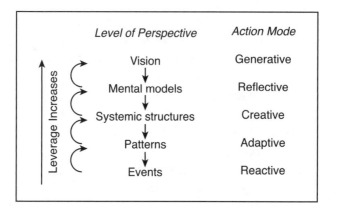

FIGURE 8–1 Levels of Perspective Framework

a fire. If the fire is the event, the reaction should be to put out the fire. The fix here is a short-term one. The fire gets put out, but you don't know who caused the fire or whether this fire was tied to other fires. It sometimes seems that the majority of the people with whom we interact are linear in their thinking and reactive to events. Although systems thinkers sometimes have to react to events, they also look for the patterns below the surface. An exploration of patterns may lead to the prevention or decrease in those events over time. This search for patterns is an adaptive action approach. A real challenge for leaders who are looking for patterns is working with others who use an event or linear approach to their problem solving.

A series of patterns may emerge that lead the systems thinker to examine systemic structures underlying these patterns. It is in the system that these thinkers must determine if certain structures cause these events and patterns. This look for systemic structures is a creative type of action (Kim, 1999). The systems thinker will explore and test whether different structures may lead to a diminution of these pattern and events. If the systems thinking leader begins to change structures, then changes in existing mental models may also occur. This clearly is a more difficult process. Reflection is necessary. Scenario planning may be critical to explore what may happen with a change in the culture and a change in mental models. As the systems thinker moves through these various stages, leverage also occurs. If a systems thinker can go through this extremely complex and painful process of thinking, a new vision may be needed which creates something that is not presently on the radar screen. Yet, systems thinking is a very powerful thing that can lead to positive change in the society as a whole. To test this model, try Exercise 8–5, which is a variation of an exercise presented in Senge et al. (1994).

LEADERSHIP AND POWER

The issue of how a leader views work within an organization or system presents an interesting view of the world through the eyes of a manager and a leader. A manager is concerned with keeping the organization or agency moving in a forward fashion within the constraints imposed on that entity from the director or from a governing or advisory board. Although the organization is a system in principle, in practice the manager usually is more linear when moving from specific problems and challenges to specific conclusions. The leader needs to see the organization as a system that has roles and responsibilities within the context of the organization as a whole or its roles and responsibilities within the context of a community.

EXERCISE 8–5 The Problem Is

Purpose: To explore different levels of thinking in the analysis of a problem

Key Concepts: Thinking modes, event, patterns of events, systemic structures, mental models, vision

Procedures:

1. Divide the class or training group into groups of 8–10.
2. Choose a public health problem to discuss related to preparedness. One way to do this is to ask each member of the group to state a problem he or she sees in their university, agency, or community.
3. The team chooses the problem.
4. Explore the problem and solutions for the following:
    A) Event
    B) Pattern of events
    C) Systemic structures
    D) Mental model
    E) Vision
5. Discuss the differences that occur at each level of thinking.

Systems and leadership can be viewed as power concerns (Oshry, 1999). Power within a system is used to transform the system and to move it in new direction. The goal of leaders is to use power to improve the system, and in public health the goal is to improve the quality of life of all residents of the community. The prepared public health leader wants to help all members of the system gain self-awareness and see that systems thinking is beneficial to improved organizational and community health. Position by itself does not guarantee power, but rather the leader who understands the organization or community and how to move the system forward in a courageous way defines the real meaning of power. Power is the management of the energy in the system (Oshry, 1999). The effective leader knows when to turn the heat up in a difficult situation and when to cool it down (Heifetz & Linsky, 2002). Heating things up brings a creative tension to the situation.

In addition, there is the critical skill of relationship building needed to improve the functioning of the system (Oshry, 1999). In addition, the whole process of systems change can be seen as a story, called an *archetype* in systems language. These archetypes help to monitor and better understand how systems work. As pointed out below, archetypes become critical analytical tools for the leader as a systems thinker. The problem for the average individual is that the parts are seen and the whole is lost. This has been labeled as *spatial blindness* (Oshry, 1995). To this can be added the concept of *temporal blindness* to refer to the fact that all systems have a history or story to tell. The blindness refers to the fact that most people live in the present but ignore the past. The goal of a successful prepared public health leader must be to see the whole world systemically.

BRIEF DISCUSSION OF THE TOOLS

Advocates of systems thinking have developed a number of tools to graphically plot out understandings of how the systems work. The tools are also used to communicate to others how these potential solutions can affect the organization or community. The tools have been developed to simplify the explanation of very complex phenomenon. Although there are many different tools for systems work, the following discussion concentrates on systems archetypes. There are three other graphic systems tool measurements including causal loop diagrams, computer simulation software packages, and microworlds (Jackson, 2003). Causal loop diagrams graphically show dynamic interrelationships in a system by tying such things as behavior of different variables over time to some systems factors (Kim, 1992). Computer simulation software include such things as computer modeling and learning laboratories. Jackson (2003) discussed microworlds as management flight simulators that were constructed from data related to computer simulation models.

Leaders who are systems thinkers view their world in terms of loops and links (Kim, 1999; Senge et al., 1994). In systems thinking, the leader believes that his tools will reflect a story (Jackson, 2003). These stories can be seen in a series of archetypes which are graphic models that help to explain reality in a systems way. The archetypes tell us something else. Certain structural patterns seem to occur over and over again (Senge, 1990). These system archetypes thus become tools for learning and also analyzing the various social structures that seem to exist in our organizational and personal lives. Although each social situation is unique, there are still enough similarities within given cultures to allow the systems thinker as leader to classify these situations. Thus, these systems archetypes, which are few in number, can be useful tools. These system archetypes were defined and discussed by Senge and colleagues (1990, 1994, 1999), and also extensively by Kim (1999, 2003).

It all seems to be about thinking in loops. All systems archetypes are based on two processes: the reinforcing process and the balancing process. These two processes are represented by a loop with feedback built into the loop. The reinforcing loop is based on a growth and collapse model (Senge, 1990; Kim, 1999). Using a simple public health scenario, Figure 8–2 shows how reinforcing loops work. If you are overweight, you tend to eat more than a person of normal weight. The more you eat, the greater your weight. Reinforcing loops also show that a change in one direction dynamically increases change in that same direction (Kim, 1999). Using the reinforcing loop process can give you other public health examples (Figure 8–3). If you already realize that obesity and other nutritional disorders are not really as simple as portrayed in Figure 8–2, then you are ready to look at balancing loops.

Balancing loops refer to processes that limit growth and generate processes of resistance (Senge et al., 1994). Balancing loops attempt to stabilize a system or bring it into equilibrium (Kim, 1999). The balancing loops also show some other things. Look at Figure 8–4. You are 50 pounds overweight relative to your height and age. The gap then is 50

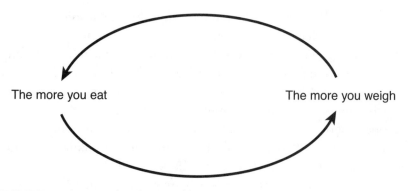

FIGURE 8-2 Example of a Reinforcing Loop

pounds that you want to lose. As you eat more, the gap between your actual and acceptable weight will increase. So what can be done? You can exercise and go on a diet (corrective action). Your weight decreases, and the gap between your actual and acceptable weight also decreases. Some diagrams make a distinction between the gap and the desired level as can be seen in Figure 8–4. Give public health examples utilizing Figure 8–5. Now you can explore an archetype approach by putting together Figures 8–2 and 8–4.

Wouldn't it be great if all situations were this easy to analyze? It is important to point out that every link in a system contains a delay. A

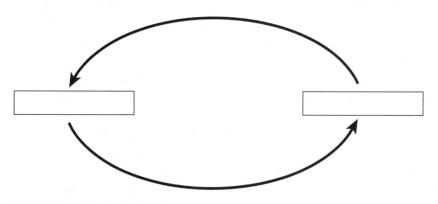

FIGURE 8-3 Reinforcing Loops

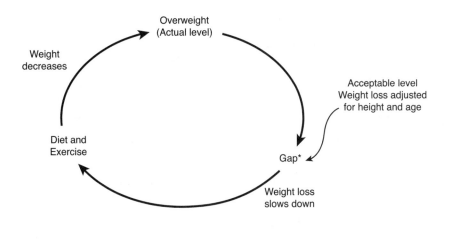

* The gap in achieving what weight is desired occurs because age and height
were not considered in the weight loss program (corrective action).

FIGURE 8–4 Balancing Loops Seek Equilibrium—Some Desired Level of Performance

delay can affect the operation of a system or other components in a system. There are four types of delay (Kim, 1999).

The first type of delay refers to delays that are physical in nature. Physical delays are time based and involve getting from here to there. For example, for some individuals, it may take 3 months to lose 10 pounds with exercise and diet. For other individuals, it may take 6 months. Thus, there is a physical delay in the time a corrective action is instituted and the desired state is actualized.

The second type of delay is transactional in that various procedural activities can slow down the change process. Using the above nutrition example, the buying of the diet products may be delayed due to delivery or production problems or even a change in price. The dieter may be affected by any of these transactional problems.

The third form of delay is informational in that there may be delays in communicating information about the physical changes that the diet and exercise may cause. The overweight person's diet may be under the supervision of a physician who is monitoring the changes through various laboratory tests or communications from a nutritionist who works for an entity that has complex procedures related to sending reports back to the doctor who has to evaluate the report before giving information to the patient or modifying the diet in light of these new results.

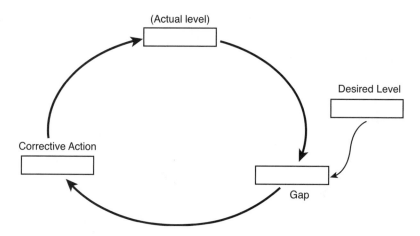

FIGURE 8–5 Balancing Loops

The final delay is perceptual in that the dieting individual may misinterpret the messages which he or she has received.

When all the above pieces are put together, we have a systems archetype. There are basically eight major systems archetypes. Figure 8–6 shows a brief description of the eight archetypes and some guidelines for using them (Kim, 2003). Exercise 8–6 will allow you to try to apply the archetypes to scenarios in a team.

A LOOK AT COMPLEXITY

As the events of September 11, 2001, have demonstrated, unanticipated events sometimes occur. Complexity science has emerged in recent years as a new methodology for dealing with the chaos and complexity of the modern world. Chaos theory is sometimes viewed as the next iteration of systems theory, with complexity science being the next point on the continuum:

Systems theory is based on nonlinearity (Lewin & Regine, 2000). However, it does not seem to explore critically the process of small

Systems theory———▶———Chaos theory———▶———Complexity science

changes leading to large effects. This latter point was a critical aspect of chaos theory. It is chaos theory that argued chaotic systems seem to develop according to verifiable rules or equations. Complexity science goes the next step. There are three system states: chaotic, stable, and a

Archetype	Description
Drifting Goals 	In a Drifting Goals archetype, a gap between the goal and current reality can be resolved by taking corrective action (B1) or lowering the goal (B2). The critical difference is that lowering the goal immediately closes the gap, where as corrective actions usually take time.
Escalation 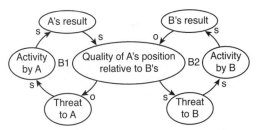	In the Escalation archetype, one party (A) takes actions that are perceived by the other as a threat. The other party (B) responds in a similar manner, increasing the threat to A and resulting in more threatening actions by A. The reinforcing loop is traced out by following the outline of the figure-8 produced by the two balancing loops.
Fixes That Fail 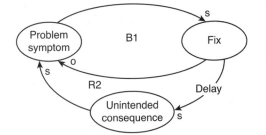	In a Fixes that Fail situation, a problem symptom cries out for resolution. A solution is quickly implemented that alleviates the symptom (B1), but the unintended consequences of the "fix" exacerbate the problem (R2). Over time, the problem symptom returns to its previous level or becomes worse.
Growth and Underinvestment 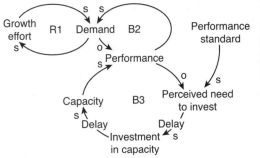	In a Growth and Underinvestment archetype, growth approaches a limit that can be eliminated or pushed into the future if capacity investments are made. Instead performance standards are lowered to justify underinvestment, leading to lower performance which further justifies underinvestment.

continues

FIGURE 8–6 Systems Archetypes at a Glance

Archetype

Description

Limits to Success

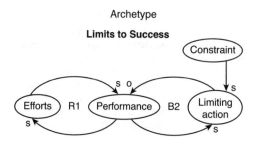

In a Limits of Success scenario, continued efforts initially lead to improved performance. Over time, however, the system encounters a limit which causes the performance to slow down or even decline (B2), even as efforts continue to rise.

Shifting the Burden/Addiction

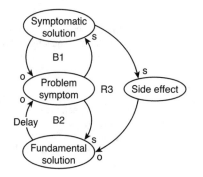

In a Shifting the Burden, a problem is "solved" by applying a symptomatic solution (B1), which diverts attention away from more fundamental solutions (R3). (See *The Systems Thinker*, September, 1990). In an Addiction structure, a Shifting the Burden degrades into an addictive pattern in which the side effect gets so entrenched that it overwhelms the original problem symptom.

Success to the Successful

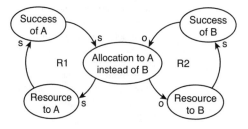

In a Success to the Successful archetype, if one person or group (A) is given more resources, it has a higher likelihood of succeeding that B (assuming they are equally capable). The initial success justifies devoting more resources to A, and B's success diminishes, further justifying more resource allocations to A(R2).

Tragedy of the Commons

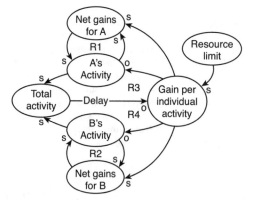

In a Tragedy of the Commons structure, each person pursues actions which are individually beneficial (R1 and R2). If the amount of activity grows too large for the system to support, however, the "commons" experiences diminishing benefits (B5 and B6).

FIGURE 8–6 *continued*

zone of adaptability somewhere between these two extremes (Lewin & Regine, 2000). In addition, systems can change.

Another aspect of complexity thinkers is that they focus on the interactions between individual agents in the system and monitor their effects on the system as a whole. There is also a strong belief that order will arise out of chaotic times. However, it is not always possible to determine what that

---

EXERCISE 8–6 Systems Archetypes

Purpose: To use systems archetypes for public health issues

Key Concepts: Systems archetypes, Drifting Goals, Escalation, Fixes That Fail, Growth and Underinvestment, Limits to Success, Shifting the Burden, Success to be Successful, Tragedy of the Commons

Procedures: Divide the class or training group into groups of 8–10. Apply each scenario to the system archetype. You can make any assumptions necessary to better understand how archetypes work.

System Archetype	Scenario
Drifting Goals	You decide to go on a diet to lose 50 pounds. After a year, you lose 25 pounds. You lower your diet goal.
Escalation	A smoking coalition talks to a local theater owner about instituting a no-smoking policy in the theater bar. The local health department tobacco control department head is threatened.
Fixes That Fail	Teenage pregnancy rates in a community are increasing. A condom distribution plan is initiated in the local high school. Rates decline for six months and then increase again.
Growth and Underinvestment	A million dollars is given to your community to build capacity to address potential disasters. Six months into the process, your budget is cut by a third.
Limits to Growth (or Success)	The federal government allocates funds to local public health agencies to make them prepared to handle bioterrorism events. Training occurs. A bioterrorism event occurs.
Shifting the Burden	In the community with an increasing rate of teenage pregnancy, the short-term solution of condom distribution does not alleviate the problem. The high school develops a program to increase self-esteem.

continues

EXERCISE 8–6 *continued*

Success to be Successful	You have been promoted to director of your local health department. The promotion means you will be away from home four nights a week. How do you balance work and family responsibilities?
Tragedy of the Commons	There is a flu vaccine shortage. You hear that 100 shots will be given at the local high school on Saturday. You go on Saturday. Everyone else has the same idea.

new order will be. However, self-organization is the basic characteristic of the universe (Kelly & Allison, 1999). Self-organizing groups come into being during periods of bounded instability. Complexity theory should prove useful to those leaders who struggle with the changes that the terrorist events of 2001 have brought.

The new leaders and managers will have to learn the skills of managing the unknowable (Stacy, 1992). When a system is undergoing dynamic change, it is not possible to study the system in terms of its parts. The dynamic system affects all the participants in it in ways that may not be predictable. It almost seems that the system is operating out of control. The traditional archetypes don't seem to apply. The prepared public health leader needs to think in terms of whole systems, interconnections between one system and another, and also view the patterns of behavior that the disorder creates in individuals. The leader has to observe the small changes that may change the whole system. Details within the system are often distracting. With the changes that complexity bring, new leadership strategies will be needed. Seven approaches can be taken (Stacy, 1992):

- The first approach relates to the change in the way a prepared public health leader gets the managers in an agency or the partners in a community collaboration to change their mental model concerning control. Traditional approaches to trying to deal with an organizational or community challenge is to increase awareness that these unexpected challenges often require innovative and sometimes either organization-wide or community-wide involvement in a possible solution. Old rules and approaches may not work. How does the manager or leader control a situation that may not have traditional rules and regulations to guide the process?

- The second issue is tied to the first and relates to the issue of power. In working collaboratively on a problem solution, existing power relationships may need to be changed to allow for a sharing of power and leadership in the solution. Conflict may also be critical in order to explore all possible issues related to resolving the unexpected occurrence.
- The third application requires that problem solving and decision making be done in self-organizing learning teams. Self-organization may well involve individuals opinions and judgments about who should be on the team relative to the skills and contributions that will be required to deal with the event (Stacy, 1992). These teams will have to define their goals and objectives for the crisis and its possible resolution.
- The fourth factor adds the complex issue of multidisciplinary or multiple cultural group involvement. It is often difficult to create a common culture or a consensus solution when different groups are impacted differently by the solutions proposed. If external experts are brought into the group as consultants or facilitators, the proposed solutions to these challenges will also be affected. Control, power, and decision making are all impacted by the composition of the problem-solving body.
- The prepared public health leader takes a sometimes calculated risk in sharing control and power with others. Creative solutions may lead to revolutionary change. It may not be possible to determine the creativity of a solution until after the event has been managed (Stacy, 1996). The issue of how much risk the leader is taking is difficult to evaluate when an event and its outcome are unpredictable and when the future seems to be unknowable because the old ways of doing things have changed. The question becomes whether any sort of preparation is possible.
- The sixth strategy (Stacy, 1992) points to the need to improve group learning skills as a prerequisite to addressing the unknowable. If we apply the learning organization perspective, then we can extend the perspective to argue that each team can determine the training and other tools that will expedite its work. Training should not be a one-shot deal. Because of the complexity of the world and the unpredictability of events, learning must be ongoing.
- The final application involves the critical leadership concern related to the time factor (Stacy, 1992). It is impossible to predict how long

it will take to address an unexpected event. Discussion and experimentation take time. It is necessary for a leader to give slack to the team so that it can carry out its work. The prepared public health leader has to determine how much slack time can realistically be allowed. The leader has to maintain stable equilibrium in times of complexity when the team needs learning time as well. Stacy (1996) summarized these reasons for a complexity approach to systemic problem solving as a way to better indicate how organizations and communities create conditions for spontaneous self-organization to generate emergent outcomes to crisis situations or other unpredictable events.

SUMMARY

This chapter emphasized the importance of systems thinking by the prepared public health leader. The leader has to move from a linear approach to problem solving and decision making and move to a systems perspective. The five levels of learning were presented. It is imperative that leaders create learning organizations to better understand the changes that are occurring in communities. The issue of leadership and power was discussed within the context of a systems perspective. The tools of systems thinking were presented with exercises from the public health field. Finally, complexity theory was introduced as the next evolution in systems thinking with new perspectives tied to unanticipated events. September 11, 2001, requires the prepared public health leader to deal with complexity issues and problem solutions.

REFERENCES

Addelson, M. (n.d.). Exploring systems thinking: A discussion of Peter Senge's fifth discipline—The art and practice of the learning organization. Psol.gmu. edu/psol/perspectives2insf

Heifetz, R. A., and Linsky, M. (2002). *Leadership on the line*. Boston: Harvard Business School Press.

Jackson, M. C. (2003). *Systems thinking*. London, England: John Wiley and Sons.

Kauffman, D. L., Jr. (1980). *Systems one: An introduction to systems thinking*. Minneapolis, MN. S. A. Carlton.

Kelly, S., and Allison, M. A. (1999). *The complexity advantage*. New York: Mc-Graw Hill.

Kim, D. H. (1999). *Introduction to systems thinking.* Waltham, MA: Pegasus Communications.

Kim, D. H. (1992). *Systems archetypes I.* Waltham, MA: Pegasus Communications.

Lewin, R., and Regine, B. (2000). *Soul at work.* New York: Simon and Schuster.

Oshry, B. (1995). *Seeing systems.* San Francisco: Berrett-Kohler Publishers.

Oshry, B. (1999). *Leading systems.* San Francisco: Berrett-Kohler Publishers.

Rowitz, L. (2001). *Public health leadership: Putting principles into practice.* Sudbury, MA: Jones and Bartlett.

Senge, P. (1990). *The fifth discipline.* New York: Doubleday.

Senge, P., Kleiner, A., Roberts, C., Ross, R., Roth, G., & Smith, B. (1999). *The dance of change.* New York: Doubleday.

Senge, P., Roberts, C., Ross, R. B., Smith, B. J., & Kleiner, A. (1994). *The fifth discipline fieldbook.* New York: Doubleday.

Stacy, R. D. (1996). *Complexity and creativity in organizations.* San Francisco: Berrett-Kohler.

Stacy, R. D. (1992). *Managing the unknowable.* San Francisco: Jossey-Bass.

Sweeney, L. B., & Meadows, D. (1995). *The systems thinking playbook* (Vol. 1). Durham, NH: Laboratory for Creative Learning.

Systems Thinker. (2002). *What is systems thinking?* Waltham, MA: Pegasus Communications.

Turning Point Leadership Collaborative. (2004). *Collaborative leadership learning modules.* Seattle: Turning Point National Program Office (R. W. Johnson Foundation).

CHAPTER 9

People Skills

The deepest wisdom and the most profound expression of your experience are rooted in compassion.

—*Ronald A. Heifetz and Marty Linsky, 2002*

Leadership is all about people and institutions. In discussing the leadership of the future, it can be stated that the legacy of the successful leader is the creation and sustainability of valued institutions that can survive the test of time (Kouzes & Posner, 2002). This does not mean that stresses will not enter the system, but rather that a strong institutional structure will survive onslaughts such as the events of September 11, 2001, and the anthrax letters that followed. Leaders are also committed to the growth and nurturance of people. These people include all members of a community whether they work directly in an organization in which the leader resides or in the surrounding community. All prepared public health leaders need to be committed to promoting healthy communities. This chapter is concerned with the skills the leader needs to work with people.

To put the content of this chapter in perspective, I want to tell you a personal story about a very special person who affected my life. I know that it is unusual for an author of a book like this one to personalize the content, but sometimes it is important to waive the rules. This book and this chapter are about personal things and feelings. The man about whom

I am going to tell you was a man who changed the direction of my professional life. His impact on me goes back almost 40 years, even before people were talking about the importance of emotions in leadership. It was the first week of my several years as a graduate student in sociology. I remember visiting the department offices in an old university building where I discovered that not all the department's professors were in this building. I also found to my amazement that I had received a graduate teaching assistantship in what was at that time an innovative 2-semester course on the relationship between society and culture. All the lectures had been taped and were to be broadcast over the university television station several times a week at different times. This course was one of the first attempts at distance education before distance education was popular. The lectures were given by Professor William Dickson of the Sociology Department. Sometimes Professor Dickson had televised discussions with other well-known campus faculty as part of the program. I was to run three discussion sections each semester. Professor Dickson was one of the brightest, most insightful teachers that I have ever known. However, if his intelligence was all that he had to offer, my story would be over.

Professor Dickson's office was in an old converted house several blocks from the departmental main offices. I remember walking over to his office on a beautiful fall day. He was seated behind a big desk with books and papers strewn all over the place. As soon as I introduced myself, he concentrated on me. He listened intently and seemed to immediately understand my nervousness and uncertainties about being a graduate student. Bill always listened intently and always seemed to understand what my fellow graduate colleagues were going through. He was always available and willing to talk about anything. It wasn't just his intelligence, it was his ability to understand all of us. We graduate students all got his attention. He mentored us, coached us, and guided us through all the complexities of graduate school. He invited us often to his home, and his wife always offered us her friendship as well as snacks for starving students. I married about a year into my graduate work, and Bill and Jane were always warm to us and invited my wife and me many times over to their home.

About halfway through my graduate work, Professor Dickson accepted another position at another university several hundred miles away. I thought that was the end of his mentoring of me. I was wrong. He continued to remain my mentor and friend till the end of his life. In fact, he offered me my first teaching job which I did not take for a number of reasons. He and Jane still remained my friends. I visited with him whenever I was in his city. We discussed the world and he always asked how my wife and children were. He was always interested in me as a person. Here clearly was a man who had great intelligence as well as strong people skills. I only hope that each of my readers experience the impact of a Bill Dickson. It can change a life.

EMOTIONALLY COMPETENT LEADERSHIP

Although intelligence and the Intelligence Quotient (IQ) seemed to be the critical requirement for leadership during the previous century, leaders of the 21st century need to have emotional intelligence as well. Today, leaders need to develop an ability and capacity to recognize their personal feelings and the feelings and emotional reactions of others (Goleman, 1998a). In addition to developing this emotional awareness, leaders need to become motivated to manage their emotions and feelings in their relationships with others as well. In his classic book on leadership, Burns (1978) said that a critical activity for leaders is to help others become aware of their feelings, feel these needs in a strong way, understand their values and how they emotionally respond to these values, and then become involved in meaningful actions based on these emotional realities. Mayer and Salovey (1993) coined the concept of *emotional intelligence* to refer to these important leadership skills. Effective leadership thus occurs within the context of emotional intelligence (Feldman, 1999). You can experiment with your view of yourself as a leader who recognizes personal feelings by doing Exercise 9–1 using a mirror.

Emotional intelligence is critical to effective leadership (Goleman, 1998b). In reviewing extensive research, Goleman pointed out that it may be technical and cognitive skills that get a person a leadership position, but it is emotional intelligence that helped leaders keep their jobs. It is also interesting to note that leaders have to rely on these emotional skills more and more as they move up the organization. These leaders promote the development of technical skills for those individuals who work in the more technical positions in the organization. It is also clear that leaders will have to be proficient in emotional intelligence as they expand their

---

EXERCISE 9–1 The Mirror

Purpose: To understand some of the characteristics that define you as a
     leader

Key Concepts: Leadership, emotional intelligence

Procedures: Hold up a hand mirror or look into a wall mirror.

1. Do you see a leader?
2. How do you feel as you view this person?
3. Is this person successful?
4. What do you think holds the person in the mirror back?
5. What are the five things you can do in the next six months to increase your success?

---

activities outside the organization in collaborative groups or other community-based activities. Emotional intelligence distinguishes the outstanding leaders and clearly is an important indicator of strong and effective performance (Goleman, 1998b). This finding was strongly supported by Mayer and Salovey (1993) to explain how two people with similar general intelligence and technical expertise can end up in entirely different parts of an organization and at different leadership levels in the organization. Exercise 9–2 will give you a chance to evaluate your leadership traits.

There is a need to become aware that the relationship between technical skills, cognitive skills including IQ, and emotional intelligence needs to be evaluated further. If we were to create a recipe for successful leadership, it would be necessary to determine the percentage of these three

---

EXERCISE 9–2 What Makes a Leader?

Purpose: To understand the traits of a successful leader

Key Concepts: Leadership, emotional intelligence

Procedures:

1. Write down the 10 traits of a successful leader.
2. How many of these 10 traits do you have?
3. How many of these traits relate to emotional intelligence?
4. What do you have to do to demonstrate more of these traits?

---

ingredients for different types of professional work. Although it seems clear that emotional intelligence increases in importance as leaders work more with others, it also seems apparent that the relationship of the three ingredients will fluctuate over time and place. Thus, the formula for effective leadership becomes:

> Technical skills (__%) + cognitive skills (__%) + emotional intelligence (__%) = successful leadership (100%)

An interesting set of issues relates to the question of whether emotional intelligence can be learned. Intelligence and emotional intelligence are separate sets of competencies (Goleman, 1995). Having a high intelligence quotient is not a guarantee of strong social skills or also high emotional intelligence. General intelligence is less flexible than emotional intelligence (Bradberry & Greaves, 2003). People do not generally increase their general intelligence over time, but emotional intelligence does increase as people become more adept at personal relationships. Emotional intelligence is not fixed at birth due to genetics (Goleman, 1998b). It clearly can grow over time. In making the argument that emotional intelligence can grow and be learned, there is evidence that emotional intelligence increases with age (Goleman, 1998b). Emotional intelligence is related to neurotransmitters in the limbic system of the brain which is tied to feelings, impulses, and drives. It will be important in the future for training programs to orient their activities to changing behavioral patterns that are associated with the limbic system. Increasing the motivation to make these changes must be a goal of training. Learning to be empathic is a critical part of the development of emotional intelligence.

EMOTIONAL INTELLIGENCE COMPETENCIES

It has become clear in the last several years that emotional intelligence skills for leaders are important for the individual leaders but also for the leader's relationships with others. This is not to denigrate the importance of technical and cognitive skills. The real concern is related to balance. The leader needs to use the head as well as the heart. An interesting view of this issue is found in an inspirational writing by Rabbi Lori Forman (1999). She was responding to a religious document called the Midrash in which ancient Jewish scholars defined the wicked as those who are controlled by their heart and the righteous have their hearts under control. Rabbi Forman explained this passage in terms of balance. It is not possible to separate our rational self from our feeling self. Our thoughts guide our feelings and vice versa. It is through the combination of thoughts and feelings that humankind address the world. Self-control is important because feelings without control can lead to chaos. It is important for the leader to realize that the mind skills and the heart skills all need to be developed if successful leadership is to occur.

Many writers have come up with frameworks for determining the important components and competencies of emotional intelligence. Three of these frameworks are discussed here. All three involve the development of personal skills as well as skills involved in dealing with others. All three models also have assessment tools tied to them which the reader can access. Table 9–1 gives a summary of the three models. The first model relates to the structure defined by Goleman (1995, 1998a, 1998b, 2001). Goleman and his colleagues in the Consortium for Research on Emotional Intelligence in Organizations have been working with this model for a number of years. The framework now has four components with 20 subcompetencies associated with each of the four categories. Two of the dimensions (self-awareness and self-management) involve personal competencies and two of the dimensions (social awareness and relationship management) involve social competency.

The self-awareness domain includes emotional self-awareness, accurate self-assessment, and self-confidence. The competencies involved here

Table 9–1 Frameworks for Emotional Intelligence

Goleman (2001)	Cooper and Sawaf (1996)	Feldman (1999)
Self-awareness	Emotional literacy	Knowing yourself
Self-management	Emotional fitness	Maintaining control
Social awareness	Emotional depth	Reading others
Relationship management	Emotional alchemy	Perceiving accurately
————	————	Communicating with flexibility

include an ability on the part of the individual to understand and recognize moods, feelings, and drives. Specifically, emotional self-awareness includes the ability to recognize moods and emotions and how it affects personal behavior. People with this competence not only understand their moods but also understand why they are feeling as they do (Goleman, 1998b). These people also recognize the link between thoughts and feelings. They also know that their performance is often affected by these feelings and thoughts. Competency in accurate self-assessment includes the knowledge of one's strengths and limitations. This skill clearly involves learning from experience. These people also are willing to accept feedback on their behavior. The third competency in self-awareness involves self-confidence. These people are willing to take a stand. They are often the risk takers. Exercise 9–3 will give you the chance to describe your risk-taking experiences.

The second component of the Goleman model involves self-management, which has several subcompetencies associated with it. This component includes the ability to not only understand one's feelings and moods, but also to use these feelings and moods to guide oneself towards personal goals and objectives. There is a strong motivational factor here in that the leader is not only aware of personal moods and feelings, but needs to stay flexible and positive in directing these moods and feelings into change (Bradberry & Greaves, 2003). The first subcomponent is emotional self-control which means that the leaders know or learn how to control feelings and emotions. People strong in this competency have also mastered the ability to stay focused. Being trustworthy is clearly an important part

---

EXERCISE 9–3 Risk Taking

Purpose: To understand how taking risks affects the emotions

Key Concepts: Emotional intelligence, risk taking, leadership

Procedures: Divide the class or training group into groups of 10.

1. Think back over the past year and see if you took a risk in some work or social situation.
2. How did you feel?
3. What was the reaction of other people?
4. Discuss with your group your risk-taking experience and have other members of the group tell you about their experience.

of self-management. Action in an ethical manner is a critical leadership responsibility. People strong in this competency also work vigorously to build trust. They also admit their mistakes and address unethical behavior in others. It is important to remember that trust takes time to build, and it can be destroyed in a moment. Part of trust is carrying through on promises, which is also involved in the competency of conscientiousness. Thus, these leaders keep their promises. Do Exercise 9–4 on building trust.

The next competency related to self-management involves the skills related to adaptability, involving flexibility in managing change. Leaders are always oriented towards the future and the changes necessary to get there. They look for new approaches and new methods for attaining goals. They are innovative and want to generate new ideas. Leaders are excellent multitaskers, and they can handle shifting priorities. They clearly are flexible. The next competency of leaders having an achievement drive is closely tied to the competency of adaptability and innovation. These people are clearly results and outcome based. They also take calculated risks to achieve the ends they seek. These people would be concerned with the tools of performance measurement. They would also want to create performance standards and then surpass them. The final competency for self-management involves initiative, which is a readiness and ability to act on opportunities whenever they present themselves. Optimism is part of this competency because leaders are positive in addressing challenges (Goleman, 1998b). If you are to seize opportunities, then a positive perspective helps. Leaders create visions and then surpass them. They will do whatever is necessary to get the job done, although they will always practice ethical standards in doing so. These people are wonderful in inspiring others to follow their lead.

The next dimension of the Goleman model (2001) addressed the issue of social awareness. An important ability of leaders is to be able to recognize and read the emotions, feelings, and reactions of others (Bradberry & Greaves, 2003). The interesting challenge here is to do this when you might feel differently than other people about a situation. There are three competencies tied to this dimension of emotional intelligence. The first critical set of skills is empathy or understanding others. Empathy requires the ability to be an active listener who is able to pick up emotional cues from other people. Empathy includes sensitivity to the needs of other people. Mentors and executive coaches need to be strong in this competency. If we as leaders are to enable others to act, then we must learn to empower others. One way to do this is to show others that we understand

EXERCISE 9–4 Building Trust

Purpose: To explore the issue of building trust in collaborative leadership

Key Concepts: Trust, collaborative leadership

Procedures: Divide the class or training group into smaller groups and have each participant fill out the self-assessment tool on trust. Score your results, and have the group answer the questions at the end of the assessment tool.

Collaborative Leadership

Building Trust

Self-Assessment Exercise

For each item, circle one rating under the Behavior Frequency column indicating your view of how often you exhibit that behavior. Your responses to this questionnaire are for your own use. You will not be asked to share your scores after you have answered. You will be asked to use your score and your responses to help you develop a personal learning plan.

Behaviors		Seldom		Sometimes		Often		Almost Always
1	I build communication processes that make it safe for people to say what is on their minds.	1	2	3	4	5	6	7
2	I refuse to engage in "rigged" processes.	1	2	3	4	5	6	7
3	I protect the group from those who would wield personal power over the collaborative process.	1	2	3	4	5	6	7
4	I create credible processes for collaborating.	1	2	3	4	5	6	7
5	I ensure that processes for exercising collaborative leadership are open to all stakeholders.	1	2	3	4	5	6	7
6	I ensure that the processes for collaborative leadership are transparent to all stakeholders.	1	2	3	4	5	6	7
7	During the first stage of creating collaborative relationships, I establish the common ground among the stakeholders.	1	2	3	4	5	6	7
8	I approach collaboration by relying heavily on building trust among stakeholders.	1	2	3	4	5	6	7
9	I "walk the talk," i.e., I do what I say I will do.	1	2	3	4	5	6	7
10	I demonstrate to my peers that I believe that trust is the foundation for successful collaboration.	1	2	3	4	5	6	7

**Your Score: Add all the circled behavior frequencies.
Write the number in the box.**

70–61 Excellent score   40–21 Opportunities for growth
60–41 Stronger score   20–1 Important to change behavior

Written Comments:
What do you think are your strengths in building trust as a collaborative leader?

What do you think are your most important areas for improvement in building trust?

their needs and desires. Good leaders make others feel strong and capable (Kouzes & Posner, 2002). In doing this, those who follow often exceed their own expectations.

The second competency area is service orientation. This competency is familiar to those who are proponents of continuous quality improvement methods. This competency involves the development of skills to anticipate, recognize, and meet the needs of others whether they be the clients of a public health agency, the residents of a community, or our community partners. Leaders competent in this area are concerned about how others react to public health decisions. Public health leaders have a strong concern for others, this is tied to the belief that all people are entitled to the best that health and public health has to offer. Social justice concerns drive the public health agenda, and yet political and budgetary decision sometimes lead to health inequities.

The final competency in the social awareness cluster involves organizational awareness. It is with this competency that we see many of these issues raised in other chapters in this book. This competency can be defined as an ability to increase awareness of the emotions and political realities of those with whom the leader works (Goleman, 2001). This competency involves the skills of networking, collaboration, influence building, and systems thinking. The leader with this competency must understand the interdependencies of groups and how feeling and emotions affect outcomes. Almost all the skills covered in Part 3 of this book require this competency to be well developed.

The fourth dimension of the emotional competency model of Goleman involves the critical sets of skills related to relationship management. In fact, the skills discussed above on social awareness are closely allied to this cluster of eight competencies. Such skills as strategic planning, conflict resolution, problem solving, decision making, and other traditional leadership and management tools are subsumed under this component of emotional intelligence (Rowitz, 2001). The value-added piece of the present discussion relates to the impact of emotions and feelings on these traditional leadership activities. A major competency involves the development of others, which appears closely allied to the empathy competency discussed previously. Leaders need to be concerned about the future and the issue of succession planning. It is important to recognize the skills and potential of others. Leaders need to be realistic. No leadership position is forever.

Being able to be influential is another competency related to relationship management. Influence and skill in persuasion are closely tied together. The leader has to become skillful in getting others to buy into his or her message. This means that complex strategies need to be developed to build consensus and support for the issues that the leader considers to be important. Successful leaders are able to put the pieces together in effective ways. They make their point and convince others of the validity of their position. It is important that the enthusiasm and positivism of the leader be contagious for others to follow the leader.

The next competency involves the ability of the leader to listen with an open mind, monitor personal emotions and feelings, and be able to send effective messages in a number of different ways. Leaders emphasize the importance of communication in all its aspects. Communication is more than interpersonal in nature and covers many things including written communication strategies and public discussion and dialogue (Rowitz, 2001). People who are strong in this competency excel at reading emotional cues in others (Goleman, 1998b). These leaders are also effective in addressing complex issues in a straightforward manner. They are good listeners and seek to understand what is said to them at both a verbal and emotional level. They foster communication, and they try to listen to information about good and bad events. It is clear that collaboration not only improves performance, it creates a strong level of trust (Kouzes & Posner, 2002). Since communication is so important, Chapter 11 will discuss this issue in more detail relative to risk and crisis communication skills.

The next competency in relationship management involves conflict management. People strong in this competency know how to handle difficult people in tense situations (Goleman, 1998b). This ability involves the use of tact and diplomacy. These leaders know how to diffuse tension and move from conflict to collaboration. They do this by addressing conflict in an open manner and encourage the voicing of diverse views. These leaders want to create win-win situations (Rowitz, 2001). The leader really needs to be able to spot trouble before it explodes in a major crisis situation. The leader also needs to determine when an objective negotiator needs to be brought in to resolve conflicts because the emotions are overtaking rational decision making.

The assumption in the present chapter has been that all these competencies are important for leaders. The competencies of visionary leadership and catalyzing change are clearly competencies of leaders. Leaders need to be able to create a vision with an awareness that emotional factors will clearly guide the vision process. To attain the vision, the leader needs to convince others to go along with the steps necessary to bring about change. Leaders are catalysts for change and need not only recognize that change is necessary, but also challenge the status quo and remove the barriers to change (Goleman, 2001). Leaders will have to get others to emotionally invest in the change process and be part of the vision that the leader has. Chapters 15 and 16 address these issues in more detail.

The next relationship management competency addresses the building of bonds between people. Building networks between people is important if strong relationships are to be built. In informal discussions with the directors of 19 state and regional public health leadership institutes around the United States, these directors have stated that one of the hidden functions of leadership development is fostering the connections and friendships that develop among the trainees. These leaders think that one of the benefits of training relates to the leadership networks that this training generates. These relationships that evolve through training or through building bonds between people in other arenas often create trust and goodwill. Strong leaders build bonds. When these bonds develop, social capital increases.

The final competency in the Goleman framework involves the competencies of teamwork and collaboration. Some of these issues were discussed in Chapter 6. At the emotional intelligence level, this competency involves the creation of a balance between the work or task to be performed and the relationships necessary to carry out the work (Goleman, 1998b). Collaboration clearly has emotional components. The sharing of information and future plans or resources can lessen stress in many situations, although not in all of them. Feelings of competition have strong emotional reactions. The goal of leaders strong in collaboration is to build positive working and personal environments. These leaders want to nurture teamwork and collaboration in coalitions, alliances, and partnerships.

Goleman (2001) has put together the emotional intelligence competencies with leadership style, impact on climate (or social context), objective of the leadership style orientation, and its effect on organizational effectiveness. Table 9–2 shows these relationships. The important thing to note in the table is the specific competencies which seem to predominate in each leadership style. Which style is your predominant style? Are you competent in the areas listed for that style? If you go through the list of the twenty

Table 9-2 Leadership Style, EI, and Organizational Effectiveness

Leadership Style	EI Competencies	Impact on Climate	Objective	When Appropriate
Visionary	Self-confidence, empathy, change catalyst, visionary leadership	Most strongly positive	Mobilize others to follow a vision	When change requires a new vision or when a clear direction is needed
Affiliative	Empathy, building bonds, conflict management	Highly positive	Create harmony	To heal rifts in a team or to motivate during stressful times
Democratic	Teamwork and collaboration, communication	Highly positive	Build commitment through participation	To build buy-in or consensus or to get valuable input from employees
Coaching	Developing others, empathy, emotional self-awareness	Highly positive	Build strengths for the future	To help an employee improve performance or develop long-term strengths
Coercive	Achievement drive, initiative, emotional self-control	Strongly negative	Immediate compliance	In a crisis, to kick-start a turn around, or with problem employees
Pacesetting	Conscientiousness, achievement drive, initiative	Highly negative	Perform tasks to a high standard	To get quick results from a highly motivated and competent team

Goleman competencies, which competencies would you say are your strong ones and which do you want to develop competence in for the future?

The second approach to emotional intelligence, as seen in Table 9–1, is built on something called the four cornerstone model (Cooper & Sawaf, 1996). As will be seen in the following discussion, the four cornerstone model clearly overlaps with the Goleman model just discussed, and yet there are some different perspectives that the authors give that can enrich the skills of the prepared public health leader. High-level executives with a strong emotional quotient (EQ) as well as a strong IQ (intelligence quotient) tend to make the best decisions and run the most dynamic and creative organizations (Cooper & Sawaf, 1996). These leaders also report that they are living very satisfying lives. The following discussion will involve a look at the four cornerstone model and the competencies associated with each of the cornerstones.

The first cornerstone relates to emotional literacy which relates to the emotional center of all our activities (Cooper & Sawaf, 1996). It is emotional literacy that affects our energy and motivation. This cornerstone, as well as each of the other three, has four competencies associated with it—emotional honesty, emotional energy, emotional feedback, and practical intuition. Many of our emotional reactions are tied to the first competency of honesty. Being true to yourself and others undergirds much of the Goleman discussion above. The way the leader is seen by others is important here. The honest leader needs to judge him or herself in an honest manner as well. Whenever a leader is asked to evaluate personal skills on a leadership assessment tool, it is assumed that the leader will be honest in filling out the form and not answer the questions in such a way that the leader thinks the tester will evaluate so that their skills are seen in a more favorable light. One little exercise that you can try to evaluate this honesty dimension is to evaluate your energy level, openness, and level of focus on a scale from one to ten for each dimension before and after a meeting that you have to attend (Cooper & Sawan, 1996). Your honesty in rating yourself on this scale from 3–30 will give you insights into your ability to address issues. If you have trouble being motivated during the meeting, evaluate the strategies that would help you become more involved.

The second competency in this first cornerstone is emotional energy. People do better when they have the energy to address tasks and develop people relationships. There are two major components to this competency. The first relates to the level of tension that the individual feels, and the second component is the level of energy itself. If the tension is high and the energy is high, the authors call this *tense-energy*. This pattern occurs when you push yourself to extremes and leave your personal needs at the doorstep. This pattern may lead to burnout. If you have low tension and high energy, you have *calm-energy* which can lead to some very productive work (Cooper & Sawaf, 1996). The unfortunate part is that leaders do not feel this state very often. When we feel calm-energy, it is more possible to be proactive that in the previous state where behavior tends to be more reactive.

The third energy pattern is high tension with low energy which can be called *tense-tiredness*. This is how we often feel after we get home from a busy day and a difficult freeway drive. The stress is high and the tiredness is great. In this state, individuals need to be careful to not overreact to the demands of family members or colleagues who need help in some matter. The final state is low tension with low energy which is the state of *calm-tiredness*. This is the good state of just feeling content and relaxed. Leaders need to understand their energy levels and how to react to them.

The third competency involves the skills related to understanding emotional feedback. Leaders need to realize that every feeling or emotion is sending a message. Leaders who understand this will become adept at managing emotional impulsivity. This competency is similar to the competencies discussed by Goleman in the area of self-awareness and self-management. The leader needs to take responsibility for his or her actions. An interesting exercise that you can do for better understanding this competency is to ask yourself, "If you were to take responsibility for a specific feeling you have, such as anger, what would happen?" (Cooper & Sawaf, 1996).

The fourth competency relates to emotional literacy and the development of intuitive skills. Intuition is closely tied to the empathy competency in the Goleman model. The empathic individual is one who can read the feelings beneath the words that are spoken. Sometimes our gut reactions to a situation should guide our behavior rather than our rational thoughts. Trust is also important here in that relationships built on trust allow others to say and show their authentic reactions to events. Exercise 9–5 on intuition will give you the chance to explore your use of intuition for making decisions.

The second cornerstone in the Cooper and Sawaf model involves emotional fitness, which includes the four competencies of authenticity, trust

---

Exercise 9–5 Intuition

Purpose: To see the relationship between intuition and decision making
Key Concepts: Intuition, leadership, decision making, emotional intelligence
Procedures: Divide the class or training group into groups of 10.

1. Can you think of a situation in which your intuition was correct but your decision was wrong?
2. Can you think of a situation in which your intuition and your decision were aligned?
3. Discuss your experiences with your team.

---

radius, constructive discontent, and resilience and renewal. Authentic power includes the issue of personal power. Authentic presence is affected by the factors of showing attentiveness to others (another aspect of empathy and building bonds), concern for others (also a part of empathy), your agenda and motives to get people involved in your vision, and the complex issue of entitlement that is affected by your organizational position or personal relationship to the other person. Authenticity also involves convincing others that you are taking discussion and dialogues seriously. The authentic leader is also one who admits to mistakes and is willing to forgive him or herself and others. The second competency which also exists in the Goleman model relates to the importance of building trust. The new wrinkle in the present model is the connection between trust and believability. In addition, there is a trust radius which answers the question of how far the leader is willing to extend his or her trust network (Cooper & Sawaf, 1996). Trust relationships take time to build, and a leader must struggle to be sociable to strangers where the trust is not yet apparent.

The third competency related to emotional fitness is constructive discontent. As a facilitator, the leader may have to create conflict in a group and get them to address an issue in a way different than they may have in the past. Creating discontent can have positive effects even though the stress and tension level will increase significantly. Goleman would have included this competency under conflict management. Some of the specifics in this constructive discontent include the process of increasing awareness, exposing problems in the group, using empathy to explore diverse views, promoting the development of trust in a group, understanding and promoting inclusion and participation when values and goals are in conflict, collaboration for creative solutions to problems, developing learning organizations with your colleagues in order to learn in action, creating an environment that promotes the enjoyment of the process, and a belief that constructive discontent leads to real problem solving and decision making.

The final competency for this cornerstone relates to resilience and renewal. The resilience factor is critical to creating change and will be discussed in more detail in Chapter 15. For now, it is enough to point out that resilience is tied to adaptability and the ability to adjust to change. Resilient people have great curiosity. The issue of renewal is important as well. Leaders need to renew themselves. Renewal may involve taking a new job in a new place. It may be a walk on the beach or sitting in a favorite chair and reading a new book. Each of us will have different ways to address renewal. The important message is that leaders need to allow time for this sabbatical experience if they are to remain effective. We spend time taking courses or going to training workshops to expand our leadership skills and we need to spend time on expanding our emotional intelligence skills as well.

The third cornerstone involves the critical concerns related to emotional depth (Cooper & Sawaf, 1996). This cornerstone is involved with the issue of character and how individuals over their lifetime become more and more adept at people relationships. How we practice the skills of emotional intelligence becomes a critical indicator of emotional depth. You can experiment with some of the issues involved in this cornerstone by exploring the technical and emotional aspects of the real purpose of leading by walking around. Why do leaders walk around their organizations and communities? What is the real meaning of this activity? The four competencies of this third cornerstone include unique potential and purpose, commitment, applied integrity, and influence without authority.

The competency related to unique potential relates to the individual who is adept at analyzing personal strengths and weaknesses. Leaders need to have a purpose—a personal vision. The ability to engage in some self-analysis often gives us insights into who we are (see Exercise 8–1). If you take out a piece of paper, here are some possible questions for you to consider:

1. What are my five greatest strengths?
2. Who are the five most important people in my life?
3. What are the five major accomplishments I have achieved in the last year?
4. What are the five personal things I want to do for myself in the next year?
5. What are the five work products I want to produce in the next year?
6. When I die, what are the five things I want people to say about me?

As you answer the above questions, ask yourself why the five things you discuss are important. What feelings are created as a result?

Commitment is another competency involved in emotional depth. When you add purpose to your level of commitment and your need to be accountable for your actions, you also need to be aware that you may have some resistance to the changes required to carry out your vision (Cooper & Sawaf, 1996). Underlying the discussion of commitment is to also abide by ethical standards of behavior. Accountability involves the practice of ethical behavior in a committed way. For Goleman (2001), commitment is significantly associated with leadership. The third competency of integrity is closely tied to the commitment and accountability competence. Integrity is clearly also a part of trustworthiness. Integrity involves the recognition of the difference between right and wrong. Cooper and Sawaf (1996) called this *discernment* and said that discernment needs to be tied to personal actions and the way words are used to explain action. Thus both the competency of commitment and the competency of integrity speak to the importance of ethical standards and how they affect thought and feelings. Integrity really gets to the heart of the question of what the leader represents to those who follow.

The final competency related to emotional depth is influence without authority. Influence must occur without manipulation or without authority (Cooper & Sawaf, 1996). Influence involves perception, relationships, innovations, setting priorities, empathy, and taking account of emotional reasons for actions and not just the logical analyses only. Successful leaders have influence regardless of the positions they occupy. People who are influential seem to have high energy and the ability to motivate others. They respond to the show of emotion in an understanding and non-threatening manner. For Goleman (2001), influence serves as the core of the relationship management component of his model. One way to demonstrate this is through the use of leadership stories (Cooper & Sawaf, 1996). When you read a story of someone whom you consider to be a leader, look specifically for the role of the influence competency in their demonstration of their leadership (review Case Study 6).

The final cornerstone in this model of emotional intelligence is emotional alchemy. Emotional intelligence is about synergy and about how to use your emotions to create more value in the things you do. The four competencies tied to this final cornerstone include intuitive flow, reflective time shifting, creating the future, and opportunity sensing. In discussing the idea of flow, Csikszentmihalyi (1990) defined *flow* as related to the positive aspects of life and human experience. Flow is demonstrated through such emotional processes as joy, creativity, total immersion in actions and all of life's experiences. Flow indicates a total concentration and involvement in what you are doing. Flow actually can be controlled and not left to chance. Intuitive flow is tied to strong feelings of self-worth and personal satisfaction (Cooper & Sawaf, 1996). The ability to experience intuitive flow is almost like an ability to see the real meaning of things, even when they seem obscured by rational thought. Leaders with this competency, learn to use the intuition they have in more effective ways.

The next competency expands the concept of self-reflection to address the issue of shifting time. People sense time in unique ways. Some of us notice changing daylight patterns. Some of us check our wrist or pocket watches on a regular basis. Some of us let another staff member or family member remind us of where we are supposed to be. With the skill of reflective time shifting, the emotionally competent leader can picture events in the past, the present, and the future. Shifting time also requires shifting perspectives on events. This competency allows the leader to learn to shift reactions and feeling states to a given situation at a moment's notice. Cooper and Sawaf (1996) called this *feeling yourself in time*. This set of competencies is very critical in visioning activities, which will be discussed in more detail in Chapter 16. The next two competencies are related to visioning as well. The first is the competency of opportunity sensing. Leaders need to sense things and to push traditional sensory limits. This can be called an *extension of the opportunity horizon* (Cooper & Sawaf, 1996). Leaders work to expand their awareness and to explore the larger field of possibilities. This is sometimes referred to as thinking (and sensing things) outside the box. The final competency relates to creating the future with a vision to guide the process. Goleman (2001) subsumed these three competencies within the general competency of visionary leadership.

The third framework listed in Table 9–1 is somewhat different from these first two discussed frameworks. The Feldman (1999) framework is very practical and built on words that are less technical than the categories discussed above. The Feldman model is also clearly based on the emotional intelligence competencies for leaders. This model integrates many of the above competencies into five core skills:

- Knowing yourself
- Maintaining control
- Reading others
- Perceiving accurately
- Communicating with flexibility

It is necessary for a leader to learn these basic skills before he or she goes on to develop higher-level skills such as learning to take responsibility, learning to generate different choices, developing and embracing a vision, having courage, and demonstrating resolve. This model is of interest because it tries to distinguish different levels of emotional intelligence. If you take the lifelong perspective on leadership that was explained in the leadership pyramid in Chapter 1, it seems obvious that different skills and competencies are needed at different points in a leader's career. If emotional intelligence skills expand over time, then it is clear that leaders should hone these skills as they go through life.

The first Feldman competency of knowing yourself is an obvious component in all emotional intelligence frameworks. It entails the recognition of personal emotional reactions, the ability to understand how emotions impact action, and also how to differentiate an emotion such as anger and how it is perceived in different social situations. My anger on a freeway shows itself in interesting ways while my anger at a coworker is displayed in entirely different ways. Look at a leadership challenge you face and the emotions you display. How does your decision-making process change when you learn to control your emotional reaction to the challenge?

This first core competency affects the second competency of controlling emotions (maintaining control). The important concern for the prepared public health leader is how the leader controls emotions during an emergency situation. Others will respond to the leader in terms of the emotions that they see displayed. Others expect their leaders to appear calm during a crisis. In fact, maintaining control is all about remaining calm when chaos reigns (Feldman, 1999). If a leader feels that his or her emotions are getting out of control, the leader needs to briefly step back from a chaotic situation and take a deep breath. The leader in stressful situations needs to think of positive outcomes.

The third competency of reading others is in many ways similar to the empathy competency in the other two frameworks. It not only involves an awareness of the emotions of other people, but it also involves the appreciation of the emotions of others as well as excitement involved in the diversity of other perspectives. Leaders increase their impact when they better understand the reactions of others to crisis as well as other noncrisis situations. This competency also requires active listening. Respect needs to be shown to others as well. The fourth competency of accurate perception is also related to this third competency. Leaders need to develop skills in assessing different types of situations. They also need to be guided by a vision as pointed out in the first two framework models. Leaders as systems thinkers need to keep their view on the big picture and try to maintain their objectivity if at all possible.

The final core competency is the importance of learning to be flexible when communicating with others (Feldman, 1999). Flexibility is all about bringing our verbal and nonverbal words and actions into alignment. The messages that we send need to be clear. Others will listen to our words, but also pay attention to our actions. Leaders need to be aware that not everyone will react to them in the same way. There are clearly many ramifications to our words and deeds.

In this section, three frameworks of emotional intelligence have been presented. The first two frameworks have assessment tools tied to the frameworks. The third framework is clearly a more practical one with guidelines for developing each of the competencies discussed. If you would like to experiment more with emotional intelligence models, look at the Bradberry and Greaves (2003) book which is close to the Goleman framework and then take the online version of the emotional intelligence assessment tool developed by the authors. Both the Goleman and the Cooper and Sawaf models also have assessment tools associated with their work.

PEOPLE-SMART STRATEGIES

Kravitz and Schubert (2000) reviewed the various models of emotional intelligence and believed that this field needs to be tied to an applied perspective that they designated *people-smart strategies*. People need to learn how to make choices in their lives. These choices extend to all the things you say and do. People-smart strategies mean you have to not only think smart but also act smart. There is a need for working smart. To think smart is to understand how you function as a person, to learn self-awareness skills, to practice optimistic thinking by thinking positively, to value the work you do, develop a support network, and learn the skills related to caring. The three aspects of being smart involve the learning of communication skills to effectively talk to others, learning to control emotions, and developing flexibility to change. People-smart strategies then are adaptive emotional intelligence which translate into the following activities:

1. Flexibility in communication
2. Personal stress management
3. Helping others who express pessimism about the future
4. Show respect for others
5. Manage work rage
6. Become a servant leader

SUMMARY

Dr. Arnold Levin, the founding President Emeritus of the Institute for Clinical Social Work in Chicago, looked at the issue of leadership and emotional intelligence. His observations on the topic can be found in Case Study 9. This chapter has viewed the evolving awareness of the importance of emotional intelligence in leadership. Three different models were reviewed related to the competencies necessary for emotional intelligence. The three models together give a comprehensive view of the topic. Many other writers are also studying and developing emotional intelligence frameworks and assessment tools. It clearly is an area of importance. The prepared public health leader will need to be a technical expert, cognitively aware, and emotionally competent.

CASE STUDY 9	A Public Health Practice Quiz for Arnold Levin

1. Why is there an increasing interest in emotional intelligence in leadership?

   Interest in emotional intelligence for leaders has been growing at least since the end of WWII, when Holly Whyte studied and wrote about "the organization man," and the widespread introduction of psychological tests to select leaders for the burgeoning expansion of corporations. Of course, Shakespeare wrote about the dangers to all when "men in high places" (e.g., leaders) exhibited signs of derangement. We seem to have achieved more sophistication than ever in defining, measuring, and predicting who will behave well as leaders, although there are some of us who remain somewhat unconvinced. Nevertheless, even among us doubters there is no question about how important emotional intelligence is in successful leadership, whether on baseball teams, assembly lines, corporate management, or among political leaders. As we have become less dependent on "seat of the pants" judgements, and attend to more "scientific" measures, increasing interest is generated.

2. What are the behavioral components in emotional intelligence?

   Probably the two most significant behavioral components in the emotional intelligence tool box are: the ability to listen to and to hear what others are communicating; and to supplement that process by attending to nonverbal communications simultaneously.

   Heinz Kohut, the psychoanalytic father of self-psychology wrote at length about the importance of *empathic* listening, and used the example of the clever auto salesman emphasizing "looks" to one customer, and the intricacies of the sound system and the engine to the next one, depending on how he read their respective interests.

3. Are emotional intelligence skills really more important than technical and cognitive skills in leaders?

   I think it depends on many factors as to which is more or less important. In a physics lab, I doubt that a clinical social worker who is extremely adept with emotional intelligence but knows nothing about Heisinger's Uncertainty Principle would be likely to command the respect of the physicist workers, and would therefore not be accepted as their leader. However, in the defined role of leader/manager of a complex organization that included physicists or mechanics, and others, he or she might well put emotional intelligence to work to establish his or herself as an acceptable leader, even without the technical skills of the personnel. Professional managers always need managerial and organizational skills.

4. Can we teach people to be more emotionally competent?

   Yes, we can teach people to be more emotionally competent.

continues

CASE STUDY 9 *continued*

5. What is your formula for a successful leader?
A successful leader
 a. Has confidence based on competence, within the parameters of his or her assigned or assumed role
 b. Uses his or her emotional intelligence to bring out creativity among those being led
 c. Is able to define the purposes of the organization in a way that permits and encourages others to join in, both in fine-tuning purposes of the organization as well as carrying them out

REFERENCES

Bradberry, T., & Greaves, J. (2003). *The emotional intelligence quickbook*. San Diego: Talent Smart.

Burns, J. M. (1978). *Leadership*. New York: Harper and Row.

Cooper, R. K., & Sawaf, A. (1996). *Executive EQ*. New York: Perigee Books.

Csikszentmihalyi, M. (1990). *Flow*. New York: Harper Perennial.

Feldman, D. A. (1999). *The handbook of emotionally intelligent leadership*. Falls Church, VA: Performance Solutions Press.

Forman, L. (1999). Directing the heart. In K. M. Ovitsky & L. Forman (Eds.), *Sacred intentions*. Woodstock, VT: Jewish Lights.

Goleman, D. (1995). *Emotional intelligence*. New York: Bantam Books.

Goleman, D. (1998a). Who makes a leader. *Harvard Business Review, 76*(6), 94–102.

Goleman, D. (1998b). *Working with emotional intelligence*. New York: Bantam Books.

Goleman, D. (2001). Emotional intelligence: Issues in paradigm building. In C. Cherniss & D. Goleman (Eds.), *The emotionally intelligent workplace*. San Francisco: Jossey-Bass.

Heifetz, R. A., & Linsky, M. (2002). *Leadership on the line*. Boston: Harvard Business School Press.

Kouzes, J., & Posner, B. (2002). *The leadership challenge* (3rd ed.). San Francisco: Jossey-Bass.

Kravitz, S. M., & Schubert, J. D. (2000). *Emotional intelligence works*. Menlo Park, CA: Crisp Learning.

Mayer, J. D., & Salovey, P. (1993). The intelligence of emotional intelligence. *Intelligence, 17*(4), 433–442.

Rowitz, L. (2001). *Public health leadership: Putting principles into practice*. Sudbury, MA: Jones and Bartlett.

Turning Point. (2004). *Collaborative leadership learning modules*. Seattle: Turning Point National Office (R. W. Johnson Foundation).

CHAPTER 10

Public Health Law and Ethics

One of the chief organizing forces for
public health lies in the system of law.

—*Bernard J. Turnock*

Norms, values, and laws give structure to our personal and social lives.
Laws define what we can do and what we are not supposed to do. In the
United States, the Declaration of Independence and the Constitution
define the structure and parameters of our way of life. The Founding
Fathers were visionary and created documents that were flexible enough
to adapt to the changes that time and events have brought. The prepared
public health leader must understand the context in which he or she lives
and works. The laws become tools to define public action and process.
Our society and way of life have been under attack for the last several
years. It is now critical for leaders to develop competencies related to
understanding the law and how to use it. This does not mean that all prepared public health leaders need to become lawyers, but it does mean that
lawyers and political scientists may need to be consulted when our understanding of the law and legal process is limited. This chapter will look at
the law and what the prepared public health leader needs to know.

On a personal note, I would like to put the following discussion in
context. As a young man, I went to law school for a year. I struggled that
year because I could not make the study of law real for me. It was too
abstract. As I have gotten older, I have discovered the importance of
understanding law within a social or work-related context. Law requires

an ecological context to become real. As a public health professional, I have learned about the need to see public health within the social fabric of our society. Norms, values, law, political structure, and community context all become integrated and thus change will occur at the intersection of all these social and political processes. Thus, public health in the United States does not look like public health structures in Africa or Asia. The prepared public health leader needs to know the territory in which he or she works. Knowing about the law and the impact of laws on our daily lives needs to be part of a lifelong learning agenda for the leader. It is very important to study the impacts of the laws and the unique forms that laws take in different local jurisdictions.

THE MEANING OF THE LAW

The word *law* relates to the legal system, the legal process, the profession of lawyers and their partners, and finally to legal knowledge and experience and training (Neuberger & Christoffel, 2002). The functions of laws and regulations are to regulate behavior, protect the rights of individuals and their property rights, define the duties and responsibilities of government and individuals, guide the judiciary, and provide strong ethical standards for the residents of the jurisdiction and the country as a whole. The law comes in several flavors: constitutionally-based law, statutory law, regulatory law, and common law. It is also important to see the differences in types of law. For example, statutory law is legislatively based, and regulatory law is more administratively based.

It is an inherent responsibility of the state to promote the health and well-being of the population (Gostin, 2000). The state needs to assure the right conditions for people to be healthy. The state does this through the identification, prevention, and amelioration of the risk factors to good health in the community. Gostin (2000) believed in the limitation of the state to "constrain the autonomy, privacy, liberty, proprietary, or other legally protected interests of individuals for protection or promotion of community health." Public health law is based then on the role of the government in promoting the health of its citizens, the importance of population-based approaches to health, the important relationships between the state and its citizens, evidence-based services and scientific methodologies, and the legal concerns related to coercion. There is an important ethical issue related to coercion: how much can the state assure conformance with health and safety standards without the use of some coercion?

The major controversy then relates to the issue of personal rights of citizens and how much the government can do to affect these rights. Much discussion relates to the issue of police powers. A review of the United States Constitution does not mention the term "police powers." Police powers are inferred from the powers that governments have to protect the health, safety, welfare, and general quality of life of the citizens of a jurisdiction (Neuberger & Christoffel, 2002). It also seems that police powers are associated with the authority of a state. States can give local governments the authority to exercise police powers. How police powers can be enacted differs in the various states. Within the public health context, police powers involved with jurisdictional variations involves all laws and regulations that have been enacted to improve morbidity and mortality within a given population (Gostin, 2000). Police powers have been used at various times to promote and preserve public health in activities ranging from injury and disease prevention to air and water quality. Police powers have also been used in vaccination, isolation and quarantine, inspection of residential and commercial premises for many health- and injury-related issues, concerns about unsanitary conditions such as rodents in restaurants, health nuisances of various kinds, air and water contamination, closing of beaches with *E. coli* problems, pure food and drinking water contamination, fluoridation issues, and licensure of health professionals (Gostin, 2000).

Much discussion has been raised in recent years about the relationship between police powers and personal freedoms. This is a very complex issue that cannot be fully discussed here. However, the issue becomes critical during emergency situations. Leaders need to be cognizant of the concerns of Americans about their civil rights. Utilizing police powers must also recognize how people will react to the loss of their personal rights when balanced against the need to protect the community as a whole. Exercising police powers carries a strong trust of the government concern with it (Gostin, 2000). There are issues in public health law between volunteerism and coercion. Leaders will struggle to gain compliance with public health protocols in communities with a volunteer approach or a police powers approach.

To better prepare public health leaders for the legal issues of public health, a new training program is being developed for state and local health professional staff (Munson, 2004). This new training program is being developed in collaboration with Dr. Richard Goodman of the

Public Health Law Program of the Centers for Disease Control and Prevention. The fundamental principles behind this new CD-ROM based course will be basic sources and authorities, ethics, and administrative law. The course, to be rolled out during 2005, is tentatively planned to include nine study modules including the following:

1. Basic Sources and Authorities
2. Ethics
3. Administrative Law
4. Roles of Legal Counsel for Public Health Agencies
5. Surveillance, Outbreak Investigations, and Emergencies
6. Privacy Issues
7. Infectious Diseases
8. Environmental and Occupational Diseases, and Injuries
9. Chronic Diseases, Birth Defects, and Other Noninfectious Conditions

The series of nine units may also be offered as well in a 1- to $1^1/_2$-day public health law conference. Other formats will also be possible.

The Public Health Training Network course by Neuberger and Christoffel (2002) is a more advanced 10-module course with a well-developed coordinator guide. This course includes the following modules:

1. Introduction
2. Data Collection and Surveillance
3. Service Delivery
4. Licensing
5. Inspections
6. Enforcement
7. Policy Development
8. Negotiation
9. Communication
10. Responsibility and Liability

This legal basis of public health course has exercises associated with each of the modules. To put some of the thinking of this course and others on the law, Exercise 10–1 will require you to do a little homework. Divide your class or training group into groups of 6–8. Find the answers to the questions delineated in the exercise. This exercise is included in the first module of the course. If you feel that you would like to review module 1

EXERCISE 10-1 Legal Research

Purpose: To use the Internet or library to learn about legal terminology

Key Concepts: Public health law, statutes, ordinance

Procedures: Use the Internet or library to answer the questions.

1. Where, in your jurisdiction, can you find the actual text of the following:
   - State statutes
   - State regulations
   - Local municipal codes
   - State judicial opinions
2. Have you ever used a law library to find such material? How would you describe the experience?
3. What do the following citations mean:
   - Fla. Stat. § 828, 12 (1987)
   - 40 CFR Subpart A, § 46.101
   - Ordinance 87-40
   - 494 U.S. 829 (1989)?
4. How would you go about determining if certain physical conditions amount to a "public nuisance"? Would you look to statute/code or the common law? Whom could you contact to get this information?

---

of the course, the module can be downloaded from the CDC Web site for the Public Health Training Network (www.cdc.gov/phtn).

PUBLIC HEALTH LAW COMPETENCIES

The major question a prepared public health leader asks is related to how much a nonlawyer working in public health needs to know. As in other parts of public health, the issue of core competencies gets raised when the law is discussed. The Center for Law and the Public's Health at Johns Hopkins and Georgetown Universities have reviewed this issue and developed a framework of core competencies for public health professionals. Input into the development of the core legal competencies document was accomplished using a multidisciplinary group of lawyers and other public health professionals who were brought together in June 2001. Prior to that meeting, further input was received from multiple respondents in a national electronic survey conducted by the Public Health Foundation in Washington, D.C., along with feedback from several national public health and public policy organizations including the Association of State and Territorial Health Officials, the National Association of County and City Health Officials, the American Public Health Association, the National Association of Local Boards of Health, and the National Council of State Legislatures.

The final list of core legal competencies is linked to the set of core public health competencies discussed in Chapter 5 (Council on Linkages Between Academia and Public Health Practice, 2001). Secondly, the competency list was stratified for three different levels of public health professionals—frontline professional staff (F), senior-level professional staff (S), and supervisory and management staff (M). The framework adds a fourth group of health officials and governance boards (O). Table 10–1 reproduces the list of core legal competencies. As can be seen, seven competency areas are designated (Center for Law and the Public's Health, 2001a):

1. Public Health Powers
2. Regulatory Authority/Administrative Law
3. Ascertaining Authority/Obtaining Legal Advice
4. Law and Public Health Services and Functions
5. Legal Actions
6. Legal Limitations
7. Personal/Contracts Law

Case Study 10–A presents an interesting mix of legal issues in which the courts, state legislatures, public health departments, and other interested parties came together on a controversial set of issues related to the Master Tobacco Settlement Agreement. The case writers presented several interesting questions as part of the case; these are included for your discussion. To these questions, it is possible to add the question of what legal competencies were necessary on the part of the public health leaders in this case.

STATE REVIEW OF PUBLIC HEALTH LAWS

A notable resolution was adopted by the National Association of Attorneys General in December 2003 urging states to review their public health laws because of all the changes in public health and the American society since September 11, 2001. The resolution can be seen in Figure 10–1. It was strongly believed that many of the state's public health laws were outdated. The Centers for Disease Control and Prevention has named public health law reform to be one of its 10 priorities for building public health infra-

Table 10–1 Public Health Law Competencies

I. Public Health Powers—Generally	Level(s)
A. Describes the basic legal framework for public health; roles of federal, state, and local governments; and the relationship between legislatures, executive agencies, and the courts	F
B. Describes the meaning, source of, and scope of states' powers to protect the public's health, safety, and general welfare (i.e., police powers) and to protect the individual from identifiable harm (i.e., parens patriae powers)	M, O
C. Identifies and applies basic provisions of the governmental unit's health code and regulations within the particular area of practice (e.g., communicable disease control, environmental health, public health nursing)	M, O
D. Describes the scope of statutory and regulatory provisions for emergency powers	O
E. Distinguishes public health agency powers and responsibilities from those of other governmental agencies, executive offices, police, legislatures, and courts	O
II. Regulatory Authority/Administrative Law	
A. Describes basic legal processes, such as how legislatures create and amend laws, how executive officials enforce laws, and how courts make and interpret laws	O
B. Determines procedures for promulgating administrative regulations	O
C. Determines procedures for obtaining mandatory or prohibitory injunctions from a court	O
D. Follows administrative procedure laws for conducting investigations, holding hearings, promulgating regulations, and provisions concerning open public records	M, O
E. Weighs options and applies, when necessary, processes to address public health problems through criminal charges for specific behaviors and civil suits for damages	O
III. Ascertaining Authority/Obtaining Legal Advice	
A. Identifies legal issues for which legal advice should be sought and knows what action to take where legal issues arise, including contacting legal advisors	M, O
B. Provides factual assistance and states basic legal issues to legal advisors	M, O

continues

Table 10–1 *continued*

III. Ascertaining Authority/Obtaining Legal Advice	Level(s)
C. Reads and comprehends basic statutory and administrative laws	M, O
D. Recognizes that legal rules do not always specify a course of conduct	M, O
E. Effectively integrates legal information into the exercise of professional public health judgement	M, O
F. Develops enforcement strategies consistent with the law and in the interest of protecting the public's health	M, O
IV. Law and Public Health Services and Functions	
A. Describes how law and legal practices contribute to the current health status of the population	O
B. Determines how the law can be used as a tool in promoting and protecting the public's health	M, O
C. Identifies the mechanisms through which law can deter, encourage or compel health-related behaviors	M, O
D. Identifies and exercises legal authorities, responsibilities, and restrictions to assure or provide health care services to populations	M, O
E. Identifies and exercises legal authority over the quality, delivery, and evaluation of health care services within the agency's jurisdictions	M, O
F. Applies ethical principles to the development, interpretation, and enforcement of laws	F, M, O
V. Legal Actions	
A. Describes how and under what circumstances legal searches of private premises can be performed	S, M, O
B. Knows how and under what circumstances legal seizures of private property for public health purposes can take place	S, M, O
C. Describes the limits of authority for legally closing private premises	S, M, O
D. Identifies legal authority for compelling medical treatment or instituting mandatory screening programs	S, M, O
E. Knows legal authority for imposing quarantine, isolation, or other restrictions on the movement or placement of persons	S, M, O
F. Identifies provisions for the issuance, revocation, or suspension of licenses, and decides what actions to take to protect the public's health	S, M, O

continues

Table 10–1 *continued*

V. Legal Actions	Level(s)
G. Adheres to confidentiality laws in the collection, mainte-nance, and release of data	S, F, M, O
VI. Legal Limitations	
A. Recognizes prominent constitutional rights implicated through the practice of public health (e.g., freedom of speech, right to assemble, freedom from unreasonable searches and seizures, right to privacy, due process, equal protection) and the analytic techniques courts use in enforcing these rights	S, M, O
B. Recognizes federal, state, and local statutes or ordinances and major federal or state cases granting rights to individuals and limiting public health authority	S, M, O
C. Describes legal protections regarding minors and incompetent persons	S, M, O
D. Acknowledges the sources of potential civil and criminal liability of public health workers	S, M, O
VII. Personnel/Contracts Law	
A. Implements practices to legally hire, discharge, and discipline employees	M, O
B. Applies essential tenets of antidiscrimination laws, such as the Americans with Disabilities Act (ADA) affecting employment practices and the delivery of services	F, M, O
C. Develops contractual terms when contracting for the delivery of essential public health services that serve to protect the public's health	M, O
D. Negotiates, develops, complies with, and terminates contracts with other persons, organizations, and agencies for the provision of essential public health services	M, O

F = frontline professional staff; S = senior-level professional staff; M = super-visory and management staff; O = health officials and governance boards

structure and improving public health outcomes (CDC, 2001). In recent years, a number of states have been updating or revising their public health laws. One interesting example of this is discussed below in the Illinois experience. However, the updating and revision of these laws has not been a consistent enterprise across the country (Gostin & Hodge, 2002).

States have defined public health in different ways in their laws and statutes. Table 10–2 presents some of these statutory definitions of public

CASE STUDY 10-A   Master Tobacco Settlement Agreement: A Three-State Comparison of the Allocation of Funds

Case Study in Policy Development
Red, White, and Glue Year 10 Team
Jo Ambrose
Karen Kunsemiller
Emil Makar
Phyllis Pelt
Charlene Stevens
Laura Thomas

Tobacco use is the single most preventable cause of death and disease in our society. Cigarette smoking causes heart disease, several kinds of cancer (lung, larynx, esophagus, pharynx, mouth, and bladder), and chronic lung disease. Cigarette smoking also contributes to cancer of the pancreas, kidney, and cervix. Smoking during pregnancy can cause spontaneous abortions, low birth weight, and sudden infant death syndrome. Annually, tobacco use causes more than 430,000 deaths and costs the nation between $50–73 billion in medical expenses alone. These expenses have increasingly become a critical responsibility for the states to attempt to address.

In November 1998, 46 states, the District of Columbia and five U.S. territories settled their Medicaid lawsuits against five of the largest tobacco manufacturers (Phlegm Balls Inc., Money Suckers Group, Breath Rotters, Cancerettes, and Malignant Tumors). The industry committed to pay the states approximately $206 billion over the next 25 years for recovery of their tobacco-related health care costs. The tobacco settlement, known as the Master Settlement Agreement (MSA), presented the states with an opportunity to reduce the terrible burden exacted by tobacco on the states' economies. In the MSA, there was no obligation for the states to spend this money on tobacco control programs, which would ultimately lead to a reduced death toll from tobacco. However, most states promised to use a significant portion of the settlement funds to attack the public health problem posed by tobacco in the United States.

The Centers for Disease Control and Prevention (CDC) recommended that states establish tobacco control programs that were comprehensive, sustainable, and accountable. The four main goals were to prevent the initiation of tobacco use by young people, promote cessation among adults, eliminate nonsmokers' exposure to secondhand smoke, and eliminate disparities related to tobacco among various population groups. To reduce smoking rates considerably, each state needed to invest a substantial amount in new or expanded integrated tobacco control initiatives. Specific

continues

CASE STUDY 10-A *continued*

funding ranges and programmatic recommendations were provided for each state. Approximate annual costs to implement all of the recommended program components were estimated to range from $6 to $17 per capita in medium-sized states.

Each state legislature had the opportunity to make the decision regarding how to spend the money that was received from the MSA. The decisions made by three of the states will be presented. These states were State of Confusion, State Wanna Be, and Exemplary State. These are medium-sized states with comparable populations. State of Confusion received $300 million for year 2000-2001, State Wanna Be received $304 million, while Exemplary State received $306 million. For each of the three states, the final decisions made by the state legislatures for the 2000-2001 fiscal year regarding the MSA moneys will be presented as well as how these allocation decisions were reached.

State of Confusion

For five years prior to the MSA, State of Confusion was spending approximately $8 million annually on tobacco prevention and control programs such as prevention of youth initiation, smoking cessation, and prevention of secondhand smoke exposure. Since establishing these programs, there was no substantial decrease in the use of tobacco and no significant reduction in the number of deaths due to tobacco. The Centers for Disease Control and Prevention's recommended range of funding for tobacco prevention and control programs for the State of Confusion was $65-181 million annually.

In March 2000, the General Assembly of the State of Confusion met to discuss how to distribute the $300 million the state had received. The meeting was limited only to members of the General Assembly. No members of outside groups such as the public health department, smoking prevention advocate groups, health care providers such as hospitals, and managed care organizations were allowed to witness the proceedings. Representative Upfore Reelection was the first speaker. He started the discussion by stating that most of the settlement money if not all of it should go back to the taxpayers. It belongs to them because they already paid and continue to pay for the tobacco-related health care costs. This money is a payback to them for what they already spent and continue to spend. It does not mean we should add more dollars to prevent smoking because this money was not given to the state for that reason. "I recommend we allocate the money to be used as a tax credit and urge you to support this decision," said Representative Upfore Reelection. Representative Veri Sensible, a school of public health graduate, objected to her colleague's

continues

CASE STUDY 10-A   *continued*

opinion. She stated that spending extra dollars on smoking prevention would save the taxpayers a tremendous amount of money in the future. The conclusive evidence is that comprehensive state tobacco prevention and control programs can reduce tobacco use and the economic burden of tobacco-related diseases. This type of heated discussion continued until July 2000.

During the discussions, the State of Confusion did not include any of the essential public health services to determine how to allocate the money. No tobacco experts were consulted with to determine how the funds should be divided. The legislators made all of the decisions.

Distribution of Dollars State of Confusion

Tobacco Settlement Funds (TSF) Received 2000–2001: $300 Million
CDC Recommendation for Tobacco Prev. and Control: $65–181 Million

Programs that have a direct effect on tobacco prevention and control:

Amount Allocated ($ millions)	Description
5	Youth Prevention
5	Adult Cessation
3	Eliminate Secondhand Smoke Exposure

TOTAL	$13 million
% of TSF	4.3%
% of CDC Minimum	20.0%

Programs that have an effect on public health:

Amount Allocated ($ millions)	Description
12	HIV/AIDS Research
20	Diabetes Research
25	Gang Prevention

TOTAL	$57 million
% of TSF	19.0%

Programs that do not have an effect on tobacco prevention and control nor public health:

Amount Allocated ($ millions)	Description
40	Rainy Day Fund
40	State Prisons
50	State Tobacco Farmers
100	Tax Credit

TOTAL	$230 million
% of TSF	77.0%

continues

CASE STUDY 10-A *continued*

State Wanna Be

State Wanna Be was an industrial state and had suffered recently from a slowing economy, which led to a significant increase in the number of people with incomes below poverty level. According to Healthy People 2010, individuals who are poor are significantly more likely to smoke than individuals of middle or high income (34% compared to 21%). Before the MSA, State Wanna Be was spending about $20 million annually on tobacco prevention and control programs. A major source of funding was a cigarette excise tax. Data from Healthy People 2010 indicated that (1) increasing excise taxes on cigarettes is one of the most cost-effective short-term strategies to reduce tobacco consumption among adults and to prevent initiation among youth and (2) the ability to sustain lower consumption increases when the tax increase is combined with an anti-smoking campaign. Since establishing these programs, the rate of tobacco use had been slightly decreasing steadily. The Centers for Disease Control and Prevention's recommended range of funding for tobacco prevention and control programs for State Wanna Be was $63–177 million annually.

In April 2000, the General Assembly of State Wanna Be met to discuss how to distribute the $304 million the state had received through the MSA. The initial meetings were limited only to members of the General Assembly. However, the Master Settlement Agreement State Committee had several public meetings in order to listen to various groups' points of view and how the groups thought the money should be spent. Represented at the hearings were members of the public health department, nonprofit health organizations, the highway safety and control commission, police and fire departments, state and private universities, and students and administrators from grade schools, junior highs, and high schools across the state. Mr. Keepa Low Profile, the Director of the State Wanna Be Public Health Department, was unable to completely express how he thought the money should be divided due to the fact that this topic was a very political issue. His proposal was very similar to the one the Governor was promoting. The nonprofit health organizations pushed for the money to follow the CDC recommended guidelines for "best practices." The highway safety and control commission articulated that there was a real need for the highways of the state to be repaired. Policemen and firemen thought the money should be used for new patrol cars with the latest technology and new fire trucks. They felt this would keep the residents of State Wanna Be safe. The state and private universities suggested a new scholarship fund be set up for the residents, who would otherwise be unable to attend college. The reasoning was that this would allow those individuals

continues

CASE STUDY 10-A   *continued*

that were poor to receive an education and therefore be less likely to smoke. Students spoke on how they were the targets of the tobacco industry and they would like to see the money spent on youth prevention and cessation.

A total of two hearings were held, one in May and the other in June. The legislators took into account what the members of their state said; however, in the long run the ultimate decision still rested on the legislators. The final allocations were decided on in July of 2000. State Wanna Be, through the assistance of the nonprofit health organizations, used the essential public health service of evaluating the effectiveness, accessibility, and quality of personal and population-based health services. In addition from the students' recommendations, the state developed policies and plans that supported community health efforts.

Distribution of Dollars State Wanna Be

Tobacco Settlement Funds (TSF) Received 2000–2001: $304 Million
CDC Recommendation for Tobacco Prev. and Control: $63–177 Million

Programs that have a direct effect on tobacco prevention and control:

Amount Allocated ($ millions)	Description
13	Youth Prevention
9	Adult Cessation
7	Eliminate Secondhand Smoke Exposure
11	Eliminate Disparities Related to Tobacco
TOTAL $40 million	
% of TSF 13.0%	
% of CDC Minimum 63.0%	

Programs that have an effect on public health:

Amount Allocated ($ millions)	Description
5	Dental Research
15	Diabetes Research
25	Cardiovascular Disease Prevention Improvement of Health Care System for
50	Low SES Individuals
TOTAL $95 million	
% of TSF 31.0%	

continues

CASE STUDY 10-A *continued*

Programs that do not have an effect on tobacco prevention and control nor public health:

Amount Allocated ($ millions)	Description
35	Restructuring of Selected Golf Courses
34	State Highway Safety and Control Commission
100	College Scholarship Fund
TOTAL $169 million	
% of TSF 56.0%	

Exemplary State

Exemplary State had relatively no experience or knowledge concerning the state's tobacco problem. Before the MSA, Exemplary State was indirectly spending money on tobacco prevention but no true dollar amount could be calculated. The Centers for Disease Control and Prevention's recommended range of funding for tobacco prevention and control programs for Exemplary State was $64–176 million annually.

In February 2000, the General Assembly of Exemplary State met to discuss how to distribute the $306 million the state had received through the MSA. The initial meetings were limited only to members of the General Assembly, however a few concerned senators and representatives investigated and consulted with national, state, and local tobacco authorities. Senator Pre Vention stated that an initial assessment needed to be done to ascertain where and which programs were needed. Statistics on current cigarette use by youth and adults and the average annual deaths related to smoking were gathered for each county. Next, Representative Breathe Easy spoke about the need to develop policies and plans. This would ensure that the money that was received over the next 25 years would be put to the best possible use. One of the policies he felt strongly about was eliminating exposure to secondhand smoke in workplaces, restaurants, and homes. After doing some of his own investigating, Representative Elimi Nate Cancer thought that focusing on adult cessation would ultimately lead to youth prevention. Senator Oso Smart agreed with her colleagues and added that there was a definite need for a competent tobacco prevention workforce. This workforce should not only be in the community offering direct services but also mobilizing the community to sustain the comprehensive tobacco prevention and control efforts once the tobacco workforce had left the community. After these initial discoveries the state held three hearings that were open to the public and many members of the

continues

CASE STUDY 10-A *continued*

state attended. The final decision of how to spend the $306 million was decided in June of 2000.

Exemplary State decided to follow the CDC recommended guidelines for how to spend their money. Since the state is an exemplary state it followed several of the essential public health services. Representative Pre Vention ensured that the health problems of the community were identified and diagnosed. She had her staff members research the impact tobacco has had on the state. Representative Breathe Easy made certain that there were policies and plans in place that supported individual and community tobacco efforts. A competent public health workforce was put in place due to Senator Oso Smart's insight.

Distribution of Dollars Exemplary State

Tobacco Settlement Funds (TSF) Received 2000–2001: $306 Million
CDC Recommendation for Tobacco Prev. and Control: $64–176 Million

Programs that have a direct effect on tobacco prevention and control:

Amount Allocated ($ millions)	Description
20	Community Programs to Reduce Tobacco Use
5	Chronic Disease Programs to Reduce Burden of Tobacco Related Diseases
13	School Programs
10	Enforcement
10	Statewide Programs
21	Countermarketing
47	Cessation Programs
16	Surveillance and Evaluation
8	Administration and Management

TOTAL $150 million
% of TSF   49.0%
% of CDC Minimum   234.0%

Programs that have an effect on public health:

Amount Allocated ($ millions)	Description
11	Prescription Drugs for the Elderly
20	Cancer Research
25	Cardiovascular Disease Prevention
50	Health Insurance Improvements

TOTAL $106 million
% of TSF   35.0%

continues

CASE STUDY 10–A *continued*

Programs that do not have an effect on tobacco prevention and control nor public health:

Amount Allocated ($ millions)	Description
20	College Scholarship Fund
30	Trust Fund
TOTAL $50 million	
% of TSF 16.0%	

These three states along with the other 43 states have the task of deciding how the money should be spent for the next 24 years. Every year the state legislatures will decide how the money will be allocated. Various organizations will lobby the legislators to vote in their favor for funding. With such large amounts of money to be spent and no obligations to spend it on tobacco, the states have an extremely important role in deciding their future responsibilities: the state's economy, and tobacco's toll on themselves and their residents.

CASE STUDY Questions

Master Tobacco Settlement Agreement: A Three-State Comparison of the Allocation of Funds

The intent of the Master Tobacco Settlement Agreement was to enable states and other participants to recover money that had been spent for the treatment of tobacco-related health problems. To this end, states will receive approximately $206 billion dollars over the next 25 years. However, every year each state will determine how the money is allocated. This case study presents a comparison of the allocation of first-year tobacco settlement dollars by three states receiving similar awards.

1. The core public health function of policy development involves advocating for public health, building community constituencies, and identifying resources in the community to meet identified needs. Discuss the policy development activities, or lack thereof, of the three states presented in this case study. What are the strengths and weaknesses of each approach?

2. Additional policy development activities include setting priorities and developing plans to address the health needs of the community. Using the allocation tables in the case study, discuss evidence of these activities in each state's decision-making process.

continues

CASE STUDY 10-A *continued*

3. Discuss all factors that could influence the prioritization process and allocation of tobacco settlement dollars. In what ways do you think the tobacco industry influences the decision-making process?

4. What influence should the CDC guidelines have on the prioritization and allocation process?

5. What can public health advocates, including taxpayers, do to influence decisions regarding the use of tobacco settlement dollars in future years? What strategies should be developed now to sustain tobacco prevention efforts beyond 25 years and protect future generations?

6. Tobacco settlement dollars are intended to replace money used for tobacco-related health problems and to influence future tobacco use. However, other lobbyists can argue that many worthy state projects did not get funded because of tobacco-related expenses and, therefore, should be considered when doling out settlement funds. As a public health advocate, how would you respond to this argument?

Adopted
National Association of Attorneys General
December 2–6, 2003
Williamsburg, Virginia

WHEREAS, every state (territory) has enacted laws to allow for proper response by health officials to public health conditions; and

WHEREAS, the majority of those statutes were passed several decades ago, and, fortunately, have been seldom needed and therefore seldom used, and so are little known; and

WHEREAS, given changes in medical and public health circumstances, the status quo is no longer satisfactory; and

WHEREAS, with the ever increasing mobility of persons, animals and products between towns, states and nations, we have been increasing levels of concern regarding contagion and increasing numbers of public health incidents, such as those involving SARS and *Monkeypox* disease; and

WHEREAS, many of those statutes address limited and previously known health conditions, but are not flexible to address present medical and disease circumstances;

NOW, THEREFORE, be it resolved that the National Association of Attorneys General;

1) encourages states to undertake a review of their public health laws *and the Model State Public Health Act*, and to update those laws to reflect present circumstances; and

2) encourages the education of public health authorities and their counsel on the constitutional and statutory laws related to public health response to assure the best response and preparedness in an emergency; and

3) authorizes its Executive Director to transmit these views.

FIGURE 10-1 A National Resolution on Public Health Laws.

Table 10–2 Statutory Definitions of Public Health in Select States

ST	Stat. Cite	Statutory Definition of Public Health
AL	Ala. Code § 22-21-311; § 22-11A-1; § 22-2-8 (1982).	Public health includes: care of sick, injured, physically disabled or handicapped, mentally ill, retarded or disturbed persons; the prevention of sickness and disease; care, treatment and rehabilitation of alcoholics; and care of elderly persons. Public health includes protection from diseases and health conditions of epidemic potential.
AK	Alaska Stat. § 18.05.010 (2000).	The Department of Health and Social Services shall administer the laws and regulations relating to the promotion and protection of the public health, control of communicable diseases, programs for the improvement of maternal and child health, care of crippled children, and hospitalization of the tuberculous and shall discharge other duties provided by law.
AZ	Ariz. Rev. Stat. § 36-104 (1993).	Public health support services include: (i) Consumer health protection programs, including the functions of community water supplies, general sanitation, vector control and food and drugs; (ii) Epidemiology and disease control programs, including the functions of chronic disease, accident and injury control, communicable diseases, tuberculosis, venereal disease and others; (iii) Laboratory services programs; (iv) Health education and training programs; and (v) Disposition of human bodies program.
CA	Cal. Gov't Code § 855.4 (1995).	Public health of the community includes preventing disease or controlling the communication of disease.
CO	Col. Rev. Stat. § 25-1-107	The department has, in addition to all other powers and duties imposed upon it by law, the following powers and duties: (a) (I) To investigate and control the causes of epidemic and communicable diseases affecting the public health. (II) For the purposes of this paragraph (a), the board shall determine, by rule and regulation, those epidemic and communicable diseases and conditions that are dangerous to the public health.

continues

Table 10–2 *continued*

ST	Stat. Cite	Statutory Definition of Public Health
DE	Del. Code Ann. tit. 29, § 7904(b) (2000).	"Public health and preventative services" are defined as activities that protect people from diseases and injury. They include activities that: (i) prevent and control communicable disease epidemics; (ii) promote healthy behaviors to control chronic disease; (iii) monitor the health of the population through data analysis and epidemiological studies; (iv) result in policies to promote the health of the public; (v) assure quality health services and systems for the population; (vi) result in the setting of standards for the protection of the public's health; (vii) provide assistance during disasters; (viii) assess environmental health risks; and (ix) offer health protection strategies to environmental control agencies.
GA	Ga. Code Ann. § 31-2-1 (2000).	In order to safeguard and promote the health of the people of this state the department is empowered to: (1) Provide epidemiological investigations and laboratory facilities and services in the detection and control of disease, disorders, and disabilities and to provide research, conduct investigations, and disseminate information concerning reduction in the incidence and proper control of disease, disorders, and disabilities; (2) Forestall and correct physical, chemical, and biological conditions that, if left to run their course, could be injurious to health; (3) Regulate and require the use of sanitary facilities at construction sites and places of public assembly and to regulate persons, firms, and corporations engaged in the rental and service of portable chemical toilets; (4) Isolate and treat persons afflicted with a communicable disease; (5) Manufacture drugs and biologicals which are not readily available on the market and not manufactured for commercial purposes; (6) Promote health aspects of civil defense; (7) Detect and relieve physical defects and deformities and provide treatment for mental and emotional disorders and infirmities; (8) Protect dental health; (9) Determine the presence of disease and conditions deleterious to health; and (10) Provide education and treatment in order to prevent unwanted pregnancy.

continues

Table 10–2 *continued*

ST	Stat. Cite	Statutory Definition of Public Health
KY	Ky. Rev. Stat. Ann. § 211.180 (2000).	Matters of public health include detection, prevention, and control of communicable, chronic and occupational diseases; the control of vectors of disease; the safe handling of food and food products; the safety of cosmetics; the control of narcotics, barbiturates, and other drugs as provided by law; the sanitation of public and semipublic buildings and areas; the licensure of hospitals; protection and improvement of the health of expectant mothers, infants, preschool, and school-age children; the practice of midwifery, including the issuance of permits to and supervision of women who practice midwifery; and protection and improvement of the health of the people through better nutrition.
MA	Mass. Gen. Laws ch. 111, § 5 (1996).	The department shall take cognizance of the interests of life, health, comfort and convenience among the citizens of the commonwealth; shall conduct sanitary investigations and investigations as to the causes of disease, and especially of epidemics, and the sale of food and drugs and adulterations thereof; and shall disseminate such information relating thereto as it considers proper. It shall advise the government concerning the location and other sanitary condition of any public institution. It may produce and distribute immunological, diagnostic and therapeutic agents as it may deem advisable.
MI	Mich. Comp. Laws § 333.2221 (1992).	The department shall continually and diligently endeavor to prevent disease, prolong life, and promote the public health through organized programs, including prevention and control of environmental health hazards; prevention and control of diseases; prevention and control of health problems of particularly vulnerable population groups; development of health care facilities and agencies and health services delivery systems; and regulation of health care facilities and agencies and health services delivery systems to the extent provided by law.

continues

Table 10–2 *continued*

ST	Stat. Cite	Statutory Definition of Public Health
MO	Mo. Rev. Stat. § 192.011 (1996).	The department shall monitor the adverse health effects of the environment and prepare population risk assessments regarding environmental hazards including but not limited to those relating to water, air, toxic waste, solid waste, sewage disposal and others. The department shall make recommendations to the department of natural resources for improvement of public health as related to the environment. . . . The department of health shall develop a comprehensive disease prevention plan to expand existing and to develop new programs.
NE	Neb. Rev. Stat. §§ 71-7504, 71-7508 (1992).	Community public health services shall mean services designed to protect and improve the health of persons within a geographically defined community by (1) emphasizing services to prevent illness, disease, and disability, (2) promoting effective coordination and use of community resources, and (3) extending health services into the community. Such services shall include, but not be limited to, community nursing services, home health services, disease prevention and control services, public health education, and public health environmental services. Disease prevention and control services shall mean epidemiology, immunization, case finding and follow-up, continuing surveillance and detection, and prevention of communicable and chronic diseases.
NH	N.H. Rev. Stat. Ann. §§ 125:9, 126-A:4[I] (1995).	The commissioner of the Department of Health and Human Services shall: I. Take cognizance of the interests of health and life among the people; II. Make investigations and inquiries concerning the causes of epidemics and other diseases, the sources of morbidity and mortality, and the effects of localities, employments, conditions, circumstances, and the environment on the public health. The Department shall ". . . provide a comprehensive and coordinated system of health and human services as needed to promote and protect the health, safety, and well-being of the citizens of New Hampshire."

continues

Table 10–2 *continued*

ST	Stat. Cite	Statutory Definition of Public Health
NJ	N.J. Stat. Ann. § 59:6-3 (1992).	Promoting the public health of the community includes preventing disease or controlling the communication of disease within the community.
NY	N.Y. Pub. Health § 602 (1990).	Services that promote the public health (including enhancing or sustaining the public health, protecting the public from the threats of disease and illness, or preventing premature death) include (1) family health services; (2) disease control, which shall include activities to control and mitigate the extent of non-infectious diseases, particularly those of a chronic, degenerative nature, and infectious diseases; (3) health education and guidance, which shall include the use of information and education to modify or strengthen practices that will promote the public health and prevent illness; (4) community health assessment; and (5) environmental health, which shall include activities that promote health and prevent illness by ensuring sanitary conditions in water supplies, food service establishments, and other permit sites, and by abating public health nuisances.
OK	Okla. Stat. tit. 63, § 1-206 (1996).	1. Maintain programs for disease prevention and control, health education, guidance, maternal and child health, including school health services, health in the working environment, nutrition and other matters affecting the public health; 2. Provide preventive services to the chronically ill and aged; 3. Maintain vital records and statistics.
OR	Or. Rev. Stat. § 431.416 (1999).	Local public health authorities or health district shall assure activities necessary for the preservation of health or prevention of disease in the area under its jurisdiction . . . including: (a) Epidemiology and control of preventable diseases and disorders; (b) Parent and child health services, including family planning clinics; (c) Collection and reporting of health statistics; (d) Health information and referral services; and (e) Environmental health services.

continues

Table 10–2 *continued*

ST	Stat. Cite	Statutory Definition of Public Health
SC	S.C. Code Ann. § 44-1-140 (1988).	The Department may adopt rules and regulations requiring and providing: sanitation of public places; regulation of milk and milk products; sanitation of meat markets and bottling plants; sanitation in handling mollusks, finfish, and crustaceans; control of disease-bearing insects; control of industrial plants; care and isolation of people having a communicable disease; regulation of disposition of garbage and sewage; thorough investigation and prevention of all diseases; education to prevent disease.
TX	Tex. Health & Safety § 12.031 (1992).	"Public health services" means: (1) personal health promotion, maintenance, and treatment services; (2) infectious disease control and prevention services; (3) environmental and consumer health protection services; (4) laboratory services; (5) health facility architectural plan review; (6) public health planning, information, and statistical services; (7) public health education and information services; and (8) administration services.
WI	Wis. Stat. § 160.05 (1998).	Public health concerns. (a) The department shall designate which of the substances in each category are of public health concern and which are of public welfare concern. (b) In determining whether a substance is of public health concern, the department shall take into account the degree to which the substance may: 1. Cause or contribute to an increase in mortality; 2. Cause or contribute to an increase in illness or incapacity, whether chronic or acute; 3. Pose a substantial present or potential hazard to human health because of its physical, chemical or infectious characteristics; or 4. Cause or contribute to other adverse human health effects or changes of a chronic or subchronic nature even if not associated with illness or incapacity. (c) In determining whether a substance is of public health concern, the department may consider other effects not specified under par. (d) if those effects are reasonably related to public health.

health to demonstrate the diversity in definitions (Gostin & Hodge, 2002). The other important finding from their survey can be seen in Table 10–3 pointing to the different models various states have used to carry out their public health functions. A survey of state public health deputy directors was undertaken in which 24 states responded (Gostin & Hodge, 2002). Some of their findings include the following:

1. More than 70% of the respondents reported that public health infrastructure bills were introduced in their state legislators although three respondents said the bill had failed to pass.
2. Forty-six percent of the deputy directors reported that their states had not developed comprehensive public health reforms.
3. Hot topics for legislative action as seen by the deputy directors included such topics as tobacco control, HIV/AIDS, minority

Table 10–3 Classification of State and Local Distribution of Public Health Functions

Distributional Approach	Brief Description	States	Total
Centralized (top-down) Approach	The state public health agency either performs directly or regulates the level and extent of public health services provided at the local county or city levels.	AR, FL, LA, MS, NM, SC, VA	7
Decentralized (bottom-up) Approach	The authority and direct responsibility for many public health functions lies at the local county or city level of government.	AZ, CO, CT, ID, IN, IA, ME, MO, MT, NE, NV, NJ, ND, OR, UT, WA, WI	17
Hybrid Approach	The direct responsibility for public health functions are shared between state and local governments.	AL, AK, CA, GA, IL, KA, KY, MD, MA, MI, MN, NH, NC, NY, OH, OK, PA, SD, TN, TX, WV, WY	22

health issues, bioterrorism, emerging infections, immunization rates and registries, cancer prevention, oral health, privacy issues, West Nile virus, and children's health care coverage.

4. State legislatures have considered a variety of comprehensive or limited public health laws since the early 1990s.

The survey was concluded by noting the complexity of the public health laws in America (Gostin & Hodge, 2002). This diversity was a reflection of the variations in the society as a whole. However, the diversity in the laws also complicates the political process. The prepared public health leader needs to learn the laws of his or her jurisdiction both at the local and the state level. The differences in laws are also demonstrated in the different forms that the public health system takes in different areas of the country. The reform of the state and eventually the local public health system will involve not only the modernization of the legal bases of public health practice, but innovative ways to implement any changes proposed in a rather fragmented health care system. A proposal was presented for the development of a model state public health act within a national public health system. This model act is discussed in the next section of this chapter.

MODEL STATE PUBLIC HEALTH ACT

To clarify the role of public health in the 21st century and to better understand the diversity of laws defining state and local public health requirements, the Turning Point Public Health Statute Modernization National Collaborative (funded by the Robert Wood Johnson Foundation) undertook the development of a model state public health act. The purpose of the model act was to create an act based on modern constitutional, statutory, and case-based law at the national and state levels. The act was also to reflect current scientific and ethical principles which are the foundation of contemporary public health practice. The model act has nine articles with numerous subsections. The act builds on the organization and provision of the core public health functions and the essential public health services. Table 10–4 is an outline of the model act and its many subsections. Many of the topics of this act are reflected in chapters of this book, all of which prepared public health leaders need to grasp—from public health infrastructure concerns to the general orientation to emergency preparedness and response.

Table 10–4 Outline of the Model State Public Health Act

Article I. Purposes and Definitions

Section

1-101. Legislative Purposes
1-102. Definitions

Article II. Mission and Functions

Section

2-101. Mission Statement
2-102. Essential Public Health Services and Functions
2-103. Roles and Responsibilities
2-104. Public Health Powers—In General

Article III. Public Health Infrastructure

Section

3-101. Public Health Infrastructure
3-102. Public Health Workforce
3-103. Performance Management
3-104. Accreditation of State or Local Public Health Agencies
3-105. Incentives and Evaluations
3-106. Public Health Planning and Priority Setting
3-107. Public Health Advisory Council

Article IV. Collaboration and Relationships with Public and Private Sector Partners

Section

4-101. Relationships Among Federal, Tribal, State, or Local Public Health Agencies
4-102. Relationships Among Public and Private Sector Partners
4-103. Relationships Among Participants in the Health Care System

Article V. Public Health Authorities/Powers

Section

5-101. Prevention and Control of Conditions of Public Health Importance
5-102. Surveillance Activities—Sources of Information
5-103. Reporting
5-104. Epidemiologic Investigation
5-105. Counseling and Referral Services for Persons Exposed to Contagious Diseases
5-106. Testing, Examination, and Screening
5-107. Compulsory Medical Treatment
5-108. Quarantine and Isolation
5-109. Vaccination
5-110. Licenses
5-111. Public Health Nuisances
5-112. Administrative Searches and Inspections

The second major model act relates to state emergency health powers. The reason for such an act is to address the issue of public health powers (including police powers) for state and local public health authorities to make sure that there are strong and effective emergency prevention, preparedness, and response mechanisms in place. The model act addresses the issue of the public health role in emergencies as well as the issue of rights of the public and how these rights can be respected. This model state emergency health powers act (see Table 10–5 for an outline of the model act) was developed by the Center for Law and the Public's Health

---

Table 10–5 Model State Emergency Health Powers Act

Article I   Title, Findings, Purposes and Definitions

Section 101-Short Title—Model State Emergency Health Powers Act
Section 102-Legislative Findings
Section 103-Purposes
Section 104-Definitions

Article II   Planning for a Public Health Emergency

Section 201-Public Health Emergency Planning Commission
Section 202-Public Health Emergency Plan

Article III Measures to Detect and Track Public Health Emergencies

Section 301-Reporting
Section 302-Tracking
Section 303-Information Sharing

Article IV Declaring a State of Public Health Emergency

Section 401-Declaration
Section 402-Content of Declaration
Section 403-Effect of Declaration
Section 404-Enforcement
Section 405-Termination of Declaration

Article V   Special Powers During a State of Public Health Emergency—Management of Property

Section 501-Emergency Measures Concerning Facilities and Materials
Section 502-Access to and Control of Facilities and Property Generally
Section 503-Safe Disposal of Infectious Waste

continues

Table 10-5 *continued*

with support from the Alfred P. Sloan Foundation (2001b). The model act has as a requirement the development of a plan to provide a coordinated response to a public health emergency. The model act itself recommended the reporting and collection of information, the immediate investigation of a threat by giving investigators access to an individual's health information under specified circumstances, the appropriation of property or other resources that may be necessary for the care, treatment, and housing of patients, and the allowance of public health authorities to provide care, test, and vaccinate residents who are ill or who have been exposed to a contagious disease, and to quarantine people when necessary. The model act has already been used by a number of state and local legislators as a guide for addressing public health reforms.

The model has already been introduced in whole or in part in over forty states. Hodge (2004) has reviewed the progress of the states in this endeavor in a report available from the Center for Law and the Public's Health. Thirty-three states and Washington, D.C., have passed bills or resolutions which include provisions or sections of the model act. To look at the process of developing a state act, Munson in Case Study 10-B presents a view of the Illinois experience.

Before leaving this section it is interesting to note the development of a "memorandum of understanding" model which is available in some states to develop a local public health mutual aid and assistance system. The goal of this approach is to have local governmental public health entities work together as partners during an emergency event. What these memoranda do is establish a statewide system. Depending on the plan, the personnel, equipment, supplies, and services of a local health entity from another community than the one in which the crisis occurs will come into the jurisdiction of another local public health department to help them during the emergency.

HEALTH INSURANCE PORTABILITY AND ACCOUNTABILITY ACT OF 1996 (HIPAA)

The issue of privacy of records and the protection of individual rights lead to a brief discussion of HIPAA. The prepared public health leader must always be aware of the issue of privacy and the protection of individual rights. Today, there is increasing concern about the government or other entities being able to access the health record of individuals without their express approval. At least 20% of Americans believes that a health care provider, insurance company or plan, government agency, or employer has accessed personal health information in an improper manner (Lumpkin, 2002). What people are concerned about is how this information is used. It has become easier to access information in the modern computer age (Sweeney, 2002). To this must be added the "collect more" phenomenon. There has also been an increase in the collection of person-specific data where earlier data was collected more in an aggregated form.

CASE STUDY 10-B

Cloaking Public Health Leaders with Authority to Respond to Bioterrorism Threats or Events: One State's Struggle

By
Judith W. Munson

Introduction

When the anthrax attacks occurred in the fall of 2001 immediately after the terrorist attacks of September 11, public health found itself in the unrelenting glare of the national media spotlight. It did not do well. Public health agencies, responding to the anthrax victims and determined to prevent further spread of the infecting bacteria, found that they were working with new and unfamiliar partners, most notably, the private medical community, postal authorities, and law enforcement agencies at every level: local, state, and national. They scrambled for answers to questions about the behavior of the anthrax spores and sought confirmation in laboratory after laboratory that this was, in fact, *Bacillus anthracis* they were confronting. At first, assuming it was naturally occurring, they searched for the sites where *B. anthracis* could have been contracted. They were stunned to discover that it came through the mail and that it escaped through the pores of envelopes. Then, they were amazed to learn that it was dispersed throughout the post office by the sorting machines and the high-pressure cleaning devices used to maintain them.

Public health agency directors all around the nation watched the events as they unfolded; first in Florida, then in Washington, then in New York, and finally, in Connecticut. After it had finally played out, there were 18 confirmed cases of anthrax (11 inhalational, seven cutaneous), five deaths, and more than 30,000 individuals on prophylaxis.

Public health professionals including agency directors, physicians, epidemiologists, environmental health practitioners, public health nurses, and many others, were horrified by what they and the nation were witnessing. They faced difficult questions. If it happened within their jurisdictions, did they have the legal authority to act? Did they have any emergency powers? Would they be able to act immediately to close a building contaminated by anthrax? Did they have the authority to detain everyone in the building for testing? Did they have the legal authority to require each exposed individual to be vaccinated? Or to command the administration of antibiotics? Or to isolate those infected and to quarantine those exposed? Suddenly, the newly hired Chief Counsel at the State Department of Public Health in Upper Midwestern State was bombarded by so many questions that he didn't know where to start. He had just moved into his

continues

CASE STUDY 10-B *continued*

new office on September 4, 2001, the day after Labor Day—one week before September 11—and now this.

The legal foundational authority of public health officials and public health agencies shot to the top of the national agenda. The nascent Public Health Law Program at the Centers for Disease Control and Prevention (CDC) in Atlanta became the fulcrum for this national initiative. By grant to Georgetown University Law Center and Johns Hopkins School of Public Health, the Center for Law and the Public's Health, a legally focused academic think tank sprang into action. Within a few short weeks after the terrorist attacks on the World Trade Center and the Pentagon—and the anthrax attacks up and down the East Coast, now identified as incidents of bioterrorism—a model state emergency health powers act was drafted, vetted, revised, and circulated. Its provisions were responsive to the needs of public health agency directors to act authoritatively and with expanded powers within their jurisdictions in the event of a bioterrorism threat or event. The final version was ready for deployment in late December 2001. Within approximately six months, by June 2002, it was estimated that 34 states had introduced bills based on the provisions of this model act.

In Upper Midwestern State (UMS), the response to this model act was immediate: a high-profile senator sponsored a bill introducing the legislation in the state senate; and, a highly respected state representative, a champion of public health legislation over the years, introduced it in the House of Representatives. Virtually duplicate bills, they were immediately criticized as threats to civil liberties. In addition to opposition from the group called Another Conscientious Legal Undercover Agent (ACLUA), other groups posted summaries of provisions they found objectionable in the bills. Their objections included most elements of the model act. Here is a sampling of their objections:

(The bills) create the Upper Midwestern State Emergency Health Powers Act and each of them;

- Authorizes $50,000,000 for expenses, approved by the governor, for any fiscal year
- Allows the governor, by executive order, to declare a public health emergency if specific conditions are met
- Gives the governor broad, unilateral emergency powers, including financial powers
- Designates the state public health department as the public health authority and the department of state police as the public safety authority;
- Provides for detecting, reporting, and tracking public health emergencies, and for disseminating information
- Authorizes special powers over persons including medical exams,

continues

CASE STUDY 10-B *continued*

diagnostic tests, vaccinations, isolation and quarantine, and access to patients health records
- Provides for penalties and for trial courts to review quarantine orders and refusals to submit to vaccinations
- Authorizes special powers for licensing and appointing health personnel
- Provides for immunity from liability
- Provides that the act overrules conflicting laws and regulations
- Preempts home rule powers
- Exempts actions from the reimbursement requirements of the State Mandate Act
- Amends the code of civil procedure to authorize quick-take powers of eminent domain
- Becomes effective immediately upon passage of law

Not only were civil liberty concerns driving the opposition to these bills, but turf issues were heightened when the UMS Emergency Management Agency perceived encroachment into the "emergency responsibility" arena by the UMS Department of Public Health. Public health was new to front-line response. Statutorily grounded emergency responders were unaccustomed to even having public health at the table, let alone in charge. The 2001 anthrax attacks had changed forever the nature of public health agencies, but other vested interests were not ready to yield authority—not just yet.

The end result was that, despite the five deaths and the 18 confirmed cases of anthrax on the East Coast, the model act was not going anywhere in Upper Midwestern State. The senate bill was permanently stalled in the Senate rules committee and the House bill ultimately suffered the same fate as well.

BTGAME

Upper Midwestern State was designated as a BTGAME site for the 2002–2003 bioterrorism simulation cycle. Congressionally funded, the exercise was designed to involve the heads of agencies at the federal, state, county, and municipal levels at two sites. BTGAME was designed as a 5-day exercise involving a WMD incident in Major Metro City in Upper Midwestern State and an explosion of radioactive material (a "dirty bomb") in a West Coast venue. Both sites involved governmental entities at multijurisdictional levels, including border issues with another country.

The BTGAME scenario in UMS featured the simultaneous release of a biological agent—pneumonic plague (*Yersinia pestis*)—at three locations in the Major Metro City area: the Big Game Center, the Major International

continues

CASE STUDY 10–B *continued*

Airport, and the Downtown Train Station. The attack would take place on Mother's Day, Sunday, May 11, 2003. The exercise would then play out over the next week, May 12–16, 2003. But, the planning for the events of that week began almost a year in advance. During the course of the year-long planning process, Upper Midwestern State would experience a changeover in the governorship of the state—from Republican to Democratic—the first such changeover in 25 years; and an entirely new federal department would be created and come into being. The United States Department of Homeland Security was created in November 2002 and activated into operation on January 24, 2003. It was the largest governmental reorganization in 50 years and would be an oversight agency for many of the activities in the BTGAME drill. By the time it became operational, the planning year was already half over.

The BTGAME exercise was preplanned. There were to be no surprises. The federal, state, county, and municipal levels of governmental agencies (e.g., public health, emergency management, and law enforcement)—as well as the participating private entities (e.g., hospitals)—were given scripts in advance. Some referred to BTGAME as an "open book" exam.

One important element of the exercise surfaced early because of the participation of the UMS Department of Public Health's chief counsel. He was concerned about the legal authority of the participating agencies: Did they have the authority to do what they were scripted to do? Did the legal foundations exist? For example, was the statute, or rule, or ordinance, or attorney general opinion or judicial decision in place for the agencies to engage in a particular activity without exceeding legal bounds? If yes, then no problem; if no, then gaps needed to be identified and a legal bypass would be required, such as the drafting of executive orders for the governor to sign. The chief counsel could readily find the answers to these questions for the agency he advised—the UMS Department of Public Health—but were the legal counsels to the other agencies asking the same questions? These questions were considered to be of such importance that he decided to take action.

In an effort to address these issues and to be prepared to respond quickly when questions of legal authority were posited during the course of the exercise, the Chief Counsel convened a BTGAME legal team. The BTGAME legal team consisted of attorneys who provide legal counsel and services to the federal, state, county and municipal governmental agencies involved in the drill, as well as attorneys for private health care providers, professional associations, and academic institutions. It also included attorneys representing the interests of border state agencies. Nearly 30 agencies were invited to send their attorneys to attend the legal team meetings.

continues

CASE STUDY 10–B *continued*

At the first BTGAME legal team meeting, the participants voted to meet monthly and quickly established subcommittees to address legal issues pertinent to

1. Emergency management/public health issues

2. Law enforcement issues

3. Border issues

Work proceeded continuously from September 2002 through April 2003. It was in April, the month before the exercise was to take place, that the result of all these efforts was produced in the form of a 4-inch binder.

But during the course of the BTGAME legal team's early deliberations, much was going on in the General Assembly and the governor's office of Upper Midwestern State. In December 2002, the state representative who had always championed public health issues introduced HB 6. It was ready for first reading in January when the new General Assembly began its deliberations. After taking into consideration the many voices in disaster preparedness and response in UMS, the bill passed both houses and was signed into law in July 2003. Basically, the bill defined "public health emergency" and put the UMS Department of Public Health into the playing field for emergency response in the state, but that was all. No new powers for public health were included.

Another bill—introduced in the Senate in February 2003 by a leading senator and cosponsored by the president of the Senate—suffered a different outcome. This bill, SB 1742, initially simply a "shell" bill, was amended to allow the UMS Department of Public Health to isolate or quarantine without the prior consent of the individual or without a prior court order. Although the bill, as amended, was adopted in the House on May 31, 2003, (barely two weeks after the BTGAME exercise was concluded), it was referred to the Senate rules committee on the same day and did not resurface before the legislative session ended on July 1. No agreement on enhanced public health powers could be reached. It was dead.

On January 13, 2003, the new governor was sworn in. The first female attorney general in UMS took office on the same day. She was the former senator who was the first to introduce the State Emergency Health Powers Act into the Senate in November 2001—just a year earlier.

The BTGAME legal team binder contained the federal and state constitutions and all statutes, rules, regulations, court decisions and opinions of the attorney general which had been identified for relevancy. For each of the items, a digest of the pertinent provisions was prepared and included as the first information sheet under each tab in the notebook. In the front

continues

CASE STUDY 10–B *continued*

cover pocket of the notebook, the BTGAME legal team emergency contact list was placed. By agency, it listed the name, the title, the phone, fax, cell or pager numbers and e-mail addresses of each participating member—in other words, of all the attorneys for all the agencies taking part in the exercise. The notebook was titled, *BTGAME Legal Team Handbook, April 2003*.

Compiling and assembling the *BTGAME Legal Team Handbook, April 2003* was a monumental effort. It involved months of work on the part of the many attorneys participating in the legal team. It became the most valuable resource during the exercise—not only for the legal resources and analyses it contained, but for the ability to contact any other legal team member on a moment's notice. In addition, because of the meetings, they had met and were acquainted with the person they would be calling. They knew each other's names and recognized each other's faces.

But the notebook took on an importance in another context: by its comprehensiveness, it clearly identified where no law existed and where coverage was essential if Upper Midwestern State was to be prepared to respond instantly and effectively to a real-life bioterrorism threat or event. It highlighted the gaps of the present statutory scheme. It made the inadequacies of the public health legal authorities self-evident. It became the *raison d'etre* for revisiting the legal foundations of public health authority in Upper Midwestern State.

Still, with a new governor in the state capital, revisiting, updating, and reinforcing public health's legal authority was not high on the agenda. The BTGAME exercise took place. Public health laws remained the same. The gaps remained, except for the passage of HB 6 which defined public health emergency and made the UMS Department of Public Health a player in the emergency response capability of the State.

Monkeypox

The BTGAME exercise was barely concluded—the report on how well the Upper Midwestern State had performed would not be forthcoming for months—when a much more real and immediate threat surfaced. Unusual illnesses were being reported in the state. The illnesses signaled the emergence of a zoonotic infectious disease—in other words, a disease and infection which is transmitted between animals and humans. It was a rare viral disease. It had a name: it was monkeypox.

Monkeypox had never been seen in this country until it emerged in late May and early June 2003, in three nearby states (later, other states would report cases within their borders, as well). Before June 2003, monkeypox was known as the cause of the smallpox-like human illnesses found only in Africa—and that was in 1970—more than 30 years earlier.

continues

CASE STUDY 10-B   *continued*

Upper Midwestern State's Department of Public Health provided the following description of monkeypox on its Web site:

> In humans, the signs and symptoms of monkeypox are similar to small-pox, but usually milder. About 12 days after people are infected with the virus, they may get a fever, headache, muscle aches and backache, swollen lymph nodes and a general feeling of discomfort and exhaustion. Within one to three days after development of a fever, they will get a rash. The rash typically develops into raised bumps filled with fluid. It often starts on the face and spreads to other parts of the body, but can origi-nate on other areas of the body. The bumps go through several stages before they get crusty, scab over, and fall off. A person is considered to be infectious to others until their lesions are crusted. The illness usually lasts for two to four weeks. If an exposed person does not develop signs or symptoms by the 21st day after the last exposure, they are unlikely to develop monkeypox.

In June of 2003, monkeypox was traced to prairie dogs which were being sold by an exotic pet dealer in a suburb of Major Metro City. The disease was also linked to imported Gambian rats and other exotic animals. Monkeypox, closely akin to smallpox, required public health to act—and to act quickly. There was one major impediment: the UMS Department of Public Health had no authority over animals. UMS, and its sister states facing the same dilemma, looked to the federal level for help.

Federal Legal Action

The Secretary of the U.S. Department of Health and Human Services had authority over the introduction of communicable diseases from foreign countries and their spread from one state to another. Consequently, the CDC and the Food and Drug Administration (FDA) promulgated an interim final rule in November 2003 superseding a previous order issued by the agencies in June 2003.

The rule (paraphrased here) contains the following general prohibitions: It prohibits the importing of any rodents, whether dead or alive, obtained from Africa, or whose native habitat is Africa; plus any products derived from such rodents, or, any other animal whose importation has been pro-hibited by order, plus any products derived from such animals. The rule's import prohibition is intended to make clear that it covers any rodents (or other prohibited animals) that were caught in Africa and then shipped directly to the United States or shipped to other countries before being imported to the United States. The prohibition also applies to rodents whose native habitat is in Africa, even if those rodents were born else-

continues

CASE STUDY 10–B   *continued*

where. This would apply to a Gambian giant pouched rat, for example, even if that animal was born outside Africa.

But the (now) well-seasoned chief counsel to the UMS Department of Public Health took the initiative on the state level, as well.

State Legal Action

On June 7, 2003, the governor of Upper Midwestern State issued an executive order. Prepared by, and submitted to the Governor by the UMS Department of Public Health chief counsel, it identified the source of the orthopox (the family of viruses that includes monkeypox) virus as prairie dogs that had been in close proximity with Gambian rats, and it gave to the UMS Department of Public Health the lead responsibility in developing and implementing a plan for handling animals infected with or exposed to the orthopox virus. This included possible isolation or quarantine until the threat to the public's health had passed.

In addition, the executive order provided that

> Effective immediately, the following is prohibited in Upper Midwestern State with respect to prairie dogs or Gambian rats until the UMS Department of Public Health determines that the threat to the public health no longer exists: importation, sale or distribution, public display, or any other activity that could result in unnecessary human contact.

The executive order also gave the UMS Department of Public Health the responsibility for evaluating the presence of the virus in places that housed the infected animals and implementing a plan for their disposition. In addition, the UMS Department of Public Health was to immediately undertake all appropriate epidemiological investigations and communicable disease precautions to protect the public. UMS Department of Public Health was to consult with the UMS Department of Agriculture, and all other state agencies were directed to assist in the implementation of the order.

At no time during the outbreak was there any evidence of person-to-person transmission of the disease. In all cases, the infected individual had contact with an infected prairie dog. At the time of the order, there was one human case of monkeypox in Upper Midwestern State; there were 12 cases in the state bordering on the north. There were no deaths from monkeypox at any time during or after the outbreak.

The executive order was an unusual step for the governor to take—to give the state public health agency all of these powers. Still, no legislation was introduced that would provide the UMS Department of Public Health with the ongoing authority to act in circumstances such as these, where an

continues

CASE STUDY 10–B *continued*

emerging infectious zoonotic disease—never before seen in the Unified States—was threatening the health of the people of the state.

SARS

Severe acute respiratory syndrome (SARS) made its public debut on the world stage in February of 2003. It later developed that cases had been occurring in China's Guangdong Province since November 2002. The World Health Organization (WHO) stated that it was to be the "first severe and readily transmissible new disease to emerge in the 21st century." SARS emerged as an atypical pneumonia, baffling doctors and public health experts. Symptoms included high fever, dry cough, myalgia, and mild sore throat. These are not high-alert symptoms. It was when these symptoms quickly developed into bilateral pneumonia and then into acute respiratory distress—followed by death, in some cases—that alarms went off. Cases were being diagnosed in Hong Kong and Vietnam. According to WHO:

> SARS was carried out of Guangdong Province on 21 February by an infected medical doctor who had treated patients in his home town. He brought the virus to the ninth floor of a four-star hotel in Hong Kong. Days later, guests and visitors to the hotel's ninth floor had seeded outbreaks of cases in the hospital systems of Hong Kong, Vietnam, and Singapore. Simultaneously, the disease began spreading around the world along international air travel routes as guests at the hotel flew home to Trendy City, Canada, and elsewhere, and as other medical doctors who had treated the earliest cases in Vietnam and Singapore traveled internationally for medical or other reasons.

In March 2003, the disease broke out among health care workers in hospitals in Hong Kong and Hanoi. These developments prompted the first WHO global alert on March 12, 2003. Within days, the new disease had spread around the world, from Hong Kong to Vietnam to Singapore and to Trendy City. When it became obvious that SARS was being spread by air travel, the WHO issued a heightened global health alert, including a rare "emergency travel advisory."

SARS, its virulence and its transmissibility, were being watched by public health professionals around the world, including those at the UMS Department of Public Health. SARS was new, and it was deadly. There was no vaccine to prevent it, and there was no known medicine that would cure it. No one was yet sure they knew all the ways in which transmission occurred. No one was yet sure what caused the disease. What was known almost immediately, however, was that the health care workers treating patients in the hospitals were at great risk. Infection control measures and

continues

CASE STUDY 10–B *continued*

the control tools dating back to the earliest days of empirical microbiology—isolation and quarantine—were pressed back into service.

The WHO worked tirelessly to combat this new disease: electronically interconnecting public health professionals and laboratories; establishing electronic reporting of new cases and deaths on a daily basis; deploying teams expert in infection control to hot spots; and, at the end of March, recommending airport screening.

But for Upper Midwestern State, it was the news on March 14 that had the most immediate significance: the Canadian government reported that "there were four cases of atypical pneumonia within a single family in Trendy City that had resulted in two deaths." Not only was SARS now in North America, it was just north of the border of a nearby state. If it could get there, it could get anywhere—even to Upper Midwestern State.

SARS in Trendy City, Canada

The news from north of the border was alarming:

- On April 23, 2003, the WHO recommended persons planning to travel to Trendy City consider postponing all but essential travel. The warning was lifted a week later but the damage to the city's tourism industry was devastating. Canadian Broadcasting System (CBS) News reported that "[p]reliminary estimates put initial losses for hotels and restaurants at tens of millions of dollars."
- On May 31, 2003, Trendy City went back on the WHO list of areas with local transmission for the second time. Canada reported 26 suspected and eight probable cases of the disease linked to four Trendy City hospitals.
- On July 2, 2003, WHO again removed Trendy City from its list of areas with recent local transmission.

But the total assessment of the economic damage that SARS inflicted upon Trendy City was yet to come. In August 2003, it was reported that:

> The provincial conservative government is being forced to withdraw $1 billion from its reserve and contingency funds because of the economic impact of SARS.

This was sobering news, especially to Upper Midwestern State where the Major Metro City area attracts close to 30 million visitors each year, and those visitors spend nearly $9 billion annually. This produces $500 million in tax revenue for UMS and the greater Major Metro City area. The possibility of a Trendy City-type economic setback on Upper Midwestern State and Major Metro City was highly disturbing.

continues

CASE STUDY 10–B *continued*

Legal Responses to SARS

The final tally of SARS cases and deaths around the globe was relatively small: on September 26, 2003, the WHO reported a total of 8098 cases with a total of 774 deaths from SARS for the period November 2002 to July 31, 2003. By contrast, it is generally known that an average of 36,000 people die from influenza-related complications each year in the United States. Nonetheless, public health scrambled to contain and defeat an epidemic of a newly emerging disease with legal authorities that were outdated, outmoded, obsolete, and inadequate. This was true at all intervention levels: international, national, state or province, and local.

The International Front

The WHO, at the time of the SARS epidemic, found its own International Health Regulations (IHR) to be in urgent need of revision and updating. The last major revision was in 1969. This new undertaking is of such importance that the first European Union (EU) Commissioner of Health and Consumer Protection has been appointed special envoy for the WHO for the revision of the IHR. Final revisions are expected to be presented to the World Health Assembly at its meeting in May 2005. Working towards the goal of containing the international spread of disease, the IHR revisions will improve upon early detection of threats, the response and management of the threats through global cooperation and collaboration, and the communication among institutions and member states and the WHO office. The need for these improvements came from the SARS experience.

The National Front

In the United States, on the national level, the president issued an executive order on April 4, 2003, that added Severe Acute Respiratory Syndrome (SARS) to the list of quarantinable communicable diseases under the National Public Health Act. Although the WHO's tally of SARS cases globally reflected that, in the United States, there were 29 cases and no deaths from SARS as of July 31, 2003, others counted far fewer, claiming there were only eight laboratory confirmed cases of SARS corona virus with all the patients recovering. Nonetheless, the listing of diseases for which quarantine was legally provided was updated. Months later, on Tuesday, January 13, 2004, the Secretary of the United States Department of HHS announced the immediate embargo on the importation of civets to the United States, the animal suspected of transmitting SARS to humans.

In Canada, where the total number of SARS cases as of the end of July 2003 was 251 with 43 deaths, legal action was more immediate and definitive. The first action was to designate SARS a communicable, virulent, and

continues

CASE STUDY 10–B   *continued*

reportable disease. Without this designation, the Ministry of Health had no authority to quarantine people or to require reports to be submitted. A second change was to amend the Public Health Protection Act to permit a judge to order an individual quarantined in a facility other than a hospital.

The State Front

On the state level, legal actions took a variety of turns.

In the provinces of Canada, the provincial chief medical officers for health have been granted greater independence. No longer appointed by the minister of health, they are appointed by the lieutenant governor. The chief medical officers can now take action when presented with a public health emergency.

In Upper Midwestern State, the governor's office asked the chief counsel of the UMS Department of Public Health to reconvene the BTGAME legal team and to work with the state representative who championed public health causes to get needed legislation through the General Assembly.

UMS Department of Public Health's chief counsel responded quickly. For this particular task, the reconvened BTGAME team would take on a new name. The bioterrorism exercise was over and now it was time to address the realistic threat posed by the SARS experience around the globe. The group became the Public Health Emergency Preparedness Legal Team. A legislative subcommittee was established to craft a bill which would give public health the legal authorities needed to address not only bioterrorism threats or events but newly emerging and zoonotic infectious diseases as well.

The legislative subcommittee, greatly encouraged by the unprecedented participation of the state representative who had initially introduced the Model State Emergency Health Powers Act into the House, went right to work. Seeking to maximize the potential for enacting enhanced public health emergency powers, the subcommittee invited those early detractors to participate this time. For example, the group called Another Conscientious Legal Undercover Agent (ACLUA), so vocal in opposition in the past, was a willing participant this time around. Also invited were representatives from the associations of private medical practitioners and trial lawyers. From time to time, the group was joined by the chief legislative assistant to the Speaker of the House. In UMS, this was truly unprecedented. It signaled a level of importance to the deliberations that was felt throughout the room.

Established in October 2003, the subcommittee met often: sometimes fortnightly, sometimes monthly; sometimes in person; sometimes via teleconference; and, sometimes by video conference. The subcommittee was chaired by the chief counsel to the UMS Department of Public Health.

continues

CASE STUDY 10–B *continued*

The subcommittee drafted a 47-page bill that was introduced into the House by the state representative in January 2004. It established the following new public health powers:

- To order a person or a group of persons to be quarantined or a place to be closed and made off limits to the public on an immediate basis without prior notice or prior consent or court order if, in the reasonable judgment of the Department, immediate action is required to protect the public from a dangerously contagious or infectious disease
- To order physical examinations, tests, vaccinations, collection of laboratory specimens, medications, or observation and monitoring
- To examine, test, disinfect, seize, or destroy animals or other related property believed to be sources of infection in order to prevent the spread of a dangerously contagious or infectious disease in the human population
- To gain emergency access to medical records
- To develop a statewide system for syndromic data collection
- To share information with law enforcement
- To modify the scope of practice for licensed or certified professionals

At every stage, care and attention was directed to due process concerns and protecting the civil liberties of the citizens of UMS. Other interests represented in the deliberations were heard as well. Whenever someone insisted upon a particular position and tensions were heightened in the room, the state representative reminded everyone of the specter of the public health threat which was the motivating energy behind this effort. The chief counsel, as chair, would initiate a move towards the positions of the detractors. When the meetings were concluded, there was consensus around the table.

The state representative introduced the bill hammered out in this deliberative process. Because potential voices of organized opposition had been heard in the meetings, there were no objections raised during the deliberations in the General Assembly. The bill passed the House unanimously. When it arrived in the Senate, it was sponsored by a rising star on the national stage and, once again, no opposition emerged. That meant it passed in the Senate unanimously, as well. It went to the governor. It was signed into law on July 28, 2004, and it became effective immediately.

Conclusion

The Upper Midwestern State (UMS) Department of Public Health finally has the statutory authority it needs. The statutes now provide that it can respond quickly and authoritatively to bioterrorism threats or events and

continues

CASE STUDY 10–B   *continued*

to "dangerously contagious or infectious disease(s)" whether from an animal or human source. But it took three years to do it. Why so long? Was it the specter of an anthrax attack that was the motivation behind these new authorities? Or was it the threat of another bioterrorism pathogen, e.g., pneumonic plague, as in the BTGAME exercise? Or was it the possibility of an outbreak of another zoonotic disease never before seen on this continent (e.g., monkeypox) directly within its own borders—right in its own front yard? Or was it directly in response to a newly emerging infectious disease of global implications (SARS) that prompted these enhancements to public health's legal foundational authorities? Possibly not; possibly none of them was enough, by itself, to provide the motivation for these changes.

Looking at the sequence of public health emergencies in UMS since 9/11, and the fits and starts of legislative initiatives designed to address them, it appears that it was the economic devastation that SARS brought to Trendy City, Canada, that ultimately accomplished what all the other dramatic events could not. SARS was barely even in this country and certainly not within UMS at all. So the disease itself was not, by itself, the motivator. Possibly, just possibly, it was the economic meltdown of Trendy City's tourism industry—the impact of SARS on all those businesses and all those jobs closely associated with them—that provided the impetus to make the necessary changes in the laws of UMS. Whatever the ultimate motivating factor might have been, the conclusion has now been written: the governor's office, the state representative, the legislative assistant to the Speaker of House, the rising star of the Senate, and the entire General Assembly backed the efforts of the chief counsel of the UMS Department of Public Health. They all acted swiftly, thoroughly, and definitively. Now, at last, Upper Midwestern State is legally prepared for any foreseen (and, it is hoped, for any unforeseen) public health emergency.

However, data are not always readily released. They are released in a limited way to a more widely distributed audience. It is possible to think of data release on a continuum from limited to no-restrictions release.

Another issue relates to the identification of data and the anonymity of individuals (Sweeney, 2002). There is also the availability of personal information on the Internet to consider. The critical issue thus becomes how can data be protected. Sweeney (2002) discussed several different methods. A few examples are the following:

1. Scrambling information
2. Encryption (scrambling data and hiding the key to unscrambling it)

3. Utilization of partial identifying information, such as using a birth year but not the birth date
4. Datafly (replacement of social security number with a one-way encryption, for example, so that longitudinal data can be collected but specific identifiers are hidden)
5. Safe Harbor (list of data fields that cannot be released).

There are many different approaches to protecting data.

HIPAA was an attempt to deal with the issue of confidentiality. Public health leaders are clearly caretakers of personal information. There needs to be guidelines for the protection of the rights of individuals and their personal information. The primary purpose of HIPAA initially was to make sure that individuals could maintain insurance coverage even in those circumstances where they needed to change jobs (Mool, 2002). The act (Health Insurance Portability and Accountability Act—PL 104-191) includes provisions to administratively simplify and streamline the health services contacts that an individual has and the method of payment of these services. The act also provides for the establishment of privacy and security standards that were adjudged necessary to protect health information about individuals. A privacy rule was published by the United States Department of Health and Human Services in December 2000. The privacy rule mandated that security methods must be in place to protect health information by April 14, 2003.

The important concern for the prepared public health leader is the need to know the details of HIPAA and how to address these privacy and security issues. The concerns over emergency preparedness and response also require a look at these same issues when police powers are implemented to address a crisis. The release of certain types of information may be critical during a terrorist act when people are injured and it is necessary to gain access to personal health information that can affect the treatment plan of the injured.

PUBLIC HEALTH ETHICS

In recent years, there has been much discussion about the importance of ethical standards and its importance for every civilized society. The difficulty of developing an ethics code for public health is partially related to the population-based focus of the field. It is difficult to make the jump from the ethical behavior of a person to the ethical behavior of the population as a whole (Mariner, 2000). The ethics of public health professionals should not be perceived as different from the ethical behavior of any other governmental official or any other health professional. The place to look for an existing set of ethical principles is the Universal Declaration of Human Rights, adopted by the United Nations in 1948. The declaration is reproduced in Figure 10–2. In addition, there is a need for a public health ethics statement (Mariner, 2000). The values of public health can serve as the foundation for such a set of ethical principles. However, the development of such a set of ethical principles would not be an easy task. The way to address ethics in public health is to not stress the abstractions of codes and principles, but rather to look at the way professionals practice public health for the knowledge of the real ethical principles that guide our work (Swartzman, 2000).

In examining the issue of public health ethics, there are a number of moral considerations that need to be made (Childress et al., 2002). There is first the question of the benefits of the public health services to be provided to the public. Public health professionals have to be careful to avoid or prevent harmful activities from happening. There is clearly the additional consideration of public health equity and the provision of services and programs to all people in the community regardless of background. Public health professionals need to remain cognizant that people have choices and the freedom to make them. The privacy and confidentiality of the service population also needs to be guaranteed. It is important also to keep our promises and commitments to the public and to our partners in health. Public health professionals must always be truthful and work to maintain the trust of our constituents.

A very interesting experiment was undertaken by the Public Health Leadership Society (PHLS), an organization made up of alumni of the national Public Health Leadership Institute. The society has developed a set of ethical principles for public health. There were some underlying assumptions to the 12 ethical principles in the code. The developers believed that people are interdependent and this interdependence is the critical element in the growth of communities. Public health needs to see this relationship between people and their communities. Health of the public is tied to their life in the community. It was also stated that the code was intended for governmental public health and related agencies in the United States. Table 10–6 lists the 12 Principles for the Ethical Practice of Public Health. These principles are based on the following 11 values and beliefs of American society (PHLS, 2002):

Adopted and proclaimed by General Assembly resolution 217 A (III) of 10 December 1948

On December 10, 1948 the General Assembly of the United Nations adopted and proclaimed the Universal Declaration of Human Rights the full text of which appears in the following pages. Following this historic act the Assembly called upon all member countries to publicize the text of the Declaration and "to cause it to be disseminated, displayed, read and expounded principally in schools and other educational institutions, without distinction based on the political status of countries or territories."

PREAMBLE

Whereas recognition of the inherent dignity and of the equal and inalienable rights of all members of the human family is the foundation of freedom, justice and peace in the world,

Whereas disregard and contempt for human rights have resulted in barbarous acts which have outraged the conscience of mankind, and the advent of a world in which human beings shall enjoy freedom of speech and belief and freedom from fear and want has been proclaimed as the highest aspiration of the common people,

Whereas it is essential, if man is not to be compelled to have recourse, as a last resort, to rebellion against tyranny and oppression, that human rights should be protected by the rule of law,

Whereas it is essential to promote the development of friendly relations between nations,

Whereas the peoples of the United Nations have in the Charter reaffirmed their faith in fundamental human rights, in the dignity and worth of the human person and in the equal rights of men and women and have determined to promote social progress and better standards of life in larger freedom,

Whereas Member States have pledged themselves to achieve, in co-operation with the United Nations, the promotion of universal respect for and observance of human rights and fundamental freedoms,

Whereas a common understanding of these rights and freedoms is of the greatest importance for the full realization of this pledge, **Now, Therefore THE GENERAL ASSEMBLY proclaims THIS UNIVERSAL DECLARATION OF HUMAN RIGHTS** as a common standard of achievement for all peoples and all nations, to the end that every individual and every organ of society, keeping this Declaration constantly in mind, shall strive by teaching and education to promote respect for these rights and freedoms and by progressive measures, national and international, to secure their universal and effective recognition and observance, both among the peoples of Member States themselves and among the peoples of territories under their jurisdiction.

Article 1. All human beings are born free and equal in dignity and rights. They are endowed with reason and conscience and should act towards one another in a spirit of brotherhood.

Article 2. Everyone is entitled to all the rights and freedoms set forth in this Declaration, without distinction of any kind, such as race, colour, sex, language, religion, political or other opinion, national or social origin, property, birth or other status. Furthermore, no distinction shall be made on the basis of the political, jurisdictional or international status of the country or territory to which a person belongs, whether it be independent, trust, non-self-governing or under any other limitation of sovereignty.

Article 3. Everyone has the right to life, liberty, and security of person.

Article 4. No one shall be held in slavery or servitude; slavery and the slave trade shall be prohibited in all their forms.

Article 5. No one shall be subjected to torture or to cruel, inhuman or degrading treatment or punishment.

FIGURE 10–2 Universal Declaration of Human Rights

FIGURE 10–2 *continued*

Article 6. Everyone has the right to recognition everywhere as a person before the law.

Article 7. All are equal before the law and are entitled without any discrimination to equal protection of the law. All are entitled to equal protection against any discrimination in violation of this Declaration and against any incitement to such discrimination.

Article 8. Everyone has the right to an effective remedy by the competent national tribunals for acts violating the fundamental rights granted him by the constitution or by law.

Article 9. No one shall be subjected to arbitrary arrest, detention or exile.

Article 10. Everyone is entitled in full equality to a fair and public hearing by an independent and impartial tribunal, in the determination of his rights and obligations and of any criminal charge against him.

Article 11. (1) Everyone charged with a penal offence has the right to be presumed innocent until proved guilty according to law in a public trial at which he has had all the guarantees necessary for his defence.

(2) No one shall be held guilty of any penal offence on account of any act or omission which did not constitute a penal offence, under national or international law, at the time when it was committed. Nor shall a heavier penalty be imposed than the one that was applicable at the time the penal offence was committed.

Article 12. No one shall be subjected to arbitrary interference with his privacy, family, home or correspondence, nor to attacks upon his honour and reputation. Everyone has the right to the protection of the law against such interference or attacks.

Article 13. (1) Everyone has the right to freedom of movement and residence within the borders of each state. (2) Everyone has the right to leave any country, including his own, and to return to his country.

Article 14. (1) Everyone has the right to seek and to enjoy in other countries asylum from persecution.

(2) This right may not be invoked in the case of prosecutions genuinely arising from non-political crimes or from acts contrary to the purposes and principles of the United Nations.

Article 15. (1) Everyone has the right to a nationality.

(2) No one shall be arbitrarily deprived of his nationality nor denied the right to change his nationality.

Article 16. (1) Men and women of full age, without any limitation due to race, nationality or religion, have the right to marry and to found a family. They are entitled to equal rights as to marriage, during marriage and at its dissolution.

(2) Marriage shall be entered into only with the free and full consent of the intending spouses.

(3) The family is the natural and fundamental group unit of society and is entitled to protection by society and the State.

Article 17. (1) Everyone has the right to own property alone as well as in association with others. (2) No one shall be arbitrarily deprived of his property.

Article 18. Everyone has the right to freedom of thought, conscience and religion; this right includes freedom to change his religion or belief, and freedom, either alone or in community with others and in public or private, to manifest his religion or belief in teaching, practice, worship and observance.

continues

FIGURE 10–2 *continued*

Article 19. Everyone has the right to freedom of opinion and expression; this right includes freedom to hold opinions without interference and to seek, receive and impart information and ideas through any media and regardless of frontiers.

Article 20. (1) Everyone has the right to freedom of peaceful assembly and association.

(2) No one may be compelled to belong to an association.

Article 21. (1) Everyone has the right to take part in the government of his country, directly or through freely chosen representatives.

(2) Everyone has the right of equal access to public service in his country.

(3) The will of the people shall be the basis of the authority of government; this will shall be expressed in periodic and genuine elections which shall be by universal and equal suffrage and shall be held by secret vote or by equivalent free voting procedures.

Article 22. Everyone, as a member of society, has the right to social security and is entitled to realization, through national effort and international co-operation and in accordance with the organization and resources of each State, of the economic, social and cultural rights indispensable for his dignity and the free development of his personality.

Article 23. (1) Everyone has the right to work, to free choice of employment, to just and favourable conditions of work and to protection against unemployment.

(2) Everyone, without any discrimination, has the right to equal pay for equal work.

(3) Everyone who works has the right to just and favourable remuneration ensuring for himself and his family an existence worthy of human dignity, and supplemented, if necessary, by other means of social protection.

(4) Everyone has the right to form and to join trade unions for the protection of his interests.

Article 24. Everyone has the right to rest and leisure, including reasonable limitation of working hours and periodic holidays with pay.

Article 25. (1) Everyone has the right to a standard of living adequate for the health and well-being of himself and of his family, including food, clothing, housing and medical care and necessary social services, and the right to security in the event of unemployment, sickness, disability, widowhood, old age or other lack of livelihood in circumstances beyond his control.

(2) Motherhood and childhood are entitled to special care and assistance. All children, whether born in or out of wedlock, shall enjoy the same social protection.

Article 26. (1) Everyone has the right to education. Education shall be free, at least in the elementary and fundamental stages. Elementary education shall be compulsory. Technical and professional education shall be made generally available and higher education shall be equally accessible to all on the basis of merit.

(2) Education shall be directed to the full development of the human personality and to the strengthening of respect for human rights and fundamental freedoms. It shall promote understanding, tolerance and friendship among all nations, racial or religious groups, and shall further the activities of the United Nations for the maintenance of peace.

(3) Parents have a prior right to choose the kind of education that shall be given to their children.

Article 27. (1) Everyone has the right freely to participate in the cultural life of the community, to enjoy the arts and to share in scientific advancement and its benefits.

(2) Everyone has the right to the protection of the moral and material interests resulting from

continues

FIGURE 10–2 *continued*

any scientific, literary or artistic production of which he is the author.

Article 28. Everyone is entitled to a social and international order in which the right and freedoms set forth in this Declaration can be fully realized.

Article 29. (1) Everyone has duties to the community in which alone the free and full development of his personality is possible.

(2) In the exercise of his rights and freedoms, everyone shall be subject only to such limitations as are determined by law solely for the purpose of securing due recognition and respect for the rights and freedoms of others and of meeting the just requirements of morality, public order and the general welfare in a democratic society.

(3) These rights and freedoms may in no case be exercised contrary to the purposes and principles of the United Nations.

Article 30. Nothing in this Declaration may be interpreted as implying for any State, group or person any right to engage in any activity or to perform any act aimed at the destruction of any of the rights and freedoms set forth herein.

1. Humans have a right to the resources necessary for health.
2. Humans are inherently social and interdependent.
3. The effectiveness of institutions depends heavily on the public's trust.
4. Collaboration is a key element to public health.
5. People and their physical environment are interdependent.
6. Each person in a community should have an opportunity to contribute to the public discourse.
7. Identifying and promoting the fundamental requirements for health in a community are of primary concern to public health.
8. Knowledge is important and powerful.
9. Science is the basis for much of our public health knowledge.
10. People are responsible to act on the basis of their personal knowledge.
11. Action is not based on information alone.

A BRIEF NOTE ON ADVOCACY

An important responsibility for the prepared public health leader is to not only advocate for public health, but also be a spokesperson for the role of public health in crises. The Trust for America's Health (2003) has defined the advocate as an individual who defends and fights for the cause or petitions of others. If you as a leader want to be an effective advocate, it is important to follow the five listed steps:

1. Identify who you want to persuade.
2. Know facts and do your homework.
3. Start to communicate with policy makers.

Table 10–6 Principles of the Ethical Practice of Public Health

1. Public health should address principally the fundamental causes of disease and requirements for health, aiming to prevent adverse health outcomes.

2. Public health should achieve community health in a way that respects the rights of individuals in the community.

3. Public health policies, programs, and priorities should be developed and evaluated through processes that ensure an opportunity for input from community members.

4. Public health should advocate and work for the empowerment of disenfranchised community members, aiming to ensure that the basic resources and conditions necessary for health are accessible to all.

5. Public health should seek the information needed to implement effective policies and programs that protect and promote health.

6. Public health institutions should provide communities with the information they have that is needed for decisions on policies or programs and should obtain the community's consent for their implementation.

7. Public health institutions should act in a timely manner on the information they have within the resources and the mandate given to them by the public.

8. Public health programs and policies should incorporate a variety of approaches that anticipate and respect diverse values, beliefs, and cultures in the community.

9. Public health programs and policies should be implemented in a manner that most enhances the physical and social environment.

10. Public health institutions should protect the confidentiality of information that can bring harm to an individual or community if made public. Exceptions must be justified on the basis of the high likelihood of significant harm to the individual or others.

11. Public health institutions should ensure the professional competence of their employees.

12. Public health institutions and their employees should engage in collaborations and affiliations in ways that build the public's trust and the institution's effectiveness.

4. Begin to advocate this very day.

5. Always follow up.

SUMMARY

This chapter has pointed to the critical concern that knowledge of the law is an important set of competencies for the prepared public health leader.

The legal competencies were reviewed as well as model public health practice statutes. The concern over the loss of personal rights is an important issue. How a state and local health agency exercises its police powers during emergencies is also a concern. A discussion of HIPAA was also presented. This was followed by a discussion of public health ethics with the ethics code developed by the Public Health Leadership Society. Finally, the issue of advocacy was briefly presented.

REFERENCES

Centers for Disease Control and Prevention. (2001). *Public health's infrastructure: A status report.* Atlanta: CDC.

Center for Law and the Public's Health. (2001a). *Core legal competencies for public health professionals.* Baltimore: Author.

Center for Law and the Public's Health. (2001b). *Model state emergency health powers act.* Baltimore: Author.

Childress, J. F., Gaare, R. D., Gostin, L. O., Kahn, J., Bonnie, R. J., Kass, N. E., et al. (2002). Public health ethics: Mapping the terrain. *Journal of Law, Medicine, and Ethics, 30,* 170–178.

Council on Linkages between Academia and Public Health Practice. (2001). *Core competencies for public health professionals.* Washington, DC: Public Health Foundation.

Gostin, L. O. (2000). *Public health law.* Berkeley, CA: University of California Press.

Gostin, L. O., & Hodge, J. G., Jr. (2002). *State public health law: Assessment report.* Baltimore: Center for Law and the Public's Health.

Hodge, J. G. (2004). *The model state emergency powers act: State legislative activity.* Baltimore: Center for Law and the Public's Health.

Lumpkin, J. (2002) . HIPAA in context, *Leadership in Public Health, 4*(4), 3–12.

Mariner, W. K. (2000). The search for public health ethics, *Leadership in Public Health, 5*(3), 3–13.

Mool, D. (2002). Overview of the HIPAA colloquium: Implementation in Illinois, *Leadership in Public Health, 4*(4), 1–2.

Munson, J. D. (2004). *The Public Health Law 101 Series (introductory workshop).* Chicago: University of Illinois at Chicago Summer Institute.

Neuberger, B., & Christoffel, T. (2002). *The legal basis of public health.* Atlanta, GA: CDC (Public Health Training Network).

Public Health Leadership Society. (2002). *Principles of the ethical practice of public health.* New Orleans: PHLS.

Swartzman, D. (2000). Finding ethics in public health. *Leadership in Public Health, 5*(3), 14–15.

Sweeney, L. (2002). Sharing data under HIPAA. *Leadership in Public Health, 4*(4), 13–27.

Trust for America's Health. (2003). *You, too, can be an effective public health advocate.* Washington, DC: Author.

Turning Point. (2003). *Model state public health act: A tool for assessing public health laws.* Seattle, WA: Author.

United Nations General Assembly. (1948). *Universal Declaration of Human Rights, Resolution 217 A (III).* New York: United Nations.

CHAPTER 11

Risk and Crisis Communication

$$1N = 3P$$

(One negative statement is equal to three positive statements)

—Vincent Covello, Speaker
National Public Health Leadership Network, April 2003

Public health leadership requires skills in building relationships, and it is by becoming competent in the many different areas of communication that a leader will be successful in building such relationships. Even with an awareness that public health leaders need to develop the many important competencies related to communication, this may turn out to be a difficult marketing challenge. About 10 years ago, a training initiative at my university targeted communication skills as an important leadership issue. A 1-day workshop on communication skills training was planned. A communication specialist was contacted to teach the workshop. The workshop was marketed to all health departments in one midwestern state for a 1-day workshop on a Saturday. An interesting thing happened. Very few public health people registered for the workshop. It was cancelled. We undertook a telephone survey to determine what happened. First, many of the people we surveyed told us that they were already expert at communication and didn't need to be trained. A second finding was that these professionals felt that workshops held on a Saturday was a mistake. Over the last few years, leaders have learned that they do need more training on communication skills. I am still not sure if a workshop on Saturday would fly though. This chapter will explore some important communication skills related to risk and crisis communication. In addition, the issue of social marketing as a strategy will be explored.

RISK AND RISK COMMUNICATION

When we talk about risk, we are often talking about it from a perspective of a type of event we or others have experienced in the past. Our perceptions of these emergency events give us clues to how we might handle the occurrence of a similar event in the future. Thus, our past gives us clues to potential events in the future. In addition to this awareness of a past event and its consequences, anger or discontent enters the picture over the potentiality of another similar event. If the hazard or emergency event of the past was a serious one, then a sense of outrage occurs if a second event ensues. People also feel their personal space has been invaded. One interesting example of this is the feelings that go along with the effects of a hurricane when a person's house and all his or her belongings are destroyed. The upset and outrage was also demonstrated by the families of victims of September 11, 2001. There is also the emotional factor of vulnerability that people feel as a result of these crisis events. Our feeling of risk are thus affected by several factors:

Risk sensitivity = memory of past emergencies + vulnerability + outrage

The above formula is clearly an oversimplification of a very complex process. Our level of risk sensitivity is affected not only by our personal reactions to a potential hazardous event, but it clearly is also affected by how this potential risk is communicated to us. The issue of how much we trust the communicator also becomes part of the formula. Specifically, the National Research Council (1989) described risk communication as an interactive process in which information and opinions are exchanged among individuals, groups, and institutions. Risk communication also involves the relaying of multiple messages about the nature and severity of the risk and nonrisk messages that address the concerns of the public, opinions, or reactions to the risk messages. There are four major risk communication theories which were described by Covello, Peters, Wajtecki, and Hyde (2001). All the theories need to be seen within the context of big concern situations.

Trust Determination Theory

The trust determination theorists point to the fact that people who are upset tend to distrust the messenger (Association of State and Territorial Health Officials [ASTHO], 2002). It is critical that professionals responsible for risk communication build trust with their publics over time. Trust must be built if the effects of high-concern situations are to be lessened. The communicator needs critical skills related to active listening because people with high risk sensitivity do not believe that the communicator is listening to their concerns. The importance of trust has been discussed earlier in this book, and it is clear that trust includes many of the skills of emotional intelligence discussed in Chapter 9. Covello (1992, 1993) has demonstrated that the four factors of empathy and caring, competence and expertise, honesty and openness, and dedication and commitment are associated with the public assessment of trust in the communicator. Crisis situations are often seen to be examples of high-concern and low-trust situations. To gain some clarity of the issue of concern and trust, look at Figure 11–1, which is a graphic contingency table related to concern and trust. Exercise 11–1 asks you to develop four scenarios demonstrating each of the four possible combinations of trust and concern.

Mental Noise Theory

Theorists who support a mental noise model (ASTHO, 2002) discovered that people under stress who are upset have difficulty in hearing and

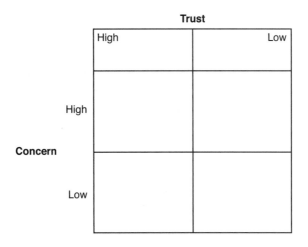

FIGURE 11–1 Trust and Concern in Risk Situations

EXERCISE 11–1   Developing Scenarios on Trust and Concern

Purpose: To explore risk communications issues related to trust and concern

Key Concepts: Risk communication, trust, concern, scenario building

Procedures: Divide the class or training group into groups of 10. Utilizing
    Figure 11–1, develop four scenarios demonstrating:

1. High trust and high concern
2. Low trust and high concern
3. High trust and low concern
4. Low trust and low concern

---

understanding the messages being sent by a communicator. This theory posits the sending of no more than three key messages at a time, keeping messages to 10 seconds or no more than 30 words, and repeating the messages, and using visuals when possible. Mental noise situations are greatest in high-concern situations (Covello, et al., 2001). Body language may negate a verbal message (ASTHO, 2002). It is the emotional reaction to the high-concern event that generates strong feelings, from fear to anger to rage, that creates the mental noise that then affects the ability of the individual to engage in rational conversations.

Negative Dominance Theory

The negative dominance theorists have stated that when people are under stress, they tend to see the world in negative ways. It mirrors as the Covello quote at the beginning of this chapter that negative statements seem to have greater weight than positive statements. People who are communicating with the public need to be careful not to use too may negative words in their messages because stressed people in high-concern situations will increase the real value of these negative words. Communicators need to present their messages in terms of what is being done rather than on what is not being done (Covello, et al., 2001).

Risk Perception Theory

The fourth model has been called risk perception, which relates to how risks are perceived by people. Covello and his colleagues (2001) looked at risk perception in the context of high-concern situations and stated that the level of concern tends to be strongest when people define the situation as involuntary, not equitable, not beneficial, out of a person's immediate control, associated with adverse potential or real outcomes, and as shown above in trust determination arguments as being associated with untrustworthy individuals or organizations. It seems clear that the issue of risk perception is an important aspect of risk communication strategies. In fact, all four theories are really interrelated and cover slightly different perspectives on the issue of trust and concern as well as the important relationship between the communicator and the recipient of the communication message.

Covello and Allen (1988) have summarized these various theories into the seven cardinal rules of risk communication:

1. Accept and involve the public as a partner.
2. Plan carefully and evaluate your efforts.
3. Listen to the public's specific concerns.
4. Be honest, frank, and open.
5. Work with other credible sources.
6. Meet the needs of the media.
7. Speak clearly and with compassion.

These discussions often simplify what in many ways may be a more complex set of reactions. Fischoff and his colleagues (1981) studied how people's reactions to the magnitude of a risk are affected by many factors. If a risk is seen as something that a person or group can voluntarily control, the risk may be more acceptable than a risk which is out of the control of the individual or group. Second, if a person feels that he or she can control the risk, then he or she would handle it, in contrast to experiencing feelings related to situations that were out of control. If the risks are seen as beneficial, they are more acceptable than risks that seem to not be so. Individuals also react more fairly when they perceive that a risk is evenly distributed among a population than a risk that is seen to be unfairly distributed. This might be labeled the "why me" phenomenon.

Risk or crises that are natural in origin are often more acceptable than man-made risks. We respond strongly to both, but more strongly to such things as terrorist events. If a risk is generated by a trusted person or resource, then people tend to be more accepting of it than when the risk comes from an untrusted person or source. Risks perceived to be familiar, such as a tornado or hurricane in a place where these natural events often occur, are more acceptable than risks that are more unusual. We also react more strongly to risks that affect children than to risks that affect adults.

It is important to see risk from a reaction perspective as well as from who will be most impacted by the risk. Perhaps, it would be possible to rate the reaction through the following formula:

Risk reaction indicator = Actual risk + rumor + level of concern + emotional reaction divided by 4

Rate each factor in the formula from 1–100 and then divide by 4 to get the risk reaction indicator. This will help the prepared public health leader who is responsible for working and communicating with an individual or group gauge the audience that he or she is addressing. It may also affect the message that is to be given. The emotional reaction to the potential risk is also affected by whom the risk is seen to impact the most. A risk to a given person is seen in a different light to a risk to other family members. A work risk is different than a risk to home. A community risk is also different than personal or family risks. Finally, a risk to a society or to national security is different again to other types of risk.

There are many myths that stand in the way of the development of effective risk communication programs (Chess, Hance, & Sandman, 1988). It is important to address these myths with action to improve communication strategies. Table 11–1 presents these myths and action steps.

Chess and his colleagues have also pointed out the critical nature of community input into the risk communication process. It is important to involve the community earlier and to involve community organizations and leaders in the decision-making process. The decisions to be made will affect the lives of people living in the community. It should be clear by now that people affected by the risk situation will respond differently than those who are not directly affected. In other words, the audiences for a risk message may each have different reactions and needs. The prepared public health leader needs to develop different messages for different audiences. In this case, one size does not fit all. As pointed out above, people's values and feelings are important. The trustful leader will understand this and acknowledge these realities.

Keeping in mind the above discussion, it is now useful to discuss the issue of the message. The prepared public health leader as communicator has to craft a message or series of messages that in essence take the crisis

Table 11–1 Risk Communication: Myths and Actions

Belief in some common myths often interferes with development of an effective risk allow communication program. Consider the myths and actions you can take.

Myth: We don't have enough time and resources to have a risk communication program.
Action: Train all your staff to communicate more effectively. Plan projects to include time to involve the public.

Myth: Telling the public about a risk is more likely to unduly alarm people than keeping quiet.
Action: Decrease potential for alarm by giving people a chance to express their concerns.

Myth: Communication is less important than education. If people knew the true risks, they would accept them.
Action: Pay as much attention to your process for dealing with people as you do to explaining the data.

Myth: We shouldn't go to the public until we have solutions to environmental health programs.
Action: Release and discuss information about risk management options and involve communities in strategies in which they have a stake.

Myth: These issues are too difficult for the public to understand.
Action: Separate public disagreement with your policies from misunderstanding of the highly technical issues.

Myth: Technical decisions should be left in the hands of technical people.
Action: Provide the public with information. Listen to community concerns. Involve staff with diverse backgrounds in developing policy.

Myth: Risk communication is not my job.
Action: As a public servant, you have a responsibility to the public. Learn to integrate communication into your job and help others do the same.

Myth: If we give them an inch, they'll take a mile.
Action: If you listen to people when they are asking for inches, they are less likely to demand miles. Avoid the battleground. Involve people early and often.

Myth: If we listen to the public, we will devote scarce resources to issues that are not a great threat to public health.
Action: Listen early to avoid controversy and the potential for disproportionate attention to lesser issues.

Myth: Activist groups are responsible for stirring up unwarranted concerns.
Action: Activists help to focus public anger. Many environmental groups are reasonable and responsible. Work with groups rather than against them.

reaction out of the emergency situation. In a talk at the annual American Public Health Association meetings in 2004, Vanderford discussed messages in terms of three elements. First, there is the content element which relates to presenting explicit information. Second, there is the relational element which involves such concerns as respect and caring for the recipients of the message. It also involves the implicit statements related to the power of the person giving the message. The third element is the contextual element, which looks for other competing messages and what associations are made with the message being given.

MESSAGE MAPPING

A very useful tool for prepared public health leaders in his or her role as a risk communicator involves the use of message-mapping techniques. All of the previous discussion discussed the critical issue of how the public perceives a risk and how the communicator tells the public about the risk and what to expect. It should be clear that an informed public will be better able to listen to the message than the uninformed public. If you were to conduct a simple nonrandom survey of your neighborhood, apartment building, workplace, or residence at a university and ask people what they know about potential natural or man-made crises that might occur in their jurisdiction and secondly what their community and residence has done to prepare for these possible crises, what would you discover? I would guess that most of our family, friends, and colleagues are not very well informed about these potential risks. This lack of knowledge and information may explain the foundation for the issues raised in the last section of this chapter.

An informed public will change the message. In fact, the involvement of community people in risk assessment and communication as a partnership can have benefits. In a recent Agency for Toxic Substances and Disease Registry (ATSDR) report for citizens (2004), it was discussed that community input can help in the identification of local facts which might clarify the risk determination process. Community input might also improve the determination of how great the risk will be for the community. Community involvement may also simplify the planning process and communication strategies in that an informed community may well be better able to understand the risks. This process may mean that different communication issues can be addressed which go far beyond the messages needed when people are uninformed. Community involvement may also help gain acceptance and support for the emergency response activities because they know what will happen during an emergency. For example, if police powers are required, the public will understand the reasons more readily.

The interesting missing link in this discussion relates to the prepared public health leader who often serves as the voice of his or her community. The prepared public health leader is the one that often has the responsibility or delegates the responsibility for relaying information about an emergency to the public as well as to the media. Here it becomes evident that the leader has to read his or her own personal emotions and perceptions, as well as the emotions and perceptions of the people who work in the agency, the community that is served, the elected community officials, and finally, the concerns of the media to report the latest news. Covello and his colleagues from the Center for Risk Communication (date unavailable) have come up with a list of the 77 most frequently asked questions of the person who relays the latest information about the crisis. These questions, which have been reproduced in Table 11–2, are extensions of the traditional journalist questions of who, what, when, where, why, and how. These questions are intended to find out about the causes and extent of the crisis as well as its impact on the population and community. These questions as well as the early discussion on trust and concern all guide the message-mapping process. The other element of importance that prepared public health leaders need to recognize is that the skills of conflict management are also important in any discussion of crisis management.

There are eight goals related to the use of message maps in risk communication (Covello, 2002):

1. Determine who the key stakeholders are early in the process.
2. Attempt to forecast the questions and concerns of stakeholders before they verbalize them.
3. Integrate thought and feeling processes to more accurately develop prepared questions related to stakeholder fears, perceptions, and concerns.
4. As clearly and concisely as possible, assemble supporting information to go with the key messages.
5. Create an open environment for dialogue and discussion both within the agency and outside it.

Table 11-2 77 Questions Commonly Asked by Journalists During a Crisis

---

What is your name and title?

What are your job responsibilities?

What are your qualifications?

Can you tell us what happened?

When did it happen?

Where did it happen?

Who was harmed?

How many people were harmed?

Are those that were harmed getting help?

How certain are you about this information?

How are those who were harmed getting help?

Is the situation under control?

How certain are you that the situation is under control?

Is there any immediate danger?

What is being done in response to what happened?

Who is in charge?

What can we expect next?

What are you advising people to do?

How long will it be before the situation returns to normal?

What help has been requested or offered from others?

What responses have you received?

Can you be specific about the types of harm that occurred?

What are the names of those that were harmed?

Can we talk to them?

How much damage occurred?

What other damage may have occurred?

How certain are you about damages?

How much damage do you expect?

What are you doing now?

Who else is involved in the response?

Why did this happen?

What was the cause?

Did you have any forewarning that this might happen?

Why wasn't this prevented from happening?

What else can go wrong?

continues

Table 11–2 *continued*

If you are not sure of the cause, what is your best guess?

Who caused this to happen?

Who is to blame?

Could this have been avoided?

Do you think those involved handled the situation well enough?

When did your response to this begin?

When were you notified that something had happened?

Who is conducting the investigation?

What are you going to do after the investigation?

What have you found out so far?

Why was more not done to prevent this from happening?

What is your personal opinion?

What are you telling your own family?

Are all those involved in agreement?

Are people overreacting?

Which laws are applicable?

Has anyone broken the law?

How certain are you about the laws?

Has anyone made mistakes?

How certain are you about mistakes?

Have you told us everything you know?

What are you not telling us?

What effects will this have on the people involved?

What precautionary measures were taken?

Do you accept responsibility for what happened?

Has this ever happened before?

Can this happen elsewhere?

What is the worst-case scenario?

What lessons were learned?

Were those lessons implemented?

What can be done to prevent this from happening again?

What would you like to say to those that have been harmed and to their families?

Is there any continuing danger?

Are people out of danger? Are people safe?

Will there be inconvenience to employees or to the public?

How much will all this cost?

continues

Table 11–2 *continued*

Are you able and willing to pay the costs?

Who else will pay the costs?

When will we find out more?

What steps are being taken to avoid a similar event?

What lessons have you learned?

What does this all mean?

---

6. Devise user-friendly approaches for key communicators in your organization if you are not to be the spokesperson.
7. Guarantee that the messages to be given are consistent and trustworthy.
8. Always have your agency speak with one voice.

Message mapping provides a process for understanding communication in high-risk situations. There are seven steps in the construction of message maps (Covello, 2002):

1. Identify the key stakeholders.
2. Determine a complete list of specific concerns (SCs) of each stakeholder group that is identified.
3. Analyze the list of SCs to determine what are the underlying general concerns (GCs) of each stakeholder group.
4. Develop three key messages of less than three seconds or less than nine words for each key message related to what most stakeholders need to know, want to know, or are most concerned about relative to both SCs and GCs.
5. Provide or discover supporting facts for each key message.
6. Undertake systematic testing of the message utilizing standardized procedures.
7. The spokesperson presents the prepared message maps through various communication channels.

Covello's (2002) template for message mapping can be found in Figure 11–2. Exercise 11–2 gives you the chance to experiment with message mapping for three stakeholder groups concerned about a terrorist attack in Los Angeles in the next year.

There has been increasing interest in recent years in logic models. The logic model approach would be an interesting variation on the message-mapping approach. In logic models, you create a chart divided into five

Stakeholder: Question or Concern:		
Key message 1	Key message 2	Key message 3
Supporting fact 1-1	Supporting fact 2-1	Supporting fact 3-1
Supporting fact 1-2	Supporting fact 2-2	Supporting fact 3-2
Supporting fact 1-3	Supporting fact 2-3	Supporting fact 3-3

FIGURE 11–2 Message Map Template

portions (Kellogg, 2000). In the first column, you list the inputs, including information about the crisis, specific concerns, and general concerns (see Figure 11–3). In the second column, you list the activities to be carried out, including the structure of the message, the various media to be contacted, and any other stakeholder activities. The third column shows the outputs that are the products of the previous column. The fourth column allows the analysis of the outcomes of the communication activities, and the final column determines the impact of all the activities done on the various stakeholders and the community as a whole. The major advantage of the logic model approach is that it can be used for all sorts of problem analysis by the prepared public health leader. You can contrast

---

EXERCISE 11–2 The Risk of Terrorism in Los Angeles

Purpose: To utilize message-mapping techniques to examine the possibility of
        a terrorist event in a large metropolitan area
Key Concepts: Risk communications, message mapping
Procedures: Divide the class or training group into groups of 10.

1. Divide your group into the following three stakeholder groups:
   a. The community
   b. Elected officials
   c. The media
2. Task is to develop a message map (see Figure 11-2) on the risk of a terrorist attack in Los Angeles in the next five years. Before undertaking the mapping process, develop a specific and general concerns list to guide you in the process.
3. Present your findings to the entire group.

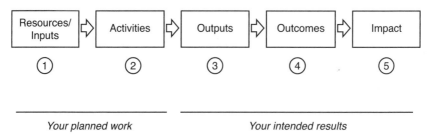

FIGURE 11–3 Logic Model Example

this logic model approach with the message-mapping model approach by redoing Exercise 11–2.

CRISIS COMMUNICATION

Sometimes it is difficult to evaluate a potential crisis because nothing like it has happened before. Perhaps the crisis occurs unexpectedly and it must be addressed. Crisis communication strategies have been developed for these types of events. Crisis communication has been defined first to describe how an agency or organization faces a crisis and has to communicate to various stakeholders about the event (Reynolds, 2002). Underlying the definition just given is an awareness that the organization, and by inference the community, is facing a crisis that requires, and in fact demands, a response. The agency that is required to respond may also feel a lack of control relative to the crisis situation. Because crises go through phases, it is critical for the communicator to understand these phases as the response will change depending on the stage of the crisis. Figure 11–4 demonstrates this through the crisis communication lifecycle with key communication points related to each stage. Reynolds's work is an excellent resource for all aspects of crisis communication with detailed charts and evaluation techniques related to the skills necessary to carry out a well-developed crisis communication plan.

All crises have some things in common (Fernandez & Merzer, 2003). There is always confusion and chaos at the occurrence of the event. There needs to be immediate response to the media and the public when a crisis occurs. Crisis events seem to escalate in intensity during the early hours and days after the event. Information tends to be limited and sometimes misleading. The public is interested at the outset but often loses interest if

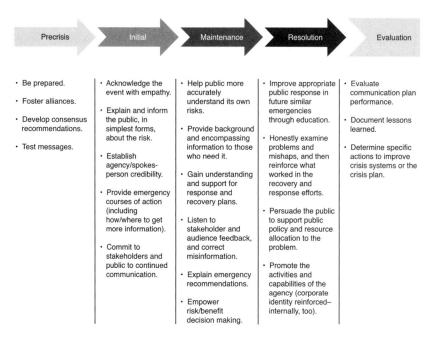

Precrisis	Initial	Maintenance	Resolution	Evaluation
• Be prepared. • Foster alliances. • Develop consensus recommendations. • Test messages.	• Acknowledge the event with empathy. • Explain and inform the public, in simplest forms, about the risk. • Establish agency/spokesperson credibility. • Provide emergency courses of action (including how/where to get more information). • Commit to stakeholders and public to continued communication.	• Help public more accurately understand its own risks. • Provide background and encompassing information to those who need it. • Gain understanding and support for response and recovery plans. • Listen to stakeholder and audience feedback, and correct misinformation. • Explain emergency recommendations. • Empower risk/benefit decision making.	• Improve appropriate public response in future similar emergencies through education. • Honestly examine problems and mishaps, and then reinforce what worked in the recovery and response efforts. • Persuade the public to support public policy and resource allocation to the problem. • Promote the activities and capabilities of the agency (corporate identity reinforced–internally, too).	• Evaluate communication plan performance. • Document lessons learned. • Determine specific actions to improve crisis systems or the crisis plan.

FIGURE 11–4 Crisis Communication Lifecycle

they are reassured that the event is being controlled and handled well. The influence of the media and its needs to monitor the crisis can increase and exacerbate the concern by the public and all other stakeholders. It should be possible to plan for these unanticipated events. A crisis communication plan is important and the creation of a crisis communications team is also critical (Fernandez & Merzer, 2003).

The Seven-Step Communication Response Plan

It is possible to follow a seven-step communications response plan (Fernandez & Merzer, 2003). The seven steps, reworded for clarification, are described in the following sections.

Create and Appoint the Crisis Communications Team

The development of a multiprofessional team made up of individuals from throughout an organization is important if the team is to be representative of the organization as a whole. The team may include external stakeholders as well. A team leader and spokesperson needs to be determined. The team leader will have multiple responsibilities to the senior leadership of the organization as well as to external stakeholder groups and residents of the community. The team leader will lead the effort of developing the crisis communication plan. It will be the crisis communication team (CCT) that will activate this plan in concert with the organization emergency preparedness and response plan.

Collect and Validate Critical Information about the Crisis

It is within the first day of the emergency that an organization will discover its credibility and trust level with the internal and external stakeholders. The CCT needs to establish liaisons outside the organization to gather factual information. Some research will be needed as well as a general monitoring of the media. The information needs to be sorted, analyzed, and evaluated relative to the public health impact of the emergency.

Determine the Seriousness of the Crisis Event

The seriousness of the emergency also needs to be determined in consultation with external liaisons. It is also important to carry out a situational assessment to make certain that all parties addressing the emergency are doing it from the same set of facts.

Identify the Key Stakeholders

The major reason that it is important to define the key stakeholders is that differently worded messages may be necessary for different audiences. The order of informing stakeholders may also be important if there are casualties. Families need to be informed before the media. As discussed in earlier chapters, families should not receive bad news from the media. The humanitarian response team needs to be working with families early.

Develop, Design, and Implement a Communications Strategy for the Local Jurisdiction

Fernandez and Merzer (2003) stated that the CCT needs to learn to balance the needs of the organization with all of its external communications. If a crisis has community-wide implications, it may be necessary to create a crisis communications center or as it is sometimes called a joint information center (JIC). The JIC will usually be under the supervision of the incident commander. However, the lead agency will designate who will speak for the JIC. The key messages need to work towards allaying the fears of the public. The messages need to take a positive tone. There are two types of messages. Position key messages give the organization or the JIC view of the nature of the incident and the response that is being given to the event. Instructional key messages direct stakeholders to do something or to take a specific action.

Develop Background and Supporting Information

Some of the background information relates to policies and procedures of the organization for giving out information. For example, many universities will not allow faculty to talk to the media without getting the approval of the administration of their university. This is not as clear-cut as it may first appear because some faculty believe that this approval process is not appropriate and is an infringement of academic freedom policy and procedures. This small example raises the concern about how conflicting policies can impact getting needed information out to the public. When messages and procedures for delivering them are determined, JIC members will need to get supporting documentation to back up their messages.

Inform and Develop a Protocol for Delivering Messages and Reacting to Stakeholder Concerns

The obvious final step is the delivery of the message based on the plan and protocol worked out in the rest of the plan. A media log should be utilized to keep abreast of all requests for information as well as the responses to these requests and who gave it. The way the message is reported in the media also needs to be monitored.

In reality the techniques of risk communication and crisis communication overlap. Some of these overlaps are discussed by media advocacy expert and consultant Robert Howard in Case Study 11. This is a very complex area and the prepared public health leader will often not have the time to learn all the ins and outs of these communication approaches. The communication specialist will have to work closely with these leaders and coordinate their preparedness and response activities as well as the noncrisis activities in a coordinated way.

A BRIEF OVERVIEW OF SOCIAL MARKETING

The previous discussion demonstrates the need for the prepared public health leader to become proficient in the skills of communication. If the goal of public health is to influence people to change their behaviors to more

CASE STUDY 11   A Public Health Practice Quiz for Robert Howard

1. **How are risk communications and crisis communications related and different?**

    The best example that comes to mind is the people who live along the Mississippi flood plain and continue to do so year after year despite multiple years of having their homes and belongings swept away and yet they remain in these homes. For years, government and service agencies have sought to instruct these fine people that their existence along this plain puts them at a distinct *risk*. This *risk* of course becomes a *crisis* when the flood waters begin to rise, as spring and summer rains inevitably cause the water levels to rise and these people, their homes, farms, businesses, and livelihoods are literally swept downstream. During those times there is a significant outreach and increase in the effort to reach these persons and warn them of the impending, potentially deadly crisis they face due to rising waters. Upstream and downstream, literally every possible means of communications are employed to inform these persons of the looming threat and risk they face from this crisis. Efforts range from sophisticated media campaigns to the practically biblical form of shouting at people from high-water marks, including helicopters, to leave the area of risk. Many dry off and stay until the next year . . . and the next flood.

    We inform people in virtually every possible way on a daily basis of the risks of smoking, including writing on the packages of the very products they buy that the product will undoubtedly be harmful to them. We even inform them of the genuine national crisis we face of losing tens of thousands of citizens through continued use of these products, but it does not mean they will act on the messages in a casual or critical atmosphere. It seems that legislation has the best possibility of actually getting people to act on or against risk with any regularity. This was certainly the case with seat belts when the industry and government combined over a period of time to make the nonuse of seat belts so financially and socially unacceptable that now many Americans have been driven into using these unquestionably life-saving devices. It wasn't until public safety, government, and industry came together with public health and advertising to inform, educate, legislate, and change behaviors.

    This principal applies across the board to any number of habits, practices, and behaviors including drug use, HIV-AIDS, and other STDs, handgun ownership, obesity, and high blood pressure. The mere fact that you have identified both a risk and the point at which it becomes a "crisis" or critical public health event *does not mean* that you

continues

CASE STUDY 11   *continued*

have successfully reached into the minds of those impacted and changed their behavior. For each person, that trip switch is something different. It is through a *broad use of all possible media*, informed spokespersons who will affect all races, sexes, nationalities; combined with intelligent and broadly dispersed repetition of the message, targeting the message at especially high-risk groups and varying the delivery of the message through clever and eye-catching techniques that cause the person at risk or in crisis to understand the outcome of continuing their usual behaviors. Even then, it is extraordinarily helpful to have the aid and support of legislation to assist.

Of course, laws do not always make or change behavior patterns, as we see each year with deaths due to drunk driving, speeding, and certain forms of drug use. Society can however make a determination that a particular risk or behavior is so unacceptable that lawmakers must take innovative and broad-reaching measures that employ multiple layers of risk communications at all levels to impact change in that risk behavior. The ultimate aim being to lower that risk bar to a level where it is no longer possible of creating or rising to a crisis level. We have seen this work in areas of risk including child labor, alcohol sales to minors, seatbelt "click-it-or-ticket" campaigns and some food safety issues such as homogenization of milk and chlorination of water.

I believe, in the end . . . unless laws tell them otherwise, people will determine what is too risky for them and what constitutes a life-changing or crisis environment for them and their life styles, tastes, and families. And yet in spite of those daunting challenges and slim likelihood of the actions of politicians, we in public health have an *absolute moral obligation* to *stand atop the high ground and shout out* to those at risk in both times of high risk and low risk that there is risk involved and options are available.

2. **How is recovery possible when mental health issues remain even after the last communication message is given?**

We have to get beyond the concept that we will, in any critical event, achieve a level of complete and absolute mental health recovery. The make up of each of our own personal histories is so complex that no level of expert can predict what impact an event or crisis may have on us in a given situation.

We must instead move toward a program of *recovery and recognition*. We must recover and resume our lives as best we can with the support of community and family following a crisis. Some person will "bootstrap" wonderfully and recover with little or no assistance, while others will need a vast range of both physical and emotional support in getting through a crisis. As an example, a family of seven who recovers from a horrific tornado with all family members intact, but loses a beloved

continues

CASE STUDY 11 *continued*

family pet will certainly mourn the loss of that pet, but have the strength and support of the family unit to get through the crisis of losing the animal. On the other hand, an 80-year-old woman who loses her only pet of 20 years that served as her only physical and emotional manifestation of love and caring may be devastated. Have we recognized the impact that loss has on her and how can we get her through that event?

In public health we must look for ways to aid, identify, and help these families, *each*, get through this crisis. Let there be no mistake that the walking wounded with the thousand-yard stare, but no apparent physical injury, may well turn out to be as much a health risk in both the short and long term than the person with a fractured leg.

The emotional scars left behind in each of us from past events are the platform from which we dive into each event in our life, especially crises where life-changing events occur. It is incumbent that we recognize how the past shapes the future. This underscores the need for each of us to support and understand the mental health programs in our community and the level of mental health of those we love, care for, employ, and neighbor with, and how changes with life experiences, age, events, and illness can result in a need to shape our message of risk communication and risk recovery. We must additionally understand that there must be a constant and ongoing effort to understand which media entities our community and family employ. Have we developed a way to use not just billboards and TV in a critical event, but radio, flyers, bulletin boards, the Internet, and community meetings? This must be an ongoing campaign to stay aware of the aging of our community, the influx of new peoples, and the social and economic factors in our hometowns. Who do we go to when we want to reach everyone in our community? How do we best use all of this media not just for the quick impact, but the long-running communications efforts in understanding that all persons heal in a unique fashion?

This question goes to the core of every disaster, critical event, or crisis, and that is that there is always some level of mental or emotional impact, and in some cases that impact is life changing. In public health we must be alert to that fact and train all of our workers, volunteers, and administrators to recognize it not only in the victims but in the workers. It is important to remember that in both the Oklahoma City explosion and in the World Trade Center disaster, 70% of the volunteers ultimately developed emotional problems that required some level of treatment. If *volunteers* are impacted, then we must expect some level of harm to the *victim* and be attuned and prepared to deal with the way and manners in which these behaviors manifest themselves. With that

continues

CASE STUDY 11   *continued*

in mind we must develop systems and plans and *sensitive communications* to deal with them in both the long and short term.

3. **How is communication affected by community literacy concern?**

It isn't the community literacy concern I have, but the community literacy **reality**. The fact that your community is literate does not mean they read in the conventional manner, or are impacted by messages the way we of some 50 years ago received data in public service announcements and brochures. What are those in my community who are most at risk going to most benefit from, and how can I best reach them with print and broadcast material? If I am dealing with low literacy in the local community, I may well want to go to the use of comic books or other graphic media that have a simple theme with easy to read language and illustrations.

Is it really worth my while to publish messages in *The Wall Street Journal* to young boys and girls with no regular interest in this publication's content? We must understand the level of literacy in the audience we are trying to reach, and the reality of the media that reaches into the homes, glove boxes, purses, and nightstands of these people I want to understand and touch. When I know the reality of the literacy range and which media are being listened too, watched, or read, I know that I am at least halfway on my way to getting into that audience. If you are managing a publicity or awareness campaign to reduce morbidity and mortality in your community, you better quickly find out what the *most at risk* are reading, listening to, and taking home.

By the way, this should include the often overlooked media of public gatherings such as churches, community meetings, and public events. These are legitimate and truly literate moments to reach and teach.

4. **How important is message mapping?**

Message mapping is as *critical as ring vaccination was to the smallpox effort.* This is not an overstatement or hyperbole. When you immunize a person with intelligent and lasting information they will take that message home. It will have the same impact as herd immunity. What is vital is the important and frequent "booster shot" of data and information that reminds and underscores the original message. A grid method of reaching your community in which you seek to reach all persons within a given area is an intelligent and appropriate approach. It also recognizes the realities of the ethnic and racial makeup of neighborhoods and communities and gives you a chance to plan a strategy prior to going into that community and attempting the communications equivalent of "carpet bombing" where messages just fall everywhere and have no focus or target and we just hope they are picked up.

continues

CASE STUDY 11   *continued*

Message mapping makes you ask, "Where are my most at risk communities? What media do they most often use or listen to?" Message mapping also forces you to *track, maintain, and monitor* those to whom you have reached out.

Effective public health campaigns in the year 2005 simply cannot be done without smart, targeted message mapping. In this day and age of precious and few health care resource dollars, we do not have the benefit of shotgunning information out and hoping it lands in the right spot. We must map, must target, and must deliver a smart, clever, and understandable SOCO (single overriding communication objective).

5. **What are the most common mistakes in health communications?**

One word—hubris. Far too many public health professionals clad in our Birkenstocks and jeans feel that we have seen it all and heard it all. We have failed to understand that there is a primal and basic reason we were given one mouth and two ears. We need to listen twice as much as we speak. We fail to understand the power and emergence of new forms of communications such as urban contemporary radio, blogging, and 15-second advertising. We have published papers, run programs, and dug into our data like ticks, often never poking our heads up to see what is really new, effective, and appropriate. We have forgotten our listening skills because we have initials after our names.

On more occasions than I can count I have been in the back of a room where a presenter is describing a "new and innovative program to reach young people" only to have those very same young people in the back of the room saying, "Who is this guy and who has he been talking to?" In most cases he or she has been listening to those members of his or her staff who tell them what they want to hear (after all, they do sign the paychecks) what a right-wing or left-wing predisposed position dictates, and have shaped a program around that. The effort is invariably a failure, and the official is rarely held accountable or led to understand by means of savvy and articulate critique where he or she went wrong.

We *must not and cannot rely* on a political appointee who completely lacks in any level of health expertise to deliver health messages to an American public desperate for critical, accurate, and timely data, as was the case in the post 9/11 anthrax attacks. People want their health information in those critical moments from a doctor, nurse, or health care professional, and it is only hubris that allowed a politician to decide that he was the best person to deliver that data and then handle difficult and complex questions from the highly articulate and well-educated medical media on hand. Where was the Surgeon General in the early days of that event and why was he not used? Our initial mes-

continues

CASE STUDY 11   *continued*

sages were so confusing and disjointed that many Americans were calling anthrax a virus and were convinced that the initial patient had
acquired the illness by drinking water from a stream in North Carolina
as stated by the Secretary of Health and Human Services. To this day,
as an epidemiologist, I have sought out the conditions where a person
can contract "inhaled" anthrax by drinking water. The Secretary must
have access to data the rest of the scientific world lacks. Or he simply
possessed such hubris that he was unable to simply defer to a qualified
health care expert who could have assisted him.

Hubris stops us and blocks us from opening our minds to the idea
that there may well be someone else in our stable of experts or health
care professionals who is better equipped to deliver this message. Many
appointed officials have *true health care thoroughbreds* at their disposal,
but overlook them because of hubris and the love of the sound of their
own voice and seeing their own face on TV or in a newspaper.

Hubris stops us from *reaching out and seeking out* experts and professionals who may rightly and accurately tell us *that the way we are doing
business at that moment is off-center,* but can be corrected with adjustments and assistance. Hubris stops us from asking for and accepting
assistance.

Hubris is the enemy of effective communication at all levels and must
be actively sought out in ourselves and our colleagues and addressed in
an aggressive yet sensitive manner. Hubris blocks millions of health care
communications dollars from going where they need to go and in the
end is quite simply, a killer.

healthy ones to improve the health of the community, then the prepared
public health leader needs to learn the skills of social marketing (Turning
Point Social Marketing Collaborative, 2003a). Social marketing is first
about knowing your audience. There is a concern for developing strategies for social and behavioral change implied in a social marketing plan.
The plan needs to motivate people to act and will be most effective in
those situations in which people have a reason to want to change. There is
also the "installment plan" approach to change in that people are not
aware at first that a change is necessary. This is followed by a second stage
when people know they need to change, but don't change their behavior
for all sorts of personal or social reasons. Social marketing attempts to
remove the barriers that prevent change from taking place.

There are six phases of social marketing (Turning Point Social Marketing Collaborative, 2003b):

1. Describe the problem.
2. Conduct the market research.
3. Create the marketing strategy.
4. Plan the intervention.
5. Plan program monitoring and evaluation.
6. Implement the intervention and evaluation.

Although the health communication issues in social marketing are not dissimilar to the techniques of risk or crisis communication, marketing concerns often go beyond communication to implementing programs to change behaviors.

SUMMARY

It is clear that the prepared public health leader needs to learn the basics of risk communication, crisis communication, and social marketing (ATSDR, 2003). It is not possible in one chapter to cover the complexities of these three communication approaches in more than a superficial way. The leader needs to understand the approaches discussed here and go beyond them to the increasing number of government manuals, books, and articles on these topics. Leaders will need to work with communication specialists when they do not take on that role themselves. Communication specialists need to be part of the leadership team addressing emergency preparedness and response as well as all other major public health concerns.

REFERENCES

Agency for Toxic Substances and Disease Registry. (2004). *Citizen's guide to risk assessment for public health assessments.* Atlanta: CDC.

Agency for Toxic Substances and Disease Registry. (2003). *A primer on health risk: Communication principles and practice.* Atlanta: CDC.

Association of State and Territorial Health Officials. (2002). *Communication in risk situations.* Washington, DC: Author.

Chess, C., Hance, B. J., & Sandman, P. M. (1988). *Improving dialogue with communities: A short guide to government risk communication.* Trenton, NJ: New Jersey Department of Environmental Protection.

Covello, V. T. (1992). Risk communication, trust, and credibility, *Health and Environmental Digest, 6*(1), 1–4.

Covello, V. T. (1993). Risk communication, trust, and credibility, *Journal of Occupational Medicine, 35*, 18–19.

Covello, V. T. (2002). Message mapping: World Health Organization Workshop on bioterrorism and risk communication. Geneva, Switzerland: WHO.

Covello, V. T., & Allen, F. (1988). *Seven cardinal rules of risk communication.* Washington, DC: United States Environmental Protection Agency, Office of Policy Analysis.

Covello, V. T., Peters, R. G., Wojtecki, J. G., & Hyde, R. C. (2001). Risk communication, the West Nile Virus epidemic, and bioterrorism. *Journal of Urban Health: Bulletin of the New Academy of Medicine, 78*(2), 382–391.

Covello, V. T., Wojtecki, J. G., & Peters, R. (Unavailable). *77 Questions asked by journalists during a crisis.* New York: Center for Risk Communications.

Fernandez, L., & Merzer, M. (2003). *Jane's crisis communications handbook.* Alexandria, VA: Jane's Information Group.

Fischoff, B., Lichenstein, S., Slovik, P., & Keeney, D. (1981). *Acceptable risk.* Cambridge, MA: Cambridge University Press.

W. K. Kellogg Foundation. (2000). *Logic model development guide.* Battle Creek, MI: Author.

National Research Council. (1989). *Improving risk communication.* Washington, DC: National Academy Press.

Reynolds, B. (2002). *Crisis and emergency risk communication.* Atlanta: CDC.

Rowitz, L. (2001). *Public health leadership: Putting principles into practice.* Sudbury, MA: Jones and Bartlett.

Turning Point Social Marketing Collaborative. (2003a). *Basics of social marketing.* Seattle, WA: Turning Point National Office (R.W. Johnson Foundation).

Turning Point Social Marketing Collaborative, Centers for Disease Control and Prevention, and Academy for Educational Development. (2003b). *CDCynergy: Social marketing edition* [Computer software]. Atlanta: CDC Office of Communication.

Vanderford, M. (2004, November 9). *Leading through crisis-new threats, new leadership skills.* Presentation given at the annual meeting of the American Public Health Association, Washington, DC.

CHAPTER 12

Tipping Point Awareness

> There is nothing in the world, large or small, from the
> invisible electron to the most massive bodies in infinite space,
> which has no bounds with its fellows or with unlike bodies.
>
> —*David Ben-Gurion, first prime minister of Israel*

There is nothing in time and space that is not connected. All the things that happen to us start from a small seed or event and continue to grow over time. We are not always aware of the changes, but in retrospect everything seems clear and we can track the changes that have occurred. It is sometimes difficult to determine when our awareness was increased and we became aware of things and events to which we had previously been oblivious. The one thing that we can be sure of is that the connections between people and events are very much interrelated. In this chapter, we look at an important set of skills for a prepared public health leader. These skills are tied to the search for seminal events that define our reality. The concepts behind Gladwell's book on tipping points were not written specifically about the field of public health, although many public health examples were given and are based on the field of epidemiology (Gladwell, 2000). This chapter will view the concepts of the tipping point as a set of useful and important skills for the prepared public health leader. The other issue relates to how leaders can increase their awareness of the potential for epidemics and those events that may tip the balance toward crisis.

FOUNDATIONS OF EPIDEMIOLOGY

Many defining events in our society can be looked at in a similar fashion to epidemics (Gladwell, 2000). For example, there have been terrorist acts around the world for a long time, but at some point these acts create major reactions related to controlling these events more overtly. Gladwell described terrorism as being like a growing virus that reached an epidemic status on September 11, 2001, and gave an example of a yawn as a specific example of his comparison to a virus. One person yawns, and it seems to become contagious with many other people nearby who then yawn as well. I have noticed this phenomenon as well at concerts or plays when one person coughs and within minutes, many people are coughing.

With regard to terrorist activities, it sometimes seems that one terrorist event triggers many more such events. This phenomenon is seen daily in our newspapers and on our television sets where each day bring new terrorist activities in Iraq and in the Middle East. However, it seems that September 11, 2001, created the tipping point where terrorism was now clearly seen as a worldwide threat that needs to be controlled in a systematic way. An important consideration is that a tipping point may be interpreted in different ways by different groups. Terrorist groups might see the event as justification for further terrorist activities. The recipients will see the event as a need to protect the country and institute security measures as well as strategies for finding the terrorists. A vicious cycle is created when terrorist attacks lead to further security measures and hunts for the terrorists that lead to further terrorist attacks and on and on.

There are three characteristics of epidemics: (1) the level of contagiousness, (2) small facts or events that have large and long-lasting consequences, and (3) changes which can occur suddenly or at a dramatic moment like September 11, 2001. The interesting issue is related to the question of why certain events create epidemics and other events do not. It does appear that leaders need to constantly look for clues in their communities or, in fact, elsewhere on this planet to events that may trigger an epidemic. The prepared public health leader needs such skills to put many factors together to determine the chances for certain events happening. Exercise 11–2 in the last chapter is an important set of tools for this activity as are many of the skills discussed in this book.

Epidemics are seen in terms of the following triad:

- Agent—Those people who spread infectious agents
- Host—The infectious agent itself
- Environment

The tipping point then relates to the event that triggers the crisis. It becomes a disruption of the equilibrium. When we began to note the occurrence of dead birds at the start of the West Nile virus epidemic, the concern was not great, but a point was reached when the Centers for Disease Control and Prevention and other federal agencies thought that there was a crisis. In other words, when did the tipping point occur? Gladwell (2000) created a 3-rule metaphor to better explain the relationship between agent, host, and environment. He called these change agents "The Law of the Few" (the agent), "The Stickiness Factor" (the host), and "The Law of Context" (the environment).

The Law of the Few points to the fact that it is often a few exceptional people that lead the way to potential epidemics or change. It becomes important for the prepared public health leader to find these people. The interesting factor is that there are really only a small number of these people. In the terrorist arena, Osama Bin Laden is one of these. The nature of the messenger *is* important. The messages that he or she gives are often contagious. Gladwell (2000) described three types of agents: Connectors, Mavens, and Salespeople. Connectors are people who seem to know many important people and also know how to bring them together. They are extremely social in that they are socially aware, have high emotional intelligence, and are very intuitive about people. They also are good at remembering names and places. They know people in many different areas of endeavor. They would meet you, talk to you for a few minutes, and then say, "There is someone that you need to meet." They also are excellent at spreading messages that are true as well as false.

One way to determine if you are a connector is to answer the next few questions:

1. If you see a good movie, how many people do you recommend to go see it?
2. If you read a good book, do you recommend it to others?
3. Do you bring friends with similar interests together, or do you keep your friends isolated from one another?

If everyone you recommend a movie or book to goes to the movie or buys and reads the book and they recommend it to others, you may have helped create a high-grossing film or a best seller even when the reviews were not so good.

Mavens are information specialists. They seem to know everything and they are willing to share the information. They like to help others solve their problems. They mainly want to teach and help others by introducing them to new information. They also want to get information in return so that they can give that information to others. In some situations, Mavens appear arrogant to others. They also love to see the reaction of others to their supposed expertise. Some Mavens are also Connectors, although this is not always the case. Mavens tend not to be persuaders like Salespeople are. Salespeople are wonderful at convincing us to buy the message that they are delivering. They strongly believe that small things can make as large a difference as bigger things.

The Stickiness Factor refers to the host in the epidemiologic triad and is the second rule of the tipping point (Gladwell, 2000). The question here is: what makes a specific message catch on with some people, but not with others? The message and its presentation may affect how great the impact or stickiness is. Tinkering with the message may change its impact, although the general content of the message may not have changed. Finding the best way to transmit the information is critical. Exploring factors that create stickiness are critical in the long run. If you think about the recent flurry of activity related to the harmful effects of secondhand smoke in the workplace and the attempt to convince people of this fact, what are five ways to create a sticky message related to this? Write out a public announcement to create such a message, and then present it to a group to determine who is influenced enough by your message to support a change in a local ordinance related to outlawing smoking in all workplaces in your community.

The final tipping point rule relates to the power of context. Epidemics are strongly impacted by local conditions in a community or neighborhood. Sometimes it seems like a small incident or factor affects the outcome. Such factors as the demographic characteristics of the area, urban and rural differences, level of family life in terms of whether areas are predominantly family based or not, socioeconomic factors, streetlighting, transportation hubs, values, cultural issues, and so on can affect the spread of an epidemic. Some of the environmental tipping points can be changed. For example, if there is no streetlighting, adding streetlighting can affect the incidence of crime. Creating a block club in an inner city can also change social relationships in a community. Case Study 12 is a question-and-answer session which was written by Gladwell to explain his interpretation of why the tipping point approach is so important. To give you a chance to experiment with these three tipping point rules, Exercise 12–1 on the Broccoli Diet presents an example of such an experiment.

CASE STUDY 12

An Interview with Malcolm Gladwell

What is *The Tipping Point* about?
It's about change. In particular, it's an idea that presents a new way of understanding why change so often happens as quickly and as unexpectedly as it does. For example, why did crime drop so dramatically in New York City in the mid-1990s? How does a novel written by an unknown author end up as national bestseller? Why do teens smoke in greater and greater numbers when every single person in the country knows that cigarettes kill? Why is word-of-mouth so powerful? What makes TV shows like Sesame Street so good at teaching kids how to read? I think the answer to all those questions is the same. It's that ideas and behavior and messages and products sometimes behave just like outbreaks of infectious disease. They are social epidemics. *The Tipping Point* is an examination of the social epidemics that surround us.

What does it mean to think about life as an epidemic? Why does thinking in terms of epidemics change the way we view the world?
Because epidemics behave in a very unusual and counterintuitive way. Think, for a moment, about an epidemic of measles in a kindergarten class. One child brings in the virus. It spreads to every other child in the class in a matter of days. And then, within a week or so, it completely dies out and none of the children will ever get measles again. That's typical behavior for epidemics; they can blow up and then die out really quickly, and even the smallest change—like one child with a virus—can get them started. My argument is that it is also the way that change often happens in the rest of the world. Things can happen all at once, and little changes can make a huge difference. That's a little bit counterintuitive. As human beings, we always expect everyday change to happen slowly and steadily, and for there to be some relationship between cause and effect. And when there isn't—when crime drops dramatically in New York for no apparent reason, or when a movie made on a shoestring budget ends up making hundreds of millions of dollars—we're surprised. I'm saying, don't be surprised. This is the way social epidemics work.

Where did you get the idea for the book?
Before I went to work for *The New Yorker*, I was a reporter for the *Washington Post* and I covered the AIDS epidemic. And one of the things that struck me as I learned more and more about HIV was how strange epidemics were. If you talk to the people who study epidemics—epidemiologists—you realize that they have a strikingly different way of looking at the world. They don't share the assumptions the rest of us have about how and why change happens. The term *tipping point*, for example, comes from the world of epidemiology. It's the name given to that moment in an epidemic

continues

CASE STUDY 12   *continued*

when a virus reaches critical mass. It's the boiling point. It's the moment on the graph when the line starts to shoot straight upwards. AIDS tipped in 1982, when it went from a rare disease affecting a few gay men to a worldwide epidemic. Crime in New York City tipped in the mid 1990s, when the murder rate suddenly plummeted. When I heard that phrase for the first time I remember thinking—wow. What if everything has a tipping point? Wouldn't it be cool to try and look for tipping points in business, in social policy, in advertising, or in any number of other nonmedical areas?

Why do you think the epidemic example is so relevant for other kinds of change? Is it just that it's an unusual and interesting way to think about the world?
No. I think it's much more than that, because once you start to understand this pattern you start to see it everywhere. I'm convinced that ideas and behaviors and new products move through a population very much like a disease does. This isn't just a metaphor, in other words. I'm talking about a very literal analogy. One of the things I explore in the book is that ideas can be contagious in exactly the same way that a virus is. One chapter, for example, deals with the very strange epidemic of teenage suicide in the South Pacific islands of Micronesia. In the 1970s and 1980s, Micronesia had teen suicide rates 10 times higher than anywhere else in the world. Teenagers were literally being infected with the suicide bug, and one after another they were killing themselves in exactly the same way under exactly the same circumstances. We like to use words like *contagiousness* and *infectiousness* just to apply to the medical realm. But I assure you that after you read about what happened in Micronesia you'll be convinced that behavior can be transmitted from one person to another as easily as the flu or the measles can. In fact, I don't think you have to go to Micronesia to see this pattern in action. Isn't this the explanation for the current epidemic of teen smoking in this country? And what about the rash of mass shootings we're facing at the moment—from Columbine through the Atlanta stockbroker through the neo-Nazi in Los Angeles?

Are you talking about the idea of memes, which has become so popular in academic circles recently?
It's very similar. A meme is an idea that behaves like a virus—that moves through a population, taking hold in each person it infects. I must say, though, that I don't much like that term. The thing that bothers me about the discussion of memes is that no one ever tries to define exactly what they are, and what makes a meme so contagious. I mean, you can put a virus under a microscope and point to all the genes on its surface that are

continues

CASE STUDY 12 *continued*

responsible for making it so dangerous. So what happens when you look at an infectious idea under a microscope? I have a chapter where I try to do that. I use the example of children's television shows like Sesame Street and the new Nickelodeon program called Blues Clues. Both of those are examples of shows that started learning epidemics in preschoolers, that turned kids onto reading and "infected" them with literacy. We sometimes think of Sesame Street as purely the result of the creative genius of people like Jim Henson and Frank Oz. But the truth is that it is carefully and painstakingly engineered, down to the smallest details. There's a wonderful story, in fact, about the particular scientific reason for the creation of Big Bird. It's very funny. But I won't spoil it for you.

How would you classify *The Tipping Point*? Is it a science book?
I like to think of it as an intellectual adventure story. It draws from psychology and sociology and epidemiology, and uses examples from the worlds of business and education and fashion and media. If I had to draw an analogy to another book, I'd say it was like Daniel Goleman's *Emotional Intelligence*, in the sense that it takes theories and ideas from the social sciences and shows how they can have real relevance to our lives. There's a whole section of the book devoted to explaining the phenomenon of word of mouth, for example. I think that word of mouth is something created by three very rare and special psychological types, whom I call Connectors, Mavens, and Salesmen. I profile three people who I think embody those types, and then I use the example of Paul Revere and his midnight ride to point out the subtle characteristics of this kind of social epidemic. So just in that chapter there is a little bit of sociology, a little psychology, and a little bit of history, all in aid of explaining a very common but mysterious phenomenon that we deal with every day. I guess what I'm saying is that I'm not sure that this book fits into any one category. That's why I call it an adventure story. I think it will appeal to anyone who wants to understand the world around them in a different way. I think it can give the reader an advantage—a new set of tools. Of course, I also think they'll be in for a very fun ride.

What do you hope readers will take away from the idea of the tipping point?
One of the things I'd like to do is to show people how to start "positive" epidemics of their own. The virtue of an epidemic, after all, is that just a little input is enough to get it started, and it can spread very, very quickly. That makes it something of obvious and enormous interest to everyone from educators trying to reach students, to businesses trying to spread the word about their product, or for that matter to anyone who's trying to create a change with limited resources. The book has a number of case stud-

continues

CASE STUDY 12 *continued*

ies of people who have successfully started epidemics—an advertising agency, for example, and a breast cancer activist. I think they are really fascinating. I also take a pressing social issue, teenage smoking, and break it down and analyze what an epidemic approach to solving that problem would look like. The point is that by the end of the book I think the reader will have a clear idea of what starting an epidemic actually takes. This is not an abstract, academic book. It's very practical. And it's very hopeful. It's brain software.

Beyond that, I think that *The Tipping Point* is a way of making sense of the world, because I'm not sure that the world always makes as much sense to us as we would like. I spend a great deal of time in the book talking about the way our minds work—and the peculiar and sometimes problematic ways in which our brains process information. Our intuitions, as humans, aren't always very good. Changes that happen really suddenly, on the strength of the most minor of input, can be deeply confusing. People who understand *The Tipping Point*, I think, have a way of decoding the world around them.

EXERCISE 12–1 The Broccoli Diet

Purpose: To understand the tipping point model utilizing the three Gladwell laws

Key Concepts: Tipping point, Law of the Few, Stickiness Factor, Law of Context

Procedures: Dr. I. M. Green has conducted major research on the effects of eating specific vegetables as a method for losing weight. After 15 years, he has discovered the weight-loss effect of eating broccoli as part of each meal. As a result of his research, he has created the Broccoli Diet and a new recipe book for using broccoli in many food recipes. He has created an entire line of spices that include powdered broccoli as part of the spice mixture.

1. Divide the class or training group into groups of 10.
2. Using the three Gladwell laws, discuss how quickly the Broccoli Diet will become the predominant diet plan in America.
3. How will your group know that the tipping point has been reached?

LEADERSHIP AND THE TIPPING POINT

Figure 12–1 looks at the issue of complexity and the tipping point in public health from the leadership perspective. If we imagine the tipping point as the balancing part of a seesaw, it is first necessary to realize that the foundation for change is always within the context of the community in which it occurs. If a particular event is to become sticky (Gladwell, 2000), then an understanding of external events that are labeled *societal* in the figure needs to be balanced against strategic public health concerns that impact the given community. From a slightly different perspective, Figure 12–2 examines the public health response to a crisis from the external pressures on a community from the larger state or national perspectives, the community crisis itself, and the relationship of this crisis to the priorities of the community—such as health and safety concerns, national agenda issues that emergency responders need to act within, and those strategic challenges discussed below that affect the messages that get developed.

Societal pressures are all those factors in the culture of the community that affect such things as its power structure, its social capital infrastructure, its organizational structure, its views of public health, its concerns about personal rights and freedoms, its fear level related to a disruption in the quality of community life as perceived by its residents, and so on. There are many strategic challenges facing public health in the 21st cen-

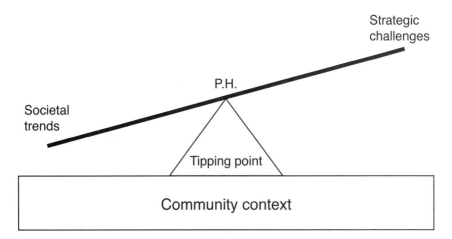

FIGURE 12–1 Public Health Complexity Issues: Leadership Demands

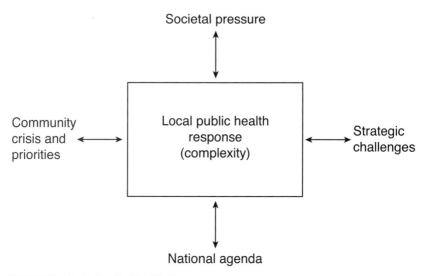

FIGURE 12–2 Public Health Response

tury. Table 12–1 lists some of the major challenges facing public health today. When this list was developed by Lenihan in 1998, public health had been going through a reevaluation of the field and a policy reevaluation of how public health fits into the organization of public services at the state level. The creation of human services superagencies was a major activity in the 1990s. As we look at the strategic challenges after September 2001, the challenge related to emergency preparedness and response clearly rises to the top of the list. In addition, the issue of health disparities is also a key issue of this new century. All these strategic challenges affect the public health system and how it is influenced by specific events. With regard to new and reemerging diseases, we now have West Nile virus, SARS, monkeypox, and the reemergence of pertussis to contend with.

The national public health agenda and new initiatives are also a factor in public health response. Table 12–2 lists some of these national agenda concerns. There are many discussions occurring about the certification of public health professionals and the accreditation of public health agencies. These discussions involve the factors to be considered in the development of these certification programs. Agreement on all the factors to be considered is not an easy process. Increasing concern with management and leadership development programs has become a reality (Rowitz, 2001). The Health Alert Network and its rapid dissemination of information and

Table 12–1 Today's Public Health Challenges

- Emergency preparedness and response
- Eliminating health disparities
- Growth of managed care
- Privatization
- Welfare reform
- Emphasis on accountability and performance
- Steering versus rowing versus navigating
- Invisibility of public health
- Government and health department reorganization
- Explosion of information technology
- Emergence of new and reemergence of old diseases
- Changing demographics
- Enhanced role of prevention
- Growing number of uninsured
- Shifting public expectations

homeland security concerns are major parts of the agenda, as is increasing emphasis on evidence-based public health practice. There is also emphasis on workforce development, which has been covered extensively in this text. New tools for community assessment are being developed, such as MAPP (Mobilizing for Action through Planning and Partnership) and the

Table 12–2 National Agenda Concerns

- Public health credentialing and accreditation
- Health Alert Network
- Public health leadership
- Essential public health services
- Workforce development
- Public health infrastructure
- National performance standards
- Public health informatics
- MAPP assessment
- Evidence-based public health
- Homeland security

National Public Health Performance Standards program, which is based on performance tied to the 10 essential public health services.

The prepared public health leader is always looking for clues based on the above factors that might tip the scales and move public health in new directions. It thus becomes a question as to whether it is possible or not to develop an awareness to potential shifts that certain types of events may cause. We now know that a terrorist act or potential terrorist or bioterrorist act is one of these events. We also know that a judicial decision at the Supreme Court level may also create such a tipping point. Exercise 12–2 will give you the chance to interpret American history, tipping points, and the impacts of these events.

Gladwell (2005) has now added to this discussion with his concept of *Blink*. Sometimes, leaders have to make decisions so rapidly that the emo-

---

EXERCISE 12–2 Historical Tipping Points

Purpose: To understand the tipping points of history

Key Concepts: Tipping point

Procedures: Divide the class or training group into groups of 10.

1. Utilizing the chart below, have each person list five American historical events that each individual feels were tipping point occurrences. Two of the five should be public health tipping points.
2. Each small group will look at each member's list and come up with a list of 10 events of which 5 relate to public health tipping points.
3. Explain with notes on the chart below why each event is a tipping point.
4. Present your list to the class or training group as a whole.

Historical Event	Tipping Point	Explanation

tional component does not seem to impact the decision. Rapid cognition is the kind of decisions that are made on the spot as a situation occurs. It is only after the event and the Blink that emotions and other reactions enter the picture. Each individual carries a cognitive map of all his or her previous life experiences into each new situation (Rowitz, 2001). Each new situation builds on previous ones. Thus, an important question relates to this cognitive historical map we carry around with us and its relationship to a rapid cognition decision.

SUMMARY

This short chapter presents the beginning of a discussion of a set of critical skills for the prepared public health leader related to tipping point awareness. It builds on public health's epidemiological tradition and shows how the skills of epidemiology may be useful in better predicting and understanding the relationship of emergency events, their causes, outcomes, and impacts on a community. Over the next few years, it is expected that more will be learned about techniques for better predicting unusual events and how to determine the effects of these events on a community.

REFERENCES

Gladwell, M. (2000). *The tipping point.* Boston: Little, Brown.

Gladwell, M. (2005). *Blink.* Boston: Little, Brown.

Lenihan, P. (1998). Personal communication.

Rowitz, L. (2001). *Public health leadership: Putting principles into practice.* Sudbury, MA: Jones and Bartlett.

CHAPTER 13

Forensic Epidemiology: A New Partnership

The changes which break up at short intervals the prosperity of man
are advertisements of a nature whose law is growth.

—*Ralph Waldo Emerson*

The emerging new field of forensic epidemiology gives the prepared public
health leader the opportunity to practice the skills discussed in previous
chapters of this book in a new context. At its foundation, forensic epidemiology is about collaboration with many new partners. It is also about
the necessity of bringing traditional epidemiologic principles, public
health law, and the principles of crime scene investigations together within
a context of bioterrorism and terrorism. It is about exercises and drills with
these new partners. It is about understanding the work of public health
through laboratories and crime laboratories. It is also about working across
jurisdictional boundaries when federal, state, and local people need to
work together. It is about building social capital through these new partnerships to better prepare for emergencies and our responses to it. It is
about rapid cognition and making decisions quickly before our gut reactions slow us down. It is critical to also take emotional reactions into
account once the realities of a crisis take hold. Forensic epidemiology also
concerns the critical skills of communication and how to communicate
with partners who have a different lexicon and a different view about handling crisis situations. It is about knowing the law, protection of personal
rights, police powers, and other legal and judicial considerations. This

chapter will look at this new field, review the Centers for Disease Control and Prevention (CDC) curriculum for forensic epidemiology, and give you the chance to experiment with one of the case studies in its curriculum.

Forensic epidemiology requires a relationship between public health investigations of a crisis and the parallel criminal investigation of the same event. Goodman and his colleagues (2003) stated that public health and law enforcement agencies including local and state police, Federal Bureau of Investigation (FBI) agents, and local fire professionals need to work together when there may be evidence that an event may be criminal in nature and when detection of the event may be tied to laws that make the event a possible crime. One example Goodman et al. gave was related to an HIV-infected individual who knowingly exposes others to HIV by having sex without appropriate protection. Utilizing the various approaches discussed by Goodman and his colleagues, we can define forensic epidemiology as the utilization of epidemiologic methods to uncover the causes of an event or series of events which appear to have possible intentional or criminal behavior factors associated with the event. The epidemiologic investigation must thus be coordinated with criminal investigation methods. Forensic epidemiology requires a collaboration and a coordination of investigations. Table 13–1, which Goodman and his colleagues presented as a background for the development of a forensic epidemiology training program, emphasizes the issues of criminal and epidemiological investigative methods, operations and procedures, and communications.

A NEW PARADIGM

A paradigm is a model that provides parameters around which the work of an organization gets done (Barker, 1992). What we have in forensic epidemiology is a situation in which conflicting paradigms clash. One possible solution is a paradigm shift in which there is a new model to drive the action. A new game is created with new rules. A second solution is for one of the conflicting groups to superimpose its model on other groups through a power grab. A third possibility is to bust an existing paradigm and start over. A fourth approach is the one we seem to be taking in forensic epidemiology. We seem to be blending the paradigms of public health and epidemiology by creating this new synthesis called forensic epidemiology. Yet, this blend still recognizes the need for each of the existing paradigms to continue to work in a setting in which crises are not the norm.

Table 13-1 Course Objectives for Epidemiology Training

Criminal and Epidemiological Investigative Methods
Demonstrate an understanding of the similarities and differences in public health and law enforcement investigative goals and methods.

Show an understanding of crime scene procedures.

Describe specimen collection and establishment of chain of custody of evidence.

Demonstrate an understanding of environmental testing.

Understand the inclusion of *intentionality* in the epidemiologic differential diagnosis and investigation.

Operations and Procedures
Demonstrate an understanding of controlling laws and sources of authorities for actions.

Demonstrate an understanding of legal issues surrounding bioterrorism.

Determine jurisdictional lead responsibilities.

Identify additional resources to call and when to call.

Recognize when to involve the other discipline after the problem is acknowledged.

Coordinate public health and law enforcement during responses and investigations.

Coordinate local, state, and federal resources.

Describe on-scene control measures and interventions.

Communications
Communicate and share information between law enforcement and public health.

Differentiate between treatment of information (e.g., privacy, confidentiality, public discosure).

Describe media relations and risk communication.

Since the various terrorist events of 2001, there has been an increasing probability that public health and law enforcement will need to work together and coordinate their investigative activities. The emergence of these new relationships creates a change in the paradigm that affected investigations in the past. This new emerging partnership paradigm can be viewed in terms of overt and covert events (Butler et al., 2002). If the crisis event is overt, the agent declares that he or she is responsible for the terrorist event. The event itself may also, by its very nature, imply or lead the way to the agent perpetrator. Law enforcement—police or FBI agents—will often detect and announce the event. The flow chart shown in Figure 13–1 shows the likely scenario for communication related to an event. This chart also shows a possible connection between public health and law enforcement in response to a bioterrorism or terrorist event. The collaboration occurs at several points in time:

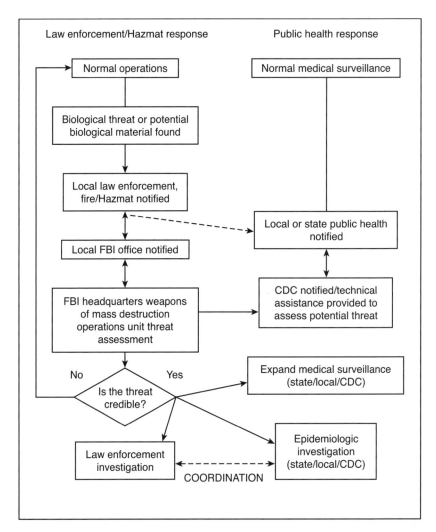

FIGURE 13–1 Flow of Communication During Overt Bioterrorism or Terrorism Event

- Notification of the local or state public health agency of the event
- During technical assistance from CDC in evaluating the potential threat
- With increased medical and public health surveillance
- Possible need for epidemiologic investigations

Covert events involve unannounced or not recognizable releases of a foreign agent where people becoming ill leads to the recognition of an emergency (Butler et al., 2002). In covert events, possible criminal intent may take time to ascertain. In these events, public health usually begins the initial inquiry, which concentrates on such activities as diagnosis, medical care, and epidemiologic investigations. Figure 13–2 shows these activities. A look at this chart shows the collaboration between public health and law enforcement is almost the reverse of the activities in a overt event. Here public health notifies the local FBI office of the event and their belief that there may have been a crime committed. After that point, there will have to be a coordination between the epidemiologic and the criminal investigation activities.

There are differences in investigation approaches of public health and law enforcement (Butler et al., 2002). Utilizing an inductive approach, public health takes a scientific method approach to its investigations. The process often takes more time than criminal investigation, which tends to be deductive in nature because of the need to conduct surveys, analyze and evaluate the results, and relate the findings to similar activities and events in the past. The scientific method process is also more open, whereas the criminal investigation may need to be more confidential and secretive in nature. Prepared public health leaders often need to learn the skills related to being an expert witness if there is ever a criminal trial. These leaders will also need to keep information confidential that they may have been able to reveal to the public in the past. From a criminal investigation perspective, respondents now become witnesses and potential suspects. Leads are followed, evidence is collected and carefully documented and tracked through chain-of-evidence protocols. The endgame is to find and arrest the person or persons who carried out the terrorist or bioterrorism event.

The major advantage of this new partnership between public health and law enforcement is that a synergistic effect occurs. By blending the investigation approaches of both these entities, more information is collected and a more comprehensive evaluation of information and evidence

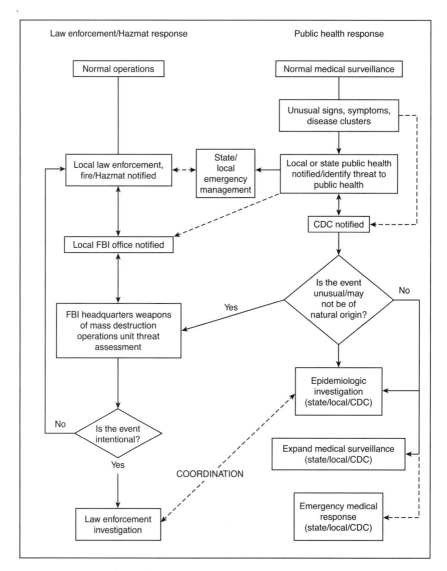

FIGURE 13–2 Flow of Communication During Covert Bioterrorism or Terrorism Event

occurs as a result. Both public health and law enforcement have similar goals in mind in collaborative investigation (FBI, 2002). Their goals are to first protect the public, prevent or stop the spread of disease, determine and identify those agents responsible for threat or attack on the public, and finally to protect their employees during a crisis and in the response phase of those crises. Law enforcement and public health must be part of the response team in these terrorist and bioterrorism events. They need to share the types of information they will each need to carry out their individual investigations. They can coordinate their investigation and information gathering when their mutual interests are compatible. Effective information exchange is the goal. Tables 13–2 and 13–3 summarize the information relevant to public health and law enforcement.

ROLE OF THE LABORATORY

An important set of partners in forensic epidemiology are representatives from public health laboratories and from forensic crime laboratories (CDC, 2004). Public health state laboratories are reference laboratories in a state. In some states, there are also county and city laboratories. These laboratories have a great deal of experience in investigating all kinds of biological agents which are of concern, as well as epidemiologic outbreak investigations. These laboratories will have a critical role to play in terrorist and bioterrorist situations. These laboratories also have links with CDC and other federal agencies. Specifically, the state public health laboratory is involved in such reference services as additional and definitive testing on isolates and other specimens (CDC, 2004). These laboratories are also involved in all kinds of environmental testing, rapid testing, applied research, improvement of clinical laboratories throughout their respective states, and support of disease surveillance and epidemiology investigations. With regard to emergency preparedness and response, the state laboratories have several other critical tasks including the monitoring of community health status, assessment of diseases of public health significance, early intervention and detection of diseases, assurance activities related to safe and disease-free communities, and many other responsibilities.

Forensic laboratories are laboratories tied to law enforcement and criminal investigations. Many people have some idea of what these laboratories do thanks to the popular CSI (Crime Scene Investigation) television shows of the first decade of the 21st century. These shows demonstrate the connection between police, crime scene investigators, coroners, and laboratory specialists working together on complex cases. Some of the services conducted by forensic laboratories include fingerprinting and maintaining national databases that can be searched for fingerprints of suspects. Analyses of hair, DNA samples, blood types, other tissue samples, and

---

Table 13-2 Information Important to Public Health Personnel During an Investigation into a Biological Attack

---

Personal/Family Health Information
- What does the victim think made him or her ill?
- When (date/time of onset) did the victim start feeling sick?
- Does the victim know of anyone else who has become ill or died (e.g., family, coworkers, etc.)?
- Has the victim had any medical treatment in the last month? What is the name of the health care provider? Where was the victim treated?
- Does the victim have any allergies to medications?

Activities Information
- Where does the victim live and work or go to school?
- Did the victim attend a public event (i.e., sporting event, social function, visit a restaurant, etc.)?
- Has the victim or the victim's family members traveled more than 50 miles in the last 30 days?
- Has the victim or the victim's family members had any contact with individuals who had been in another country in the last 30 days?

Agent Dissemination Information
- Has the victim detected any unusual odors or tastes?
- Has the victim noticed any sick or dead animals?

Medical Information
- Is the victim's disease contagious?
- When did the victim first seek treatment for the illness?
- What are the laboratory results?
- Who collected, tested, analyzed, and had access to the samples?

Personnel Safety Information
- What precautions should criminal investigators take?
- What physical protection from the disease/agent is needed?
- Is the agent communicable by person-to-person exposure? How is the disease spread?

Epidemiological Investigation Information
- Who is the point of contact in the public health community?
- Where should the sick be referred?
- What makes this case suspect?
- What is the spectrum of illness the law enforcement community could be seeing (case definition)?

---

other human materials can also be done. These laboratories will also perform microscopic and chemical analyses of fiber, paper, and other materials. Some laboratories can also do ballistics testing involving projectile characterization, weapon analysis, and explosive debris analysis.

Table 13-3 Information Important to Law Enforcement Personnel During an Investigation Into a Biological Attack

---

Personal Information

- Victim's name
- Victim's age/date of birth
- Victim's sex
- Victim's address
- Victim's Social Security number
- Victim's driver's license number
- Victim's occupation/employer
- Victim's religious affiliation
- Victim's level of education
- Victim's ethnicity/nationality
- Record any personal property (bag & tag)
- Common denominators among victims/patients (e.g., race, socioeconomic status, sociopolitical groups and associations, locations, events, travel, religion, etc.)

Travel Information

- Whether the person has traveled outside of the United States in the last 30 days
- Whether the person traveled away from home in the last 30 days.
- The person's normal mode of transportation and route to and from work everyday
- The person's activities for the last 30 days

Incident Information

- Whether interviewee heard any unusual statements (e.g., threatening statements, information about biological agents)
- Did the victim see an unusual device or anyone spraying something?
- Were there any potential dispersal devices/laboratory equipment/ suspicious activities?
- Identification of the biological agent: is the agent's identity suspected, presumed, or confirmed?
- The victim's account of what happened or how he or she might have gotten sick
- The time/date of exposure. Is the time/date suspected, presumed, or confirmed?
- The number of victims: Is the number suspected, presumed, or confirmed?
- Whether there is a cluster of casualties: Is the cluster suspected, presumed, or confirmed?

continues

Table 13–3 *continued*

- The potential methods of exposure (e.g., ingested, inhaled, skin contact)
- The exact location of the incident: Is this location suspected, presumed, or confirmed?
- Whether the biological event is a single incident or involves multiple releases: Is this suspected, presumed, or confirmed?
- The case distribution: What are the names, dates of birth, and addresses of the cases?
- The types of physical evidence that should be sought
- Any witnesses to a suspicious incident. What are their names, dates of birth, and addresses?

Safety Information

- What makes this case suspect?
- The presence of any information that would indicate a suspicious event
- Any safety or security issues for the public health personnel

Criminal Investigation Information

- Who is the point of contact in the law enforcement community?
- To whom should potential witnesses be referred?
- Any chain of custody needs

The other critical concern relates to the implementation of a process called *chain of custody* where all specimens that are collected are carefully documented as to when received and whoever handled the specimen at any time. There are procedures related to the containers in which the specimens are to be held. A complete record for each specimen is collected. This type of detail is not usual in state or local public health laboratories. Chain-of-custody protocols become critical if a case goes to court. Lock-and-key protocols also need to be followed both in the field and in the laboratory to avoid tampering or accidental interference. The police or laboratory technician may also be required to testify in court. In the case of terrorist and bioterrorist events, public health laboratory technicians may also have to testify.

By now, it should be clear that the concept of a case can also differ. In public health, a case refers to an individual and whether that individual has a particular disease or health-related condition. The determination of this is made by a health professional examining the presenting symptoms of the individual, clinical and laboratory testing and findings, and personal or family background factors. A case in the civil and criminal realm involves everyone and everything connected with an event. It includes such things as all activities related to the event, interviews with witnesses and others, evidence and its collection, and so on. There is also a clear differentiation between the victim and the case. Another term often used is *suspect*, which is a person who may be responsible or an accessory to the event.

FORENSIC EPIDEMIOLOGY COURSE

This course was developed for both managers and leaders. The prepared public health leader needs to not only develop the relationships necessary to work in this new field, but must also understand the interrelationships between forensic epidemiology concerns and many of the other topics and skills required to work in the new public health arena. The main goal of the CDC course on forensic epidemiology is to enhance the collaboration and effectiveness between law enforcement and public health during terrorist and bioterrorist events by training both groups together for a 2-day period, although variations in the course have been done in different places. The course involves three fact-based case studies that small groups made up of both law enforcement and public health professionals work on together. Each team has public health personnel including epidemiologists, laboratory representatives, program directors, public health information officers, emergency room staff, infection control nurses, other health and safety personnel, and possibly state or local health department personnel. On the law enforcement side, there may be state and local police, FBI agents, fire professionals, judges, lawyers and U.S. attorneys, and forensic laboratory people. Some teams have also included public health faculty as well.

A second part of the course includes talks by experts from both sectors. Some of these talks are specific to the two groups. For example, law enforcement people are introduced to public health, and public health professionals are introduced to law enforcement. In a typical course, the first half day is given over to formal presentations. The first afternoon and the second day involve the experiential activity of going over the case study examples. To give you a better idea about the process, Case Study 13 includes one of the cases in the course. The case study entitled "Anthrax in Florida" is based on a true case that occurred in that state in

CASE STUDY 13   Anthrax in Florida

Objectives/Topics for Case Study 13

1. Understanding public health investigations, including:
    - Defining exposed population(s)
    - Providing prophylaxis to exposed persons
    - Identifying the source (e.g., perpetrators/reservoir)

2. Understanding how a public health investigation differs from and is similar to a criminal investigation

3. Addressing communication challenges, including media relations and risk communication (including public health needs vs. law enforcement restriction)

4. Addressing interagency communication

5. Maintaining simultaneous epidemiological and criminal investigations

6. Defining jurisdictional issues

7. Understanding issues related to the law surrounding entry into and sampling of homes and workplaces

Facts and Questions

Facts I: On October 2, 2001, the Palm Beach Health Department was notified by an infectious disease physician about unusual test results using gram stain (a special dye used to identify bacteria) for a patient with meningitis (bacterial infection of the tissues covering the brain); the patient was a county resident. The state epidemiologist was contacted and a team of local epidemiologists began an investigation. The state made arrangements for further laboratory testing in the state laboratory. On October 3, specimens were sent to the state laboratory and further information suggested that this case could be a suspect case of systemic anthrax (i.e., anthrax bacteria in the blood). The state epidemiologist notified the CDC about this case according to established protocol. The CDC notified the FBI headquarters in Washington, DC, of the situation in Florida, and the FBI field office in Miami dispatched personnel to assist in assessing this unfolding situation.

Question 1: What are the implications of one or more suspected or confirmed cases of anthrax in the United States?

Question 2: How is a suspected case of anthrax confirmed and where are human samples sent?

Facts II: Early on the morning of October 4, the state laboratory, part of the US Laboratory Response Network (LRN), determined that the organism in the patient's specimen was anthrax bacteria—*Bacillus anthracis*, or *B. anthracis* for short. Although the tests were deemed to be conclusive, this rare finding needed independent confirmation. Arrangements were made

continues

CASE STUDY 13   *continued*

for samples to be transported to CDC's national reference laboratory in Atlanta, which later verified the Florida results. That same morning, state and federal investigators joined the local staff to conduct an intense investigation of the possible source of the patient's infection. From the public health perspective, this single case of confirmed anthrax is considered to be an epidemic because this form of infection is so rare.

Question 3: What are the goals of this phase of a public health investigation of an epidemic?

Question 4: At this point, how should the investigators handle media relations in terms of what the public needs to know?

Facts III: Because the patient's medical condition had deteriorated such that he could not be interviewed, public health and FBI investigators interviewed his wife and daughter. Investigation of the patient's history revealed that he had traveled by car from Florida to North Carolina and back to Florida in the week prior to his admission to the hospital. The incubation period (i.e., the time interval between the initial infection and the onset of clinical features of disease) for systemic anthrax is believed to range from 1 to 60 days, but is usually from 3 to 7 days. The information collected to this point suggested that the patient's potential exposure could have occurred in either state or any point in between. This information led to environmental investigations (including outdoor activity locations, and residential and work settings) in both North Carolina and Florida in an attempt to identify the possible source of the patient's infection. In addition, because of the potential for this case to have resulted from a criminal act, by October 4, law enforcement officials in both state had been notified. In Florida, local and state law enforcement, the FBI, and public health were now joined in the investigation.

Question 5: Based on the information above, at this stage of the investigation what are the roles of public health officials and law enforcement authorities in the investigation, and under what circumstances might the respective roles of public health and law enforcement officials change?

Question 6: What is the law surrounding entry into and sampling of homes and workplaces?

Question 7: What are the requirements for training and protection of those who may be asked to enter facilities to collect environmental samples?

Facts IV: From October 5–8, public health and law enforcement officials continued the investigation, defining the patient's activities in greater detail and conducting additional environmental testing for the presence of *B. anthracis*. On October 8, the Florida Department of Health's laboratory

continues

CASE STUDY 13   *continued*

reported the detection of *B. anthracis* from environmental samples obtained from a mailbox in the patient's workplace, the surfaces in the workplace mailroom, and the patient's computer workstation keyboard. Based on this information, mail was implicated as the potential source of the patient's infection.

Question 8:   Does this investigation now become a criminal investigation and, if so, how does this change the role of public health and law enforcement investigators?

Question 9:   Who is responsible for determining whether a building should be evacuated and sealed and, if so, when it can be reentered?

Question 10:   What are the responsibilities of law enforcement in protecting such a crime scene for the purposes of further investigations and possible prosecution?

Question 11:   What are the responsibilities of public health authorities in preventing further cases of anthrax in workers and in visitors to the original case's workplace?

Question 12:   Who is in charge of the investigation at the patient's workplace and residence?

Facts V: On October 8, the Palm Beach County Health Department issued an order closing the building in which the patient worked. The building's management voluntarily closed the building when informed of the impending order. Within hours, the FBI declared the building a crime scene and took control of the building.

Based on building plan information, the building's air supply system, and the incubation period of anthrax, the decision was made to offer antibiotic prophylaxis from the National Pharmaceutical Stockpile to all employees and visitors who had been in the patient's workplace building during August 1 through October 7 (this number was approximately 1114 persons). On October 12, the New York City Department of Public Health reported a suspected case of cutaneous anthrax in an office worker at a large broadcast media outlet in New York City. The onset of illness in that worker appeared to predate that of the case in Florida, and the New York City patient recalled having received a letter with suspicious contents approximately 11 days prior to onset of disease. The letter was retrieved by the FBI, and its contents were confirmed to include *B. anthracis* spores.

Question 13:   How does the FBI coordinate among local, state, and federal law enforcement efforts during a national investigation?

Question 14:   How does health coordinate among local, state, and federal public health efforts during a national investigation?

2001. The case study has five sets of facts and 14 questions. Exercise 13–1 involves a role play situation where you will go through this case. Appendix A includes the answers to the questions posed in the case.

CONSEQUENCE MANAGEMENT

Those of us who are committed to lifelong learning ask the question: what types of new learning will we encounter in the future? The developers of the CDC's forensic epidemiology curriculum are addressing the issues related to what's next. A second-level training is being developed that covers the emerging area of consequence management, which is a military concept being applied to emergency preparedness, health law preparedness, and response activities. From a public health preparedness perspective, consequence management includes measures needed to protect public health and safety, applications and changes in public health laws and their implementation, procedures required to restore essential

---

Exercise 13–1 Anthrax in Florida

Purpose: To work collaboratively to address a bioterrorist event using forensic epidemiology

Key Concepts: Forensic epidemiology, collaboration, law enforcement, public health, investigations

Procedures. You will use Case Study 13 for this activity.

1. Divide your class or training group into groups of 10–12 people. Half of your group will represent public health representatives (for example, state laboratory director, local health official, state epidemiologist, environmental health specialist, public health nurse, and public health lawyer). Half of your group will represent law enforcement (for example, local FBI agent, police chief, sheriff from a small rural county, forensic laboratory director, fireman, and state's attorney).
2. Pick one member of your team to be a group facilitator.
3. Pick someone to be a recorder for the group and to prepare findings and recommendations of your group discussions
4. Go through the case study and answer the 14 questions presented from the viewpoint of your home state.
5. Each team will have 90 minutes to go through the process.
6. Reports will be presented to the group as a whole.

---

governmental services, and also interventions necessary to provide emergency relief to governments, businesses, and community residents who were impacted by a terrorist or bioterrorist event or series of events. If there were an actual or potential event, Federal Emergency Management Agency (FEMA) would take the lead in the response to the event.

Consequence management (CM) evolved out of a concern by Congress in 1997 related to the proliferation of weapons of mass destruction (WMD) (Taylor, Rowe, and Lewis, 1999). CM arose out of the need to coordinate activities of over 40 federal agencies who are involved in and share responsibility for emergency preparedness and response activities. Despite an awareness of the need to coordinate these agency activities at both the federal and state levels, there is as yet no agreement what this emerging field will look like. One area of agreement is that CM relates to those actions necessary for a coordinated response to a disaster. There will need to be a clear delineation of who is responsible for what. FEMA takes responsibility after an incident has occurred. It is clear that a combined response will be necessary. It will only be through planning prior to an event, coordination of strategies, and training of all partners in the endeavor that a timely response to an unexpected disaster will occur. Thus, the next step in training will be a training activity for prepared public health leaders and their preparedness partners that addresses the issues of consequence management and the leadership needed to make these new perspectives more reality based.

SUMMARY

Forensic epidemiology creates an opportunity for professionals from public health to meet and work with professionals from various types of law enforcement agencies at the federal, state, and local levels. The techniques discussed in this chapter offer these new partnerships skills related to working together in emergency preparedness and response initiatives. The next step after the implementation of forensic epidemiology programs involves the concerns related to the coordination of response activities involved in consequence management and legal preparedness.

REFERENCES

Barker, J. A. (1992). *Future Edge (Paradigms)*. New York: Will Morrow.

Butler, J. C., Cohen, M. L., Friedman, C. R., Scripp, R. M., and Watz, C. G. (2002). Collaboration between public health and law enforcement: New paradigms and partnerships for bioterrorism planning and response, *Emerging Infectious Disease, 8*(10), 1152–1156.

Centers for Disease Control and Prevention. (2004). *Forensic epidemiology: Course manager's guide*. Atlanta: Author.

Federal Bureau of Investigation. (2002). *Criminal and epidemiological investigation handbook*. Washington, DC: Department of Justice.

Goodman, R. A., Munson, J. W., Dammers, K., Lazzarin, Z., and Barkeley, J. P. (2003). Forensic epidemiology: Law at the intersection of public health and criminal investigation, *Journal of Law, Medicine, and Ethics, 31*, 684–700.

Taylor, S. R., Rowe, A. M., and Lewis, B. M. (1999). Consequence management in need of a timeout, *Joint Force Quarterly, 22*, 78–85.

CHAPTER 14

Building Communities

The pursuit of happiness is never ending—
the happiness lies in the pursuit.

—*Saul D. Alinsky, political activist, 1969*

The prepared public health leader spends more of his or her time in the community than he or she serves than inside the agency that he or she leads. Public health today is about community and community relationships. It is also about building social capital as was discussed in detail in Chapter 2, and about new partnerships as was discussed in Chapter 6. The positive orientation of the leader will serve as a guide through the good times and also through the times of crisis. In a book of reflections on his leadership experiences told as short vignettes, Magee (2000), who is a physician, stated that positive leaders stand on principle and these principles then have a visible impact on all those with whom they interact. Positive leadership is clearly needed in times of crisis. Leaders need to see beyond the crisis at the lessons to be learned and to the important tasks related to healing. The goal of leadership is to learn the skills necessary to make our communities safe and also to always respect every individual who lives within these communities. This chapter will look at additional skills that are needed by leaders as they face the challenges of public health in the 21st century in a positive way (Magee, 2000).

OVERVIEW OF COMMUNITY BUILDING

There has been much discussion in recent years about the importance of building community. It is strongly believed that a strong community is a community that can address any attack on its infrastructure. There has also been discussion about the concern that our communities are disintegrating because people who live within a jurisdiction do not relate to that community in anything other than a superficial manner. It is clear that communities grow when there is collaboration and commitment to that community. The prepared public health leader needs to work with all community groups to create an environment for positive social change through collaboration. Mattesich and Monsey (1997) have enumerated 15 factors that can help the process of community growth and development. These factors include the following characteristics:

1. It is important to get widespread community involvement and participation.
2. Good, if not great, communication skills are critical to successful community building.
3. Collaboration to support community development is better than competition.
4. It is important to develop a community identity and agreement on community priorities.
5. Community residents need to see and feel that they are benefiting from any changes that occur.
6. Community development is tied to building relationships with others and offers events and accomplishments that support the relationship-building activities.
7. Communities that succeed have relationships with organizations and communities other than themselves.
8. Community growth begins small and simple and becomes bigger and more complex over time.
9. It is important to monitor changing needs of community residents as well as any other gauge of community reaction or concern.
10. Community residents and leaders need to be offered training and informational meetings so that they can learn and better understand what is occurring.
11. Community organizations with long tenure in the community need to be involved in any community-building activity.
12. Technical assistance and consultation should be utilized to expedite change and to help residents to better understand why changes and growth are necessary.

13. It is important for communities on the move to grow new leaders.
14. Residents and their trustee community leaders need to be able to control any decisions that need to be made.
15. There needs to be a balance between internal and external resources to promote community growth.

COMMUNITY LEADERS

As prepared public health leaders extend their work into the community, it is becoming increasingly clear that the involvement of community residents becomes more and more important. Most leaders with positional authority are not willing or lack understanding of the ways to interact with community people in a collaborative way. Part of the challenge relates to that abstract phenomenon referred to as *sharing power*. Because many community people lack leadership training, it is important for the public health leader to work with the community in developing their leaders who will become trustees in the sense that they will represent other community residents. Empowering the community to train its representatives as leaders involves working with people rather than doing the work for them (Kellogg, 1995). These grassroots leaders will often be part of a community-based coalition or organization. They also need to see themselves as community trustees.

A trustee becomes involved in what has been called community ownership. Community ownership involves taking responsibility for the challenges that a community needs to take. Community leaders will thus define the issues of concern for community health. Not only will they help to define the issues, these grassroots leaders, in collaboration with the public health leaders, will help to define and implement the solutions and the strategies for carrying them out. These leaders need the training and the tools necessary to make these solutions work. Trust can easily erode when community leaders are not involved in the implementation of the strategies or when the professionals take over and disenfranchise the community leaders.

The leaders in the community come from several places (Kellogg, 1995). Formal community leaders include elected or appointed officials, heads of community agencies, direct service providers, and civic leaders. These leaders often represent specific constituents in the community and have the power to speak for a group or groups of community residents. A second key group of leaders are volunteers. These leaders are community residents with grassroot constituencies. They clearly have the trust of their constituencies, where formal leaders may not have the same level of community trust. The third group of community leaders are informal leaders. This group often includes people with high community respect but without an active constituency. They include those people who know the history of the community, people who will always give you advice when you have a problem, and the person who will just listen to you and not give you advice.

All communities have organized sectors with people who are seen as leaders in that sector. In other words, it is possible to create a list of these organized sectors in a specific community. These sectors include leaders from police and fire departments, elected offices, youth and senior centers and agencies, health care organizations, and so on. Since many communities are in a state of flux, there may also be developing community sectors from a variety of places including a new industry, new gangs, a new church, and so on. Exercise 14–1 will give you the opportunity to explore community sectors and some ways to increase community outreach (Kellogg, 1995).

Exercise 14–1 Community Sectors

Purpose: To identify community resources for building communities

Key Concepts: Community sectors, community building

Procedures: Look at your home community and identify the community sectors. Determine how you can increase community outreach. What are the outcomes that you would like to obtain? If you are a member of a community collaborative, the collaborative can do this exercise.

Community Sectors	Possible Outreach Activities	Potential Outcomes

Some community outreach strategies for the prepared public health leader include the following (Kellogg, 1995):

1. Identify and reach out to community leaders in all three sector groups.
2. Contact organized and developing community sector groups through public and house meetings and door-to-door contact.
3. Perform street outreach by going to the sector sites.
4. Set up information tables at community meeting sites, such as supermarkets.
5. Attend community meetings and speak at the open portion of a meeting, if possible.
6. Do community assessment or community participatory research.

Another dimension of working with community leaders relates to why a community leader may want to participate in the endeavors being supported by public health leaders. Kaye and Wolff (1997) stated that there are six reasons (The Six Rs) that people participate in all types of groups or community-based endeavors:

1. People participate for *Recognition* of their leadership. Recognition can be shown through such activities as award dinners.
2. People want *Respect*, which involves the respect of their peers or neighbors. Involvement also needs to occur in nonwork hours when community people who work during the day can attend.
3. Community leaders like to have a specific defined *Role* in a community initiative. These roles also need to have some power and authority associated with them.
4. Community leaders will become involved in community activities because they have a *Relationship* with others who are involved.
5. There need to be *Rewards* for being a member of a coalition or involved in a community-based activity that outweigh the costs of involvement.
6. Community leaders want to see *Results*. As business people will state, there needs to be a demonstrable product out of the interaction.

There are many tools available for evaluating community involvement. In addition to the two sources described in this section, Ayre, Clough, and Norris (2000) have developed a manual that examines change in communities from the vantage point of community readiness for change, the importance of energy in team activities, the importance of building successes into the program, motivating the community, setting direction for the change that is proposed, and then implementing the change.

An interesting set of issues relate to the self-determination part of community leadership. A very interesting Web site that is utilized by many community leaders is the Community Toolbox. Axner (no date) has studied the issue of learning how to be a community leader. People who become community leaders are those who have strong concerns about where their communities are going. They also want to improve their communities. Community leaders need to think that they can make a difference. Leadership development is a growth activity, and there really is not a limit on how many community leaders there can be in a community. There are several issues for potential community leaders to take into consideration including the following (Axner, no date):

1. It is important to create a personal vision for a community in a *big picture* way.
2. Listening skills are very important because the community leader needs to know what the concerns of other community members are.
3. It is critical that the potential leader agrees to serve a community in a leadership role.
4. Leaders need to turn their vision into a set of goals.
5. Leaders need to protect the interests of other people in their community group.
6. Leaders also have to look at their collaborative in terms of what is best for the community as a whole and be able to justify their position to others.
7. Leaders guide the process of developing and proposing programs and policies.
8. Follow-through is important—the work needs to get done.
9. Leaders need to nurture the leadership potential of other community residents.

LEADERSHIP WHEEL

In my earlier book on public health leadership, I introduced a systems approach to the tasks of leadership in organizations (Rowitz, 2001). This diagram has come to be called the *leadership wheel*, and it can now be expanded to include the tasks of leaders in communities (see Figure 14–1).

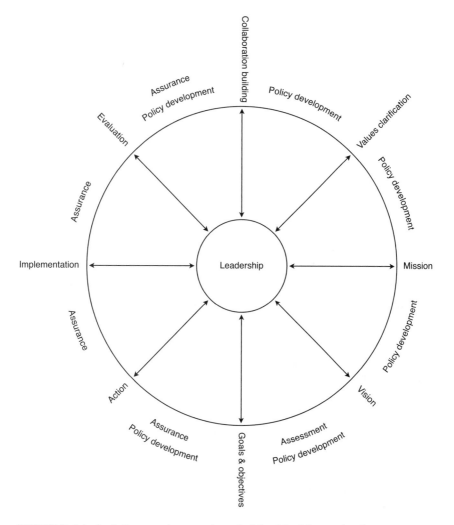

FIGURE 14–1 A System Approach to Public Health Leadership Including the Core Functions

The wheel not only utilizes the activities of groups in communities, but applies these activities to the core public health functions of assessment, policy development, and assurance. It is some community challenge, crisis situation, or community-building process that brings the prepared public health leader together with community leaders and all the emergency preparedness and response officials. In a collaborative group, these leaders will form themselves into a coalition, alliance, or partnership. It is usually some community need (assessment) as defined qualitatively or quantitatively with some policy considerations that bring the collaboration into being. Skills in collaboration with a strong commitment to address the community need serve as catalysts for the leadership process required.

The first half of the wheel represents a strategic planning approach with the addition of a values-clarification stage as well as potential for feedback at every stage of the wheel. Values clarification is often ignored as a stage in community collaboration. It is important to understand the cultural and organizational diversity that every collaboration entails. Exercise 14–2 will give your collaboration the chance to tie values to agendas. Try to understand the policy implications of the exercise. If your group takes the values-clarification task seriously, then the job of developing a mission and vision statement will be greatly simplified. Mission and vision are also part of the public health core function of policy development. Chapter 16 will give you the chance to experiment with visioning as an important leadership activity. Once the mission and vision are discussed and agreed upon, then specific goals and objectives need to be developed to make the vision a reality. Goals and objectives are the link

---

Exercise 14–2 Cascading Values

Purpose: To utilize values as a framework for collaboration

Key Concepts: Values, collaboration, agenda setting

Procedures: This exercise has been developed for you in your work with a community group.

1. Have each member of your collaborative group, whether it be a coalition, alliance, or a partnership, write down on a 3×5 index card three values that each member sees as related to their involvement in such a community activity.
2. Write all the values on a large sheet of paper (flip chart).
3. Discuss each value with the group as a whole to see how the group sees the collaboration.
4. On a second 3×5 index card, write three statements that reflect how each member sees the agenda for the group.
5. Write the agenda items on a large sheet of paper as you did for the values.
6. Match the values to the agenda items.
7. Discuss the results.
8. Create a value statement and a 6-month agenda protocol for the collaborative as a whole.

---

between the mission of today and the vision of tomorrow. If the goals and objectives do not reflect this linkage, then there is a disconnect between the mission and the vision. Goals and objectives also connect the core function of policy development with the assessment function, as goals and objectives are often tied to information gleaned from the needs assessment that brought the collaborative group into being.

The steps thus far are often where strategic planning ends and action begins. It is possible to develop a series of action steps for each goal and objective. Action planning is closely related to the important considerations related to goals management, performance measurement, and performance standards. Goals management and performance measurement tell us how effective we are in tying our action steps to addressing goals and objectives. Performance standards are benchmarks to measure our progress and successes and failures. This step is often not given the time and effort it needs to create a viable implementation (Johnson, Grossman, and Cassidy, 1996).

Action planning requires a series of steps for the creation of an action plan. The first step is determining the underlying reasons for the plan by relating it back to both vision and overall goals and objectives. Next, it is important to develop a framework based on the core functions and essential public health services. A series of design meetings can then be held to create the plan. The plan should be written down so that there will be no confusion about its components. Validation will be needed not only from members of the collaborative, but also from any other affected stakeholders. Finally, the plan needs to be disseminated to the community as well as to all the agency partners.

The plan then needs to be implemented, which will bring the core function of assurance into play. Here is where the real action occurs. All activities should be evaluated as well. The next stage is for the group to begin discussions about next steps and whether the group should continue, disband, or restructure itself and start the planning and implementation process again. It is difficult to determine how long the entire cycle will take. It will vary from community to community.

MULTICULTURAL CONSIDERATIONS

It is important to take into consideration the multicultural diversity of a community in any community-building process. Multicultural representatives should be part of any community-based activity. It is important to have different social and cultural groups involved in shaping a community collaboration, making decisions that will impact the community in which these groups live, and making sure that the collective interest is supported and nurtured (Kaye & Wolff, 1997). If public health leaders want to build effective community coalitions, alliances, and partnerships, several steps need to be followed. These steps include the following (Kaye & Wolff, 1997):

1. It is important to create a vision for any collaborative activity, taking into account that trust needs to be built through values clarification.
2. A conscious effort to be as inclusive as possible in membership recruitment is critical.
3. It is important to respect cultural differences and to create rules for the collaboration that do not undermine these differences. A safe and nurturing environment is required.
4. Whatever structure is created for the collaboration, it needs to reinforce social and cultural equity.
5. Communication rules need to be developed that reflect language differences as well as cultural etiquette so that people do not feel threatened.
6. Leadership opportunities need to be created for every member of the collaboration regardless of gender, race, or ethnic identity.
7. All action plans and program implementation strategies need to be culturally sensitive.

ASSETS-PLANNING MODEL

An important set of techniques of great utility to the prepared public health leader, especially in this age of fear of terrorism or bioterrorism, is the need to better understand the strengths of our communities and how to use these strengths in confronting all types of crises. Public health leaders have traditionally tended to take a problem focus in their data collection activities. A negative approach slows down the process of affecting change. In working with communities, it is important to build on the strengths and resources of the community. If these resources are mobilized effectively, then all sorts of community challenges can be addressed from this important community perspective.

There are differences between a problem-oriented focus and an assets-based focus (Kretzmann & McKnight, 1993). If we were to map the problems in a community, we would have to consider such things as unemployment, school truancy, rates of literacy, lead paint in old buildings, school dropouts, gang activity, adult crime, domestic and child abuse, broken families, number of people on welfare, and on and on. Each of these problems creates a community need for a solution. If we were to determine the assets of the community in terms of individuals, community collaborative efforts, associations, and public and private organizations, it would be possible to determine an interesting balance of resources against needs. On the assets side, we would create a map of such resources as schools, churches, libraries, parks, businesses, community colleges, health care resources, local health department (if one exists), citizen organizations, cultural groups, artists, and so on. To these assets can be added the personal gifts of community people, in terms of talent or money, and special gifts of people in different age groups (Kretzmann & McKnight, 1993). It is important to not only recognize the assets of the community, but also to mobilize the resources in such a way that community growth becomes more possible.

There are five steps involved in assets planning (Kretzmann & McKnight, 1993). First, it is necessary to create an assets map of the community that delineates the capacities and gifts of individuals in the community, citizens' organizations and other entities, and local institutions (see sample map in Figure 14–2). Once this mapping process is tentatively completed, the next step in assets planning involves the building of new community relationships between local assets in order to better develop strategies and programs to address community needs. In reality, assets maps are constantly changing as the community changes. It is important to mobilize these community assets for community-building activities. The third step in the assets-planning process is to expand mobilization activities for economic and social development. It is also important to increase information-sharing activities with all community assets categories. Fourth, community leaders need to convene a group of people from all assets categories to build a community vision and plan for community growth and development. Finally, it is important to leverage internal community resources with likely external resources, possibly through grants, contracts, and gifts to support the assets-based planning and development activities.

Communities need to develop a toolbox filled with techniques for community-building activities (Kretzmann & Green, 1998). There are

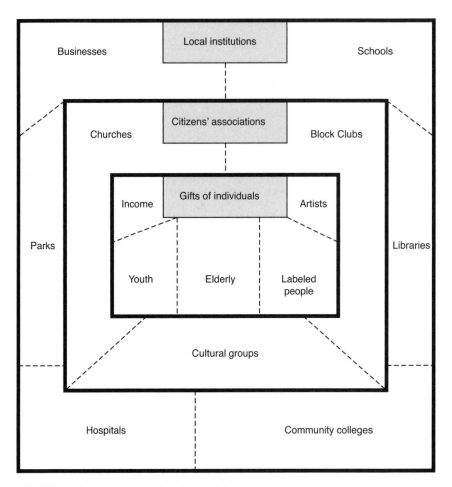

FIGURE 14–2 Community Assets Map

several tools to help in carrying out assets-planning and development activities. First, there is the assets map just discussed with the addition of a capacity inventory that adds information about the given assets and ways that different individuals and groups can better work together. The important question to be answered is whether a given community has enough assets and capacity to address all the needs that exist in that community. A second set of tools is based on self-help techniques similar to the 12-step program of Alcoholics Anonymous where peer groups form to address needs utilizing some self-help model. A third tool employs something called a *circle of support* that is used in Canada where people in need find a group of people who support them through difficult times. A fourth tool is also an expansion of the map to discover any small associations or groups in the community that were not caught in the mapping process but are groups that can address community needs . Finally, a business inventory is also useful for helping community residents address employment issues within the community. Ayre and his colleagues (2000) would add some sort of civic index process which would specifically pull together the preferred vision for the community, community governance factors, strategies for community collaboration, and information needed to help the community to better address community needs.

NATIONAL PUBLIC HEALTH PERFORMANCE STANDARDS

To bring the above discussion back to public health, it is useful to briefly review a program that was developed to determine how well communities are addressing public health issues (CDC, 2003). The four major goals of this program build on many of the skills already discussed in this book and in my earlier book (Rowitz, 2001). First, the standards assume that public health is the community's business and not just the work of a local public health agency. The larger view is clearly a systems perspective, and all the standards are built on a systems foundation. This means that a community collaborative of some kind representing the major groups and organizations undertakes the process of evaluating the performance of that community relative to the public health performance standards. The entire system of standards is built on how well the system is carrying out the core functions and essential public health services. Next, the program assumes that public health needs to be customer focused and community focused, which means that the goal is quality and accountability. Thus, the program assumes a continuous quality improvement orientation will occur. Finally, public health practice at all levels must be built on a science base. This goal has been expanded upon in the recent acceptance of evidence-based practice considerations.

The National Public Health Performance Standards are based on three instruments. The first instrument is the state public health system assessment tool, which is oriented to state public health agencies and other partners who contribute to public health services at the state level. These various state partners, which will vary from state to state, establish the parameters for public health in the state, set directions for public health practice, and implement the core functions and essential public health services for their respective states. Each of the 10 essential services have a number of indicators. For example, all the essential services in the state instrument have four indicators associated with them. These indicators are planning and implementation, technical assistance and support, evaluation and quality improvement, and resources. Under each indicator are a number of questions that the performance standards team discusses and then scores. For example, Table 14–1 shows the questions for Essential Service 1 on monitoring health status to identify health problems and Indicator 1.1 related to planning and implementation. Once the entire form is filled out, the state can transmit the instrument electronically to

---

Table 14–1 Example of Performance Standards for a State Public Health System

---

Essential Service #1: Monitor Health Status to Identify Health Problems

This services includes:

- Assessment of statewide health status and its determinants, including the identification of health threats and the determination of health service needs
- Attention to the vital statistics and health status of specific groups that are at higher risk for health threats than the general population
- Identification of community assets and resources that support the SPHS in promoting health and improving quality of life
- Utilization of technology and other methods of interpret and communicate health information to diverse audiences in different sectors
- Collaboration in integrating and managing public health-related information systems.

Indicator 1.1 Planning and Implementation

SPHS Model Standard:

The SPHS measures, analyzes, and reports on the health status of the state. The state's health status is monitored through data describing critical indicators of health, illness, and health resources that are collected in collaboration with local public health systems and other state partners

To accomplish this, the SPHS:

- Develops and maintains population-based program that collect health-related data to measure the state's health status
- Organizes health-related data into a state health profile that reports trends in health status, risk factors, and resource consumption

continues

Table 14–1 *continued*

- Tracks the state's health-related data and compares them to national health objectives and other benchmarks
- Compiles and analyzes data for local, state, and national health surveillance efforts
- Collaborates with data-reporting entities such as local health departments, hospitals, physicians, and laboratories to assure the timely collection, analysis, and dissemination of data
- Develops and manages a uniform set of health status indicators that are derived from a variety of sources (e.g., hospitals, managed care organizations, health departments, universities) and accommodates state and local health-related data needs
- Protects personal health information by instituting security and confidentiality policies that define protocols for health information access and integrity

Please answer the following questions related to Indicator 1.1:

1.1.1 Has the SPHS developed any surveillance programs for measuring the state's health status?

If so, do these programs:

1.1.1.1 Identify the data elements required for monitoring health status?

If so, do these data include:

1.1.1.1.1 Demographic characteristics?

1.1.1.1.2 Socioeconomic characteristics?

1.1.1.1.3 Mortality?

1.1.1.1.4 Natality?

1.1.1.1.5 Infectious disease incidence?

1.1.1.1.6 Chronic disease prevalence?

1.1.1.1.7 Injuries?

1.1.1.1.8 Mental health and substance abuse?

1.1.1.1.9 Behavioral risk factors?

1.1.1.1.10 Environmental risks?

1.1.1.1.11 Occupational risks?

1.1.1.1.12 Availability of personal health care services?

1.1.1.1.13 Utilization of personal health care services?

1.1.1.1.14 Availability of population-based public health services?

1.1.1.1.15 Utilization of population-based public health services?

continues

Table 14–1 *continued*

    1.1.1.1.16 Barriers to health services?

    1.1.1.1.17 Health insurance coverage?

    1.1.1.1.18 *Healthy People 2010* leading health indicators?

  1.1.1.2 Identify the methods for data collection and storage?

  1.1.1.3 Identify the roles of state and local governmental agencies and relevant nongovernmental agencies in the collection of health data?

  1.1.1.4 Facilitate access to the health-related data among state and local public health and constituent groups?

1.1.2 Does the SPHS organize health-related data into a state health profile?

If so , is the profile used to:

  1.1.2.1 Identify emerging health problems?

  1.1.2.2 Report trends in health status?

  1.1.2.3 Report changes in the prevalence of health risk factors?

  1.1.2.4 Report changes in health resource consumption?

1.1.3 Does the SPHS track the state's health-related data over time?

If so, are state data compared to:

  1.1.3.1 National health objectives?

  1.1.3.2 Benchmarks from previous state health profiles?

1.1.4 Does the SPHS compile and provide locally collected data to organizations conducting local, state, and national health surveillance?

If so, does the SPHS operate:

  1.1.4.1 A data warehousing capacity that links data from diverse sources, (e.g., universities, hospitals, managed care organizations, and health departments)?

  1.1.4.2 Protocols that meet the standards for compiling vital statistics and vital records?

  1.1.4.3 Geographic information systems (GIS) to analyze geocoded health data?

  1.1.4.4 Population health registries?

1.1.5 Does the SPHS collaborate with organizations or individuals that report health information to help assure the timely collection, analysis, and dissemination of data?

If so, does the SPHS collaborate with:

  1.1.5.1 Local health departments?

  1.1.5.2 Hospitals?

  1.1.5.3 Ambulatory care sites?

  1.1.5.4 Laboratories?

continues

Table 14–1 *continued*

    1.1.5.5 Professional health organizations (e.g., state medical and nursing societies, state hospital associations)?

1.1.6 Does the SPHS develop a uniform set of health indicators to describe the health of the state's population?

If so,

    1.1.6.1 Do these indicators provide data specific to local jurisdictions?

    1.1.6.2 Are these indicators compiled from a variety of sources?

1.1.7 Does the SPHS enforce established laws and the use of protocols to protect personal health information and other data with personal identifiers?

If so, do these protocols include procedures to:

    1.1.7.1 Protect personal identifiers?

    1.1.7.2 Specify access for confidential and nonconfidential health information?

1.1.8 How much of this SPHS Model Standard is achieved by the state public health system collectively?

        0–25%   26–50%   51–75%   76–100%

    1.1.8.1 What percent of the answer reported in question 1.1.8 is the direct contribution of the state public health agency?

        0–25%   26–50%   51–75%   76–100%

CDC, which will analyze the data and return a report for the state. The state can then use the form for all types of statewide planning activities. It is clear that the state tool provides the prepared public health leader and his or her partners with all sorts of data that can clearly influence public health practice in the state. It will also be possible to determine how the state is performing relative to each of the 10 essential public health services. In addition, state by state comparisons also become possible.

The local public health system assessment instrument brings together the local public health department and its community and health partners to contribute to the delivery of the core functions and essential public health services at the local level. It is evident that the local public health department will have a key role in the process, but there is no reason why some other entity may not be the lead agency. In many ways, it is true that public health is mostly carried out in local communities. As can be seen in Table 14–2, the indicators tied to each essential service are quite detailed

Table 14–2 Indicators for the Local Public Health System Performance Standards Instrument

Essential Service 1—Monitor health status to identify community health problems
  Indicator 1.1—Population-based community health profile
  Indicator 1.2—Access to and utilization of current technology to manage, display, analyze, and communicate population health data
  Indicator 1.3—Maintenance of population health registries

Essential Service 2—Diagnose and investigate health problems and health hazards in the community
  Indicator 2.1—Identification and surveillance of health threats
  Indicator 2.2—Plan for public health emergencies
  Indicator 2.3—Investigate and respond to public health emergencies
  Indicator 2.4—Laboratory support for investigation of health threats

Essential Service 3—Inform, educate, and empower people about health issues
  Indicator 3.1—Health education
  Indicator 3.2—Health promotion activities to facilitate healthy living in healthy communities

Essential Service 4—Mobilize community partnerships to identify and solve health problems
  Indicator 4.1—Constituency development
  Indicator 4.2—Community partnerships

Essential Service 5—Develop policies and plans that support individual and community health efforts
  Indicator 5.1—Governmental presence at the local level
  Indicator 5.2—Public health policy development
  Indicator 5.3—Community health improvement process
  Indicator 5.4—Strategic planning and alignment with the community health improvement process

Essential Service 6—Enforce laws and regulations that protect health and ensure safety
  Indicator 6.1—Review and evaluate laws, regulations, and ordinances
  Indicator 6.2—Involvement in the improvement of laws, regulations, and ordinances
  Indicator 6.3—Enforce laws, regulations, and ordinances

Essential Service 7—Link people to needed personal health services and assure the provision of health care when otherwise unavailable
  Indicator 7.1—Identification of populations with barriers to personal health services
  Indicator 7.2—Identifying personal health services needs of populations

continues

Table 14–2 *continued*

Indicator 7.3—Assuring the linkage of people to personal health services

Essential Service 8—Assure a competent public and personal health care workforce
Indicator 8.1—Workforce assessment
Indicator 8.2—Public health workforce standards
Indicator 8.3—Lifelong learning through continuing education, training, and mentoring
Indicator 8.4—Public health leadership development

Essential Service 9—Evaluate effectiveness, accessibility, and quality of personal and population-based health services
Indicator 9.1—Evaluation of population-based health services
Indicator 9.2—Evaluation of personal health services
Indicator 9.3—Evaluation of the local public health system

Essential Service 10—Research for new insights and innovative solutions to health problems
Indicator 10.1—Fostering innovation
Indicator 10.2—Linkage with institutions of higher learning and/or research
Indicator 10.3—Capacity to initiate or participate in timely epidemiological, health policy, and health systems research

and cover many activities not seen in the state instrument previously shown. Since the issue of local emergency preparedness and response is one of the underlying themes in this book, Table 14–3 shows how the performance standards address the issue of planning for public health emergencies.

Table 14–3 Example of Performance Standards for a Local Public Health System

Essential Service #2 Diagnose and Investigate Health Problems and Health Hazards in the Community

Indicator 2.2   Plan for Public Health Emergencies

LPHS Model Standard:

An emergency preparedness and response plan describes the roles, function, and responsibilities of LPHS entities in the event of one or more types of

continues

Table 14–3 *continued*

---

public health emergencies. Careful planning and mobilization of resources and partners prior to an event is crucial to a prompt and effective response. LPHS entities, including the local public health agency, law enforcement, fire departments, health care providers, and other partners work collaboratively to formulate emergency response plans and procedures. The plan should create a dual-use response infrastructure, in that it outlines the capacity of the LPHS to respond to all pubic health emergencies (including natural disasters), while taking into account the unique and complex challenges presented by chemical hazards or bioterrorism.

To plan for public health emergencies, the LPHS:

- Defines and describes public health disasters and emergencies that might trigger implementation of the LPHS emergency response plan
- Develops a plan that defines organizational responsibilities, establishes communication and information networks, and clearly outlines alert and evacuation protocols
- Tests the plan each year through the staging of one or more mock events
- Revises its emergency response plan at least every two years

Please answer the following questions related to Indicator 2.2:

2.2.1   Has the LPHS identified public health disasters and emergencies that might trigger implementation of the LPHS emergency response plan?

2.2.2   Does the LPHS have an emergency preparedness and response plan?

If so,

2.2.2.1   Is the emergency preparedness and response plan in written form?

2.2.2.2   Is there an established chain-of-command among plan participants?

Does the plan:

2.2.2.3   Describe the organizational responsibilities and roles of all plan participants?

2.2.2.4   Identify community assets that could be mobilized by plan participants to respond to an emergency?

2.2.2.5   Describe LPHS communications and information networks?

2.2.2.6   Connect, where possible, to the state emergency response and preparedness plan?

2.2.2.7   Clearly outline protocols for emergency response?

If so, does the plan:

2.2.2.7.1   Build on existing plans, protocols, and procedures within the community?

continues

Table 14–3 *continued*

2.2.2.7.2	Include written alert protocols to implement an emergency program of source and contact tracing for communicable diseases and toxic exposures?
2.2.2.7.3	Include protocols to alert affected populations?
2.2.2.7.4	Include an evacuation plan?
2.2.2.7.5	Include procedures for coordinating public health responsibilities with law enforcement responsibilities?

2.2.3 Has any part of the plan been tested through simulations of one or more mock events within the past year?

2.2.4 Has the plan been reviewed or revised within the past two years?

2.2.5 How much of this LPHS Model Standard is achieved by the local public health system collectively?

0–25%	26–50%	51–75%	76–100%

2.2.5.1 What percent of the answer reported in question 2.2.5 is the direct contribution of the local public health agency?

0–25%	26–50%	51–75%	76–100%

The local public health governance performance instrument concentrates on the governing body responsible for oversight of the 10 essential services at the local level. It is the governing board that is accountable for promoting the public's health at the local level. The performance standards related to governance are based on assuring legal authority, resources, policy making, accountability through continuous quality improvement and evaluation, and collaboration. These governance functions are discussed in detail by Rowitz and Upshaw (2006, in press). Each of the 10 essential services in the governance instrument is charged with an oversight function as can be seen in Table 14–4. Table 14–5 gives an example of the indicator for Essential Service 4 with the accompanying questions.

It is important to recognize that these tools need to lead to a statewide coordinated approach to performance standards.. As can be seen graphically in Figure 14–3, the state performance standards will be clearly affected by the level of performance in every local jurisdiction. Local jurisdictions provide feedback to the state on emerging trends and challenges. The federal government influences the performance standards of the state

---

Table 14–4 Indicators for Local health Governance

Essential Service 1—Monitor health status to identify community health
        problems
    Indicator G1—Oversight to assure community health status monitoring

Essential Service 2—Diagnose and investigate health problems and health
        hazards in the community
    Indicator G2—Oversight to assure public health surveillance and
        response

Essential Service 3—Inform, educate, and empower people about health issues
    Indicator G3—Oversight of public health information, education, and
        empowerment activities

Essential Service 4—Mobilize community partnerships to identify and solve
        health problems
    Indicator G4—Oversight to assure constituency building and partner-
        ship development

Essential Service 5—Develop policies and plans that support individual and
        community health efforts
    Indicator G5—Oversight of public health policy making and planning

Essential Service 6—Enforce laws and regulations that protect health and
        ensure safety
    Indicator G6—Oversight of public health legal and regulatory affairs

Essential Service 7—Link people to needed personal health services and assure
        the provision of health care when otherwise unavailable
    Indicator G7—Oversight to assure public health outreach and enabling
        services

Essential Service 8—Assure a competent public and personal health care
        workforce
    Indicator G8—Oversight of public health workforce issues

Essential Service 9—Evaluate effectiveness, accessibility, and quality of
        personal and population-based health services
    Indicator G9—Oversight of public health service evaluation

Essential Service 10—Research for new insights and innovative solutions to
        health problems
    Indicator G10—Oversight to assure public health innovation and
        research

---

through the funding and policy mechanism. This relationship affects the state priorities as well. The state will work to implement both federal and state mandates at the local level. It is clear that there needs to be a close working relationship between the local governing body and the local public health system as well. Governance is tied to oversight by the governing

---

Table 14–5 Example of Governance Standards

Essential Service #4   Mobilize Community Partnerships to Identify and Solve Health Problems

This service includes:

- Identifying potential stakeholders who contribute to or benefit from public health and increasing their awareness of the value of public health
- Building coalitions to draw upon the full range of potential human and material resources to improve community health
- Convening and facilitating partnerships among groups and associations (including those not typically considered to be health related) in undertaking defined health improvement projects, including preventive, screening, rehabilitation, and support programs

Indicator G4   Oversight to Assure Constituency Building and Partnership Activity

Governance Model Standard:

The board of health or other governing body is responsible for creating a supportive environment that assures traditional and nontraditional partnerships are nurtured in order to draw on the full range of potential human and material resources in the cause of community health.

For effective constituency building and partnership development, the board of health or other governing body:

- Assures constituency building, partnership activities, and resource development partners to identify and solve health problems
- Assures the development, implementation, and review of policies articulating commitment to these activities
- Conducts annual evaluations of these activities and provides relevant feedback to its constituents and the community at large
- Implements strategies to enhance participation among current and potential constituents

Please answer the following questions related to Essential Service #4:

G4.1:   Does the board of health or other governing body periodically identify the individuals, agencies, or organizations providing public health leadership in constituency building and partnership activities within the community?

G4.2:   Does the board of health or other governing body assure access to national, state, or local resources that could be used for constituency building or partnership activities?

G4.3:   Does the board of health or other governing body assure the coordination of resources in the community to enhance partnerships and collaboration to achieve public health objectives?

G4.4:   Does the board of health or other governing body periodically assure the development, implementation, and/or review of written policies

continues

Table 14–5 *continued*

in support of public health constituency building or partnership activities?

G4.5: Does the board of health or other governing body annually assure that an evaluation of public health constituency and partnership activities is performed?

If so, does the board of health or other governing body:

G.4.5.1: Annually assure that feedback is provided directly to LPHS partners on community mobilization around health issues?

G.4.5.2: Assure recognition of LPHS partners for their commitment and role in addressing public health goals and objectives?

G4.6: Does the board of health or other governing body periodically implement strategies to enhance participation among current and potential constituents? (This could include activities designed to acknowledge and reward participants.)

body. The relationship between the local governing body and the state through its elected officials, state agencies, or the state board of health (if there is one) can also be important for coordinating and developing statewide relationships.

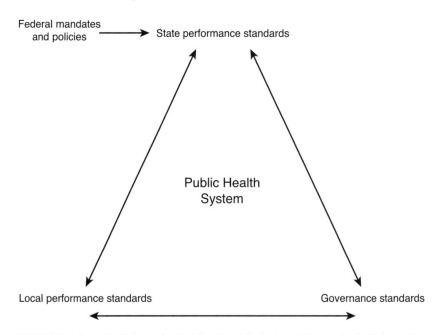

FIGURE 14–3 Building the Public Health System Through Collaboration

It should be obvious that the performance standards tools can give the prepared public health leader much information to guide planning and future action. These standards will also help in building community infrastructure. There also needs to be a connection between these standards and performance standards related to emergency preparedness and response. First, it is necessary for the emergency preparedness and response system to begin to build its programs on the core functions and essential public health services model using the instruments developed so far or by developing a special performance standards instrument for emergency preparedness. Emergency preparedness programs need to be based on the same principles that guide the performance standards programs. Assessment is part of emergency preparedness as is policy development and assurance functions. It follows that the paradigm of essential public health services would also enhance the emergency preparedness initiatives. Paul Halverson, the father of the national public health performance standards program and who is now a professor at the College of Public Health at the University of Arkansas for Medical Sciences, has addressed some of these issues in detail in Case Study 14.

CASE STUDY 14   A Public Health Practice Quiz for Paul Halverson

1. *How can performance standards help us in the community building process?*

   First of all, the National Public Health Performance Standards has been designed around the concept of the *public health system*. The public health system is broadly defined to include all stakeholders in the health of the public, including the governmental public health organization and health department, as well as any other organization, governmental or private, that has an interest, or stake, in the health of a population group. This definition is meant to be very inclusive and does, for example, specifically include the contribution made by other governmental organizations, such as the departments of social services and the departments of mental health. It is also meant to include the contributions made by hospitals, physicians, and other voluntary organizations, such as United Way, the Red Cross, and the Heart Association, as well as more informal, community-based organizations that have a compelling interest in the health of the community. This includes neighborhood associations, as well as the contributions of employers and others.

continues

CASE STUDY 14   *continued*

This public health system is a critically important construct of the performance standards, and it is this broad context in which the performance standards were developed. Using the active participation and input of all these organizations and individuals with an interest in the health of the community, the performance standards provide the opportunity for an objective look at the degree to which the community is served by an effective public health system.

The Performance Standards were developed by individuals in practice and are representative of the optimal standards of practice using the 10 essential services of public health as the organizing framework. The 10 essential services provide us with a clear idea of the breadth of public health, and build upon the work of the consensus of many different national public health organizations. The 10 essential services are not perfect, and there may be other frameworks that better describe public health. However, the decision was made in the beginning that the effort should focus on the development of specific examples of good practice in public health, rather than in developing yet another framework for providing the conceptual overview of public health.

So, in essence, the performance standards build upon a broad, inclusive definition of public health and the system in which it operates. Secondly, the performance standards provide for an objective consensus-based assessment of the current state of affairs in a particular community. And, third, given the results of the assessment, provide an avenue for discussion and prioritization of community asset building.

The process itself is often reported by communities as critically important because it opens the dialogue between all the various players and partners in the community who have been engaged in public health, and in some cases were even unaware of the efforts of others who have similar goals. In addition, it provides a context by which a community can assess its strengths and weaknesses and commit publicly to specific improvement strategies. This public and community consensus-building exercise is a critical component of the use of the performance standards program and is seen as a major benefit.

Another aspect of the community-building process is to provide comparative information by which community leaders, as well as public health professionals, can reach consensus on what is "good." For many people who are involved in public health, the concepts and goals related to public health have been diffuse and sometimes hard to gain a common understanding around specific measures of success. The performance standards attempt to provide specificity and a comparative level of performance for communities to judge how well they are able to achieve the optimal standards. Frequently, public policy decisions are

continues

CASE STUDY 14 *continued*

based upon comparative information, which can be an important component of the performance standards program. Especially when the standards process is completed on a statewide basis, individual counties may then compare their results to neighboring and what are frequently seen as "competing" jurisdictions for evaluative purposes. Likewise, communities as well as the state taken as a whole can review their data and more objectively define their areas most in need of development in a more scientific and data-based way, rather than simply choosing areas that may or may not have the greatest need.

Lastly, the performance standards program is imbedded within the MAPP (Mobilizing Action for Partnership and Planning) process. This is a very comprehensive, inclusive methodology that was developed around community health improvement and the performance standards as one of four community assessment measurements that are included. The designers of the National Public Health Performance Standards Program are committed to community building as a major reason for the conduct of the performance standards.

2. *What is the relationship between performance standards and action planning?*

Again, the assessment of the public health system is the first step in building a strong capacity within that jurisdiction's public health system. Once the assessments are completed and scores are derived, the leadership of the public health system can begin a dialogue within the context of the public health system and define the highest priority for action. This priority setting process is critically important and lends itself towards specific assignment of action steps. In many communities, the priorities that are chosen by the community public health system are then assigned leadership responsibility, and leaders within the community commit to specific action steps as part of the leadership for the community. An important indicator of the seriousness of the commitment of building a strong public health system can often be found in the degree to which community organization leaders are willing to take on leadership responsibility for solving a public health system area and including it in their organization's strategic plan. For example, if an important goal for a public health system relates to improving the health status measurement of the community and if the hospital president chooses to take on this leadership role with the public health system, the degree to which he or she is able to incorporate this health status measurement goal within the context of his or her personal performance plan and similarly includes it within the hospital strategic plan, is an important clue as to the seriousness of the commitment made for improving the public health system. In other words, the action planning is a critical next step after the completion of the performance

continues

CASE STUDY 14 *continued*

standards and should be seen as a commitment by the community to use the information obtained from the performance standards to make a difference for the community. Additionally, communities should not consider doing the performance standards unless they are willing to commit to a multiple-year strategy that includes the initial measurement, prioritizing and action planning, and then the subsequent implementation of improvement, followed by measurement and then repeating of the performance standards process. This entire process is very consistent with the quality improvement processes used throughout health care and other industries and provides an important linkage to system change.

3. *Why is there so much resistance to implementing the National Public Health Performance Standards Program at the local level?*

Actually, their resistance to implementing the performance standards program has steadily decreased over the years. First, the National Public Health Performance Standards Program was developed principally by practitioners from a variety of practice settings. The local standards, for example, were developed as part of the NACCHO-led effort to develop the MAPP process and to include the performance standards as one of the four assessments within MAPP. The NACCHO-led group consisted of public health officers from large and small jurisdictions in both urban and rural settings. In addition, the performance standards were subject to extensive field testing and were subsequently improved and changed based upon reports from the field testing activities. The performance standards program then represents a practice-based and practice-led effort by the National Public Health Partners to improve the practice of public health.

Additionally, CDC reports that now nearly half of the states in the country have committed to or completed a statewide implementation of the National Public Health Performance Standards Program. This implementation is good news and, frankly, speaks less to resistance and more towards fairly optimistic and enthusiastic adoption.

Accountability within public health is frequently seen by practitioners as inviting the opportunity to be beat up or punished. The fact of the matter is that accountability really needs to be seen as the opportunity to celebrate success and get credit for good things that have been accomplished, rather than seeing accountability as the opportunity to be punished for poor performance. We have much to celebrate in public health in terms of our success, and the performance standards provide us with the opportunity to clearly demonstrate this using nationally adopted consensus standards. That being said, however, there is pause given by all of us as it relates to the idea of being measured in terms of

continues

CASE STUDY 14 *continued*

performance. The performance standards were not developed to be used as a "report card," but rather as an instrument for quality improvement. However, there are still individuals that see public health as the sole domain of the Public Health Department, and anything negative that might surface as somehow being equivalent to pointing a finger to the health officer.

Encouraging news from the field is that more and more health officers see the performance standards as an important way to celebrate success and are voluntarily leading the way toward implementation. So, in summary, we don't see major opposition by local communities in using the performance standards, but rather a very positive movement towards using the performance standards as a way to celebrate success.

4. *What are the next steps in implementing the National Public Health Performance Standards Program?*

The next steps in implementation relate to the continuation of efforts by the national associations, principally the Association of State and Territorial Health Officers (ASTHO), the National Association of County and City Health Officers (NACCHO), the National Association of Local Boards of Health (NALBOH), the National Network of Public Health Institutes (NNPHI), and the American Public Health Association (APHA) / Public Health Foundation (PHF). These organizations are working together to provide technical assistance and support the state and local public health agencies and their boards who are interested in implementation. CDC continues to play a leadership role in providing resources to these associations to facilitate this work.

One of the important next steps is the updating of the performance standards to meet the OMB Guidance for Modernization. The commitment made by CDC at the inception of the program was that these standards would be continually updated to reflect the optimal practice of public health. This is a continuing obligation that is important for the field to acknowledge. The performance standards, should they fail to remain contemporary, would in fact be seen as a way to hold back progress and to not support growth and expansion within public health. So, the expansion and modernization of the performance standards is a critical next step, which will be led by CDC and the National Partners.

In addition, an important next step would be the use of the National Public Health Performance Standards as the basis for the development of an accreditation program. With nearly half of the state and local health departments in the country having used the performance standards and many others interested in utilizing the instruments, it is critical for us to maintain the momentum of the standards program, while

continues

CASE STUDY 14 *continued*

at the same time beginning to commit to accreditation activities. The 10 essential standards and the performance standards provide an important basis for the development of the accreditation instruments. The performance standards provide a national consensus on the optimal public health practice at the public health system level. The accreditation process should be based upon the performance of the governmental public health agency and would, in its nature, include minimum standards or minimum levels of achievement as a basis for granting an accreditation to the agency. Therefore, the performance standards have a continuing and important role in providing the beacon of optimal performance for the system and the basis for accreditation. The accreditation instruments, while providing differing levels of standards for achievement in the accreditation process, must include a minimum level of achievement, and therefore, are different from the performance standards program. Both the performance standards for optimal practice of public health within a system context and agency-based minimum standards for accreditation are critical components of system-building activities.

Indeed, one suggestion that I would have for those crafting the certification standards would be to have, as a minimum requirement, all organizations being considered for accreditation demonstrate their use of the performance standards as part of their quality improvement process. Therefore, the performance standards in the accreditation process can be tightly linked, and both can be better because of a complimentary set of standards.

An area that has frequently received attention in the interaction between accreditation and the use of the standards is the role of the agency in the building and maintaining of an appropriate and effective public health system. I can't think of a more important role for the governmental public health agency than in the development, maintenance, and continuous improvement of a vibrant and robust public health system. Indeed, it's my belief that an effective public health system is an absolute prerequisite to an effective governmental public health organization. Any health officer today who believes that the governmental public health agency can solely, within its own authority and budget, perform all of those services necessary for the community, is clearly not seeing the same picture of public health that most see in the importance of engaging the community in the practice of public health. Sustained community involvement is a critical component to the success of public health, and the public health officer's primary responsibility is to build and maintain those relationships that will enable effective system work.

continues

CASE STUDY 14   *continued*

5. *Why don't our emergency preparedness and response leaders recognize the utility of the public health core functions and essential public health services?*

In large part, the failure of emergency preparedness and response leaders to recognize the core functions and essential services lies with our inability as public health leaders to effectively communicate and utilize important examples with others in explaining public health. I am confident that communities who engage in the use of the National Public Health Performance Standards Program and complete the assessment as a community-wide organization, including emergency preparedness and response leaders in the process, would have much less difficulty gaining acceptance of the essential services framework than those who simply expect the emergency response people to know this framework without significant exposure. It would be similar to the lack of understanding by many public health officials of the framework for evaluation of corrections or fire control activities. We need to expose emergency response leaders to the 10 essential services framework and engage these leaders in helping to build an effective public health system. We need to listen carefully to the contributions they make and help them understand the role they play in building a strong and effective public health system.

It is critical that we acknowledge that emergency preparedness and response are critical components of any effective public health system. It is, therefore, incumbent upon public health leaders to assure that the full array of stakeholders engage in the public health system-building processes engendered by the National Public Health Performance Standards Program.

SUMMARY

This chapter presented a number of techniques related to building the community. Public health leaders are often not aware of many of these skills. The issue of developing and working with community leaders was discussed as was the important concern related to assets planning. Multicultural considerations were also discussed. The leadership wheel was used to show the various activities leaders need to use in working in collaborative relationships. The importance of utilizing performance standards was also discussed by reviewing the three instruments developed for the national public health performance standards program.

REFERENCES

Axner, M. (n.d.). *Developing a plan for building leadership. Community Toolbox.* Retrieved from http://ctb.ukan.edu/tools/EN/sub_section_main_1119.htm

Ayre, D., Clough, G., & Norris, T. (2000). *Facilitating community change.* San Francisco: Grove Consultants International.

Centers for Disease Control and Prevention. (2003). *National public health performance standards.* Atlanta, GA: Author.

Johnson, K., Grossman, W., & Cassidy, A. (Eds.). (1996). *Collaborating to improve community health.* San Francisco: Jossey-Bass.

Kaye, G., & Wolff, T. (1997). *From the ground up.* Amherst, MA: AHEC Community Partners.

W.K. Kellogg Foundation. (1995). *Sustaining community-based initiatives: Developing community capacities.* Battle Creek, MI: Author.

Kretzmann, J. P., & Green, M. B. (1998). *Building the bridge from client to citizen: A community toolbox for welfare reform.* Evanston, IL: Northwestern University ABCD Institute.

Kretzmann, J. P., & McKnight, J. L. (1993). *Building communities from the inside out.* Evanston, IL: Northwestern University ABCD Institute.

Magee, M. (2000). *Positive leadership.* New York: Spencer Books.

Mattessich, P., & Monsey, B. (1997). *Community building: What makes it work?* St. Paul, MN: Amherst H.Wilder Foundation.

Rowitz, L. (2001). *Public health leadership: Putting principles into practice.* Sudbury, MA: Jones and Bartlett.

Rowitz, L., & Upshaw, V. (in press). *Governance in public health: Building effective boards of health.* San Francisco: Jossey-Bass.

CHAPTER 15

Change Strategies

Change is the law of life. And those who look only to
the past or present are certain to miss the future.

—John F. Kennedy

Every leadership book is about change. September 11, 2001, taught us that change is often unexpected. Leaders need to better understand the dynamics of change if they are to become change agents themselves. Mahatma Ghandi once said that it is important to "Be the change you want to be in the world." The artist Pablo Picasso said "I am always doing that which I cannot do, in order that I may learn how to do it." One of the best quotes on change from an unknown source is, "If nothing ever changed, there would be no butterflies." To put the last 14 chapters of this book in perspective, this chapter will explore change and some understanding of the process of change. The Robert Wood Johnson Foundation and the W. K. Kellogg Foundation Turning Point Initiative to build public health capacity to better improve the health of the public through collaborative partnerships began in the mid-1990s. The Turning Point projects were all about change. Case Study 15-A presents one of the interesting stories from this initiative (Turning Point, 2004).

Although it is true that change can be planned, we do live in an age where unanticipated change events such as terrorist attacks and other crises come into our lives in an unpredictable way. Most theories of change have assumed that social change is a continuous process, but the events of the past few years clearly create discontinuities in our social structure and in our personal lives. What crisis forces us to do is view these major change events in terms of explanation rather than prediction. It is necessary to trace the event backwards to garner information that will

CASE STUDY 15–A

Collaborating for
Community Health

Bob Cassa serves his community by developing the conditions that will keep the population healthy. In his case, his community is a nation within a nation, the San Carlos Apache Nation in Arizona. A public health educator with the Indian Health Service, he coordinates, organizes, and implements a variety of health promotion and disease prevention activities in the schools and community. He especially loves working to improve the health of kids because he remembers what it was like to be young and making life-altering decisions. One of those decisions led him to public health and back to the San Carlos Apache Nation.

Twenty-nine years ago, San Carlos tribal leaders saw the future of their nation in a promising kid and encouraged him to pursue higher education. When Bob first started at Arizona State University, his options were wide open, but he soon found himself in pursuit of a BA in Health Services. As a child, Bob recalls being a patient in the local hospital, where he remembers noticing the great number of nonnative doctors and nurses. His decision to go into the health field came in part from his awareness of the need to increase the number of native providers. After receiving his bachelor's degree, he followed up with a master's in Public Health from the University of Hawaii. He started his career with Indian Health Services (IHS) in 1985 in Nevada but soon found his way back home in San Carlos in 1988.

Bob had already been serving in his community for 16 years when he was asked to participate in a training program called the Academy Without Walls. Created by Arizona Turning Point and the Mel and Enid Zuckerman Arizona College of Public Health, the academy delivers training to frontline public health workers in Arizona. San Carlos was chosen as a pilot site for the academy's competency-based training in basic public health science skills, community dimensions of practice, and cultural competency. Tribal health department employees and the employees of the Indian Health Service Unit planned to participate in the academy together to strengthen communication and collaboration between the two entities.

For Bob, the experience allowed him to revisit key principles in health education and the underlying purpose of public health. For others, some or all of the information was new. The training sessions prompted Bob to identify how he could improve health education through better collaboration, communication, community assessment, and community participation. Bob recognized that although he and his colleagues valued collaboration, sometimes in the daily activities of doing their jobs, the importance of collaboration was lost.

The Academy Without Walls provided public health workers who serve the people of San Carlos with tools, resources, ideas, and the opportunity to explore collaboration. Several agencies within San Carlos had been

continues

CASE STUDY 15–A *continued*

planning programs for kids during spring break. As a result of their participation in the academy, some IHS departments and the tribal health programs collaborated with other community groups, such as the Boys and
Girls Clubs, to put on a spring break event together. The larger event
allowed them all to do more for the kids with the same resources. The
spring break event and the lessons learned from the Academy Without
Walls are living on in San Carlos. Agencies and community groups now
collaborate in other ways to improve health and are moving in a new direction to achieve public health gains—together.

allow us to prevent or better predict similar events in the future. Chaos
theories, which were briefly discussed in Chapter 8, showed that an
understanding of how to address potential crises is tied to an awareness
that unanticipated events (and the changes that occur because of them)
are now part of the social fabric of our lives. This chapter will look at the
stages of change and how transition in our lives may be as important as
our understanding of the process of change.

OVERVIEW TO CHANGE

Change is a process of moving from what has become an obsolete present
into a revitalized present with an eye on the future. Change also mean that
the old rules do not seem to be working anymore, and new rules and procedures need to be developed for the changing context in which we live
today. The quote by President Kennedy at the beginning of this chapter
reinforces these ideas. Schein (2004) clarified the issue of change and why
people are often resistant to structured and unstructured change. People
like equilibrium in their lives. The process of coping, growth, and survival
are measured against some sense of stability in their environments. Some
of this stability comes from the culture, shared values, routines, and some
ability to predict how our day-to-day activities will play out. These
assumptions are shared with the people with whom we interact.

Unanticipated change clearly disrupts the equilibrium of people,
organizations, and their communities. We now live in an age of constant
and speeded up change. The question is how to adapt to these changes or
how to live in a world of unpredictable change. When change transforms

a culture or community, people need to unlearn the old rules and also learn the new rules (Schein, 2004). Change can be incremental or slow and intense. This latter type of change is sometimes called deep change (Quinn, 1996). The good news about incremental change is that the process is so gradual that people, organizations, and communities can adapt to the changes more easily. Another advantage of incremental change is that it is possible to revert to the prechange stage more easily because the change process is so gradual. Deep change is much more profound in that it requires new ways of thinking, feeling, and behaving. It is not possible to go back. There has been a tipping point. We cannot go back to our pre-September 11, 2001, lives. Thus, deep change is a major change that breaks with the past.

Change can be seen within the context of surprises (Schwartz, 2003). We live in a world of inevitable surprises. The things that we do know are that these surprises will continue to occur perhaps at a much faster rate than in the past. Second, we know now that surprise is inevitable, but we can plan for the things that are not expected. We can, even with some degree of accuracy, predict how certain types of crisis events will play out over time. One critical set of skills is creating different scenarios for different types of events. For example, it is possible to create scenarios about the impact of a terrorist event similar to September 11, 2001, from a number of perspectives. Exercises 15–1 and 15–2 will give you the chance to explore surprises and create some scenarios for the future.

Schwartz (2003) also explored some lessons that he believed we have learned about change and these inevitable surprises. First, it is important that change agents keep looking for clarifications of a surprise event. Conversations between individuals who have been involved in similar events can often provide new information, interpretations of happenings, and new understandings of the variations in outcomes of different types of surprise events. Successful leaders also become better at prediction and timing related to surprises by watching for what factors will speed up events and which factors will slow them down or stop them in their tracks. As mentioned earlier in this book, change agents become more aware of warning indicators and are adept at developing skills related to early detection. It is possible to discard techniques and approaches that might create environments for crisis (Schwartz, 2003).

It is also important for leaders to be careful to not deny the potential for surprise events. It is important for leaders to understand how they

---

EXERCISE 15–1 Surprises

Purpose: To look at change from the perspective of events that were
surprises

Key Concepts: Change, surprises, tipping points

Procedures: Divide the class or training group into groups of 10.

1. Have each participant list on a 3x5 card five surprise events that have
   occurred between September 11, 2001, and today that have had public
   health implications.
2. Share your list with other group members and put the events on a large
   sheet of paper.
3. Present your group list to the larger group and discuss the meaning of
   surprises. Were any of the events tipping points?

---

judge things. Each of us have different learning and behavioral styles. Our
perspectives and judgments are affected by these styles. It is worthwhile
for leaders to explore these issues either through using some leadership
profile instruments or through working with executive coaches who spe-
cialize in these analyses. Once again, it is important to emphasize lifelong
learning for leaders. Different leadership tools and skills are required for
different times and events. Leaders need to better understand how their
actions are seen within their organizations and within their communities
by their partners and by community residents. It is clearly critical, as
pointed out throughout this book, that the prepared public health leader
needs to cultivate these community connections because emergency preparedness and response activities are community-wide efforts and not just
the work of one individual.

STYLES OF CHANGE

The prepared public health leader has to be both a catalyst for change and
also a reactor to change caused by unanticipated consequences. Leaders
have different change styles. Musselwhite has studied the issue of styles for
a long time. His organization developed an instrument to define and test
change styles (Musselwhite & Jones, 2004). From over 10 years of
research, three primary change styles have emerged.

EXERCISE 15–2 Scenario Building

Purpose: To use scenarios to better understand how change is impacted by terrorist events

Key Concepts: Scenario building, change

Procedures: Assume that a terrorist event similar to the events of September 11, 2001, is being planned by an extremist political group in the next three years.

1. Divide the class or training group into groups of 10.
2. Describe the public health concerns in the following situations:
   a. Scenario in which the event is prevented
   b. Scenario in which the event occurs in New York City, Los Angeles, Chicago, Washington, DC, within a 24-hour period
   c. Scenario in which a "dirty bomb" is used
   d. Try to create two alternate scenarios to the above.
3. Present your scenarios to the group as a whole. This exercise may take 3–4 hours to complete.

The Conservers

Conservers are people who are able to gauge reality in a pretty accurate way. They also like structure and tend to work well within frameworks or organizations with well-defined rules and regulations. The conservers also tend to follow continuous quality improvement techniques. When they support making changes, they want to go slow and methodically. They have many strengths in that they see the details of every situation. They are steady and reliable, they honor commitments, encourage people to follow the rules, investigate situations thoroughly, see all sides of the issue when change is contemplated, and work to protect the integrity of the organization or community. On the negative side, they tend to be so conservative that opportunities for progress may be passed by.

The Pragmatists

Pragmatists are task oriented and tend to want to get things done with clear results. They are less concerned than the conservers with maintaining the structure of the organization or with things as they presently are. They tend to focus on the action plan phase of the leadership wheel discussed in the last chapter. They want strategies for change and want to see them implemented. They also support the development of scenarios of possible outcomes. Whereas the conservers take a more evolutionary and gradual approach to change, the pragmatists react to the situation and do what needs to be done in a timely fashion. As leaders, pragmatists are very practical, open to exploring different approaches to solving problems, respect other people's opinions, build teamwork, and move teams toward making decisions. They are good facilitators who also know how to tie theory to practice. These are the people who walk the walk. However, they sometimes have trouble making decisions. They straddle the middle of the road. Their indecisiveness may lead to decisions that are not made in a timely fashion.

The Originators

Originators are the people that like to challenge the process (Kouzes & Posner, 2002). These people like to make things happen. They are innovative and creative. They also seem to search for opportunities to create change. In many ways, these leaders are revolutionaries (Musselwhite & Jones, 2004). They tend to be navigators rather than rowers or helmsmen. They are systems thinkers who are big picture thinkers and tend to be less concerned with the details of implementation. As leaders, the originators are clearly change agents, enthusiastic, visionary, tend to multitask, and are analytic, in the sense that they look for unique ways to put things and situations together. However, they do sometimes threaten their organizations and communities because they are less concerned about the status quo. This disturbs many people. Musselwhite and Jones have found that the originators make up about 25% of the population, the conservers another 25%, and the pragmatists are the most prevalent and make up the remaining 50% of the population. Exercise 15–3 will give you the opportunity to experiment with the ways leaders with the three change styles would react to a terrorist event.

UNDERSTANDING CHANGE

Over the years, there have been many theories and explanations about change and its meaning. In this section, there will be a review of two contemporary approaches to change which give prepared public health leaders two influential approaches that are useful for increasing understanding of the challenges facing public health in this new century. One proposes

---

EXERCISE 15–3 Leadership and Terrorism

Purpose: To see how leaders with different styles respond to a terrorist event

Key Concepts: Leadership, leadership style, conservers, pragmatists, originators

Procedures: Using the anthrax letters of 2001 as an example, divide the class
or training group into groups of 10.

1. Using the facts of the anthrax in Florida case (Case Study 13), discuss
   how leaders who are conservers, pragmatists, and originators would
   have addressed the facts of the case.
2. Have your small group come up with five recommendations for action by
   the three types of leaders.
3. Present your recommendations to the larger group.

---

an 8-stage approach to carry out change initiatives in organizations and
communities. The second approach presents change from the perspective
of resilience and the ability of people to adapt to change.

In reviewing older theories of change, Musselwhite and Jones (2004)
found that most of the perspectives could be boiled down to four general
stages:

- First stage involves acknowledging that a threat exists or that change
  is needed.
- Second stage is the reaction of people to the threat or change.
- The third stage is the need to investigate and determine the kinds of
  change that are needed.
- The fourth stage is the implementation phase.

The challenges that our country faces seem to be increasing. There
were many threats to our way of life prior to September 11, 2001. All
these societal and economic factors impact our organizations as well as
our communities. In 1995, Kotter pointed to technological advances,
international economic policy, expansion of global markets, maturation
of markets in developing countries, and the changing of the guard in
many countries, especially with the fall of most Communist and many
Socialist regimes, as factors affecting American communities. To this must
also be added the increase in terrorist and the potential for bioterrorist
acts around the world. People change when their behavior changes, and

their behavior changes because leaders speak to the feelings of individuals (Kotter & Cohen, 2002). It is very important when change is occurring that the solutions are seen in terms of emotions and not just changes in people's minds. Thus, the central issue in change is not just strategy, structure, culture, or systems change, but how people see the proposed change and how it affects their feelings about the changes proposed.

Kotter and Cohen (2002) looked at this perspective from the vantage point of an 8-step model (which Kotter had developed earlier) for successful large-scale change (Kotter, 1996). Whether a change is planned or unanticipated, a sense of urgency has to be generated before any change or adaptation to an unexpected change can occur. Crises clearly increase the sense of urgency. The second step involves the development of a team or coalition to guide the change or reaction to crisis process. This means that the selection of a group must also be representative of those who will be impacted by change. Third, there needs to be a vision toward which to aim. The vision will lead to the developments of goals, objectives, action plans, and implementation as pointed out in the discussion of the leadership wheel in the last chapter. Next, the change, vision, or adaptation strategy has to be communicated to all affected partners and community residents. What the prepared public health leader needs is acceptance, participation, and commitment from all the affected parties. Fifth, it is necessary to empower people to be a part of the action necessary to bring the changes into being. Sixth, it is important to emphasize short-term wins to keep people involved in the process. Seventh, it is important to maintain the momentum of the process by showing connections between the gains and the need to produce further changes so that the projected outcomes will occur. Finally, step eight involves making the changes stick and also fitting the changes into the cultural fabric of the community.

Table 15–1 presents the 8-stage model with the behavioral changes that occur at each of the stages (Kotter & Cohen, 2002). Culture and values change last and not first. In addition, the first seven stages are easy compared to step eight. Before culture can change, behavior has to change. People need to feel that the changes are necessary for the future growth of an organization or a community. It is important for behavior to change with each step of the process. Exercise 15–4 gives you the opportunity to apply the model to a community trying to improve its security-planning activities.

Conner (1992) stated that it is not enough for leaders to recognize that change is necessary. The critical issue is how individuals can adapt to

Table 15–1 The Eight Steps for Successful Large-Scale Change

Step	Action	New Behavior
1	Increase urgency	People start telling each other, "Let's go, we need to change things!"
2	Build the guiding team	A group powerful enough to guide a big change is formed, and they start to work together well.
3	Get the vision right	The guiding team develops the right vision and strategy for the change effort.
4	Communicate for buy-in	People begin to buy into the change, and this shows in their behavior.
5	Empower action	More people feel able to act, and do act, on the vision.
6	Create short-term wins	Momentum builds as people try to fulfill the vision, while fewer and fewer resist change.
7	Don't let up	People make wave after wave of changes until the vision is fulfilled.
8	Make change stick	New and winning behavior continues despite the pull of tradition, turnover of change leaders, etc.

change. Leaders are most effective and efficient when the process of change occurs at a speed at which the leader can absorb and assimilate the changes in a reasonable way. In this second perspective, the issue of changes involves the resilience of the leader and others to adapt to the changes occurring in their environment. The resilience factor is the most critical factor if successful change is to occur. As can be seen in Figure 15–1, resilience is affected by seven support patterns. What the concept of support implies is that each support pattern will aid the leader or increase the capacity of the leader to assimilate or process changes that are needed in the organization or community. Changes in one part of the world impact the lives and communities of all other people and places (Conner, 1992).

The first support pattern involves the nature of the change. For the leader, a concern is whether the change can be controlled or not. There is also the issue of whether the outcome of the change event can be predicted. The level of disruption is also a part of the nature issue. The level

EXERCISE 15–4 Terrorism and Change

Purpose: To explore public health in the context of different potential terrorist planning activities

Key Concepts: Change, emotional intelligence, security planning

Procedures: Divide the class or training group into groups of 10. Apply the
8-stage change model of Kotter and Cohen (2002) to address
the changes needed in community security planning related to
potential terrorist events where some of the issues are:

1. Smallpox vaccination program
2. Enforced curfew for the entire community in high-alert situations
3. Increase in real estate taxes for more police and firefighters
4. Anthrax prevention program
5. Implementation of police powers during all high-alert situations
6. No local support for restrictions on personal freedom

Discuss the emotional element in each stage of your group application of the
model.
Discuss the experience of the exercise with the group as a whole.

---

of disruption is greater for unanticipated events such as terrorist or bioterrorist events. Conner stated that all change have costs associated with
them. Leaders need to determine their ability to assimilate the effects of
change. It is possible to imagine that each person has a certain number of
assimilation points and that people who are resilient have more points to
use. If the change affects the individual only, this is a micro change
(Conner, 1992). Organizational change means each person in an organization or agency must change. Macrochange is when everyone has to
change whether he or she wants to or not.

The process of change is the second support pattern. Resilient leaders
see change as a process, where less resilient people see change as a yes-or-
no situation, in which change is moving from one place to another over a
period of time. There is a transition between these two end points. The
less resilient have difficulty with the ambiguity of the change process.
Resilient people accept change as a part of life and believe that it is possible to manage that process. Leaders do not worry about the ambiguity of
the process. This does not mean that the resilient leader does not feel
stressed at times. Some change events are unpredictable in terms of when

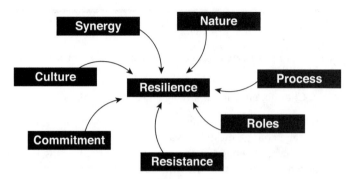

FIGURE 15–1 The Structure of Change

they occur and how they will impact all those concerned. Stress also is a part of the human condition.

The third support pattern relates to the roles of change. Resilient people are aware that the roles and relationships between people change during change events. For example, during an emergency event, the incident command system, which was discussed earlier, changes traditional roles and relationships into predetermined roles and relationships required during the emergency. There are four special roles specifically discussed during change (Conner, 1992). First, there is the *sponsor*. This is an individual who has to legitimize and sanction the change activities whether in reaction to an emergency event or in anticipation of an intended change. *Agents* are individuals or groups who are responsible for reacting to the event or for making the change if it is a planned activity. The *targets* of change are those who have to do the changing. The final role relates to the *advocate*. This is a person or group that supports the change or the implementation of a reaction procedure, but does not have the power to implement the process.

Resistance to change is the fourth support pattern. Leaders expect that there will be resistance to change or the effects of unanticipated change events. Open resistance is a healthy process that brings all issues related to the change out in the open (Conner, 1992). It is covert resistance that is not healthy. Resilient people see the positives in the change process. Less resilient people only see the negative. The issue of realistic expectations is also important in that there will be resistance if people feel that their expectations are not being met. After September 11, 2001, many people became resistant to the many security measures that needed to be imposed. I remember seeing the resistance and anger of some individuals at airports who were upset with the increased security measures. It also seems as if some people become more resistant if they think that the security precautions are permanent rather than temporary.

The next support pattern involves the issue of commitment. As mentioned earlier, change has costs. If change is to be successful, all individuals must pay those costs. Conner (1992) pointed to a number of issues that affect the level of commitment. First, the commitment will increase if people put personal resources such as time, money, and energy into the change process. Second, there needs to be allegiance to the goals that the change process is to achieve. This level of commitment needs to continue even if the changes take a long time to occur or if the proposed changes increase stress or ambiguity. Although small wins are nice, the goal always needs to be on the prize at the end of the process. Next, there may be adversity, but it is important to be steadfast. Finally, leaders know that they will need to be creative, innovative, and resourceful in solving blockages to the achievement of the end changes that need to occur.

The sixth support pattern relates to the cultural dimension, which is critical in that the outcome of any change is affected by culture, shared beliefs and values, behavior, and the ecological nature of the community and how all these factors change over time. Cultural variables are hard to change. Behavior must change first. Behavioral change will affect attitudes which, in turn, will affect beliefs and values which, in turn, will eventually affect the culture as a whole. Leaders must understand how their organizations and communities work. They must be willing to spend the time showing their organizations why change is necessary. There still needs to be a concern about the values of the community and how they can be modified to accommodate the necessary changes that need to occur. Resilient leaders also know that not all people will react to change in the same way or in the same timeframe that the leader is addressing.

The final support relates to synergy, which can be demonstrated in terms of four steps (Conner, 1992). First, there needs to be interaction among team and community members. All parties to the change need to communicate with each other and generate trust and credibility. Secondly, there needs to be "appreciative understanding," which relates to the ability to use and value diversity. The third step is integration, which relates to the blending of people with diverse backgrounds and diverse perspectives on the proposed changes. The fourth step in synergy is implementation, for which there must be successful wins. The diverse views must come together and create products of the change that add value beyond the inputs to the change. Thus, the resilient leader needs to be able to make $1 + 1 = 3$ or more.

More recently, Conner (1998) pointed out that change seems to be speeding up. Organizations and communities will have to become nimble. Crisis has meant that we live in a time of potential chaos and complexity that requires constant changes to adapt to these unexpected events. Stability seems to have gone the way of the dinosaur. For an organization or community to become nimble, they must develop strategies for success in unpredictable times and environments by implementing critical changes as effectively and efficiently as possible. The ability of the organization or community to adapt to constant change is important if these entities are to become nimble and increase their chances for successful change.

CHANGE AND ADAPTATION

Much of the discussion of change in this chapter relates to the impact of intended and unintended change on an organization or community. Although change impacts the lives of people in these entities, there does seem to be a difference in the ability of people to adapt to change and the change process itself. There are two interesting approaches to understanding adaptation in people. Conner (1998) discussed what he called the adaptation reflex in terms of a 4-step model. Initially, there is the disturbance in the equilibrium of the environment in which the individual lives or works. This disequilibrium leads to the attempt by a person to try to adjust to the changed situation to gain personal control again. An individual will explore options to gain a sense of equilibrium again. The event will either appear to be strange or will appear to be somewhat familiar (conventional). Second, a decision needs to be rendered that leads to some clarification or judgment about the meaning of the event. This is followed by a response to the situation, and finally a realignment process in which the individual develops new or modified behaviors to adjust to the change event. The response is the attempt to restore balance. The response can be adaptation with new behavior, avoidance, or assimilation of the event within the existing framework of reaction to change. In summary, the adaptation reflex involves moving from one state of equilibrium to another.

Bridges (1980) saw all adaptation as a series of transitions that occur throughout an individual's life. Transitions are clearly different from the change process itself. For the individual, all change is about a loss, (an ending stage) whether it be a loss of old ways of doing things or the loss of a loved one. The ending is almost like the death of someone. The endings create disengagement, sometimes a disorientation as to who the person really is, disenchantment with the way things used to be, and sometimes disorientation, or perhaps denial, and clearly a sense that life has been changed by the event. This sense of ending is clearly exacerbated when a terrorist or bioterrorist event occurs. The sense of loss is generally followed by a period of disorientation and confusion that varies in length for each person and for each type of change event. It is important for the individual to learn that this "neutral zone" is not an abnormal one but just a time in which the individual is learning to cope with the changes in their lives and also learning to let go of the past. Recovery can thus be a long process. This recovery period eventually leads to a new perspective which Bridges called a "new beginning." As Conner previously pointed out, individuals go through adaptation in different ways. The new beginning can be very exciting in that it offers the person new opportunities and new life possibilities.

The prepared public health leader needs to develop the skills to understand his or her adaptation responses to different types of events as well as to understand the three stages of transitions. The leader must also realize that each person experiences these things in different ways. Recovery and adaptation will be different for each member of the community. Simple expectation about change, adaptation, and transitions are complex and will impact the recovery effort after any change, crisis events, and other life-modifying occurrences.

PUTTING THE PIECES TOGETHER

Although there is not a perfect fit between the theories and perspectives discussed in this chapter, it is possible to attempt this integration although imperfect to better understand the effects of planned and unintended changes in our society. Most of the skills and perspectives discussed in this book and my previous book (Rowitz, 2001) come into play as part of the leadership toolbox that the prepared public health leader puts together over their professional careers. Figures 15–2 and 15–3 show a flowchart for the two types of change. A cursory look at the two figures show many similar processes at play during the change process. The figures show that changes during and after a crisis are complicated by the possible impact of activating the incident command system during the crisis.

Figure 15–2 looks at the process of planned change. The need for change within an organization or community requires the leader to respond to the need. Although many may be aware that changes are needed, it will be the leader who triggers the response. It is clear from our earlier discussion that different leaders will respond in various ways. The resilience factor comes into play in that the high-resilience leader will probably respond differently than the low-resilience leader. The high-resilience leader is more flexible and willing to change. The high-resilience leader will make a decision based on need and the facts at his or her disposal to either move slowly or move more quickly and comprehensively to create the changes that are necessary. This leader may move incrementally, but probably never looks back. If deep change is needed, this leader will take the risk and make it happen. The 8-stage model of

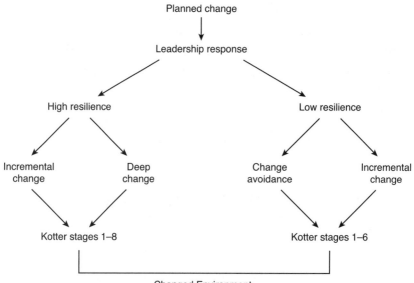

FIGURE 15–2 Integrated Model for Planned Change

Kotter could then be followed to bring about the changes and create a new environment as a result of the changes made. The leader is also aware that the changes will not be complete until most, if not all, of the affected individuals have been able to adapt to the changes by seeing that a new beginning is possible.

On the other hand, the low-resilience leader will probably treat similar needs for change in a different way. This leader will explore maintaining the status quo as a viable option, since change tends to be traumatic for people, and it appears that adaptation to the change will take too long to accomplish. The low-resilience leader always seems to be looking for a way out. Even if this leader decides change is necessary, he or she finds it hard to create a sense of urgency for change (Kotter, 1996). If change is required, the low-resilience leader will probably opt for incremental change because it allows people the chance to adapt to the change in slower steps. It also is possible under this model to return more easily to the starting point than it is with deep change. If change is needed, the process will begin. Using the Kotter model in Table 15–1, steps 1–6 will probably occur. The final steps of not letting up and making the changes stick will be very difficult for the low-resilience leader.

Although there are many similarities in the change flowchart for change due to a crisis, there are still differences. As shown in Figure 15–3, the change event comes out of a chaos perspective when the status quo is destroyed by some generally unanticipated event. This emergency event triggers the need for not only adaptive responses, but also further changes in the organization or community. There needs to be a response by the pre-pared public health leader, whether that leader is a high-resilience leader or not. The change process may need to be filtered through an overlay response that is triggered by the activation of the incident command structure of the community. However, the leaders will need to respond to guide the change process within their organizations or communities while incident command is operating. The public is already feeling a loss of the way things were, and some people will already be trying to adjust to the loss and will have entered the neutral zone that Bridges discussed.

The high-resilience leader knows that further changes are inevitable. A way of life has been altered by the emergency event. This leader will have to decide whether incremental or deep change is the best strategy. The event has had major impact. Some leaders will decide that it is necessary to slow down the change process because deep change will cause further

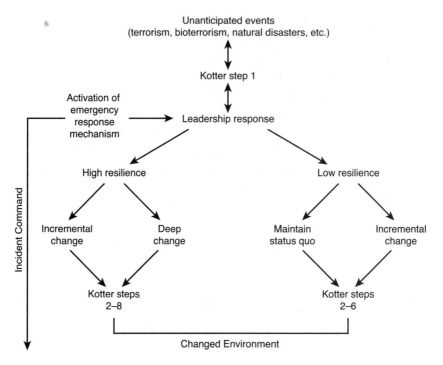

FIGURE 15–3 Integrated Model for Change During and After a Crisis

trauma. However, the nature of the event may also require deep change because incremental change will not work. The sense of urgency has already occurred with the crisis event. The high-resilience leader needs to maintain the sense of urgency as the stages of change occur. The high-resilience leader knows that it is not possible to return to the precrisis event stage. Community and organization life are forever changed.

The low-resilience leader struggles with the need for further changes as a result of the emergency event. This leader may try to maintain the status quo, even though the old status has changed. This leader may opt for no further change so as not to disrupt the lives of people too much. Sometimes, the low-resilience leader recognizes that some further change is needed even though it will be painful to bring it about. This leader will probably go for an incremental change approach without great enthusiasm associated with it. Kotter's steps 2–6 will probably occur without the final steps that will sustain the changes over time. The low-resilience leader will probably believe that it will eventually be possible to return to the way life was before the emergency.

The goal of this section has been to begin to create a perspective on change that builds on the multiple models of change that have been studied. As more is learned about change, it will be possible to add to this synergistic model presented in this section and begin to better understand how change occurs when it is planned and when it is unplanned. In public health, we often confront new crises. As an example, Case Study 15-B addresses the public health issues related to school violence and the necessity of developing new strategies tied to this issue.

CASE STUDY 15-B

Code Red: A Public Health Approach to School Gun Violence

A Case Study in Assessment and Policy Development
Gerard Castro, MPH
Carol Coughlin, MBA, BA
Diana Derige, MPH
Tamarah Duperval, MD, MPH
Suzet M. McKinney, MPH
Anne Sobocinski, BSN

Abstract

The purpose of this case study (Code Red) is to demonstrate why school gun violence is a public health issue and to draw attention to the need for policy to address it. Traditionally, the concept of "safe schools"—addressing the global problem of violence in schools—has been managed under the auspices of the school systems, the Department of Justice, and the Department of Education, along with a number of community coalitions that have investigated youth violence. However, with the publishing of *Deadly Consequences* by Dr. Deborah Prothrow-Stith and Michaele Weissman in 1991, the challenge was issued to consider the problem as a public health issue, citing, "Public health people understand that behavior is difficult to alter and that change comes not as a result of a quick fix, but following a steady barrage of interventions that erode destructive attitudes and behavior over time." Former Surgeon General of the United States, C. Everett Koop, captures the essence of their message in the book's introduction with, "the discipline of public health possesses the solution to the mounting toll of violence in this country. The public health approach seeks to prevent tragedy; it seeks to identify and treat young males who are at

continues

risk for violence before their lives and the lives of those around them are ruined. The discipline of public health provides strategies to stop violence before it maims and kills."

Public health offers a community-based approach to health promotion and prevention of injury or disease. Utilizing a primary prevention focus, practitioners assess behavioral, environmental, and biological risk factors with the goal to educate individuals and communities and to protect them from these risks. Code Red specifically addresses the assessment core function. The ensuing team discussion details the policies integrating public health that need to be developed to address school gun violence.

This case study is a fictional account of events, based on actual events (Ramsland, Handlin, Frontline, etc.), that occurred in Redtown, Midwest, as the town struggled to deal with an incident at the local high school. The case of Kirt Kunkel, 15, occurred in Redtown in May 2001 and involved the killing of Kunkel's parents followed by a separate shooting at school. Two students died and 25 were injured in the school incident. Kirt's behavior was indicative of a very troubled child with disciplinary and learning problems over an extended period of time. Kirt had a documented history of obsession with weapons, as well as many other "early warning signs" that were missed opportunities for intervention and possible prevention.

In the previous three years, two other incidents occurred in the region that involved students who brought guns to school and shot their classmates and teachers. In May of 2000, Newton Brazil, a 13-year-old student, was sent home from school, later returned with a gun, and fatally shot his English teacher. In March of 1998, Marcus Johnson, 13, and Andrew Garcia, 11, were involved in an incident that resulted in the deaths of five fellow students and the wounding of 10 others, including a teacher.

The Code Red Action Team was formed to provoke thought among public health leaders surrounding the development of policies and interventions to prevent future incidents. We challenge future public health leaders to accept the charge of determining the stakeholders, defining the problem, seeking opportunities to identify risk, developing interventions, setting priorities for action, and putting their conclusions into a plan.

The Problem of School Gun Violence

In the fall of 2003, a team of public health leaders from Redtown, Midwest, were assembled to be a part of a special commission created to address the increasing problem of school gun violence perpetuated by children. In recent years, three cases of school gun violence were noted in or near Redtown. Kirt Kunkel, Newtown Brazil, Marcus Johnson, and Andrew Garcia, youngsters between the ages of 11 and 15 years, all carried out vio-

continues

CASE STUDY 15–B   *continued*

lent acts at their schools. Their actions raised awareness of the problem in the community and prompted a call to action.

Given the nature of the recent tragedies and the public outcry, the mayor of Redtown declared a state of emergency in the area of school violence, and together with city and county leaders, legislators, community coalitions and public health leaders called a "Code Red," and established the Commission for the Deterrence and Prevention of School Violence. The public health leaders served as the lead players of the commission and were commonly known as the Code Red Action Team. The commission began with an assessment of the problem, followed by an intense investigation of the events that led up to each of the three incidents.

The Tragedy of Kirt Kunkel

The first major school violence event hit Redtown in May 2001 when Kirt Kunkel, 15, was expelled from school for having a loaded pistol in his locker. Terrified as to what his parents would say and not wanting to face causing them another disappointment, Kunkel felt his only option was to kill his parents, classmates that had previously teased and belittled him, and himself. Kirt's father picked him up from the police station that day and drove him home. Kirt went to his room and retrieved a semiautomatic weapon that he had hidden there. He then shot his father to death as the father sat at the kitchen table eating a sandwich. Kirt then called a friend and talked for a while as he waited for his mother to return home from work. He allowed her to pull into the garage and park her car. As she approached the door to enter the home, he stopped her there, told her he loved her and then shot her six times. Kirt placed homemade bombs around the house, one under his mother's body, and spent the night in the home with his parent's bodies before driving his mother's car to school the next day and firing off 48 rounds of ammunition into his classmates. Kirt killed two students and injured 25 others. He was wrestled to the ground by some other kids before he could turn the gun on himself.

From the outside, Kirt's family seemed like a very functional and happy family. Kirt's parents were both well-respected teachers; his oldest sister, Louise, was a cheerleader and honor roll student. The family traveled together and were model community residents. However, from an early age Kirt displayed signs of depression and had disciplinary problems at home and at school. Below is a chronology of some key evens in Kirt's life:

* Kirt was born in August 1985. He went to kindergarten in Spain for a year when his parents took a sabbatical from teaching in the United States. He was very frustrated in school where everyone was speaking a language foreign to him.

continues

CASE STUDY 15-B *continued*

- KK entered first grade in September 1991. In a report card, his teacher indicated he "lacked maturity and had slow emotional and physical development."
- In 1993, KK was diagnosed with learning disabilities and was placed in special education classes for reading and writing, and in gifted and talented classes for math and science.
- In 1998, KK showed an interest in explosives and weapons. He used the Internet to purchase a book about how to make bombs. Kirt's mother was concerned about the type of friends Kirt as spending time with.
- In 1999, Kirt was caught shoplifting a CD in a music store. His mother found a hidden gun in his room.
- In January 2000, KK was caught throwing rocks off of a bridge with a friend. One rock damaged a car, but there was no personal injury. KK paid for damages to the victim's car and performed community services as retribution. He showed remorse for his actions. He said his friend actually threw the stone that hit the car.
- February 2000: As a result of the rock throwing incident, Kirt's depression, and his obsession with guns and explosives, Kirt's mother decided to send him to a psychologist for counseling. He was diagnosed with "major depressive disorder" and given a prescription for Prozac.
- March 2000: Kirt continued to see the doctor for depression. The psychiatrist noted that his parents were "impressive parents" for wanting their son to take responsibility for the rock throwing incident. The doctor saw nothing out of the ordinary with Kirt or his family.
- April 2000: Kirt's psychiatrist noted that he was less depressed and handled anger better, but that he still had an interest in explosives.
- In May 2000: Kirt was suspended from school for fighting with a student in his class.
- On 6/28/2000, Kirt's father went with him to buy a gun. His psychiatrist was concerned about the gun purchase.
- Kirt's psychiatric treatment was discontinued on July 30, 2000, since he was doing well in school.
- In the summer of 2000, Kirt bought a gun from a student at school and hid it from his parents.
- Kirt entered Redtown High School in the fall of 2000. He also went off of Prozac.
- September 2000: Kirt's father bought him a semiautomatic rifle, but told him that he could only use it under his father's supervision.
- October 2000: Kirt delivers "How to Make a Bomb" speech in public speaking class.

continues

CASE STUDY 15–B *continued*

- On May 20, 2001, Kirt was expelled from school for having a gun in his locker. He was embarrassed about how his father would react to his expulsion. KK returned home from school and killed his father while he was eating at the kitchen table. KK waited for his mother to return home from work, told her he loved her, then killed her.
- On May 21, 2001, Kirt drove to school dressed in a trench coat with a semiautomatic rifle and a knife taped to his leg. He went on a rampage and killed two students and injured 25 others.

After this tragic event, much research was done to better understand why Kirt Kunkel killed and if it could have been prevented. Some retrospective thoughts about this case follow.

Even after he killed their parents, Kirt's sister, Louise, still loved Kirt very much and knew that he had struggled with learning disabilities from early on in Spain. Many said he came from a "good family" and had understanding, caring parents. His mother was said to have been very proactive about getting him in treatment after the rock-throwing incident. Some have speculated that he may have felt like a failure compared to Louise and never lived up to his parent's expectations. Some friends at school said he spoke of "voices in his head"; others said he told them that he would soon do something "memorable." He was voted by his classmates as the person "most likely to create World War III" and was obsessed with guns, explosives, and other weapons. He had trouble controlling his anger and had disciplinary issues both at home and at school. He was said to have had feelings of hopelessness and loneliness and was suicidal. Kirt was once quoted as having said "My only hope is that tomorrow will be better. When I lose hope, people die." He used Prozac, which has since been found to, in some cases, cause psychotic side effects in a small percentage of minors.

Other School Shooters

Newton Brazil, a 13-year-old student, shot and killed his English teacher on the last day of school. The shooting took place after Newton and a friend had been sent home early on the last day of school for throwing water balloons. As they were leaving, Newton told his friend he was going to get a gun and return to school to shoot the school administrator who had dismissed him. Newton arrived home and could not find his mother or grandmother to return with him to school to discuss his dismissal. Newton then took a gun and returned to the school. Newton arrived at the door of his English class and asked to speak with two friends in the hallway. The English teacher refused and sent Newton away. Newton pulled out the gun, pointed it in his English teacher's face and shot. He said he only pointed the gun to scare the teacher, but it went off accidentally.

continues

CASE STUDY 15-B *continued*

By many accounts, Newton seemed to be a well-adjusted teenager who was doing well in school. Unique to this case is that Newton held his victim in high esteem. Newton considered this teacher one of his favorites. In addition to mentioning to a friend that he planned to return to school with a gun and shoot an administrator, Newton had shown the gun to his classmates a few weeks prior. The gun in question was stolen by Newton from a family acquaintance. Some indications also suggest that Brazil was smitten with the girl he requested to see in the English class and the shooting was a youth reaction to being denied access to her.

Marcus Johnson, 13, and Andrew Garcia, 11, are cousins raised in Jonesboro, Arkansas, who carried out a plan that resulted in the deaths of five fellow students and the wounding of 10 others, including a teacher at the Westside Middle School. Marcus, the elder cousin, was the leader in this tragedy, vowing to "kill girls who broke up with [him]" following the breakup with a girl friend just two weeks before the incident. He was heard by classmates just the day prior saying that "he had a lot of killing to do," but no action was taken. On the morning of the 24th, the two cousins took the Johnson's family minivan (driven by Marcus) and headed towards the Westside Middle School armed with rifles and handguns, reportedly belonging to Andrew Garcia's grandfather. On their way to school, they stopped at two or three gas stations, but no attendant would sell them gas because of their age. But somehow they made it to the school, dressed in camouflage, and ready to attack. Andrew entered the school, tripped a false fire alarm to lure students outside and then ran back to the designated position where Marcus was waiting to open fire. As students exited the building, in response to the fire alarm, the boys mowed the students down with gunfire.

Discussion of Themes—Early Warning Signs

What makes these young people kill? The Code Red Action Team examined each case carefully, attempting to identify themes or early warning signs that were common to these cases. While there do not appear to be specific "events" that spawned these killing sprees, there are some relevant similarities that are evident among these three cases.

Child psychologist Johnathon Kellerman, author of *Savage Spawn: Reflections on Violent Children* says that a good predictor of dangerousness in children is the combination of a certain temperament with a chaotic environment. In each of these three cases, the killers had some exposure to violence. However, that violence was not openly apparent to the parents, school officials, or community members that interacted with these boys on a daily basis. Kirt Kunkel used a small collection of books to educate

continues

CASE STUDY 15–B   *continued*

himself about explosives and bomb making. He then began to stockpile firearms in his home and detonate his homemade bombs in the woods behind his home to vent his feelings of anger and frustration. Although his parents were not violent people, we believe that his strained relationship with his parents coupled with his strong desire to please them created feelings of failure and despair in Kunkel. His lack of popularity among his peers seemed to only add to the chaos that went on in the mind of this lonely, immature boy. He was holding out for hope that his world would change. In his words, "When I lose hope, people die."

Newton Brazil witnessed the physical abuse that was inflicted on his mother by her boyfriend. He often tried to rescue her from the abuse. What everyone saw each day was "a good student with little history of disciplinary problems." But domestic violence was never discussed in Brazil's home. He had no outlet for his feelings and therefore kept everything inside. Eventually, it bubbled over. In the case of Andrew Garcia and Marcus Johnson, the boys had been introduced to guns and hunting at very young ages. "Killing was made a central part of their understanding of what defines manhood."

There were other commonalities among these cases. All of these boys had troubled relationships with their fathers. Sometimes, the father was absent altogether. These boys had feelings of low self-esteem and poor social skills. They were loners or outcasts. Additionally, they had all been rejected by the young girls that were the objects of their affections. So what makes these young people kill? Dr. Helen Smith, a forensic psychologist in Knoxville, Tennessee, conducted a national survey of violent and nonviolent kids. She found that "Using guns and being violent toward others moves these kids from powerlessness to power, from nobodies to media celebrities."

Pointing Fingers: The Shift of Responsibility

In hindsight, the warning signs should have been obvious. Many blame the parents. Others blame violence in the media that youth are exposed to. Still others question the police, the school, and judicial or mental health systems that may have had run-ins with the perpetrators. The National School Safety Center has created a profile of the youngster most likely to commit school violence, based on the profiles of juveniles who already have. The 20-item checklist includes drug abuse, tantrums, threats, depression, truancy, cruelty to animals, and a fascination with weapons and violence that spills over into schoolwork.

Profiles, however, are problematic because they tend to apply a lot of kids who never become violent. Using a profile gives one the tendency to

continues

CASE STUDY 15-B *continued*

stereotype and group a large number where only a very small minority will act. And there is no guarantee that the kids most likely to kill won't be missed.

Violence in movies, TV, and video games has become pervasive in our society, and studies have shown that media violence can lead to aggressive behavior in children. By age 18, the average American child will have viewed about 200,000 acts of violence on television alone. The American Academy of Pediatrics states that violence is especially damaging to young children (under age 8) because they cannot easily tell the difference between real life and fantasy. They go on to say that media violence affects children by:

- Increasing aggressiveness and antisocial behavior
- Increasing their fear of becoming victims
- Making them less sensitive to violence and to victims of violence
- Increasing their appetite for more violence in entertainment and in real life

Additionally, media violence often fails to show the consequences of violence. This is especially true of cartoons, toy commercials, and music videos. As a result, children learn that there are few, if any, repercussions for committing violent acts.

This, however, does not explain the majority of children who are exposed to the same influences and grow up to be productive members of society. Ultimately, the media does not commit the crimes, people do.

Many have pointed to the accessibility of guns as the cause of this growing problem. Has our society taken this matter seriously? Our answer is no! The proliferation of guns in our society is startling. How many gun laws have been changed? Not enough. Even current gun laws aren't being universally enforced. Despite continued acknowledgements by school shooters that the guns they used were stolen from parents or other family members, many parents have still not disposed of their guns. Some are still traveling to the local Wal-Mart to buy rifles or guns for their children. Has every family in a school community where there has been a lethal school shooting destroyed every gun they own? Of course not, but this is a question that all community stakeholders need to consider.

Missed Opportunities

Could anything have been done to prevent the murders of Kirt Kunkel's parents, the murders of two students, and the injuries to 25 other students at the Redtown, Midwest, school? In hindsight, many of the public health leaders on Redtown's special commission on school gun violence think

continues

CASE STUDY 15–B *continued*

that there were warning signs that were missed or went unheeded in the years preceding the killings.

Kunkel exhibited many of the early warning signs at a young age: a troubled childhood, disciplinary problems, early learning disabilities, and an obsession with weapons. As a high school freshman, Kirt was caught for shoplifting and had a gun hidden in his room. A year later, he was again in trouble for rock throwing and property damage. He was diagnosed with a major depressive disorder and started on an antidepressant.

Newton Brazil was a model student and overall a "good kid." He didn't have constant and recurring disciplinary problems. However, he was constantly exposed to violence in his home, and he had no outlet for his feelings. His mother did not seek help for the domestic abuse that she was suffering. Neither did she talk with her son to reinforce the basic fact that what he was seeing was not socially acceptable. His attempts to thwart off the violence that he thought was wrong were unwanted and went unrecognized. On the occasion that Brazil became upset about something, violence was the only coping mechanism that he had. He simply was not aware of anything else.

Andrew Garcia and Marcus Johnson were hunters. They had been taught very early in life that normal rules don't apply to hunters; that hunters can attack fair game at any time. Although hunting is acceptable and welcomed in many parts of the country, we must question the most appropriate age at which children should be exposed to hunting. We submit that Andrew and Marcus were not mature enough to be allotted as much freedom around guns as they were. These boys thought it would be fun to see what would happen if they opened fire on a crowd of teachers and fellow classmates. To them, it was a game. Clearly, they did not have the proper education about guns and hunting that would have enabled them to know that the taking of human life is not only wrong, but very different from hunting animals for food.

We have found that there are similarities in almost all of the school shooters. There are also differences. They are not all loners. They are not all abused children. Anger is the most common thread. Access to guns is universal.

In hindsight, the warning signs come together to form a more complete portrait of the shooter. But in the present, how do we quantify and qualify the traits and actions of these students? The warning signs were all there. Individually, as parents, friends, teachers, police, courts, doctors, and social workers, we know something about the feelings or behaviors of these young people, but how do we put it together? The answer is simple enough: we need to develop a mechanism for pooling the information and sharing that information. The discipline of public health offers us a solution:

continues

CASE STUDY 15-B *continued*

surveillance and data sharing. Surveillance can be carried out on a daily basis in our basic interactions with students. A 2000 study conducted by researchers from the U.S. Secret Service offers some key insight: "In their own words, the boys who have killed in America's schools offer a simple suggestion to prevent it from happening again: 'Listen to us.' " How do we develop the wisdom to determine which child will go on to act out in violence and direct our limited resources to preventing that future action? The wisdom comes in learning how to recognize the warning signs and building on the information you have. Wisdom also comes in extending the information we have individually to our constituents, addressing the barriers to sharing it, understanding each other, and acting together for the good of the community. Data sharing, perhaps via a confidential databank, among stakeholders will continually provide more information upon which to build.

Communication is a key factor in preventing these tragedies. It is a well-known fact that many of these young killers often tell their friends of their plans prior to carrying them out. Therefore, fellow students sometimes know that something could happen. These students need teaching and support so that they will feel comfortable revealing their information to parents and authorities. Those students who come forth will also need respect, confidentiality, and appreciation. Their information must be valued and then evaluated, rather than filed away, buried, or ignored.

We need a process for tying all of these traits together without stereotyping a significant percentage of lonely high school students. Many students will have learning problems, insecurities, and feel alone until they move through the teenage years and out of the school environment. Many will overcome the challenges of adolescence and move on to brighter lives that stereotyping could make difficult.

We can't change their ages, but we can change their environments. We need to teach these students to cope within their climactic and unstable environments. For vulnerable students, spending seven hours a day, five days a week for years in a perceived hostile and nonsupportive environment can prove disastrous for these students and the communities in which they live. Even for students who don't become violent in school, environmental changes could help many to develop better self-esteem and be less prone to anger and violence in other areas of their lives.

Violence in the Nation—A Call to Public Health

Violence is not a new phenomenon in our nation. Recent examinations of community response, social responsibility, and societal cost to violence have allowed prevention practitioners and communities to reexamine our approach to violence. Indeed, violence is a global issue, but for the United

continues

CASE STUDY 15-B *continued*

States, violence seems epidemic. The U.S. homicide rate is three to eight times greater than that of any other Western democracy. According to the Center for the Study and Prevention of Violence, intentional violence accounts for one-third of all injuries in the United States, and intentional interpersonal violence disproportionately involves young people as predators and victims. Furthermore, homicide is the second leading cause of death for youth ages 15 to 24 years.

School violence is often at the center of discussion when examining youth violence trends. School violence is not limited to urban areas. On the contrary, in 1998, students ranging in ages from 12 to 18 years in urban, suburban, and rural locales were equally vulnerable to serious violent crime and theft at school. School violence often calls our attention to the relatively recent phenomenon known as "school shootings." And while these cases are seen as especially heinous and lend themselves well to the sensationalism of media, in examining violence in the lives of our youth, we must also keep in mind that more youth victimization happens away from school than at school. Violence is a societal issue that, like water, finds its way into all corners of our lives.

The news isn't all bad. According to the Department of Justice's Bureau of Justice and Statistics, violent crime and victimization rates have declined since 1993, reaching the lowest level ever recorded in 2000. Likewise, public health officials have taken notice. *Youth Violence: A Report of the Surgeon General* was developed by the CDC, the National Institutes of Health, and the Substance Abuse and Mental Health Services Administration. The report defines the problem, using surveillance processes designed to gather data that establish the nature of the problem and the trends in its incidence and prevalence; identifies potential causes through epidemiological analyses that identify risk and protective factors associated with the problem; designs, develops, and evaluates the effectiveness and generalizability of interventions; and disseminates successful models as part of a coordinated effort to educate and reach out of the public. Public health constituents have the opportunity to examine violence and specifically youth violence at a community health level, using both integrated models and community strategies to develop violence prevention practices.

Current public health antiviolence programs often limit their scope and resources to victims of domestic violence and abused children. While these prevention and intervention programs are crucial, we must begin to examine the wider scope of violence in society. Of concern in this examination is violence prevention focused on adolescent males and adult males who are both the perpetrators and victims of the majority of violent acts in the United States.

continues

CASE STUDY 15–B *continued*

Public health methods are essential to violence prevention. Public health practice is both systematic and concerned with the discovery, examination, perpetuation, and the root cause of disease. Public health at its core can be described as "changing behavior and changing attitudes through intervention as the base of prevention." Therefore, the nature of violence that continues to permeate our communities and degrade both community health and well-being requires a systematic response.

The public health leaders of Redtown's special commission on youth violence in schools reviewed much material, interviewed many experts, and came up with many questions. Their unanimous response to these questions is that Redtown will develop public health policy to prevent violence in schools.

Study Guide Questions

1. In your group, discuss the similarities and differences in the school shooters in these three cases.

2. What are some of the missed opportunities raised in these cases?

3. Discuss the impact of the following on these cases:
   a. Parents
   b. Drugs
   c. Availability of weapons
   d. Past violent behavior/tendencies
   e. Bullying at school
   f. Exposure to violence in the home
   g. Exposure to violent video games

4. What role should public health have in school-based violence prevention programs?

5. Discuss the various jurisdictions involved and how they could work together to develop a prevention program (criminal law, the school administration, public health, parents/teachers groups, neighborhood coalitions against violence).

6. Researchers from the U.S. Secret Service studied 37 school shootings. Of the 40 school shooters interviewed, they all offered the same suggestion for prevention of school gun violence: "Listen to us." Discuss ideas for how prevention programs can provide avenues for those contemplating violence to express their feelings, free of punishment.

continues

7. Discuss ways that public health practitioners can use tools such as surveillance and data sharing to hone in on warning signs before tragedy strikes.

Case Study 15-B References

Publications
Gellert, George A. (2002). *Confronting Violence.* Boulder, CO: Westview Press.
Prothrow-Stith, D., Weisman, M. (1991). *Deadly Consequences.* New York: HarperCollins.
Web Sites
2000 PBS Online and WGBH/Frontline. (n.d.). *Frontline: The killer at Thurston High: Who is Kip Kinkel? Chronology.* Retrieved November 2, 2003, from http://www.pbs.org/wgbh/pages/frontline/shows/kinkel/kip/cron.html
2000 PBS Online and WGBH/Frontline. (n.d.). *Frontline: The killer at Thurston High: Profiling school shooters.* Retrieved November 2, 2003, from http://www.pbs.org/wgbh/pages/frontline/shows/kinkel/profile
2000 PBS Online and WGBH/Frontline. (n.d.). *Frontline: The killer at Thurston High: An interview with Kristin Kinkel.* Retrieved November 2, 2003, from http://www.pbs.org/wgbh/pages/frontline/shows/kinkel/kip/kristin.html
2000 PBS Online and WGBH/Frontline. (n.d.). *Frontline: The killer at Thurston High: 111 years without parole.* Retrieved November 2, 2003, from http://www.pbs.org/wgbh/pages/frontline/shows/kinkel/trial/
2000 PBS Online and WGBH/Frontline. (n.d.). *Frontline: The killer at Thurston High: Placing blame.* Retrieved November 2, 2003, from http://www.pbs.org/wgbh/pages/frontline/shows/kinkel/blame/
Center for the Study and Prevention of Violence. (2002). *CSPV school violence fact sheets.* Retrieved October 27, 2003, from http://www.colorado.edu/cspv/publications/factsheets/scoolviolence/FS-SV02.html
Center for Prevention of School Violence. (2003). *Parental involvement in school safety: What every parent should know; what every parent should say.* Retrieved October 27, 2003, from http://www.ncdjjdp.org/cpsv/parent/whatparentsneed.htm
Family Education Network. (2003). *When student writings set off school alarms.* Retrieved October 27, 2003, from http://www.familyeducation.com/article/0,1120,24-21838,00.html
ERIC Clearinghouse and Urban Education. (1996). *An overview of strategies to reduce school violence.* Retrieved October 27, 2003, from http://eric=web.tc.columbia.edu/digest/dig115.asp
Constitutional Rights Foundation. (n.d.). *The challenge of school violence.* Retrieved from http://www.crf-usa.org/violence/school.html

continues

CASE STUDY 15–B   *continued*

Why Files. (n.d.). *When kids kill*. Retrieved October 27, 2003, from http://www.whyfiles.org/065school_violence/1html

PBS Newshour. (1999). *Online Newshour: Kids who kill—April 21, 1999*. Retrieved October 27, 2003, from http://www.pbs.org/newshour/bb/law/jan-june99/violence_4-21.html

O'Toole, M. E., Federal Bureau of Investigation. (1999). *The school shooter: A threat assessment perspective*.

Fox News. (1999). *Kinkel was on Prozac—Heard 'voices' in his head*. Retrieved November 7, 2003, from http://www.foxnews.com/health/healthw_ap_1113_32.sml,11-15-99.

Testimony of Dr. Helen Smith before the Arkansas House of Representatives Committee on the Judiciary. (1998). *School killings: Prevention and response*. Retrieved November 7, 2003, from http://www.violentkids.com/articles/violence_article_6.html

Eugene Register Guard, May 31, 1998. *Potentially deadly youngsters not common*, by Bob Keefer. Retrieved November 7, 2003, from http://www.oslc.org/InTheNews/youngsters.html

Children's drugs? An inquiry into the school shootings in America. Retrieved November 7, 2003, from http://www.trunkerton.fsnet.co.uk/children.htm

Ramsland, K. Court TV's crime library: Criminal minds and methods. *School killers: The list*. Retrieved November 3, 2003, from http://www.crimelibrary.com/serial_killers/weird/kids1/index_1.html?sect=19

Ramsland, K. TV's crime library: Criminal minds and methods. *School killers: Kipland Kinkel*. Retrieved December 8, 2003, from http://www.crimelibrary.com/serial_killers/weird/kids1/kinkel_2.html?sect=3

Ramsland, K. TV's crime library: Criminal minds and methods. *School killers: Copy cats*. Retrieved November 21, 2003, from http://www.crimelibrary.com/serial_killers/weird/kids1/cats_4.html?sect=19

Ramsland, K. TV's crime library: Criminal minds and methods. *School killers: What the kids say*. Retrieved November 21, 2003, from http://www.crimelibrary.com/serial_killers/weird/ kids1/say_5.html?sect=19

Ramsland, K. TV's crime library: Criminal minds and metods. *School killers: The young rampage killer*. Retrieved November 21, 2003, from http://www.crimelibrary.com/serial_killers/weird/kids1/killer_6.html?sect=19

Ramsland, K. TV's crime library: Criminal minds and methods. *School killers: School violence and the media*. Retrieved November 8, 2003, from http://www.crimelibrary.com/serial_killers/weird/kids1/media_7.html?sect=19

Animal People, May 1998. *Hunting and trapping: Teach the children well*. Retrieved December 12, 2003, from http://www.animalpeoplenews.org/98/4/hunting.html

continues

CASE STUDY 15–B *continued*

Court TV Online. *Trial report: Nathaniel Brazill says he's sorry, asks judge for leniency.* Retrieved December 12, 2003, from http://www.courttv.com/trials/brazill/072601_am_ctv.html

US Department of Health and Human Services. *Youth violence: A report of the Surgeon General.* Retrieved December 8, 2003, from http://www.surgeongeneral.gov/library/youthviolence/report.html

US Department of Health and Human Services, Office of Disease Prevention and Health Promotion. *Prevention report: Youth violence is a public health issue.* Retrieved December 2, 2003, from http://www.odphp.osophs.dhhs.gov/pubs/prevrpt/01spring/Spring2001PR.htm

US Centers for Disease Control and Prevention, National Center for Injury Prevention and Control. *Youth violence.* Retrieved December 8, 2003, from http://www.cdc.gov/ncipc/factsheets/yvfacts.htm

Chicago Department of Public Health. *A public health approach to violence prevention.* Retrieved October 30, 2003, from http://www.cocpweb3.cityofchicago.org/health/Publications/ViolencePrevention/pub_health_ap

Dedman, B. Deadly lessons: School shooters tell why. *Chicago Sun-Times.* Retrieved October 28, 2003, from http://www.suntimes.com/shoot/

Violence Prevention Center. *Where'd they get their guns? An analysis of the firearms used in high-profile shootings, 1963 to 2001.* Retrieved November 21, 2003, from http://www.vpc.org/studies/wguncont.htm

Dedman, B. Examining the psyche of an adolescent killer. *Chicago Sun-Times.* Retrieved December 28, 2003, from http://www.suntimes.com/shoot/shoot_15.html

Malone, J. "3 Paducah families ask: Why, Michael?" *Courier-Journal.* Retrieved November 22, 2003, from http://www.courier-journal.com./cjextra/schoolshoot/SCHvictims.html

SUMMARY

Although much of leadership is about change, it is important for the prepared public health leader to understand the elements of change as a process and how it works. This chapter has looked at this issue and discussed it from the viewpoint of the individual who has to adapt to the changes that are occurring in our society on a daily basis, the leaders who have to respond to the need for change or adapt to changes that are unplanned, and the need to have strategies for addressing change as a process.

REFERENCES

Bridges, W. (1980). *Transitions.* Cambridge, MA: Perseus Books.

Conner, D. R. (1992). *Managing at the speed of change.* New York: Villard Books.

Conner, D. R. (1998). *Leading at the edge of chaos.* New York: John Wiley and Sons.

Kotter, J. P. (1995). *The new rules.* New York: The Free Press.

Kotter, J. P. (1996). *Leading change.* Boston: Harvard Business School Press.

Kotter, J. P., & Cohen, D. S. (2002). *The heart of change.* Boston: Harvard Business School Press.

Kouzes, J., & Posner, B. (2002). *The leadership challenge* (3rd ed.). San Francisco: Jossey-Bass.

Musselwhite, C., & Jones, R. (2004). *Dangerous opportunity: Making change work.* Philadelphia: Xlibris.

Quinn, R. E. (1996). *Deep change.* San Francisco: Jossey-Bass.

Rowitz, L. (2001). *Public health leadership: Putting principles into practice.* Sudbury, MA: Jones and Bartlett.

Schein, E. H. (2004). *Organizational culture and leadership* (3rd ed.). San Francisco: Jossey-Bass.

Schwartz, P. (2003). *Inevitable surprises.* New York: Gotham Books.

Turning Point. (2004). *States of change.* Seattle, WA: Turning Point National Office (R. W. Johnson Foundation).

PART IV

The Future

CHAPTER 16

A View of Tomorrow

The most pathetic person in the world is
someone who has sight, but no vision.

—Helen Keller

Although leaders are oriented to change, change without a vision does not take the leader very far. Leadership is as much about learning from our experiences as it is about coping with the critical events of modern times. Covey (1996) has stated that leaders for the future will be involved in developing values and cultures that are based on the principles that guide a society. Democracy provides an excellent template for change. Our founding fathers created a system based on freedom, growth, and the ability to adapt to changing circumstances. The prepared public health leader adopts these principles and adds his or her own spin to them. They realize that the future of public health is based on preventing disease and promoting health and not just on treatment and diagnosis of the disease. Prevention is what our leaders must focus upon—not just reaction. It is important for successful leaders to be pathfinders who build our society on positive visions for the future (Covey, 1996). These leaders must also be expert in aligning our health issues with the culture and values that make our society strong. Leaders also need to empower people and empower them so that they share power, authority, and responsibility for the growth and change that will inevitably occur in our society.

Vision is not only about the future, it is a strong belief in possibilities. It is based on the concept of hope and an understanding that whatever unfortunate events occur, there are always possibilities of positive social change. Vision involves the leader's ability to picture what the future might look like. Leaders always see what is possible for people in terms of the projects they do and the activities in which they will become involved (Covey, 2004). Vision is about the discipline necessary to bring change into being, the passion to carry it out, and a moral sense of doing only what is morally correct. Vision is also about building on past experiences. It is looking to the past for the positive lessons that we have learned. It is not about holding on to past grievances or blaming others for what has happened (Johnson, 2003). Vision is as much about the present as it is about the past. It is necessary to put the past in perspective and see the present for what it really is. One critical mistake many leaders make is to think that the answer for past mistakes is to completely reinvent the wheel. Politicians make this mistake every time there is a new election outcome. The future is about making plans based upon the perspectives of *now*. Vision is about planning for possible futures.

Blanchard and Miller (2004) explored the issue of what makes leaders successful. The real secret of leadership relates to a strong belief in service to the public. Leaders always need to gain credibility and trust from the people whom they serve. The important issue relates to the true meaning of service. The definition of service embraces the following:

- See and perceive possible futures
- Engage constituents in the process of change
- Realize change is inevitable
- Accept the need to constantly reinvent the future
- Advocate for concrete outcomes while protecting values and a way of life
- Protect and embody society's values in everything that is done.

This book has discussed the critical impact of terrorist acts on our way of life and the need for leaders who are prepared to address any future emergencies that our society will face. The public health concerns are primary in many of these discussions. Our leaders need to be involved in addressing the critical issues of our times. At the same time, leaders need to lead the way toward the future by investigating and understanding the possibilities that our way of life presents. This does not mean that our lives will not be affected by these unfortunate events, but rather that we are strong enough to overcome these actions, adapt in new ways, and still promote the strengths that democracy brings to the way we live. In this last section, we explore the skills of visioning in order to better prepare for our futures.

THE PROCESS OF VISIONING

Many people talk the *vision* word these days. However, predicting the future takes more than a crystal ball. For a vision to be useful, it needs to be realistic about the realities of today as well as certain factors that are predictable for the future (Nanus, 1992). A vision must also be credible in that the future that is proposed must be possible. Finally, the vision must appear to be positive for the organization or community. A vision needs to gain adherents. The credibility of the leader will clearly be a factor in this. A vision must also seem real to the people who will strive to bring it to reality. The vision needs to set a standard for high quality (Nanus, 1992). Visions provide a link between the present and the future.

Mission and vision are also linked. If we look again at the leadership wheel in Chapter 14, vision also is connected with goals and objectives. In addition, priority setting in public health and the use of performance standards can also be a useful part of visioning. The United States Federal Highway Administration (n.d.) also viewed visioning as a way to get the public to participate in long-range planning efforts. It is also possible that visioning can be seen as a mechanism for policy development. Visioning also helps in the generation of ideas and an exploration of different possible scenarios for change. Visioning is also flexible in that it can be accomplished in retreats or as part of the general process of planning. The process of vision is useful in many ways (Federal Highway Administration, n.d.):

1. It sets the stage for both short-term and long-term planning activities.
2. It can help set some new directions for policy formulation.
3. It is possible to review current policies in light of several possible futures.
4. It helps to integrate different issues in a more organized way.
5. It allows different ideas and perspectives to be applied to potential futures.
6. It gives a perspective on problem solutions.

There are four distinct phases that delineate the process of vision. A number of questions can be posed during each of these four phases

(Nanus & Dobbs, 1999). Whatever questions are posed can then provide information to guide the next step of the visioning process. Nanus (1992) gives a possible list of questions for each of the four phases. The important issue is that the visioning process should be systematic and be carried out in a well-documented fashion.

In the first phase a vision audit puts the need for the development of a new vision in context. This audit links vision with values, cultural factors, and mission. The context is an important characteristic of the process. History, demographic changes, health status indicators, and so on become part of the vision audit. Performance measures can be useful here as well. This audit helps to define present reality and what is possible within the context of today's realities. Some urban anthropologists would equate the process with some elements of what they call a cultural audit, although the cultural audit is more intense and takes longer. The second phase is the important discussion related to the scope of the proposed vision exercise. In the third stage, leaders put the proposed vision in context of the community or organization for the long term. Finally, a scenario-building process is undertaken to explore the impact of a potential vision on the organization or community.

Because vision is so time sensitive, it should be possible to experiment with vision statements for an organization or community at different future time points. To give you some practice with the visioning process, Exercises 16–1 and 16–2 allow you to experiment with the process of the development of a vision for a public health agency that has been affected by the terrorist events of September 11, 2001, at a 5-year, 10-year, and 25-year period post event.

A PERSPECTIVE FOR LEADERS

Talking about vision is in many ways more complex than it first appears. I remember a public health agency director telling me a few years ago that he had no time to develop a vision. He was too busy putting out fires. The prepared public health leader knows that he or she must find the time to plan and use the vision as a mechanism for setting the course of the agency and the community. Planning and visioning should make our jobs easier over the long run. Many tools exist to help the leaders to improve public health practice activities (Rowitz, 2004). Many tools exist to help these leaders do their work. It is not only the formal instruments required

---

EXERCISE 16–1 Visions over Time

Purpose: To explore the factors that affect visions over the short and long term

Key Concepts: Visioning

Procedures: A number of exercises in this book have explored the terrorist acts of September 11, 2001. This exercise asks you and your partners to look at public health at different times in the future.

1. Divide the class or training group into sets of three smaller groups.
2. Group 1 will develop a vision for your local health department in 5 years based on the events of September 11, 2001, and the anthrax letters.
3. Group 2 will develop a vision for public health for the next 10 years.
4. Group 3 will develop a vision for public health for the next 25 years.
5. Discuss your visions in the larger group or do Exercise 16–2.

---

by the profession to monitor the health of the public. There are more informal tools, such as the following:

- The case studies that have been used in this book
- Calls to experts for their views
- Stories of leaders
- Many exercises and games that help better define a problem and give added perspectives to its solution
- Site visits to other communities and agencies
- Community participation in health surveys
- Team-building tools
- Using executive coaches to help leaders develop personal learning contracts
- The use of journals to document leadership experiences
- Mentoring staff to take on management and leadership responsibilities
- Learning skills from business leaders that can better structure public sector leadership activities

In other words, leaders must fill their toolboxes with all sorts of tools and gadgets to make themselves more effective.

Although this book has primarily settled on the concerns of public health leaders relative to other leaders, leaders of all kinds should also be aware that they need to develop their own personal visions for their pro-

---

EXERCISE 16–2 Expert Reactions to the Vision

Purpose: To explore reactions to the visions developed in Exercise 16-1

Key Concepts: Vision

Procedures: Take the three vision statements developed by the small groups and role play the reactions of the following leaders to these statements:

1. John F. Kennedy
2. Abraham Lincoln
3. Eleanore Roosevelt
4. Martin Luther King, Jr.
5. President of the American Public Health Association

---

fessional future. Leaders need to guide their own actions as well as those of others. A leader's emotional reaction to various situations will clearly guide others (Goleman, Boyatziz, & McKee, 2002). In fact, their reactions may stimulate similar reactions in others. When leaders are positive, others seem to become positive as a result. The reverse is also true. This leadership role of being an emotional guide to others has been recently dubbed "primal leadership." Visions also are emotional in content. It is important to address this as visions are formed.

There are many self-help books on leadership in the marketplace. It is not necessary to repeat that extensive literature here. However, it is possible to mention a few important steps to reach peak performance for leaders (McLaughlin, 1998). In the Catch Fire model, the first step is one addressed extensively in this book. Leaders need to understand the mindset that guides their actions from values, cultural issues, professional background, and emotional intelligence issues. The obvious issues of eating well and exercising to keep fit are not only role model issues for the public health leader, they are healthy lifestyle issues. Leaders need to develop methods for relieving stress and fatigue if they are to work at peak levels. Leaders also need to love to work on all sorts of challenges. Change is real, and leaders need to be resilient. If they do not like to work on problems, they are in the wrong business. Humor is clearly important. Good leaders know how to use humor to ease their own stress and the stress and fears of others. The work environment needs to be livable. People need to enter a positive and pleasant workplace.

SUMMARY

Walt Disney once said that all our dreams can come true if we have the courage to pursue them. Leaders believe in this philosophy even in the face of the tragedies of the last several years. Leadership is about learning and about growth. It is usually more than a one time event, although we have heros who do a courageous act and then move back into the anonymity of their lives. The prepared public health leader lives a life of community involvement with a commitment to the people that he or she serves. To carry out the critical responsibilities associated with this responsibility, the leader needs the tools, skills, and competencies necessary to carry out these tasks with high standards for success. Leaders need to learn the skills of leadership, but also must commit to learning these new skills over a lifetime. This book serves as a guide for the prepared public health leader who needs skills to address the new public health concerns of the last several years. The prepared public health leader has learned the basic skills of leadership and now adds the skills of this new age to those basic leadership skills (Rowitz, 2001).

This book has looked at the new world of public health from the perspective of public health preparedness. We have also looked at public health today in the context of the new dimensions of the field as outlined by the Institute of Medicine. It is through building social capital that leaders will add strength to their pursuits to working with others to improve the quality of life of all residents of the United States. The issues of emergency preparedness and response were also considered from the context of public health, mental health, community and family health preparedness, and the issue of safety. Part 3 of this book examined some of the new tools of this new world. The importance of systems thinking and the need to understand the complexities of our world were examined. The importance of emotional intelligence and people-smart strategies were discussed in detail. The need for leaders to understand law and its importance for carrying out our public health work were also discussed. The need to look for tipping points and how these points help us to better understand our world were also examined. The new field of forensic epidemiology and the partnerships that develop between law enforcement and public health help strengthen our public health agenda were discussed as well. There is also the need to emphasize our assets and not dwell on only our problems. We need to build our communities from strength rather than from weakness. Change and acceptance of it is our ongoing agenda. Finally, it is important to plan for a positive future and create visions to guide us toward this positive future.

It is important to keep looking for strategies and tools to make ourselves more effective leaders. I hope this book helps you to move in these important new directions.

REFERENCES

Blanchard, K., & Miller, M. (2004). *The secret*. San Francisco: Berrett-Kohler.

Covey, S. R. (1996). Three roles of the leader in the new paradigm. In F. Hesselbein, M. Goldsmith, & R. Beckhard (Eds.), *The leader of the future*. San Francisco: Jossey-Bass.

Covey, S. R. (2004). *The 8th habit*. New York: The Free Press.

Federal Highway Administration (n.d.). *Public involvement techniques for transportation decision making*. Washington, DC: U.S. Department of Transportation Web site. Retrieved from http://www.Fhwa.dot.gov/reports/pittd/vision.htm

Goleman, D., Boyatziz, R., & McKee, A. (2002). *Primal leadership*. Cambridge, MA: Harvard Business School Press.

Johnson, S. (2003). *The present*. New York: Doubleday.

McLaughlin, P. (1998). *Catch fire*. Denver: McLaughlin.

Nanus, B. (1992). *Visionary leadership*. San Francisco: Jossey-Bass.

Nanus, B., & Dobbs, S. M. (1999). *Leaders who make a difference*. San Francisco: Jossey-Bass.

Rowitz, L. (2001). *Public health leadership: Putting principles into practice*. Sudbury, MA: Jones and Bartlett.

Rowitz, L. (2004). Ten tools for practice learning. *Journal of Public Health Management and Practice, 10*(4), 368–370.

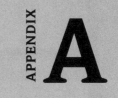
Key to Case Study 13

CASE STUDY APPENDIX 13

**Anthrax in Florida—
Answer Key**

Objectives and Topics for Case Study 13

1. Understanding public health investigations, including:
   - Defining exposed population(s)
   - Providing prophylaxis to exposed persons
   - Identifying the source (i.e., perpetrators/reservoir)

2. Understanding how a public health investigation differs from and is similar to a criminal investigation

3. Addressing communication challenges, including media relations and risk communication (including public health needs vs. law enforcement restriction)

4. Addressing interagency communication

5. Maintaining simultaneous epidemiologic and criminal investigations

6. Defining jurisdictional issues

7. Understanding of issues related to the law surrounding entry into and sampling of homes and workplaces

Problem and Questions

Question 1:   What are the implications of one or more suspected or confirmed cases of anthrax in the United States?

Answers and discussion points: In the United States, the background level of occurrence of anthrax cases is extremely low. Therefore, suspected or confirmed cases of anthrax should raise the suspicion that this biologic agent has been used as part of a deliberate bioterrorism attack and that additional cases of anthrax and additional attacks may be possible. Cases of anthrax must be investigated to determine whether they have occurred naturally (i.e., not as the result of an intentional act) and also individually evaluated as the possible result of terrorist attacks or other criminal acts. The occurrence of a confirmed case may indicate the commission of state and federal crimes. If there is suspicion that exposure was the result of an intentional act, the FBI

continues

CASE STUDY APPENDIX 13   *continued*

would assume the lead role in responding to and investigating anthrax threats and attacks.

Question 2: How is a suspected case of anthrax confirmed and where are human samples sent?

Answers and discussion points: Materials and specimens obtained from cases or suspected cases are sent to the Laboratory Response Network (LRN). (This is arranged between the health care practitioner and the public health department.) Typically, human specimens obtained in a clinical setting may be sent to a hospital or commercial laboratory. If there is suspicion regarding use of a possible bioterrorism agent, then the specimen would be forwarded to a public health laboratory which is part of the LRN network.

Question 3: What are the goals of this phase of a public health investigation of an epidemic?

Answers and discussion points: The goals involve the reinforcement of outbreak investigation principles from background lecture and other points, including:
- Verification of diagnosis
- Intensive efforts to identify and characterize additional cases
- Development and testing of hypotheses regarding potential sources or modes of spread (including examining patient's medical and recent travel history and notifying state epidemiologists in states through which patient traveled)
- Implementation of preventive and other intervention measures.

Question 4: At this point, how should the investigators handle media relations in terms of what the public needs to know?

Answers and discussion points: First, anticipate the occurrence of "leaks" of information *and* the public reporting of erroneous information. Also anticipate that the news media will demand continuous updates, including threat assessments. Anticipate that the news media will widely disseminate any details regarding an incident, some or all of which may be inaccurate or exaggerated with respect to dangers for the public.

As early as possible, public safety and public health officials should confer about and select appropriate spokesperson(s) and should make timely releases of accu-

CASE STUDY APPENDIX 13   *continued*

rate information. The establishment of a joint information center (JIC) with FBI, CDC, and state and local officials will facilitate the development of coordinated messages from public health and law enforcement. Such information must assure the public it is protected from harm while at the same time minimizing any negative impact on a related criminal investigation. The spokesperson(s) should be the only source of official information.

Question 5: Based on the information above, at this stage of the investigation what are the roles of public health officials and law enforcement authorities in the investigation, and under what circumstances might the respective roles of public health and law enforcement officials change?

Answers and discussion points: This is not yet a full-fledged criminal investigation; public health is still in the lead while the FBI and state and local law enforcement is assisting. The FBI will coordinate its threat assessment process to determine whether the situation is the result of terrorist or nation–state actors by evaluating the known facts from public health and analyzing additional law enforcement and intelligence information. At this stage of the initial response, it is unlikely that criminal intent will be evident. This assessment process will continually evaluate the additional information derived from public health, law enforcement, and intelligence sources.

Management-level public safety and public health officials should begin coordinating as soon as possible (for example, through systems such as the incident command system [ICS] or unified command system [UCS]. Such coordination enables implementation of appropriate measures to protect and treat public safety personnel who are exposed to suspect material at the scene and elsewhere, as well as to protect and treat the public.

If circumstances warrant suspicion that the event is intentional, the FBI will focus their efforts and resources on conducting the criminal investigation. This investigation is intended to identify the extent of the threat to national security and to lead to the identification, apprehension, and prosecution of the perpetrator(s). Public health officials will focus their efforts and resources on conducting an epidemiological investigation that is aimed at identifying

continues

CASE STUDY APPENDIX 13   *continued*

the source(s) and mode(s) of spread of the disease-causing agent, identifying other exposed or at-risk persons, implementing measures to prevent further exposures, and treating exposed persons.

Criminal and epidemiological investigations must be carefully coordinated to (1) avoid unnecessary exposures and duplication of efforts, (2) facilitate sharing of relevant information, and (3) otherwise complement each other. In a bioterrorism attack, the most important evidence may be the bioterrorism disease- or injury-causing biological or chemical agent itself.

For investigative purposes, the evidence may include: (1) the specific agent (weapon) itself, (2) "fingerprints" (through DNA and other analyses), or (3) trail markers (i.e., the agent material could have contaminated every place it has been stored or used by perpetrators, including containers, vehicles, and buildings). In most instances, the public health investigators who are trained to collect environmental samples and the state public health/LRN laboratory will be needed by law enforcement authorities to positively identify the bioterrorism agent, compare that specific agent with other agents, and track the path of the agent.

If the FBI determines that the act may be the result of an intentional attack, the FBI will assume the lead role in the response and criminal investigation. A joint investigation with the CDC and state and local public health will be coordinated through the joint operations center (JOC) established by the FBI. Other federal, state, and local response agencies will also be represented in both the JOC and the JIC to ensure that information is evaluated and shared within an organized response structure with connectivity to each agency's emergency operations center.

Circumstances could evolve such that the roles of law enforcement and public health have equal priority, and their functions and roles become more closely integrated as the investigation progresses. For example, with more widespread exposure to anthrax, public health's need to identify and treat exposed and infected persons and to contain the source of exposure would overlap with law enforcement's need to identify, apprehend, and prosecute perpetrator(s).

continues

CASE STUDY APPENDIX 13   *continued*

Question 6:   What is the law surrounding entry into and sampling of homes and workplaces?

Answers and discussion points:

In general

The law regarding entry to premises is governed by the Fourth Amendment to the Constitution of the United States. The law generally provides for entry with consent or with a search warrant. However, courts have recognized very specific situations when exigent circumstances are present as exceptions. Obtaining consent from a person with authority to provide such consent is often the easiest means to secure evidence that will not be legally suppressed.

Consultation with agency legal counsel is recommended in all access situations in the absence of consent. Law enforcement, public health, and public safety personnel may properly enter homes and workplaces without a warrant when circumstances represent a serious, credible, and immediate threat to the public. (These are exigent circumstances; for example, the U.S. Supreme Court has indicated that a burning building creates an exigency that justifies a warrantless entry by fire officials to fight a blaze). Law enforcement, public health, and public safety officials may be able to take samples from within those premises if such sampling is required to determine the specific nature and extent of the threat. The authority of these officials to take samples ultimately could turn on their ability to articulate the degree of seriousness and danger posed to the public, and the immediacy of that threat. In a court challenge, a judge would consider the totality of the circumstances to determine whether to admit evidence from the intrusion and the sampling, as well as other evidence discovered as a result. For example, the U.S. Supreme Court has excluded evidence of arson seized by investigators returning to the scene without a warrant six hours after the blaze had already been extinguished and the house was in the process of being boarded up. The Court ruled that the warrant requirement applies, and that any official entry must be made pursuant to a warrant in the absence of consent or exigent circumstances.

Evidence found during a warrantless search of a location may be admissible in court if the suspect has no standing

continues

CASE STUDY APPENDIX 13   *continued*

to assert that he had a reasonable expectation of privacy at the location. For example, a person who sent a letter containing anthrax to another person's workplace likely would not be able to assert a reasonable expectation of privacy at the target person's workplace. In contrast, if a person placed an envelope containing anthrax on a target coworker's desk and a warrantless search resulted in the discovery of evidence in a locked briefcase under the perpetrator's desk located in the same office suite as the target's desk, then the perpetrator may have grounds to assert that the search violated his rights to privacy because he had a reasonable expectation of privacy for items kept in his locked briefcase under his desk. The evidence might be ruled inadmissible if investigators did not obtain a search warrant for the search of the building and/or the briefcase.

Law Enforcement in Criminal Investigations

Ordinarily, if circumstances involving a warrantless intrusion by law enforcement personnel indicate that a criminal investigation is required and that the location should be processed as a crime scene, then law enforcement should delay both the sampling process and any additional processing until a search warrant for the location has been obtained, absent a reasonable belief that an immediate threat to public safety exists.

Public Health Working with Law Enforcement

One real dilemma occurs when law enforcement and public health investigations intersect. For example, if law enforcement determines that the location is a crime scene and begins the process of obtaining a search warrant, should law enforcement then restrict public health officials from entering the premises to obtain samples? Conventional law enforcement policies and procedures dictate that once a location has been designated as a crime scene (which might include evidence to be used in court), then, to limit the possibility of scene contamination, no one other than law enforcement personnel should enter the location.

State laws often address the authority of public health officials, in the absence of a criminal investigation, to proceed with or without an administrative warrant when they enter premises to inspect or to obtain samples during a disease outbreak investigation. The admissibility of evidence

continues

CASE STUDY APPENDIX 13 *continued*

collected during such inspections may vary depending upon the circumstances of the case and the legal challenges brought by the defendant at trial. Caution suggests that once a criminal investigation is begun, all sample collection from an identified crime scene be carried out jointly between public health and law enforcement with the advice and counsel of agency attorneys.

Question 7: What are the requirements for training and protection of those who may be asked to enter facilities to collect environmental samples?

Answers and discussion points: Public health and safety personnel who enter facilities to collect samples should be both *trained* and *equipped* to respond to hazardous materials incidents. However, in a suspected bioterrorism incident, FBI and public health officials should conduct the collection of environmental samples in a coordinated manner. Any environmental samples collected at the location could have important value for both the epidemiological and criminal investigations.

Question 8: Does this investigation now become a criminal investigation and, if so, how does this change the role of public health and law enforcement investigators?

Answers and discussion points: Yes. The discovery of evidence of an intentional delivery or release of anthrax indicates the possible commission of serious crimes under federal law. As such, the lead of the continuing joint public health/FBI investigation shifts to an FBI lead under national response authorities and plans.

The high priorities of both disciplines must be balanced, including those of law enforcement (to identify, apprehend, and prosecute the perpetrator) and public health (to protect the public by identifying the source or mode of spread, determining the extent of contamination and exposure, limiting further exposure, and treating those who have been exposed). Access to contaminated crime scenes should be coordinated to ensure that both law enforcement and public health objectives are met.

Federal (and, perhaps, state) statutes are violated when there has been an intentional threat involving a delivery or release of a bioterrorism agent (e.g., anthrax). Per estab-

continues

CASE STUDY APPENDIX 13   *continued*

lished national policy and authorities, the FBI is the lead federal agency for a suspected bioterrorism incident in the United States. The FBI would proceed with the criminal investigation, drawing upon the assistance of other federal, state, and local law enforcement agencies, often through established joint terrorism task forces (JTTFs).

Question 9: Who is responsible for determining whether a building should be evacuated and sealed and, if so, when it can be reentered?

Answers and discussion points: Although public safety officials might, as part of the initial threat assessment process, determine that a building should be evacuated, public health officials should be consulted and the decision made cooperatively, as soon as is possible. Once law enforcement officials have concluded their crime scene investigation and public health officials have conducted their epidemiological investigation of the site, then public health officials should make the ultimate determination as to if and when a building can be reoccupied.

Question 10: What are responsibilities of law enforcement in protecting such a crime scene for the purposes of further investigations and possible prosecution?

Answers and discussion points: Law enforcement officials in charge of the crime scene should be able to testify in court that, from the point at which they took control of the scene until the point they relinquished control to the owner or custodian, no persons entered the scene other than law enforcement officers and others who were specifically needed and authorized to be there. The purpose of this is to assure that no one could have added to or otherwise altered or contaminated the scene.

Under normal circumstances, evidence and property items removed from the scene must be inventoried, and a copy of that inventory must be provided to the owner or custodian. Typically, law enforcement officials would need to be able to describe the specific location where each item of evidence was found. Law enforcement officials (or technicians, expert witnesses, etc.) need to be able to explain what processes were used at the scene, why they were used, and what the results were. Such

continues

CASE STUDY APPENDIX 13   *continued*

information is also required for items processed and analyzed in the laboratory.

Question 11:   What are the responsibilities of public health authorities in preventing further cases of anthrax in workers in, and visitors to, the original case's workplace?

Answers and discussion points: Public health authorities will be concerned about limiting or preventing access to the location where the original patient's exposure occurred. The extent of the area of concern will depend on what is known about the locations where positive and negative environmental cultures were obtained, the usual movements of people and mail in the building, and the airflow in the building. The extent of the area may include the entire building. Further testing of environmental samples may be needed to clarify which areas are at risk.

Public health officials also will be concerned about identifying all persons with significant exposures in the building and assuring that they receive appropriate medical management, including postexposure antibiotic treatment and, perhaps, vaccination. Interviews (jointly by law enforcement and public health officials) and nasal cultures (to detect exposure to anthrax spores) of these employees and visitors also may be used to help understand the likely mode of spread, which work areas pose a risk, and which people are at risk.

Question 12:   Who is in charge of the investigation at the patient's workplace and residence?

Answers and discussion points: This could be a dynamic situation that is dependent upon the specific circumstances. When the epidemiologic investigation indicates that natural causes are not likely responsible for disease, the control of the scene would transition from public health to law enforcement officials. The scene could be secured and protected by law enforcement, and decisions about sampling and processing could be decided through a collaborative effort between public safety and public health.

To underscore points made previously, it is important to note that chain of custody does not exist in a vacuum. To understand it and to protect its intended goals, public health and law enforcement officials should keep the fol-

continues

CASE STUDY APPENDIX 13   *continued*

lowing in mind. Chain of custody exists only to assure the finder of fact (i.e., the jury in a criminal trial) that the item of evidence in question is what it is purported to be. To achieve this, the government witness, typically a law enforcement officer, needs to be able to assure that the process used to gather evidence and protect the scene from contamination is trustworthy. For this purpose, law enforcement typically will appoint an "on-scene commander." As such, the officer will be able to testify as to all relevant facts regarding the evidence-gathering process. One of the most basic needs of the on-scene commander is to know who had access to the site. Public health professionals can easily adapt their methodology by documenting who was at the scene and the locations from which all samples were taken. The on-scene commander will be able to adopt the public health report and assure the jury that the evidence is, indeed, trustworthy.

Other related discussion issues are: (1) how public health and law enforcement officials can work together to assure that each is able to collect data they need (e.g., environmental sampling); and (2) how approaches to sampling may differ between law enforcement and public health investigators.

Law enforcement authorities might utilize nonlaw enforcement experts (e.g., epidemiologists) for purposes of conducting specific processes and examinations of the scene or of evidence taken from the scene. However, before any such findings would be admitted in court, such experts may be required to testify in court regarding the what/why/how of the conduct of their examinations and specimen collections.

Based on building plan information, the building's air supply system, and the incubation period of anthrax, the decision was made to offer antibiotic prophylaxis from the National Pharmaceutical Stockpile to all employees and visitors who had been in the patient's workplace building during August 1 through October 7 (this number was approximately 1114 persons). On October 12, the New York City Department of Public Health reported a suspected case of cutaneous anthrax in an office worker at a large broadcast media outlet in New York City. The onset of illness in that worker appeared to predate that of

continues

CASE STUDY APPENDIX 13   *continued*

the case in Florida, and the New York City patient recalled having received a letter with suspicious contents approximately 11 days prior to onset of disease. The letter was retrieved by the FBI, and its contents were confirmed to include *B. anthracis* spores.

Question 13: How does the FBI coordinate among local, state, and federal law enforcement efforts during a national investigation?

Answers and discussion points: As previously noted, JTTFs help to facilitate dissemination of terrorism-related information among agencies. In the event of a bioterrorism incident, the FBI will establish a JOC and JIC to coordinate federal, state, and local law enforcement, intelligence, and public health information.

Question 14: How does public health coordinate among local, state, and federal public health efforts during a national investigation?

Answers and discussion points: The CDC has primary federal responsibility for assisting local and state authorities in outbreak investigations and in implementing control measures required to protect public health. In a jurisdiction where an outbreak is occurring, a JOC will be established to coordinate federal, state, and local efforts. The CDC has additional authority for assisting local and state health departments in a federal response to a bioterrorism event. The authority for this responsibility derives from the Federal Response Plan and the Terrorism Incident Annex. The CDC works under the direction and authority of the Department of Health and Human Services (DHHS) and its secretary. Depending on the magnitude of the response, DHHS may provide some coordination and communication support directly. If a federal state of emergency is requested by a governor and/or declared by the president, the Federal Emergency Management Agency coordinates all of the other federal agencies in assisting the local and state response to a bioterrorism event.

The CDC is the primary agency of DHHS responsible for public health communication and guidance to state

continues

CASE STUDY APPENDIX 13   *continued*

and local health departments regarding bioterrorism preparedness. The CDC works through several mechanisms in coordination. The CDC communication networks include a Web-based system, as well as several direct listserve communication mechanisms to health care providers, state public health departments, and other partner agencies. The representative committees for the state epidemiologists (the Council of State and Territorial Epidemiologists [CSTE]) and the Association of Public Health Laboratories (APHL) serve as primary points of contact. In addition, the CDC and APHL have worked on the development of the LRN.

Table of Sources

Chapter 1

Figure 1–1 Lichtveld, M., Rowitz, L., & Cioffi, J. (2004). The leadership pyramid. *Leadership in Public Health, 6(4)*, 3–8.

Figure 1–2 Centers for Disease Control and Prevention. (2002). *Public health preparedness: A status report.* Atlanta: CDC.

Table 1–1 Essential Public Health Services Working Group of the Core Functions Steering Committee. (1994). Core functions and essential public health services. Washington, DC: U.S. Public Health Service.

Chapter 2

Case Study 2 Beaman, M., Dublin, P., Lay, A., Morgan, J., Gage, R., & Vonderheide, E. (2002). A haze over Hickernoodle City: Biodefense readiness in a community. *Leadership in Public Health, 6(1)*, 13–21.

Chapter 3

Table 3–1 and Table 3–2 Lichtveld, M. Y., & Cioffi, J. (2003). Public health workforce development: Progress, challenges and opportunities. *Journal of Public Health Management and Practice, 9(6)*, 443–450.

Figure 3–1 Institute of Medicine. (2003). *The future of the public's health in the 21st century.* Washington, DC: National Academy of Sciences. Reprinted with permission.

Chapter 4

Figure 4–1 World Health Organization and Pan African Emergency Training Centre, Addis Ababa. (2002). *Disasters and emergencies: Definitions.* Geneva, Switzerland: World Health Organization.

Table 4–1 Mitroff, I. (2001). *Managing crises before they happen.* New York: Anacom.

Table 4–2 Mitroff, I. (in press). *Why some companies emerge stronger and better from a crisis.* New York: Anacom. Reprinted with permission.

Table 4–3 and Table 4–4 Trust for America's Health. (2004). *Ready or not? Protecting public's health in the age of terrorism.* Washington, DC: TFAH.

Figure 4–2 Fink, S. (2002). *Crisis management:Planning for the inevitable.* Lincoln, NE: Author's Guild Backprint.com. Reprinted with permission.

Figure 4–3 and Table 4–5 Disaster Planning Training Programme. (1994). *Disaster preparedness* (2nd ed.). New York: United Nations.

Figure 4–4 Department of Homeland Security, FEMA. (2004). *Basic incident command system (IS 195).* Emmitsburg, MD: FEMA.

Case Study 4 Black, B., Bostrom, H., Durch, J., Matucheski, H., & Peterson, J. (2003). Emergency response of public health to a train derailment and evacuation [Monograph]. In J. W. Munson (Ed.), *Case study manual. Leadership in public health*, *1*, 69–89.

Chapter 5

Table 5–1 Council on Linkages Between Academia and Public Health Practice. (2001). *Core competencies for public health professionals.* Washington, DC: Public Health Foundation.

Table 5–3 and Table 5–4 Center for Health Policy, Columbia University School of Nursing. (2004). *Curriculum toolkit: Developing curricula for public health workers.* New York: Columbia University School of Nursing.

Table 5–5 Centers for Disease Control and Prevention and Center for Health Policy, Columbia University School of Nursing. (2002). *Bioterrorism and emergency readiness: Competencies for all public health workers.* New York: Columbia University School of Nursing.

Chapter 6

Table 6–1 National Association of County and City Health Officials. (2002). *Local centers for public health preparedness: A resource catalog for bioterrorism and emergency preparedness.* Washington, DC: NACCHO.

Table 6–2 and Table 6–5 Himmelman, A. (2002). *Collaboration for a change.* Minneapolis, MN: Himmelman Consulting. Reprinted with permission.

Table 6–3 Center for Civic Partnerships. (2003). *Collaborative functions: The 12 C's of collaboration.* Sacramento, CA: Center of Civic Partnerships. Reprinted with permission.

Table 6–4 Thurman, P. (2001). *Community readiness: A promising model for community healing.* Oklahoma City, OK: University of Oklahoma Health Sciences Center, Center on Child Abuse and Neglect. Reprinted with permission.

Exercise 6–1 Turning Point. (2004). *Collaborative leadership: Collaborative leadership learning modules.* Seattle, WA: Turning Point National Office (R. W. Johnson Foundation).

Case Study 6 Willis, M. A. (2003). Creating win-win: Leveraging and strengthening coalition resources. *Leadership in Public Health, 6*(3), 11–18.

Chapter 7

Chapter 8

Chapter 9

Chapter 10

Table 10–6 Center for Law and the Public's Health. (2001b). *Model state emergency powers act.* Baltimore: Author.

Table 10–7 United Nations General Assembly. (1948). *Universal Declaration of Human Rights* (Resolution 217(A) III). New York: United Nations.

Table 10–8 Public Health Leadership Society. (2002). *Principles of the ethical practice of public health.* New Orleans, LA: PHLS. Reprinted with permission.

Exercise 10–1 Neuberger, B. & Christoffel, T. (2002). *The legal basis of public health.* Atlanta: CDC.

Chapter 11

Table 11–1 Chess, C., Hance, B. J., & Sandman, P. M. (1988). *Improving dialogue with communities: A short guide to government risk communication.* Trenton, NJ: New Jersey Department of Environmental Protection.

Table 11–2 Covello, V. T., Wojecki, J. G. & Peters, R. (n.d.). *77 questions asked by journalists during a crisis.* New York: Center for Risk Communications. Reprinted with permission.

Figure 11–2 Covello, V. T. (2002). *Message mapping: World Health Organization workshop on bioterrorism and risk communication.* Geneva, Switzerland: WHO. Reprinted with permission.

Figure 11–3 W. K. Kellogg Foundation. (2002). *Logic model development guide.* Battle Creek, MI: Author.

Figure 11–4 Reynolds, B. (2002). *Crisis and emergency risk communication.* Atlanta: CDC.

Chapter 12

Table 12–1 P. Lenihan. (1998). Personal communication.

Case Study 12–A Gladwell, M. (2000). *An interview with Malcolm Gladwell.* Reprinted with permission.

Chapter 13

Table 13–1 Goodman, R. A., Munson, J. W., Dammers, K., Lazzarin, Z., & Barkeley, J. P. (2003). Forensic epidemiology: Law at the intersection of public health and criminal investigation. *Journal of Law, Medicine, and Ethics, 31*, 684–700. Reprinted with permission.

Figure 13–1 and Figure 13–2 Butler, J. C., Cohen, M. L., Friedman, C. R., Scripps, M. R., & Watz, C. G. (2002). Collaboration between public health and law enforcement. *Emerging Infectious Diseases, 8*(10), 1152–1156.

Table 13–2 and Table 13–3 Federal Bureau of Investigation. (2002). *Criminal and epidemiological investigation handbook.* Washington, DC: Department of Justice.

Case Study 13 Centers for Disease Control and Prevention. (2004). *Forensic epidemiology: Course manager's guide.* Atlanta: CDC.

Chapter 14

Figure 14–1 Rowitz, L. (2001). *Public health leadership: Putting principles into practice.* Sudbury, MA: Jones and Bartlett. Reprinted with permission.

Figure 14–2 Kretzmann, J. P., & McKnight, J. L. (1993). *Building communities from the inside out.* Evanston, IL: Northwestern University ABCD Institute. Reprinted with permission.

Tables 14–1 to 14–5 Centers for Diseases Control and Prevention. (2003). *National public health performance standards.* Atlanta: CDC.

Chapter 15

Table 15–1 Kotter, J. P., & Cohen, D. S. (2002). *The heart of change.* Boston: Harvard Business School Press. Reprinted with permission.

Figure 15–1 Conner, D. R. (1992). *Managing at the speed of change.* New York: Villard Books. Reprinted with permission.

Case Study 15A Turning Point. (2004). *States of change.* Seattle, WA: Turning Point National Office (R. W. Johnson Foundation).

INDEX

page numbers in *italics* denote figures;
page numbers followed by t denote tables

A

Academy Without Walls, 430, 431

Accurate perception, 281

Adaptability and innovation, 268

Advocacy, public health law and ethics, 334–335

Affliative leadership style, 273t

African-American inner-city communities, research projects, 43

Agency for Toxic Substances and Disease Registry (ATSDR), 346

Agent, in terrorism, 208, 209

AIH&S (American Indian Health and Services), 181

Alabama, statutory definition of public health, 303t

Alaska, statutory definition of public health, 303t

Alinsky, Saul D., 397

Ambrose, Jo, 294

American Academy of Pediatrics, 454
  family readiness kit
    checklist of things to do, 221–222
    develop a family readiness plan, 221
    find what could happen in a disaster and the community's disaster preparedness, 221
    practice and maintain your family plan, 222

American Indian Health and Services (AIH&S), 181

American Public Health Association (APHA), 425

American Red Cross (ARC), 79, 84, 136, 219t

Analytic/assessment skills, 146t

Anger, as common thread in school shooters, 455

Anthrax attacks (2001), 112t, 315
  suspected case of cutaneous anthrax, 483–484

Anthrax in Florida (case study)
  exercise, 393
  objectives/topics, 390
  questions, answers, and discussion points, 390–393, 474–485
    does the investigation become a criminal investigation, 480–481
    goals of this investigation, 475
    handling the media, 475–476
    how does public health coordinate among local, state, and federal public health efforts, 484–485
    how does the FBI coordinate among local, state, and federal law enforcement, 484
    how is a case of anthrax confirmed; where are human samples sent, 475
    implications of one or more suspected or confirmed cases of anthrax in the U.S., 474–475
    requirements for training and protection of those entering facilities to collect samples, 480
    responsibilities of law enforcement in protecting the crime scene, 481–482